Version 6.0

EXPLORING WORDPERFECT® FOR WINDOWS™

Robert T. Grauer

Maryann Barber

University of Miami

Prentice Hall, Englewood Cliffs, New Jersey 07632

Library of Congress Cataloging in Publication Data

Grauer, Robert T. [date]
Exploring WordPerfect for Windows / version 6.0 / Robert T.
Grauer, Maryann Barber.
p. cm.
Includes index.
ISBN 0-13-079500-3
1. WordPerfect for Windows (Computer file) 2. Word processing.
I. Barber, Maryann. II. Title
Z52.5.W655G73 1994
652.5′536—dc20 94-5835
CIP

Acquisitions editor: P. J. Boardman
Editorial /production supervisor: Greg Hubit Bookworks
Interior and cover design: Suzanne Behnke
Production coordinator: Patrice Fraccio
Managing editor: Mary Cavaliere
Developmental editor: Harriet Serenken
Editorial Assistants: Renee Pelletier / Dolores Kenny

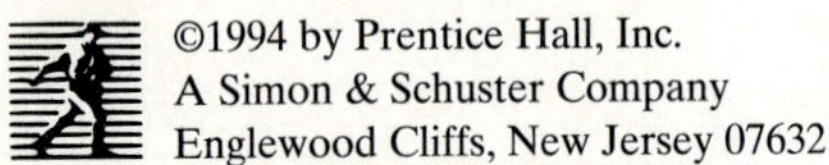

A Simon & Schuster Company
Englewood Cliffs, New Jersey 07632

Printed in the United States of America
10 9 8 7 6 5 4 3 2

ISBN 0-13-079500-3

Prentice Hall International (UK) Limited, *London*
Prentice Hall of Australia Pty. Limited, *Sydney*
Prentice Hall of Canada Inc., *Toronto*
Prentice Hall Hispanoamericano, S.A., *Mexico*
Prentice Hall of India Private Limited, *New Delhi*
Prentice Hall of Japan, Inc., *Tokyo*
Simon & Schuster Asia Pte. Ltd., *Singapore*
Editora Prentice Hall do Brasil, Ltda., *Rio de Janeiro*

Contents

4

The Professional Document: Styles and Tables 131

5

Desktop Publishing: Creating a Newsletter 173

Preface

Exploring WordPerfect for Windows 6.0 is one of several books (modules) in the Prentice Hall *Exploring Windows* series. Other modules include *Microsoft Excel 5.0, Word for Windows 6.0, Microsoft Access 2.0, Lotus for Windows 4.0,* and an introductory module, *Exploring Windows 3.1.* The books are independent of one another but possess a common design, pedagogy, and writing style intended to serve the application courses in both two- and four-year schools.

Each book in the series is suitable on a stand-alone basis for any course that teaches a specific application; alternatively, several modules can be bound together for a single course that teaches multiple applications. The initial component, *Exploring Windows 3.1,* assumes no previous knowledge and includes an introductory section for the individual who has never used a computer.

The *Exploring Windows* series will appeal to students in a variety of disciplines including business, liberal arts, and the sciences. Each module has a consistent presentation that stresses the benefits of the Windows environment, especially the common user interface that performs the same task in identical fashion across applications. Each module emphasizes the benefits of multitasking, demonstrates the ability to share data between applications, and stresses the extensive on-line help facility to facilitate learning. Students are taught concepts, not just keystrokes or mouse clicks, with hands-on exercises in every chapter providing the necessary practice to master the material.

The *Exploring Windows* series is different from other books, both in its scope as well as the way in which material is presented. Students learn by doing. Concepts are stressed and memorization is minimized. Shortcuts and other important Windows information are consistently highlighted in the many boxed tips that appear throughout the series. Every chapter contains an average of two directed exercises at the computer, but equally important are the less structured end-of-chapter problems that not only review the information but extend it as well. The end-of-chapter material is a distinguishing feature of the entire series, an integral part of the learning process, and a powerful motivational tool for students to learn and explore.

FEATURES AND BENEFITS

- *Exploring WordPerfect for Windows* presents concepts as well as keystrokes and mouse clicks, so that students learn the theory behind the applications. They are not just taught what to do but are provided with the rationale for doing it, enabling them to extend the information to additional learning on their own.
- No previous knowledge is assumed on the part of the reader as a fast-paced introduction brings the reader or new user up to speed immediately.
- Practical information, beyond application-specific material, appears throughout the series. Students are cautioned about computer viruses and taught the importance of adequate backup. The *Exploring Windows* module, for example, teaches students to extend the warranty of a new computer and points out the advantages of a mail-order purchase.
- Problem solving and troubleshooting are stressed throughout the series. The authors are constantly anticipating mistakes that students may make and tell the reader how to recover from problems that invariably occur.

- Tips, tips, and more tips present application shortcuts in every chapter. Windows is designed for the mouse, but experienced users gravitate toward keyboard shortcuts once they have mastered basic skills. The series presents different ways to accomplish a given task, but in a logical and relaxed fashion.
- A unique Buying Guide in the introductory module presents a thorough introduction to PC hardware from the viewpoint of purchasing a computer. Students learn the subtleties in selecting a configuration—for example, how the resolution of a monitor affects its size, the advantages of a local bus, and the Intel CPU processor index.

ACKNOWLEDGMENTS

We want to thank the many individuals who helped bring this project to its successful conclusion. We are especially grateful to our editor at Prentice Hall, P. J. Boardman, without whom the series would not have been possible, and to Harriet Serenkin, the developmental editor, whose vision helped shape the project. Gretchen Marx of Saint Joseph College produced an outstanding set of Instructor Manuals. Greg Hubit was in charge of production. Deborah Emry, our marketing manager at Prentice Hall, developed the innovative campaign that helped make the book a success. Delores Kenny helped coordinate all phases of the project.

We also want to acknowledge our reviewers, who through their comments and constructive criticism made this a far better book.

Lynne Band, Middlesex Community College
Stuart P. Brian, Holy Family College
Kimberly Chambers, Scottsdale Community College
Jerry Chin, Southwest Missouri State University
Dean Combellick, Scottsdale Community College
Paul E. Daurelle, Western Piedmont Community College
David Douglas, University of Arkansas
Raymond Frost, Central Connecticut State University
Vernon Griffin, Austin Community College
James Gips, Boston College
Wanda D. Heller, Seminole Community College
Ernie Ivey, Polk Community College
Jane King, Everett Community College
John Lesson, University of Central Florida
Alan Moltz, Naugatuck Valley Technical Community College
Delores Pusins, Hillsborough Community College
Gale E. Rand, College Misericordia
David Rinehard, Lansing Community College
Marilyn Salas, Scottsdale Community College
Sally Visci, Lorain County Community College
David Weiner, University of San Francisco
Jack Zeller, Kirkwood Community College

A final word of thanks to the unnamed students at the University of Miami who make it all worthwhile. And, most of all, thanks to you, our readers, for choosing this book. Please feel free to contact us with any comments and suggestions. We can be reached most easily on the Internet.

Robert T. Grauer
RGRAUER@UMIAMI.MIAMI.EDU

Maryann Barber
MBARBER@UMIAMI.MIAMI.EDU

1

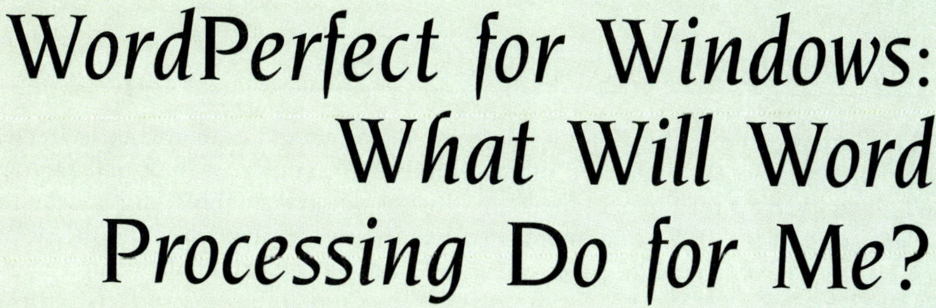

WordPerfect for Windows: What Will Word Processing Do for Me?

CHAPTER OBJECTIVES

After reading this chapter you will be able to:

1. Explain the concept of a common user interface and its advantage in learning a new application.
2. Describe the basic mouse operations; use a mouse and/or the equivalent keyboard shortcuts to select commands from a pull-down menu.
3. Discuss the function of a dialog box; describe the different types of dialog boxes and the various ways in which information is supplied.
4. Explain the functions of the minimize and maximize or restore buttons; describe the use of the scroll bar and its associated scroll box.
5. Access the on-line help facility and explain its various capabilities.
6. Define word wrap; differentiate between a hard and soft return.
7. Distinguish between the insertion and replacement (typeover) modes; explain how to switch from one mode to the other.
8. Create, save, retrieve, edit, and print a simple document using WordPerfect for Windows.

OVERVIEW

Have you ever produced what you thought was the perfect term paper only to discover that you omitted a sentence or misspelled a word, or that the paper was three pages too short or one page too long? Wouldn't it be nice to make the necessary changes, and then be able to reprint the entire paper with the touch of a key? Welcome to the world of word processing, where you are no longer stuck with having to retype anything. Instead, you retrieve your work from disk, display it on the monitor and revise it as necessary, then print it at any time, in draft or final form.

This chapter provides a broad-based introduction to word processing and ***WordPerfect for Windows.*** It begins, however, with a discussion of basic Windows concepts, applicable to Windows applications in general, and to WordPerfect for Windows in particular. The emphasis is on the common user interface and consistent command structure that facilitates learning within the Windows environment. Indeed, you may already know much of this material, but that is precisely the point; that is, once you know one Windows application, it is that much easier to learn the next.

The second half of the chapter presents (or perhaps reviews) essential concepts of word processing. The hands-on exercises at the conclusion of the chapter allow you to apply all of the material at the computer, and are indispensable to the learn-by-doing philosophy we follow throughout the text.

THE WINDOWS DESKTOP

The ***desktop*** is the centerpiece of Microsoft Windows and is analogous to the desk on which you work. There are physical objects on your real desk and there are ***windows*** (framed rectangular areas) and ***icons*** (pictorial symbols) displayed on the Windows desktop. The components of a window are explained within the context of Figure 1.1, which contains the opening Windows screen on our computer.

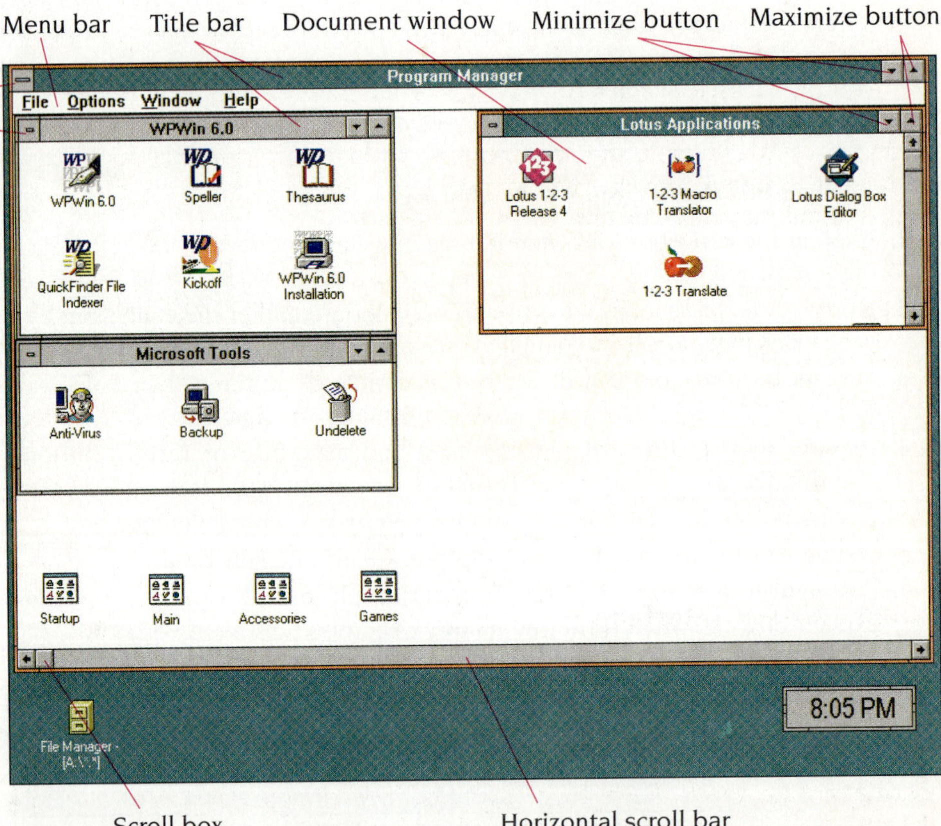

FIGURE 1.1 Program Manager

Your desktop may be different from ours, just as your real desk is arranged differently from that of your friend. You can expect, however, to see a window titled Program Manager; you may or may not see other windows within Program Manager, for example, the WPWin 6.0 and Lotus Applications windows shown in Figure 1.1.

Program Manager is a special program crucial to the operation of Windows. It starts automatically when Windows is loaded and it remains open the entire time you are working in Windows; that is, closing Program Manager closes Windows.

Program Manager is in essence an organizational tool that places applications in groups (e.g., WPWin 6.0 and Lotus Applications), then displays those groups as windows or group icons.

Regardless of the windows that are open on your desktop, every window contains the same basic elements: a title bar, control-menu box, and buttons to minimize and maximize or restore the window. The ***title bar*** displays the name of the window; for example, WPWin 6.0 in Figure 1.1. The ***control-menu box*** accesses a pull-down menu that lets you select operations relevant to the window. The ***maximize button*** enlarges the window so that it takes the entire desktop, whereas the ***minimize button*** reduces a window to an icon (but keeps the program open in memory). A ***restore button*** (a double arrow not shown in Figure 1.1) appears after a window has been maximized and returns the window to its previous size (the size before it was maximized).

Other elements, which may or may not be present, include a horizontal and/or vertical scroll bar and a menu bar. A horizontal (vertical) ***scroll bar*** will appear at the bottom (right) border of a window when the contents of the window are not completely visible. The ***scroll box*** appears within the scroll bar to facilitate moving within the window. A ***menu bar*** is found in the window for Program Manager, but not in the other windows. This is because Program Manager is a different kind of window, an application window rather than a document window.

An ***application window*** contains a program (application). A ***document window*** holds data for a program and is contained within an application window. The distinction between application and document windows is made clearer when we realize that Program Manager is a program and requires access to commands contained in pull-down menus located on the menu bar.

MICROSOFT TOOLS

The Microsoft Tools group is created automatically when you install (or upgrade to) MS-DOS 6.0. The name of each icon (Antivirus, Backup, and Undelete) is indicative of its function, and you are urged to use these programs in conjunction with your study of WordPerfect.

Common User Interface

One of the most significant benefits of the Windows environment is the ***common user interface*** imposed on all applications, which provides a sense of familiarity when you begin to learn a new application. In other words, once you already know one Windows application, even one as simple as the Paintbrush accessory, it will be that much easier for you to learn WordPerfect, because all applications work basically the same way. In similar fashion, it will take you less time to master Lotus once you know WordPerfect, because both applications share a common menu structure with consistent ways to select commands from those menus.

Consider, for example, Figures 1.2a and 1.2b, containing windows for Lotus and WordPerfect, respectively. The applications are very different, yet the windows have many characteristics in common; you might even say that they have more similarities than differences, a remarkable statement considering the programs accomplish very different tasks and were developed by different companies. There is a document window (Untitled) within the application window for Lotus, and in similar fashion, a document window (Document1) within the application window for WordPerfect.

The application windows for Lotus and WordPerfect contain the same

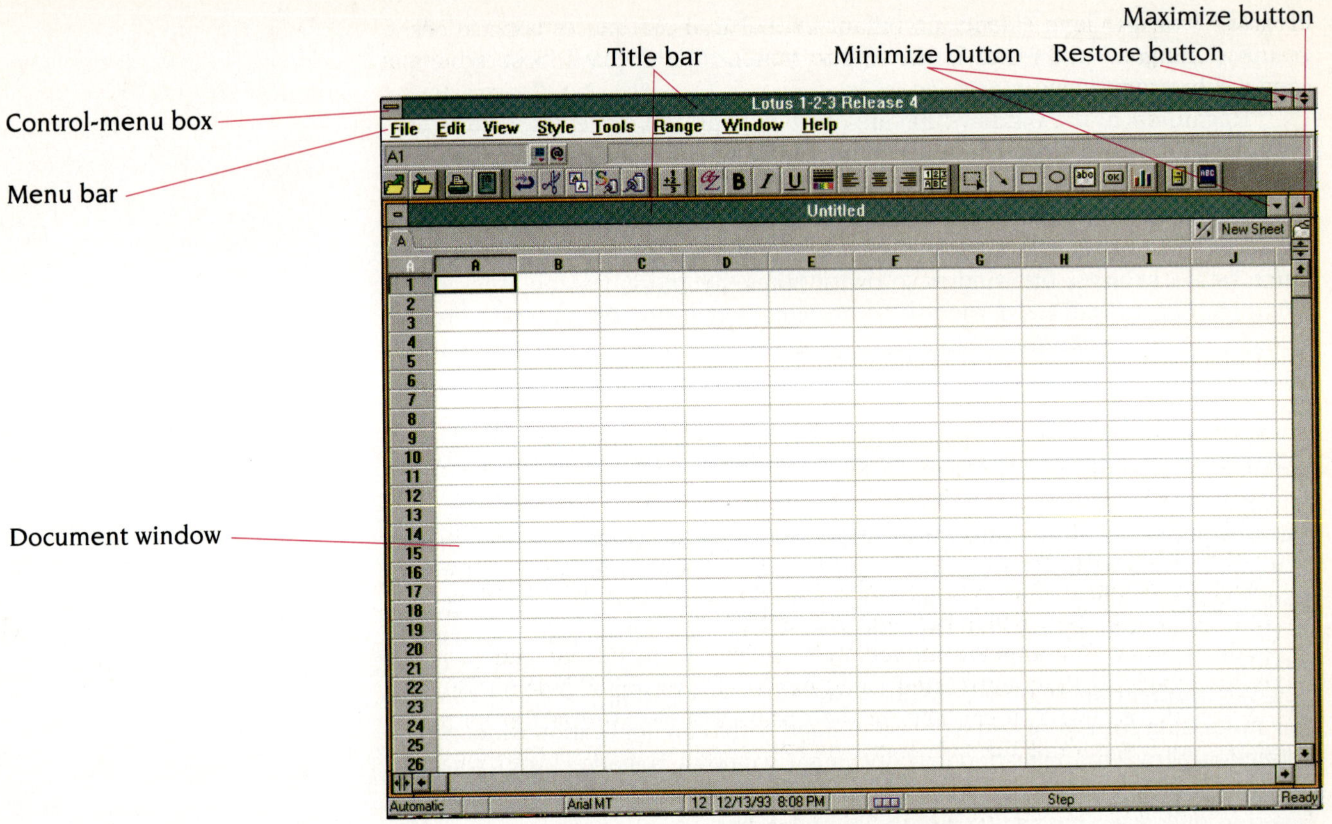

Maximize button

Title bar

Minimize button

Restore button

Control-menu box

Menu bar

Document window

(a) Lotus for Windows

Restore button

Control-menu box

Menu bar

Title bar

Minimize button

Button Bar

Power Bar

Ruler Bar

Document window

Status Bar

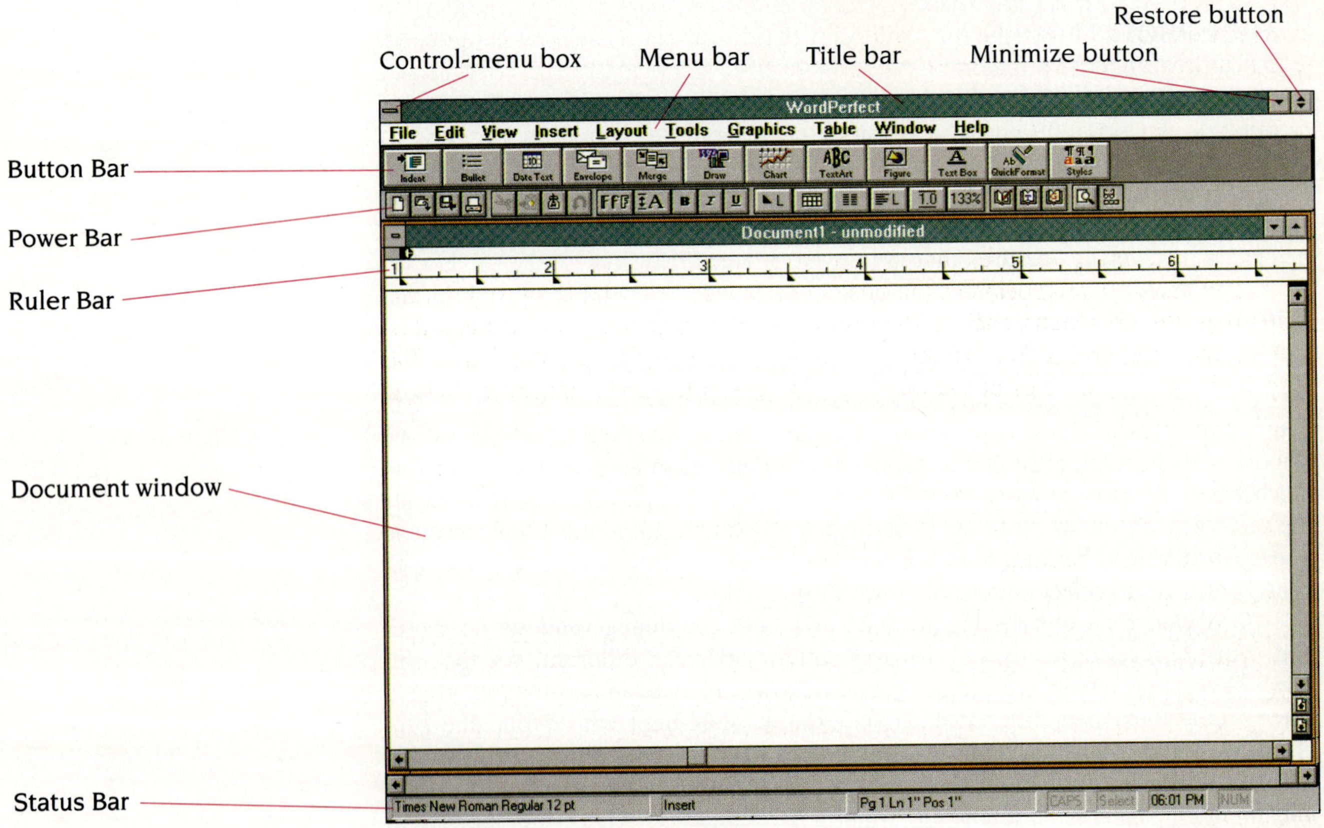

(b) WordPerfect for Windows

FIGURE 1.2 The Common User Interface

elements as any other application window: a title bar, menu bar, and control-menu box; and minimize and maximize or restore buttons. The menu bars even contain some of the same menus—for example, a File, Edit, View, Tools, Window, and Help menu, with consistent commands in both applications; that is, both File menus contain the commands to open and close a file, both Edit menus have commands to cut, copy, and paste text, and so on. The means for accessing the pull-down menus are also consistent; that is, click on the menu name (see mouse basics later in the chapter) or press the Alt key plus the underlined letter of the menu name—for example, Alt+F to pull down the File menu.

WORDPERFECT FOR WINDOWS

We concentrate now on the elements in Figure 1.2b that are unique to WordPerfect. Do not be concerned if your screen is different than ours, because WordPerfect lets you change every aspect of its environment to your personal preference. Indeed, once you start to use WordPerfect, you will want to customize it to the way in which you work. (We tell you how in Chapter 2.) What is important for the time being, is that you recognize the basic elements, which include the Button Bar, Power Bar, Ruler Bar, and Status Bar.

The ***Button Bar*** appears immediately under the menu bar and provides immediate access to frequently used menu items—for example, indentation, bullets, dates, and so on. You can change the position of the Button Bar so that it appears at the bottom of the document window, or at the left or right side of the document window. You can also display an alternate Button Bar (WordPerfect gives you twelve to choose from), or you can create your own.

The ***Power Bar*** is similar in concept to the Button Bar, but more useful for beginners as it contains more basic commands. (You cannot move the Power Bar.) The icons on the Power Bar reflect the commands they perform; for example, the printer icon (fourth from the left) will print the document. If an ***icon*** is not clear, you can determine its function by pointing to it, then reading the description that appears at the top of the screen. Perhaps the easiest way to appreciate the various icons is to view them in groups, as is done in Figure 1.3, which also gives you an indication of the most commonly used commands in WordPerfect.

The ***Ruler Bar*** enables you to change margins and/or tab stops more quickly than from pull-down menus. It also lets you make adjustments to columns and/or tables, two advanced features that are covered later in the text.

The ***Status Bar*** appears at the bottom of the window and displays information about the document, such as the position of the insertion point within a document and the current font. (Fonts are discussed in Chapter 2.) The Status Bar also indicates the settings of various keys; for example, CAPS indicates that the Caps Lock key is on.

WORKING IN WINDOWS

The next several pages take you through the basic operations common to Windows applications in general, and to WordPerfect in particular. You may already be familiar with much of this material, in which case you are already benefiting from the common user interface. We begin with the mouse and describe how it is used to access pull-down menus and to supply information in dialog boxes. We also emphasize the on-line help facility, which is present in every Windows application.

The Mouse

The mouse (or track ball) is essential to WordPerfect as it is to all Windows applications, and you must be comfortable with its four basic actions:

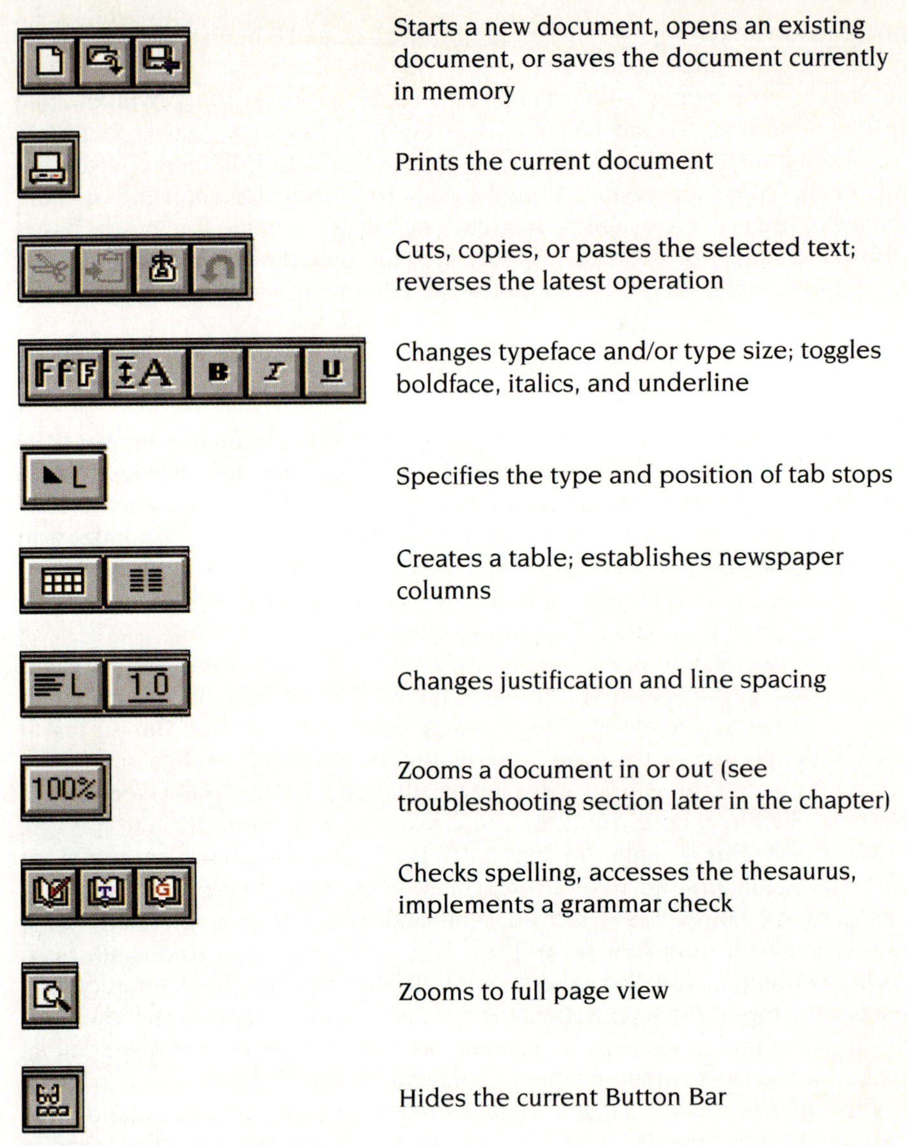

FIGURE 1.3 The Power Bar

- To ***point*** to an item, move the mouse pointer over the item.
- To ***click*** an item, point to it, then press and release the left mouse button.
- To ***double click*** an item, point to it, then click the left mouse button twice in succession.
- To ***drag*** an item, move the pointer to the item, then press and hold the left button while you move the item to a new position.

The mouse is a pointing device—move the mouse on your desk and the ***mouse pointer,*** typically a small arrow head, moves on the monitor. The mouse pointer assumes different shapes according to the nature of the current action: a double arrow when you change the size of a window, an I-beam to insert text, a hand to jump from one help topic to the next, or a circle with a line through it to indicate that an attempted action is invalid.

The mouse pointer will also change to an hourglass to indicate Windows is processing your last command, and that no further commands may be issued until the action is completed. The more powerful your computer, the less frequently the hourglass will appear, and conversely, the less powerful your system, the more you will see the hourglass.

PICK UP THE MOUSE

It seems that you always run out of room on your real desk, just when you need to move the mouse a little further. The solution is to pick up the mouse and move it closer to you—the pointer will stay in its present position on the screen, but when you put the mouse down, you will have more room on your desk in which to work.

A right-handed person will hold the mouse in his or her right hand and click the left button, whereas a left-handed individual may want to hold the mouse in the left hand and click the right button. If this sounds complicated, it's not, and you can master the mouse with the on-line tutorial provided in Windows (see step 2 in the hands-on exercise on page 17).

MOUSE TIP FOR LEFTIES

You can customize the mouse to reverse the actions of the left and right buttons. Double click on the Main group icon in Program Manager, double click on the Control Panel icon, and double click on the Mouse icon to bring up the appropriate dialog box. Click the Swap Left/Right Buttons check box.

WordPerfect is designed for a mouse, but it provides keyboard equivalents for almost every command, with the Button Bar(s), Power Bar, and Ruler Bar providing still other ways to accomplish the most frequent operations. You may (at first) wonder why there are so many different ways to do the same thing, but you will come to recognize the many options as part of WordPerfect's charm. The most appropriate technique depends on personal preference, as well as the specific situation.

If, for example, your hands are already on the keyboard, it is faster to use the keyboard equivalent. Other times, your hand will be on the mouse and that will be the fastest way. It is not necessary to memorize anything, nor should you even try; just be flexible and willing to experiment.

Pull-down Menus

Pull-down menus, such as those in Figure 1.4, are essential to all Windows applications. A pull-down menu is accessed by clicking on the menu name (within the menu bar) or by pressing the Alt key plus the underlined letter in the menu name—for example, Alt+H to pull down the Help menu. Menu options (commands) are executed by clicking on the command once the menu has been pulled down or by pressing the underlined letter; for example, press C to execute the Close command in the File menu. You can also bypass the menu entirely, if you know the equivalent keystrokes shown to the right of the command when the menu is pulled down—for example, F2 in the Edit menu to execute the Find command. A ***dimmed command*** (for example, the Copy command within the Edit menu) indicates that command is not currently executable; that is, some additional action has to be taken for the command to become available.

An arrowhead after a command indicates a ***cascade menu*** will follow with additional choices; click on the Select command in the Edit menu to produce the cascade menu shown in the figure.

Many commands are followed by an ***ellipsis*** (. . .) to indicate that additional

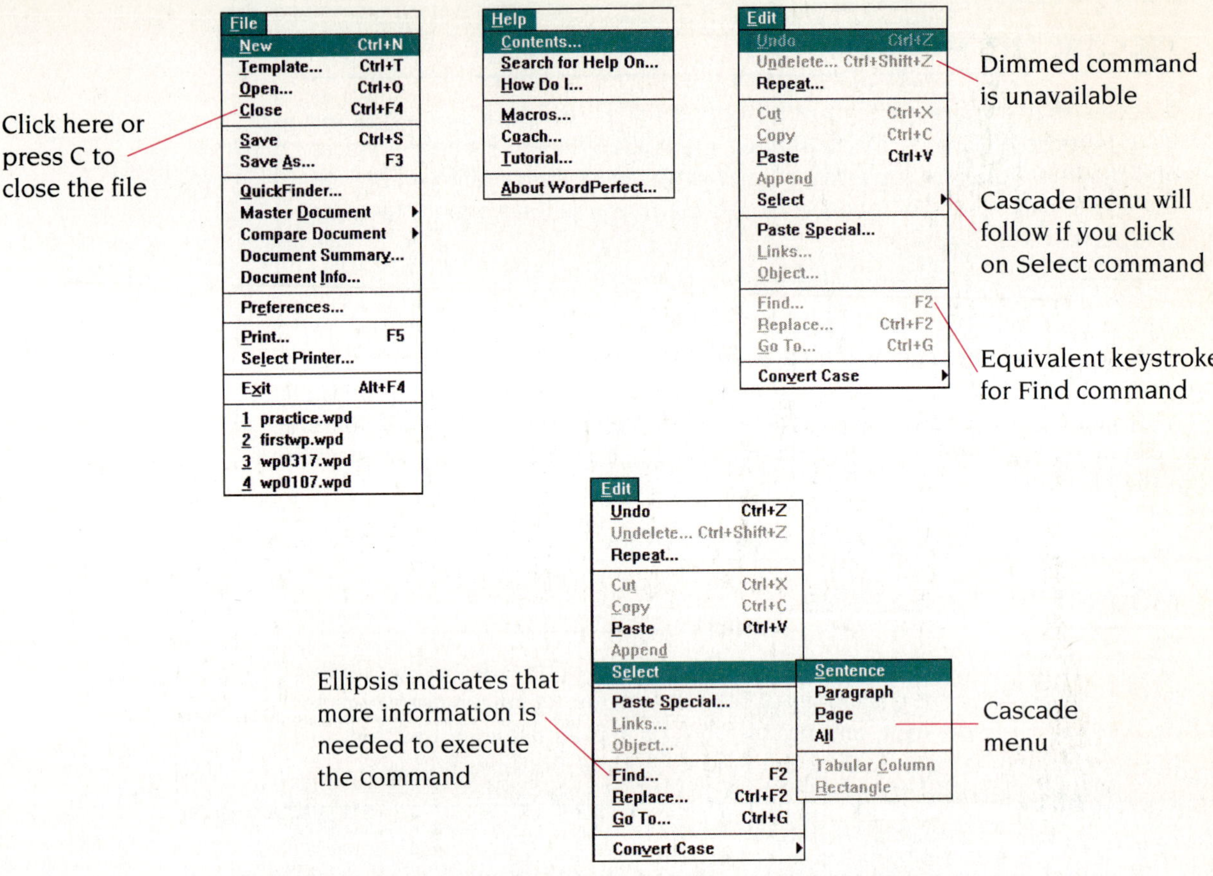

FIGURE 1.4 Pull-down Menus

information is required to execute the command; for example, selection of the Find command in the Edit menu requires the user to specify the text to be found. The additional information is entered into a dialog box, which appears immediately after the command has been selected.

> **QUICKMENUS**
>
> Point to any item in a WordPerfect document, then click the right mouse button to display a QuickMenu with commands appropriate to the item you are pointing to. Click the left mouse button to execute a command within the QuickMenu. Press the Esc key or click outside the menu to close it without executing a command.

Dialog Boxes

A ***dialog box*** appears when additional information is needed to execute a command—that is, whenever a menu option is followed by an ellipsis. There are different ways to supply the information, which in turn leads to different types of dialog boxes as shown in Figure 1.5.

The ***option buttons*** in Figure 1.5a indicate mutually exclusive choices, one of which must be chosen; for example, Documents/Backup *or* Templates *or* Spreadsheets, and so on. An option button is selected by clicking the button, which

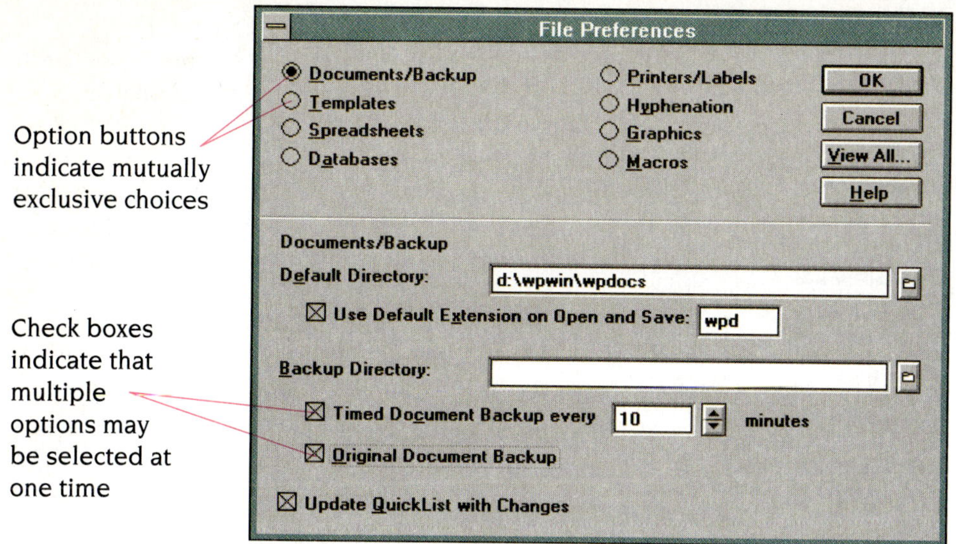

(a) Option Buttons and Check Boxes

Text box indicates that a character string is required

Find and Replace Text
Type Match Replace Direction Options
Find:
CIS
Replace With:
Computer Information Systems
Find
Replace
Replace All
Close
Help

(b) Text Boxes

FIGURE 1.5 Dialog Boxes

automatically deselects the previous button; for example, clicking Templates will remove the selection for Documents/Backup.

Check boxes are used when multiple options can be in effect simultaneously, such as requesting Timed Document Backup *and* Original Document Backup. Check boxes are selected (cleared) by clicking on the box.

A ***text box*** indicates that a character string is required, such as the find and replacement strings in the two text boxes of Figure 1.5b. Some text boxes are initially empty and display a flashing vertical bar to mark the insertion point for the text you enter. Other text boxes may already contain an entry, in which case you can click anywhere in the box to establish the insertion point and edit the entry.

An ***open list box,*** such as the list of file names in Figure 1.5c, displays the available choices, any one of which is selected by clicking the desired item. A ***drop-down list box,*** such as the list of available drives or file types, conserves space by showing only the current selection; click the arrow of a drop-down list box to produce a list of available options.

All of the dialog boxes in Figure 1.5 contain one or more ***command buttons*** to initiate an action. The function of the command button is generally apparent from its name; for example, Cancel will return to the previous screen with no action taken, while OK accepts the information and closes the dialog box.

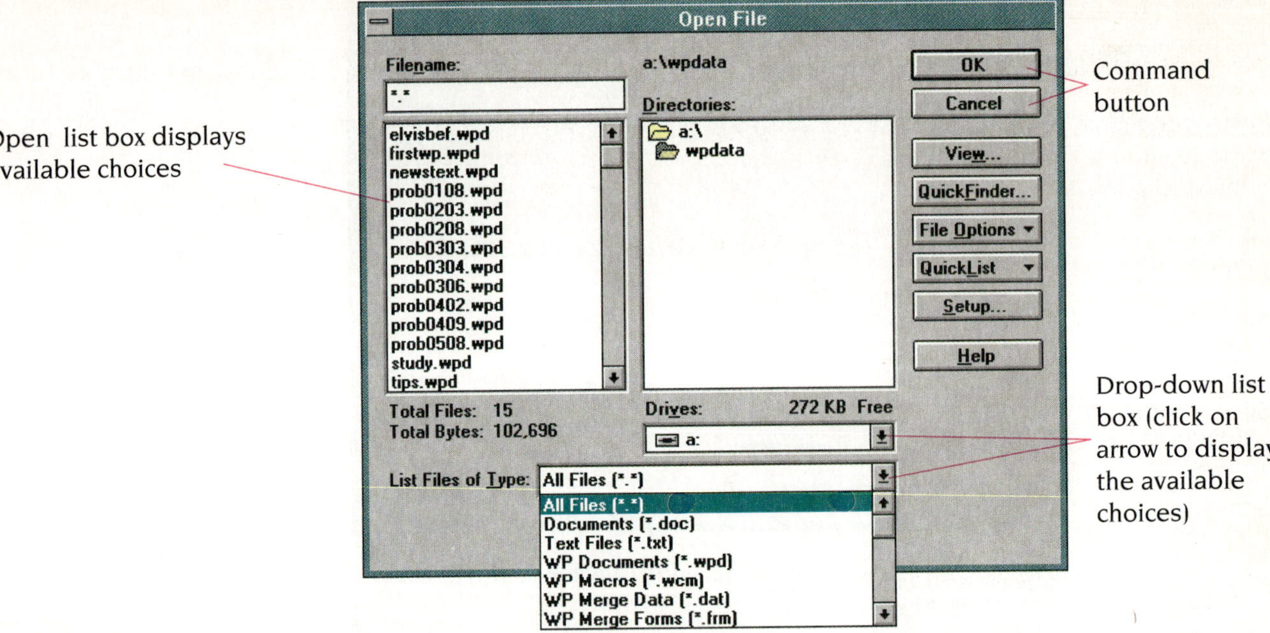

(c) List Boxes

FIGURE 1.5 Dialog Boxes (continued)

On-line Help

All Windows applications provide extensive ***on-line help,*** which is accessed by pulling down the ***Help menu.*** The WordPerfect Help menu was shown earlier in Figure 1.4 and contains the following choices:

Contents . . .	provides access to all sections within the Help facility
Search for Help On . . .	contains a list of topics for which you can request help
How Do I . . .	offers instructions for performing common tasks
Macros . . .	pertains to macros and is beyond the scope of this book
Coach . . .	a series of interactive mini-tutorials for basic features
Tutorial . . .	an introduction to WordPerfect
About WordPerfect . . .	displays version number of WordPerfect

The ***Contents command*** in the Help menu displays the screen of Figure 1.6a and provides access to all elements within the Help facility. The ***How Do I command*** produces the screen of Figure 1.6b and is especially helpful for beginners. You can obtain step-by-step instructions for any of the listed topics by clicking on that topic. Another useful feature for beginners is the ***glossary,*** shown in Figure 1.6c.

Each of the windows in Figures 1.6a, b, and c contains the elements found in any other application window: a title bar, a menu bar, minimize and maximize or restore buttons, a control-menu box, and optionally, a vertical and/or horizontal scroll bar.

The ***help buttons*** underneath the menu bar help you move around more easily; that is, you can click a button to perform the indicated function. The ***Contents button*** returns to the screen in Figure 1.6a from elsewhere within the Help facility. The ***Search button*** lets you find information on a specific topic. Click the button, then type a key word in the text box; for example, *power bar* in Figure 1.6d (or use the arrows in the open list box to scroll through the topics). Double click

Control-menu box
Menu bar
Help buttons
Title bar
Maximize button
Minimize button
WordPerfect Help
File Edit Bookmark Help
Contents Search Back History Print Close
Contents
Welcome to WordPerfect 6.0 for Windows Help
To find information, choose from the following items. To search for information and to move through Help, use the buttons along the top of the Help window.
Choose For information about
Search (Index) topics listed alphabetically
How Do I performing tasks
Glossary meanings of terms
Menu Commands features by menus
WordPerfect Bars topics by Feature Bar, Power Bar, Ruler Bar, Button Bar, and Status Bar
Keystrokes keystrokes and templates
About WordPerfect license and program dates
New Features features new to WPWin
Other Products other WPCorp products
Macros macro commands
Coach starting the Coach
Tutorial starting the tutorial
Using Help how to use Help

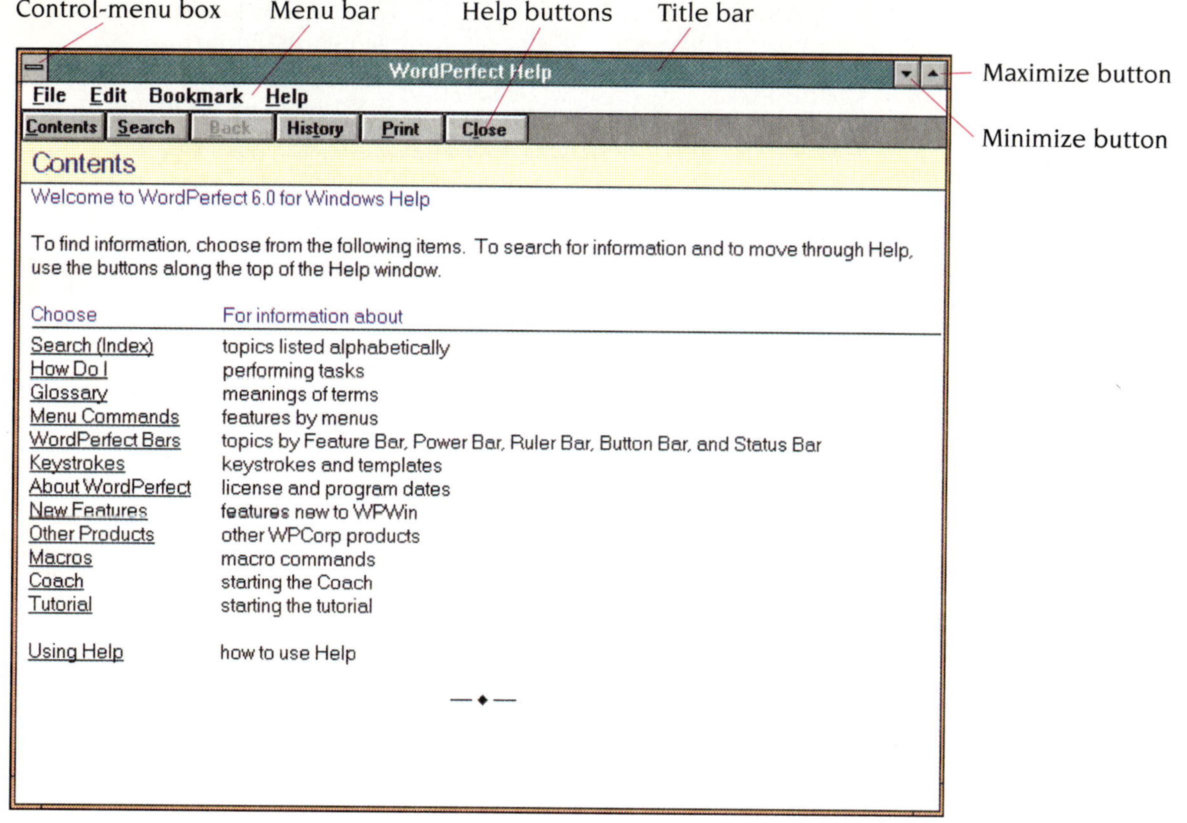

(a) Help Contents

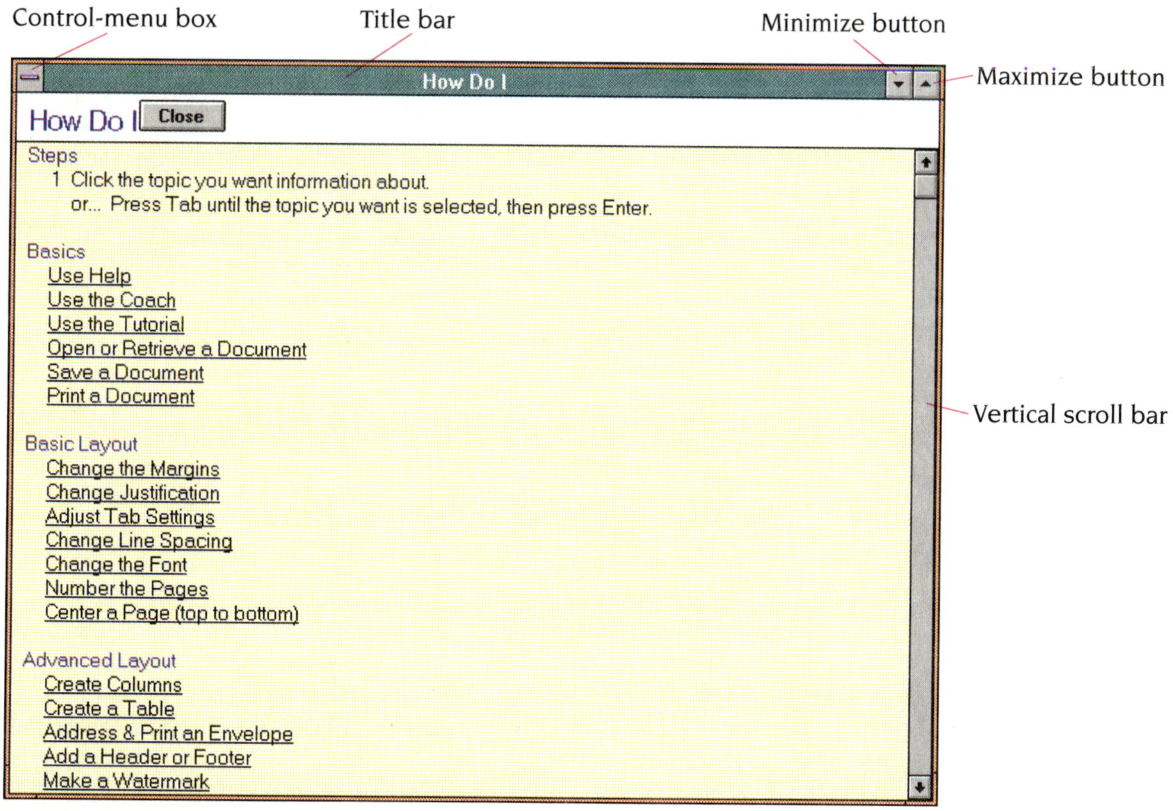

Control-menu box
Title bar
Minimize button
Maximize button
Vertical scroll bar
How Do I
How Do I Close
Steps
1 Click the topic you want information about.
or... Press Tab until the topic you want is selected, then press Enter.
Basics
Use Help
Use the Coach
Use the Tutorial
Open or Retrieve a Document
Save a Document
Print a Document
Basic Layout
Change the Margins
Change Justification
Adjust Tab Settings
Change Line Spacing
Change the Font
Number the Pages
Center a Page (top to bottom)
Advanced Layout
Create Columns
Create a Table
Address & Print an Envelope
Add a Header or Footer
Make a Watermark

(b) How Do I Screen

FIGURE 1.6 WordPerfect Help Facility

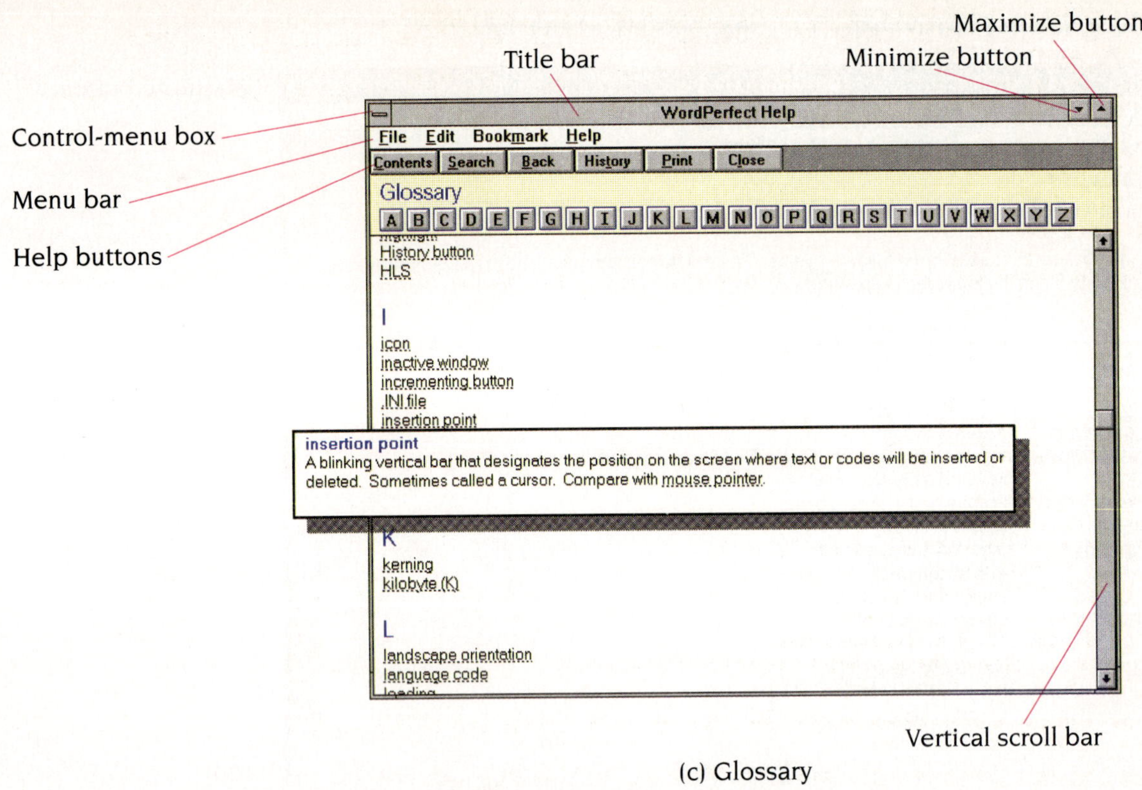

(c) Glossary

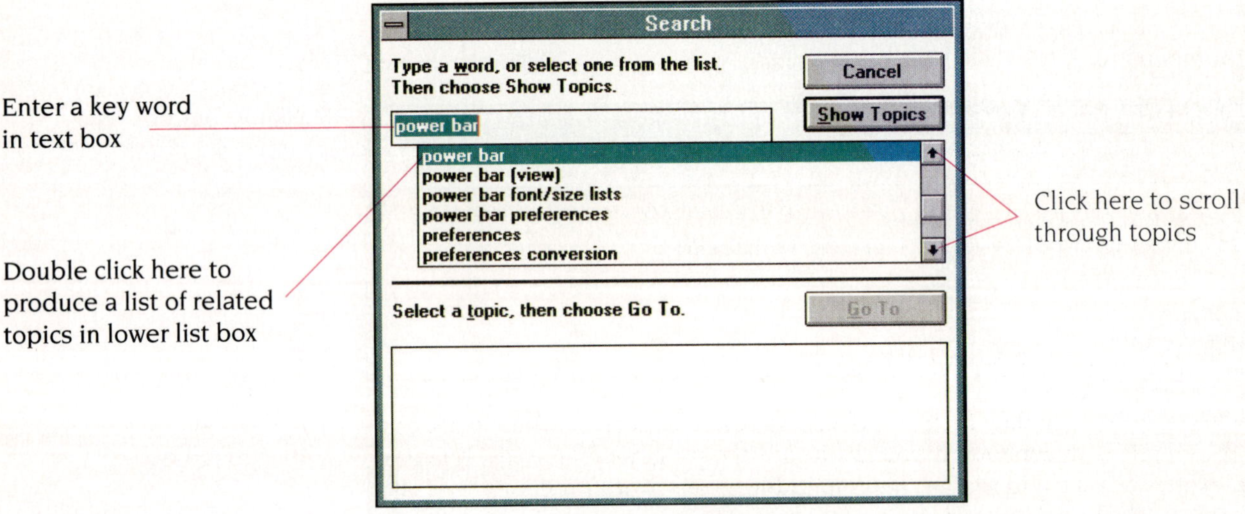

(d) Searching for a Topic

FIGURE 1.6 WordPerfect Help Facility (continued)

the highlighted topic to display information about it and/or related topics in the lower list box. Double click a topic in the lower list box to display the informational screen shown in Figure 1.6e, which describes how to customize the Power Bar (which we discuss in Chapter 2).

The ***Back button*** returns to the previous help topic. The ***History button*** is more general as it displays a list of *all* topics selected within the current session; you can return to a previous topic by double clicking on the topic. The ***Print button*** prints the current topic. The ***Close button*** closes the Help window.

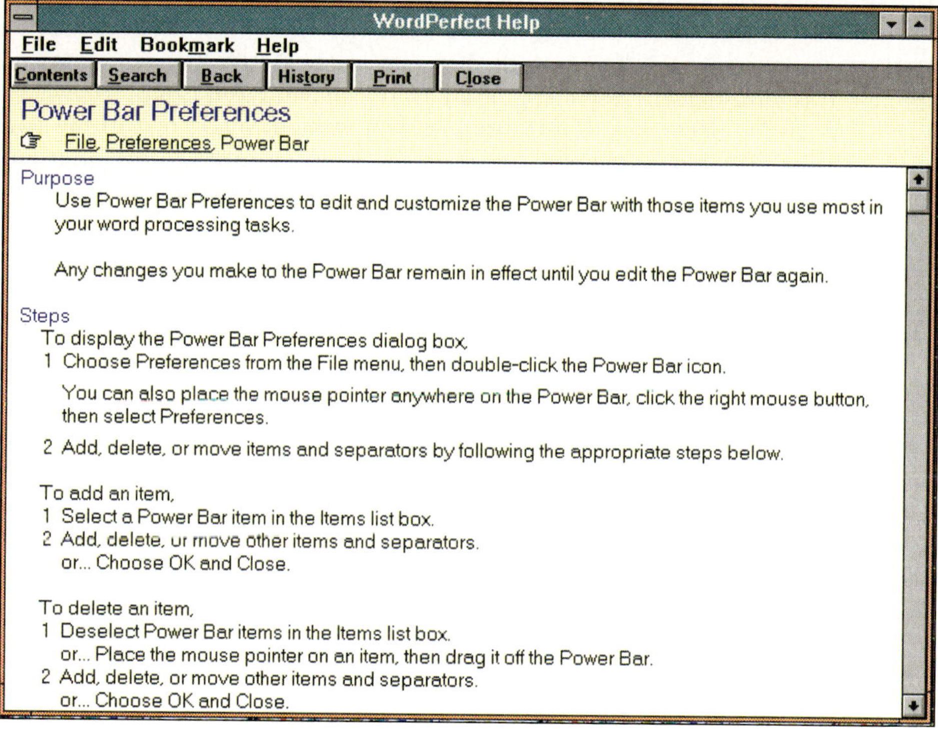

(e) Help Text

FIGURE 1.6 WordPerfect Help Facility (continued)

ON-LINE HELP

The answer to almost any question about WordPerfect is found within the Help facility if only you take the trouble to look. The Help menu also provides access to the interactive coaches that guide you through the implementation of certain features. On-line help is invaluable. Use it!

THE BASICS OF WORD PROCESSING

All word processors, be they DOS- or Windows-based, adhere to certain basic concepts that must be understood if you are to use the program effectively. The next several pages introduce ideas that are applicable to any word processor (and that you may already know). We follow the conceptual material with a hands-on exercise that gives you the opportunity to practice all that you have learned.

LEARN TO TYPE

The ultimate limitation of any word processor is the speed at which you enter data; hence the ability to type quickly is invaluable. Learning how to type is far from an insurmountable problem, especially with computer-based typing programs. As little as a half hour a day for a couple of weeks will have you up to speed, and if you do any significant amount of writing at all, the investment will pay off many times.

Insertion Point

The ***insertion point*** is a flashing vertical line that marks the position where text is entered. It is always at the beginning of a new document, but it can be anywhere within an existing document. If, for example, you wanted to add text to the end of an existing document, you would click at that position to move the insertion point, then begin typing. The insertion point often marks the starting point for the next command, as many commands begin execution at the insertion point rather than at the beginning of the document.

Toggle Switches

Suppose you are at the keyboard and type an entire sentence without pressing the Shift key, so that the sentence is in all lowercase letters. Then you press the Caps Lock key once, and retype the sentence, again without pressing the Shift key. This time the sentence is all in uppercase. You can repeat the process as often as you like, noting that each time you press the Caps Lock key the message switches from lowercase to uppercase and back again.

The point of this example is to introduce the concept of a ***toggle switch,*** a device that causes the computer to alternate between two states. The Caps Lock key is an example of a toggle switch, as it continually changes from uppercase to lowercase and back again. As we proceed in our discussion of word processing, we will see several other examples of toggle switches.

Insertion versus Replacement

WordPerfect is always in one of two modes, ***insertion*** or ***typeover*** (also known as ***replacement***) and uses a toggle switch (the Ins key) to alternate between the two. The Status Bar displays the mode you are in; for example, the insert mode was active in Figure 1.2 shown earlier in the chapter.

Press the **Ins key** once and you switch from insertion to replacement; press the Ins key a second time and you go from replacement back to insertion. Text that is entered into a document during the insertion mode causes existing text to move to the right to accommodate the material being added; text entered from the replacement mode overtypes (i.e., replaces) existing text. Text is always entered or replaced immediately to the right of the insertion point.

The insertion mode is best when you enter text for the first time, but either mode can be used to make corrections. The insertion mode is the better choice when the correction requires you to add new text; the replacement mode is easier when you are substituting one character(s) for another. The difference is illustrated in Figure 1.7.

Figure 1.7a displays the text as it was originally entered, with two misspellings. The letters *se* have been omitted from the word insertion, whereas an *x* has been erroneously typed instead of a *c* in replacement. The insertion mode is used in Figure 1.7b to add the missing letters, which in turn moves the rest of the line to the right. The replacement mode is used in Figure 1.6c to replace the *x* with a *c*.

The inrtion mode is better when
adding text that has been omitted;
the replaxement mode is easier when
you are substituting one (or more)
characters for another.

(a) Text to Be Corrected

FIGURE 1.7 Insertion and Replacement Modes

"se" has been inserted and existing text moved to the right

The insertion mode is better when
adding text that has been omitted;
the replaxement mode is easier when
you are substituting one (or more)
characters for another.

(b) Insertion Mode

"c" replaces the "x"

The insertion mode is better when
adding text that has been omitted;
the replacement mode is easier when
you are substituting one (or more)
characters for another.

(c) Replacement Mode

FIGURE 1.7 Insertion and Replacement Modes (continued)

Deleting Text

The Backspace and Del keys delete one character immediately to the left or right of the insertion point, respectively. The choice between them depends on when you need to erase a character(s); that is, the Backspace key is easier if you make the mistake as you are typing the text initially, whereas most people prefer the Del key during subsequent editing.

You can also delete a block of text by selecting it (that is, dragging the mouse over the text), then pressing the Del key. And finally, you can delete and replace text in one operation by selecting the text to be replaced and then typing the new text in its place.

THE UNDELETE COMMAND

The **Undelete command** restores the last three deleted items. Pull down the Edit menu and click Restore to retrieve the most recently deleted block of text. Click the Previous command button to view the previous deleted entry, and click it again to view the entry before that. Click the Restore command button when you find the text you want to undelete, which replaces the text in the document.

Word Wrap

Newcomers to word processing have one major transition to make from a typewriter, and it is an absolutely critical adjustment. Whereas a typist returns the carriage at the end of every line, just the opposite is true of a word processor; that is, you type continually *without* pressing the enter key because the word processor automatically wraps text from one line to the next. This concept is known as ***word wrap*** and is illustrated in Figure 1.8.

The word primitive does not fit on the current line in Figure 1.8a, and is automatically shifted to the next line, *without* the user having to press the enter key. The operator continues to enter the text with additional words being wrapped to subsequent lines as necessary. The only time you use the enter key is at the end of a paragraph, or when you want the cursor to move to the next line, and the end of the current line doesn't reach the right margin.

Word wrap is closely associated with another concept, that of hard and soft carriage returns. A ***hard return*** is created by the user when he or she presses the enter key at the end of a paragraph; a ***soft return*** is created by the word processor as it wraps text from one line to the next. The location of the soft returns changes automatically as a document is edited (for example, as text is inserted or deleted, as margins or fonts are changed, etc.). The location of the hard returns

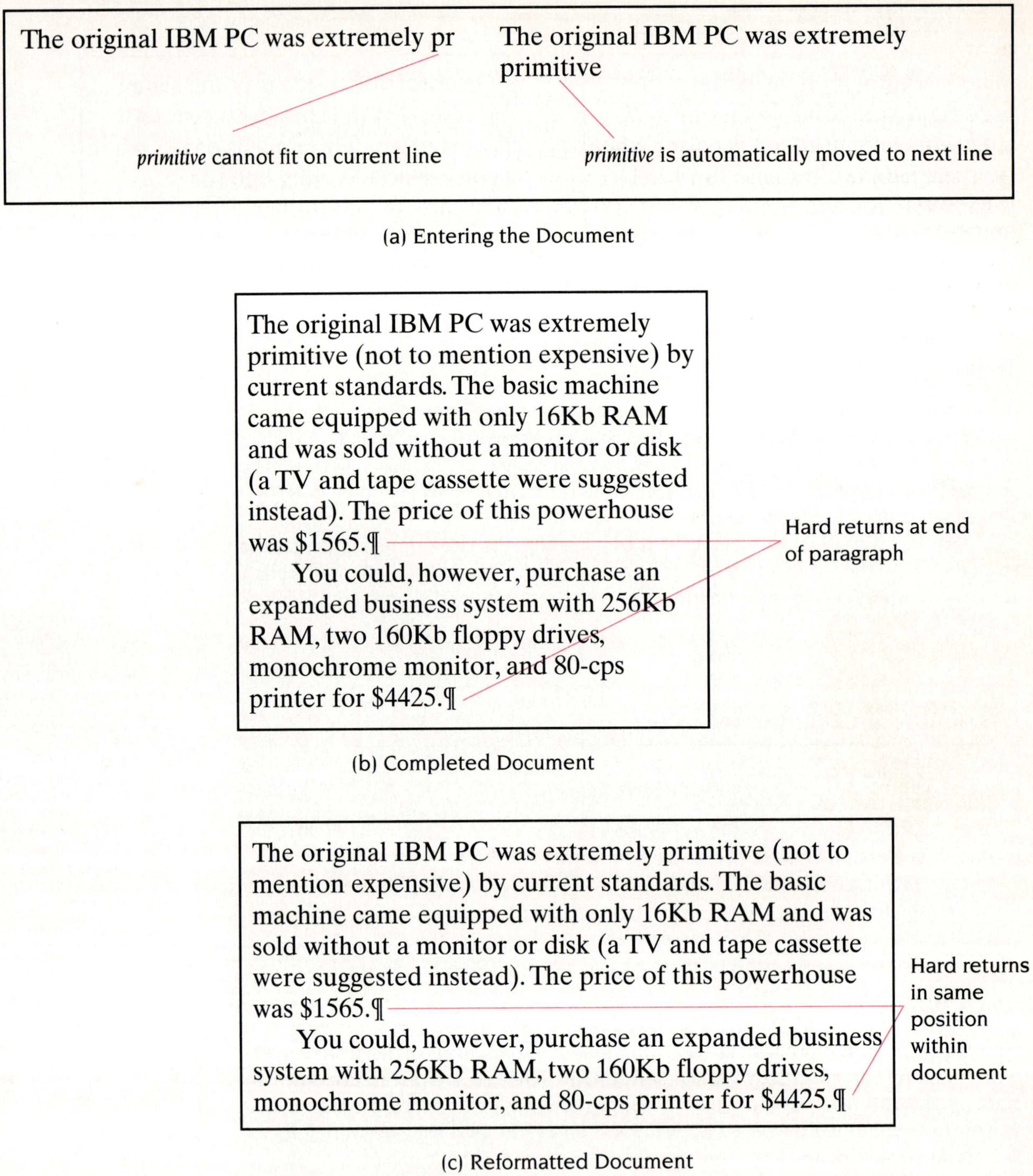

The original IBM PC was extremely pr

primitive cannot fit on current line

The original IBM PC was extremely
primitive

primitive is automatically moved to next line

(a) Entering the Document

The original IBM PC was extremely primitive (not to mention expensive) by current standards. The basic machine came equipped with only 16Kb RAM and was sold without a monitor or disk (a TV and tape cassette were suggested instead). The price of this powerhouse was $1565.¶

You could, however, purchase an expanded business system with 256Kb RAM, two 160Kb floppy drives, monochrome monitor, and 80-cps printer for $4425.¶

Hard returns at end of paragraph

(b) Completed Document

The original IBM PC was extremely primitive (not to mention expensive) by current standards. The basic machine came equipped with only 16Kb RAM and was sold without a monitor or disk (a TV and tape cassette were suggested instead). The price of this powerhouse was $1565.¶

You could, however, purchase an expanded business system with 256Kb RAM, two 160Kb floppy drives, monochrome monitor, and 80-cps printer for $4425.¶

Hard returns in same position within document

(c) Reformatted Document

FIGURE 1.8 Word Wrap

can be changed only by the user, who must intentionally insert (or delete) each hard return.

There are two hard returns in Figure 1.8b, one at the end of each paragraph. There are seven soft returns in the first paragraph (one at the end of every line except the last) and four soft returns in the second paragraph. Now suppose the margins in the document are made smaller (that is, the line is made longer) as shown in Figure 1.8c. The numbers of soft returns drop to five and two (in the first and second paragraph, respectively) as more text fits on a line and fewer lines are needed. The revised document still contains the two original hard returns, one at the end of each paragraph.

LEARNING BY DOING

We believe strongly in learning by doing, and thus there comes a point where you must use the computer if the discussion is to have real meaning. The two exercises that follow are linked to one another in that you create a simple document in exercise 1, then retrieve and edit that document in exercise 2. The ability to save and retrieve a document is critical, and you do not want to spend an inordinate amount of time entering text, unless you are confident in your ability to retrieve it later.

The first exercise also introduces you to the *data disk* that accompanies this text that you can use to store the documents you create. (You can also store the documents on a hard disk if you have access to your own computer.) The data disk contains a variety of documents that are referenced later in the text.

HANDS-ON EXERCISE 1:

Creating a Document

Objective To load WordPerfect for Windows, then create, save, and print a simple document. The exercise introduces you to the data disk that accompanies the text and reviews basic Windows operations: pull-down menus, dialog boxes, on-line help, and the use of a mouse. Use Figure 1.9 as a guide in doing the exercise.

Step 1: Load Windows

- Type **WIN** and press the **enter key** to load Windows if it is not already loaded.
- The appearance of your desktop will be different than ours, but it should resemble Figure 1.1 at the beginning of the chapter. You will most likely see a window containing Program Manager, but if not, you should see an icon titled Program Manager near the bottom of the screen; double click on this icon to open the Program Manager window.

Step 2: Master the mouse

- A mouse is essential to the operation of WordPerfect as it is to all Windows applications, and it is important that you master its operation. The easiest way to practice is with the mouse tutorial found in the Help menu of Windows itself.
- Click the **Help menu.**
- Click **Windows Tutorial.**
- Type **M** to begin, then follow the on-screen instructions.
- Exit the tutorial when you are finished.

ABOUT PROGRAM MANAGER

If you are unable to find the on-line tutorial, it may be because you are using an older version of Windows, such as Windows 3.0 rather than Windows 3.1. Pull down the **Help menu** and select **About Program Manager** to display information about the program, including the release in use. A similar screen is available for every Windows application.

Step 3: Install the data disk

- Do this step *only* if you have your own computer and want to copy the files from the data disk to the hard drive.

- Place the data disk in drive A (or whatever drive is appropriate).
- Pull down the **File menu.**
- Click **Run.**
- Type **A:INSTALL C** in the text box. Click **OK.** (The drive letters in the command, A and C, are both variable. If, for example, the data disk were in drive B and you wanted to copy its files to drive D, you would type the command **B:INSTALL D.**)

Step 4: Load WordPerfect

- Double click the icon for the group containing WordPerfect for Windows if that group is not already open, then double click the program icon labeled **WPWin 6.0.**
- Click the **maximize button** (if necessary) so that the application window containing WordPerfect takes the entire screen.
- Click the **maximize button** in the document window (if necessary) to produce a screen similar to Figure 1.9a although no text has yet been entered.
- Pull down the **View menu.** Click **Draft.** Do not be concerned if your screen is different than ours as we include a troubleshooting section immediately following this exercise.

DOUBLE CLICKING FOR BEGINNERS

If you are having trouble double clicking, it is because you are not clicking quickly enough, or more likely, because you are moving the mouse (however slightly) between clicks. Relax and try again.

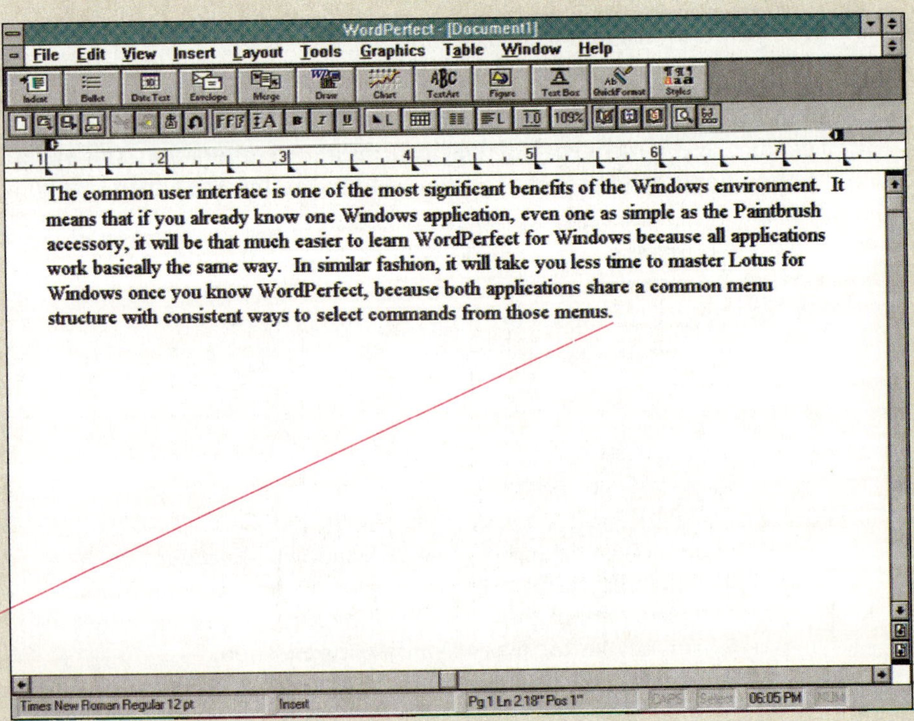

(a) Create the Document (step 5)

FIGURE 1.9 Hands-on Exercise 1

Step 5: Create the document

- Create the document in Figure 1.9a by typing just as you would on a typewriter with one exception—do *not* press the enter key at the end of a line. WordPerfect will automatically begin a new line as necessary.
- Press the **enter key** at the end of the paragraph.
- Proofread the document and correct any errors. Use the **Ins key** to toggle between the insertion and replacement (typeover) modes as appropriate.

THE INSERT/TYPEOVER MODE INDICATOR

If you do not see the Insert/Typeover indicator on the Status Bar, you need to customize the Status Bar. Pull down the File menu, click Preferences, and double click the Status Bar icon. Check the box for Insert mode. Click OK. Click Close. Now press the Ins key and the indicator on the Status Bar will toggle between Insert and Typeover.

Step 6: Save the document

- Pull down the **File menu.** Click **Save.**
- Alternatively, you can press **Alt+F** (to pull down the File menu), then type the letter **S,** or you can execute the Save command from the Power Bar by clicking the **Save icon** (the third icon from the left).
- Regardless of how you save the document, you should see the dialog box in Figure 1.9b.

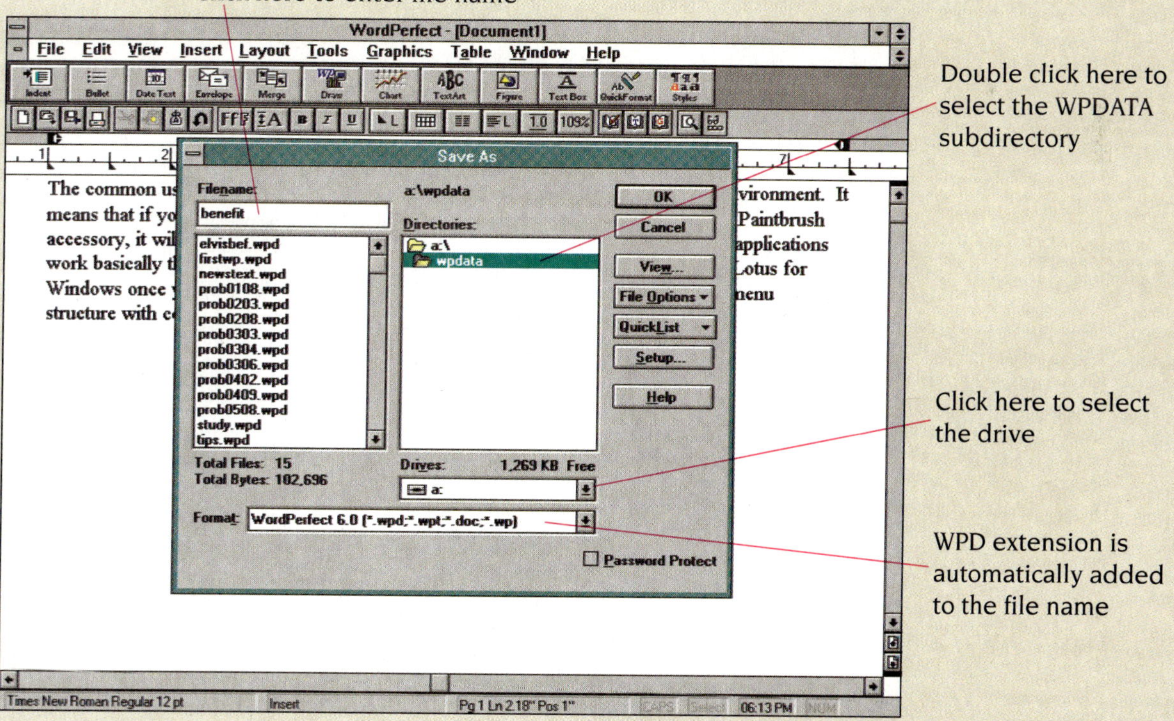

(b) The SAVE Command (step 6)

FIGURE 1.9 Hands-on Exercise 1 (continued)

- Click on the drop-down list box in the middle of the screen to specify the appropriate drive, drive C or drive A, depending on whether or not you installed the data disk in step 3.
- Scroll through the directory list box until you come to the **WPDATA** directory.
- Double click this directory to make it the active directory.
- Click in the text box for file name.
- Type **BENEFIT** as the name of the document (the WPD extension is added automatically).
- Click **OK** or press the enter key.

DISPLAY THE HARD RETURNS

Pull down the View menu and click Show ¶ to display the hard returns and other nonprinting characters contained within a document. The command functions as a toggle switch; that is, the first time you click the command the hard returns are displayed and a check mark is subsequently shown next to the command in the View menu. The second time you click the command the returns are hidden and the check mark disappears.

Step 7: Print the document

- Pull down the **File menu.**
- Click **Print** to produce the dialog box of Figure 1.9c.
- Click the **Print command button** to print the document.

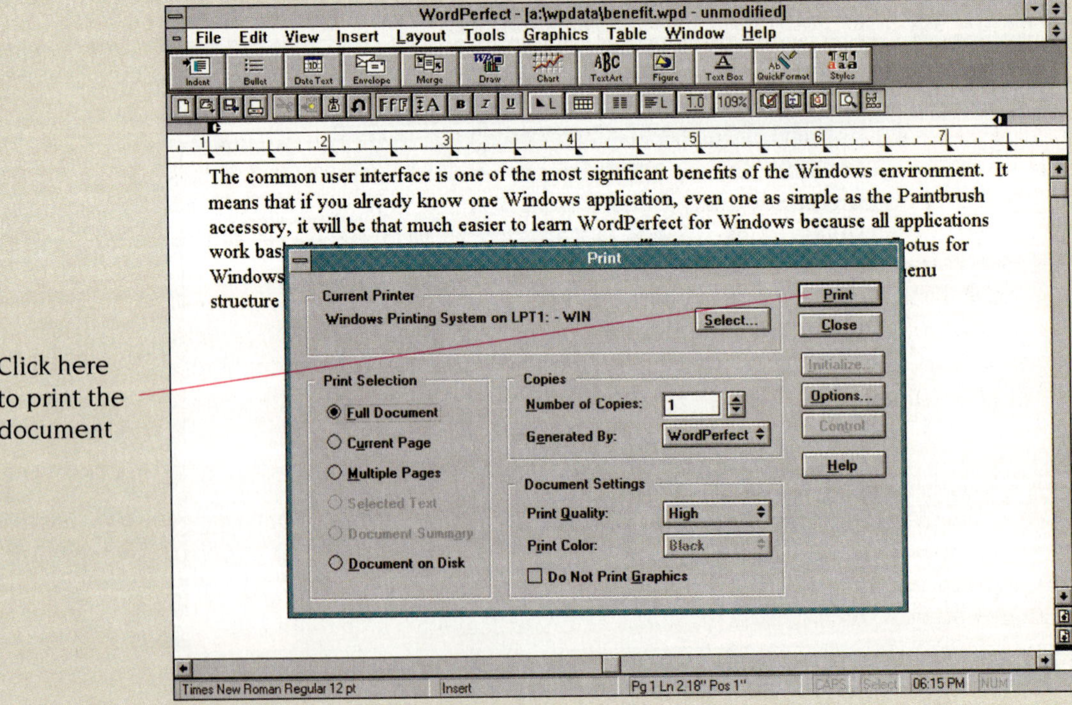

(c) The Print Command (step 7)

FIGURE 1.9 Hands-on Exercise 1 (continued)

TIP: EXECUTE COMMANDS QUICKLY

The quickest way to select a command from a pull-down menu is to point to the menu name, then drag the pointer (i.e., press and hold the left mouse button) to the desired command and release the mouse. The command is executed when you release the button.

Step 8: Exit WordPerfect

- The easiest way to exit (close) WordPerfect is to double click on the **control-menu box** at the left of the title bar. Alternatively, you can pull down the **File menu** and click **Exit,** or you can press **Alt+F4** prior to pulling down the File menu.
- Exit WordPerfect and return to Program Manager.

Step 9: Exit Windows

- The consistent command structure within Windows means that the same operation is accomplished the same way in different applications; that is, you can exit from Program Manager by using any of the techniques described in the previous step.
- Pull down the **File menu** in Program Manager.
- Select the **Exit Windows** command; this time, however, you will see an informational message indicating that you are leaving Windows, and requiring that you click the **OK** command button to confirm the operation.

TROUBLESHOOTING

We trust that you completed the hands-on exercise without difficulty, and that you were able to create, save, and print the document of Figure 1.9. There is, however, one area of potential confusion in that WordPerfect offers different views of the same document depending on the preferences of the individual user. It is unlikely that your screen will match ours completely, and, indeed, there is no requirement that it should. The *contents* of your document, however, should be identical to ours.

Figure 1.9 displayed the document in the view we prefer, called ***Draft view.*** Figure 1.10 displays an entirely different view of the same document in ***Page view.*** Your screen may or may not match either figure, and you will undoubtedly develop preferences of your own. The following suggestions will help you match the screens of Figures 1.9 and 1.10.

- If the application window for WordPerfect does not take the entire screen, and/or the document does not take the entire window within WordPerfect, click the maximize button in the application and/or the document window. Note the presence of two restore buttons in Figure 1.9a, indicating that both the application window and its associated document window have been maximized.
- If the text does not come up to the top of the screen—that is, you see the top edge of the page (as in Figure 1.10)—it means that you are in the Page view. Pull down the View menu and click Draft to match the document in Figure 1.9a.
- If the text seems unusually large or small, it means that you or a previous user elected to zoom in or out to get a different perspective on the document. Pull

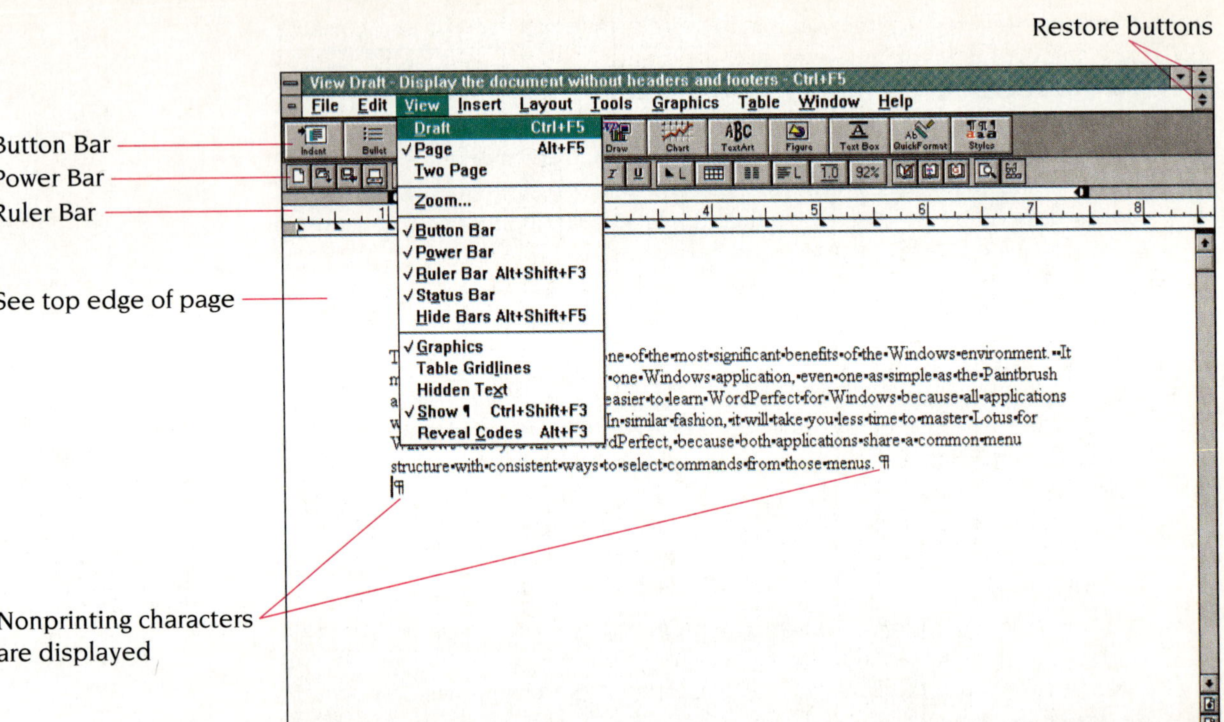

FIGURE 1.10 Troubleshooting

down the View menu, click on Zoom, then click Margin Width or Page Width, choosing whichever you prefer.

- If you see the ¶ and other nonprinting symbols, it means that you or a previous user elected to display these characters. Pull down the View menu and click on Show ¶ to remove the check. (The Show command functions as a toggle switch; that is, click the command once and the check appears; click the command a second time and the check disappears.)
- If the Power Bar, Ruler Bar, and/or Button Bar is not displayed, pull down the View menu and click the appropriate item. These commands also function as toggle switches; that is, clicking the command places a check next to the indicated item and displays it on the screen. Clicking the command a second time removes the check from the menu and the item from the screen.

Keyboard Preferences

One other difficulty you may encounter is associated with the keyboard. WordPerfect comes with two predefined keyboards, one for DOS and one for Windows. These are not keyboards in the physical sense, but software-controlled keyboards, which determine the effect of a specific keystroke combination.

The keyboard is selected during the installation of WordPerfect, but you can switch at any time (see the tip following step 4 in the ensuing exercise). You should not, however, switch back and forth continually because the keyboards are very different, and you will only confuse yourself. If, for example, you press Ctrl+End and the Windows keyboard is selected, you move to the end of the document, just as you would if you used the same keystroke combination in any Windows application. Pressing Ctrl+End with the DOS keyboard, however, deletes the line.

Individuals familiar with the DOS-based version of WordPerfect may be tempted to stick with the older keyboard to take advantage of what they already know. Although this strategy may be useful in the short term we advise against it, because it will only delay your getting used to Windows conventions. All keyboard references in this text are for the Windows keyboard.

HANDS-ON EXERCISE 2:

Retrieving a Document

Objective To retrieve an existing document, revise it, and save the revision; to demonstrate on-line help. Use Figure 1.11 as a guide in the exercise.

Step 1: Retrieve a document

- Repeat the necessary steps from the first exercise to load WordPerfect.
- Pull down the **File menu.** Click **Open** to produce a dialog box similar to the one in Figure 1.11a.

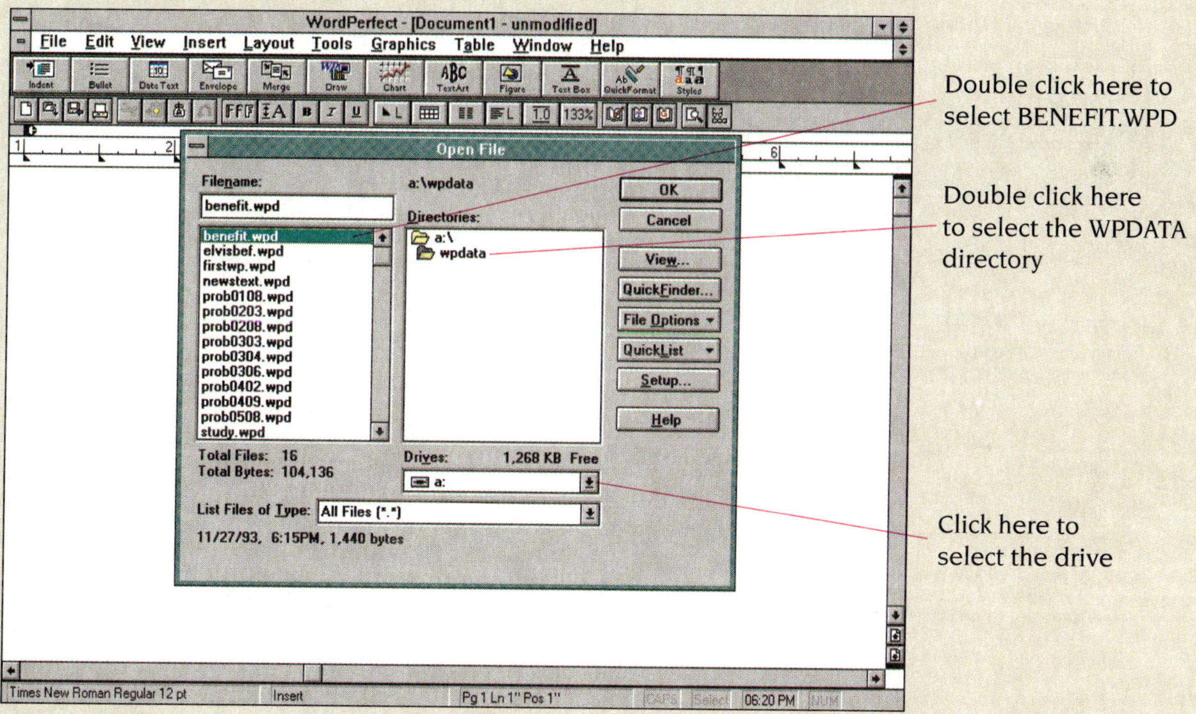

(a) The Open Command (step 1)

FIGURE 1.11 Hands-on Exercise 2

- Alternatively, you can press **Alt+F** (to pull down the File menu), then type the letter **O,** or you can execute the Open command from the Power Bar by clicking the **Open icon** (the second icon from the left).
- Click on the appropriate drive, drive C or drive A, as in the first exercise.
- Double click the **WPDATA** directory to make it the active directory.
- Double click **BENEFIT.WPD** to retrieve the document from the first exercise.

Step 2: The view menu (troubleshooting)

- Pull down the **View menu** and verify that there is a check mark next to the Power Bar, Button Bar, Status Bar, and Ruler Bar, so that these elements are displayed on the screen. If not, click the unchecked item(s) to display the element(s) on the screen.

- Click **Zoom.**
- Click **Margin Width.** Click **OK.** Your document should match the display shown earlier in Figure 1.9a. Do *not* be concerned if your typeface is different from ours or if you get more or less text on a line; these are differences in formatting and will be addressed in Chapter 2.

Step 3: Display the hard returns

- Pull down the **View menu.**
- Click **Show ¶** to display the hard returns and other hidden characters (e.g., the spaces between words).
- Pull down the **View menu** a second time. Click **Show ¶** a second time to suppress the display of the hard returns. Toggle the display of the hard returns on or off as you prefer.

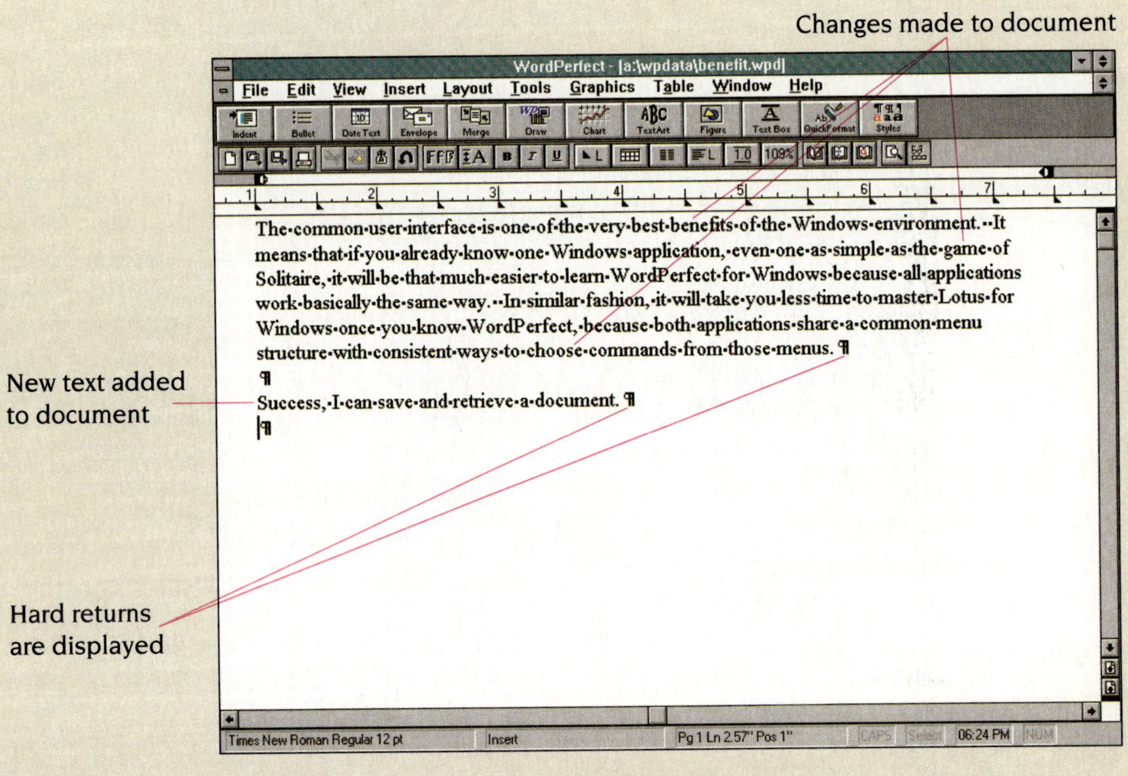

Changes made to document

WordPerfect - [a:\wpdata\benefit.wpd]

File Edit View Insert Layout Tools Graphics Table Window Help

The·common·user·interface·is·one·of·the·very·best·benefits·of·the·Windows·environment.··It means·that·if·you·already·know·one·Windows·application,·even·one·as·simple·as·the·game·of Solitaire,·it·will·be·that·much·easier·to·learn·WordPerfect·for·Windows·because·all·applications work·basically·the·same·way.··In·similar·fashion,·it·will·take·you·less·time·to·master·Lotus·for Windows·once·you·know·WordPerfect,·because·both·applications·share·a·common·menu structure·with·consistent·ways·to·choose·commands·from·those·menus.¶
¶
Success,·I·can·save·and·retrieve·a·document.¶
¶

New text added to document

Hard returns are displayed

Times New Roman Regular 12 pt | Insert | Pg 1 Ln 2.57" Pos 1" | 06:24 PM

(b) The Corrected Document with Paragraph Markers (steps 2, 3, and 4)

FIGURE 1.11 Hands-on Exercise 2 (continued)

Step 4: Modify the document

- Press **Ctrl+End** to move to the end of the document.
- Press the enter key once or twice to add a blank line(s).
- Add the sentence, **Success, I can save and retrieve a document!**
- Make the following additional modifications to practice editing.
  — Change the phrase, *most significant* to **very best.**
  — Change *Paintbrush accessory* to **game of Solitaire.**
  — Change the word *select* to **choose.**
- Switch between the insertion and typeover modes as necessary.

WHICH KEYBOARD ARE YOU USING?

If Ctrl+End deletes a line instead of moving the cursor to the end of the document, it is because you are using the WordPerfect DOS keyboard instead of the Windows keyboard. Pull down the **File menu,** click **Preferences,** and double click the **Keyboard icon.** Click **WPWin 6.0 Keyboard,** click the **Select command button,** then click the **Close command button.**

Step 5: Save the changes

- It is very, very important to save your work repeatedly during a session.
- Pull down the **File menu** and click **Save** (or click the **Save icon** on the Power Bar).

THE POWER BAR

To determine the function of a Power Bar icon, just point (don't click) to the icon. A description of the icon (known as a help prompt) will appear at the upper left of the WordPerfect window.

Step 6: Deleting text

- Point to the first character in the document. The pointer is an I-beam.
- **Press and hold the left mouse button** as you drag the mouse over the first sentence including the two spaces at the end of the sentence.
- Release the mouse.
- The sentence should remain highlighted (selected) as in Figure 1.11c. The selected text is the text that is affected by the next command.
- Click anywhere else in the document to deselect the text.
- Repeat the process to reselect the first sentence.
- Press the **Del key** to delete the highlighted text (the first sentence) from the document.

THE INSERTION POINT VERSUS THE I-BEAM

The I-beam indicates only that you are pointing to an area in a document; it is very different from the insertion point, which marks the position in a document where the text will be entered. You must **click the left mouse button** to change the insertion point after using the mouse to scroll through a document. The insertion point changes automatically if you use the keyboard to move through a document.

Step 7: The Undelete command

- Pull down the **Edit menu** as in Figure 1.11d.
- Click on **Undelete.** The sentence returns to the document and the Undelete dialog box opens.

➤ Click the **Restore command button** to restore the text.

➤ Pull down the **View menu** and remove the check next to Show ¶.

Selected text is affected by next command

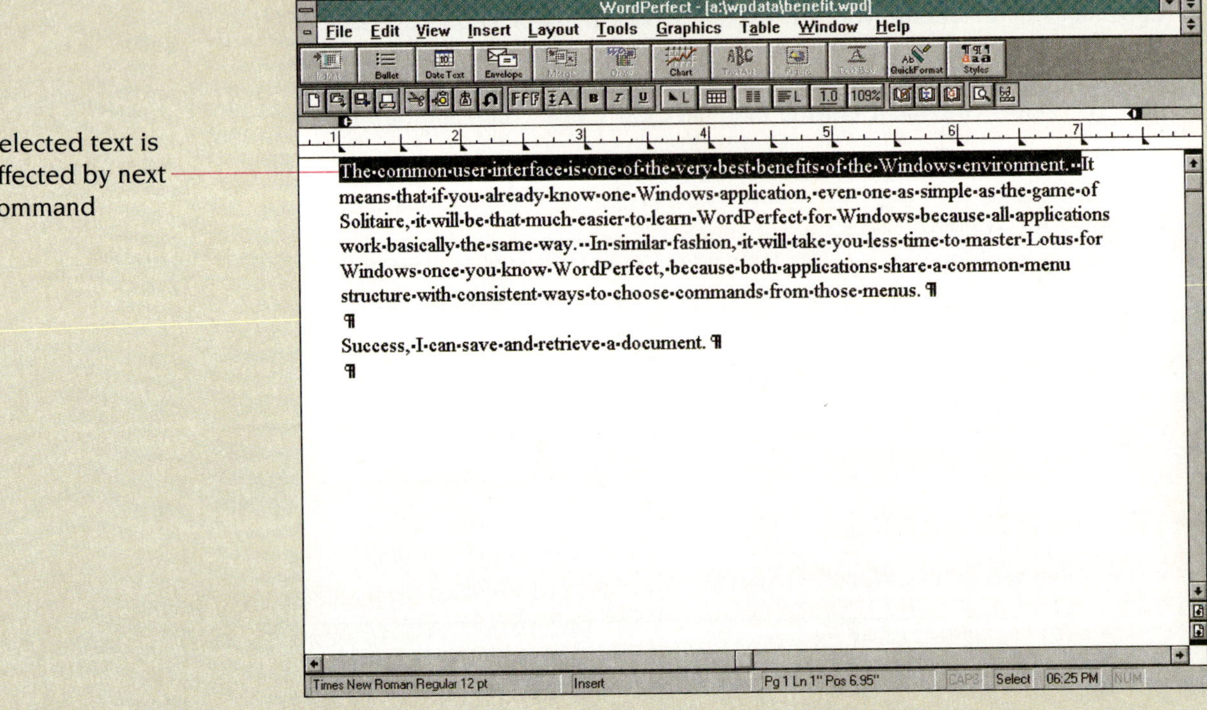

(c) Deleting the Text (step 6)

Undelete will restore deleted text

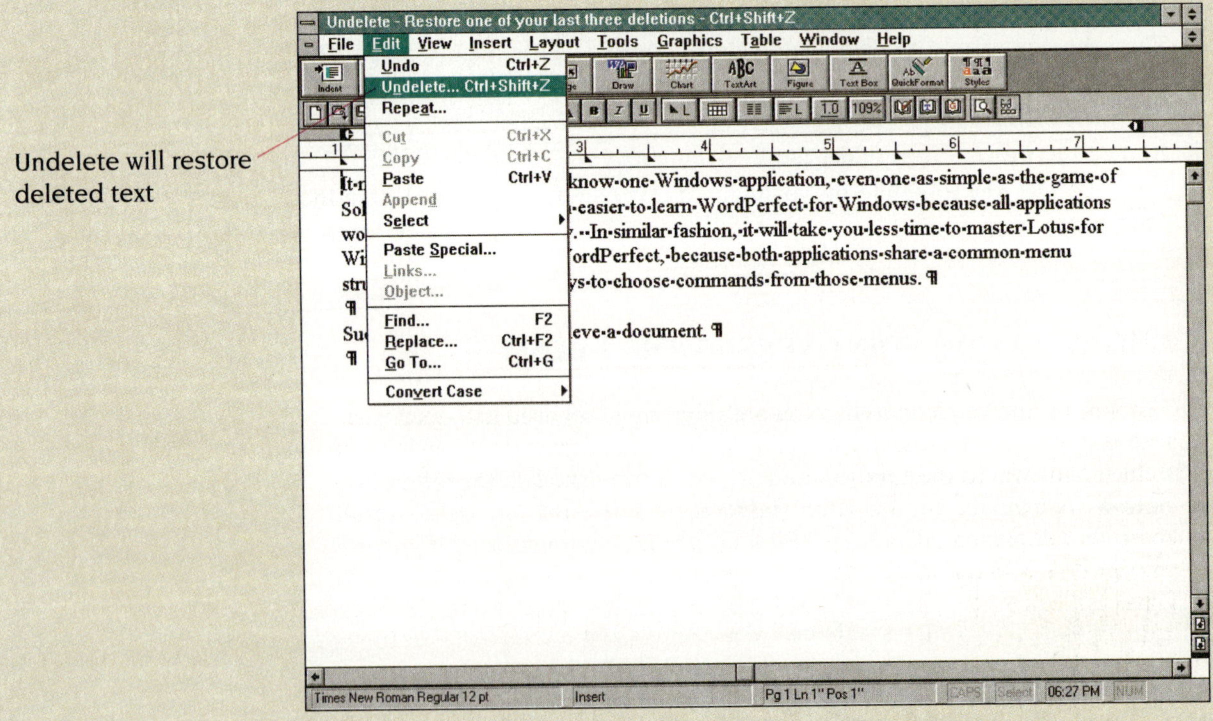

(d) The Undelete Command (step 7)

FIGURE 1.11 Hands-on Exercise 2 (continued)

Step 8: On-line help

- Pull down the **Help menu.**
- Click **Search for Help On** to produce the dialog box in Figure 1.11e.
- Type **un**delete (you have to type only the first two letters before the Help facility locates the entire word).
- Double click **undelete** when it appears in the top list box to display the related help topics in the lower list box.
- Double click **undelete** in the lower list box to display the related informational screen.
- Click the **maximize button** in the Help window. Click the **restore button** to return the window to its previous size.
- Click the **Print command button** to print the Help Topic.
- Click the **Close command button** to exit Help and return to your document.

Step 9: Print the revised document

- Save the document a final time. Print the revised document.
- Exit WordPerfect as you did at the end of the previous exercise.

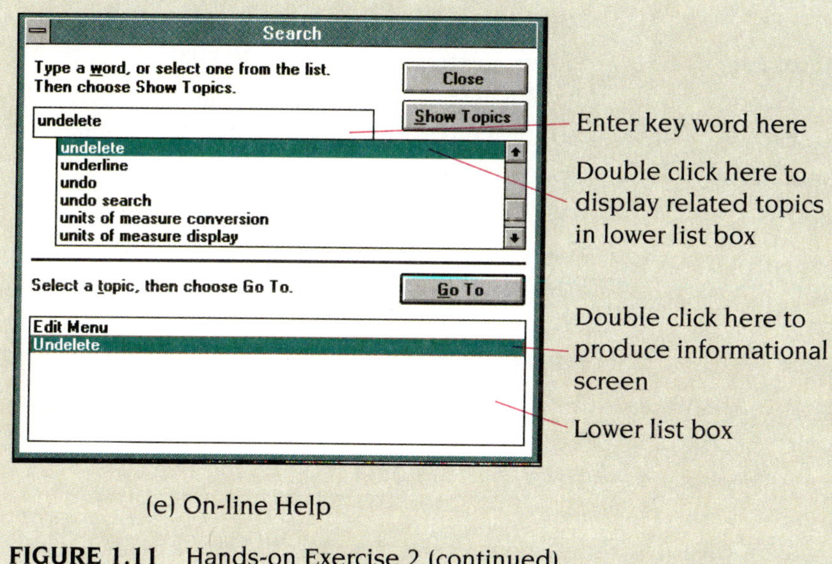

(e) On-line Help

FIGURE 1.11 Hands-on Exercise 2 (continued)

SUMMARY

The common user interface ensures that all Windows applications are similar in appearance and work basically the same way, with common conventions and a consistent menu structure. It provides you with an intuitive understanding of any application, even before you begin to use it, and means that once you learn one application, it is that much easier to learn the next.

The mouse is essential to WordPerfect as it is to all Windows applications, but keyboard equivalents are provided for virtually all operations. The Power Bar, Button Bar(s), and Ruler Bar provide yet another way to execute common commands. On-line help provides detailed information about all aspects of WordPerfect.

Any word processor is always in one of two modes, insertion or replacement (also known as typeover), and uses a toggle switch (the Ins key) to alternate between the two. The insertion point marks the place within a document where text is added or replaced.

The enter key is pressed only at the end of a paragraph, rather than the end of every line because WordPerfect automatically wraps text from one line to the next. A hard return is created by the user when he or she presses the enter key; a soft return is created by the word processor as it wraps text from one line to the next.

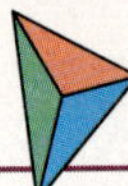

Key Words and Concepts

Application window
Button Bar
Cascade menu
Check box
Click
Command button
Common user interface
Contents command
Control-menu box
Desktop
Dialog box
Dimmed command
Document window
Double click
Drop-down list box
Draft view
Drag
Ellipsis
Glossary
Hard return
Help buttons
Help menu
How Do I command
Icon
Insertion mode
Insertion point
Keyboard preferences
List box
Maximize button
Menu bar
Minimize button
Mouse pointer
On-line help
Open list box
Option button
Page view
Point
Power Bar
Program Icon
Program Manager
Pull-down menu
QuickMenu
Replacement (typeover) mode
Restore button
Ruler Bar
Scroll bar
Scroll box
Soft return
Status Bar
Text box
Title bar
Toggle switch
Undelete command
Windows
WordPerfect for Windows
Word wrap

Multiple Choice

1. When entering text within a document, the enter key is normally pressed at the end of every:
(a) Line
(b) Sentence
(c) Paragraph
(d) All of the above

2. Which of the following is true regarding scrolling?
(a) You can scroll a document in a vertical direction
(b) You can scroll a document in a horizontal direction
(c) Both (a) and (b)
(d) Neither (a) nor (b)

3. Which of the following will execute a command from a pull-down menu?
(a) Clicking on the command once the menu has been pulled down
(b) Typing the underlined letter in the command
(c) Both (a) and (b)
(d) Neither (a) nor (b)

4. The File Open command:
   (a) Brings a document (file) from disk into memory
   (b) Brings a document (file) from disk into memory, then erases the document on disk
   (c) Stores the document (file) in memory on disk
   (d) Stores the document (file) in memory on disk, then erases the document from memory

5. The File Save command:
   (a) Brings a document (file) from disk into memory
   (b) Brings a document (file) from disk into memory, then erases the document on disk
   (c) Stores the document (file) in memory on disk
   (d) Stores the document (file) in memory on disk, then erases the document from memory

6. What is the easiest way to change the phrase, *revenues, profits, gross margin,* to read *revenues, profits, and gross margin?*
   (a) Use the insertion mode, position the insertion point before the *g* in *gross,* then type the word *and* followed by a space
   (b) Use the insertion mode, position the insertion point after the *g* in *gross,* then type the word *and* followed by a space
   (c) Use the typeover (replacement) mode, position the insertion point before the *g* in *gross,* then type the word *and* followed by a space
   (d) Use the typeover (replacement) mode, position the insertion point after the *g* in *gross,* then type the word *and* followed by a space

7. What happens if you press the Ins key *twice in a row?*
   (a) You will be in the insertion mode
   (b) You will be in the replacement mode
   (c) You will be in the same mode you were in before pressing the key at all
   (d) You will be in the opposite mode you were in before pressing the key at all

8. What is the significance of three dots next to a menu option?
   (a) The option is not accessible
   (b) A dialog box will appear if the option is selected
   (c) A help window will appear if the option is selected
   (d) There are no equivalent keystrokes for the particular option

9. What is the significance of a menu option that appears faded (dimmed)?
   (a) The option is not currently accessible
   (b) A dialog box will appear if the option is selected
   (c) A help window will appear if the option is selected
   (d) There are no equivalent keystrokes for the particular option

10. Which of the following elements may be found within a help window?
   (a) Title bar, menu bar, and control-menu box
   (b) Minimize and maximize or restore buttons
   (c) Vertical and/or horizontal scroll bars
   (d) All of the above

11. A document has been entered into WordPerfect with a given set of margins, which are subsequently changed. What can you say about the number of hard and soft returns before and after the change in margins?
    (a) The number of hard returns is the same, but the number and/or position of the soft returns is different
    (b) The number of soft returns is the same, but the number and/or position of the hard returns is different
    (c) The number and position of both hard and soft returns are unchanged
    (d) The number and position of both hard and soft returns are different

12. Which of the following is an example of a toggle switch within WordPerfect?
    (a) The Ins key
    (b) The Caps Lock key
    (c) Both (a) and (b)
    (d) Neither (a) nor (b)

13. Which of the following is true regarding a dialog box?
    (a) Option buttons indicate mutually exclusive choices
    (b) Check boxes imply that multiple options may be selected
    (c) Both (a) and (b)
    (d) Neither (a) nor (b)

14. Which of the following will exit WordPerfect and return to Windows?
    (a) Double clicking the control-menu box in the title bar for WordPerfect
    (b) Pressing Alt+F4 from anywhere within WordPerfect
    (c) Pulling down the File menu and clicking on Exit
    (d) All of the above

15. Which of the following actions will end a Windows session?
    (a) Double clicking on the control-menu box of the Program Manager
    (b) Double clicking on the control-menu box of WordPerfect
    (c) Both (a) and (b)
    (d) Neither (a) nor (b)

ANSWERS

1. c	**4.** a	**7.** c	**10.** d	**13.** c
2. c	**5.** c	**8.** b	**11.** a	**14.** d
3. c	**6.** a	**9.** a	**12.** c	**15.** a

EXPLORING WORDPERFECT

1. Use Figure 1.12 to identify the elements of a WordPerfect screen by matching each element with the appropriate letter.

____ Restore button	____ Minimize button
____ Control-menu box	____ Horizontal scroll bar
____ Power Bar	____ Vertical scroll bar
____ Button Bar	____ Menu bar
____ Ruler Bar	____ Status Bar

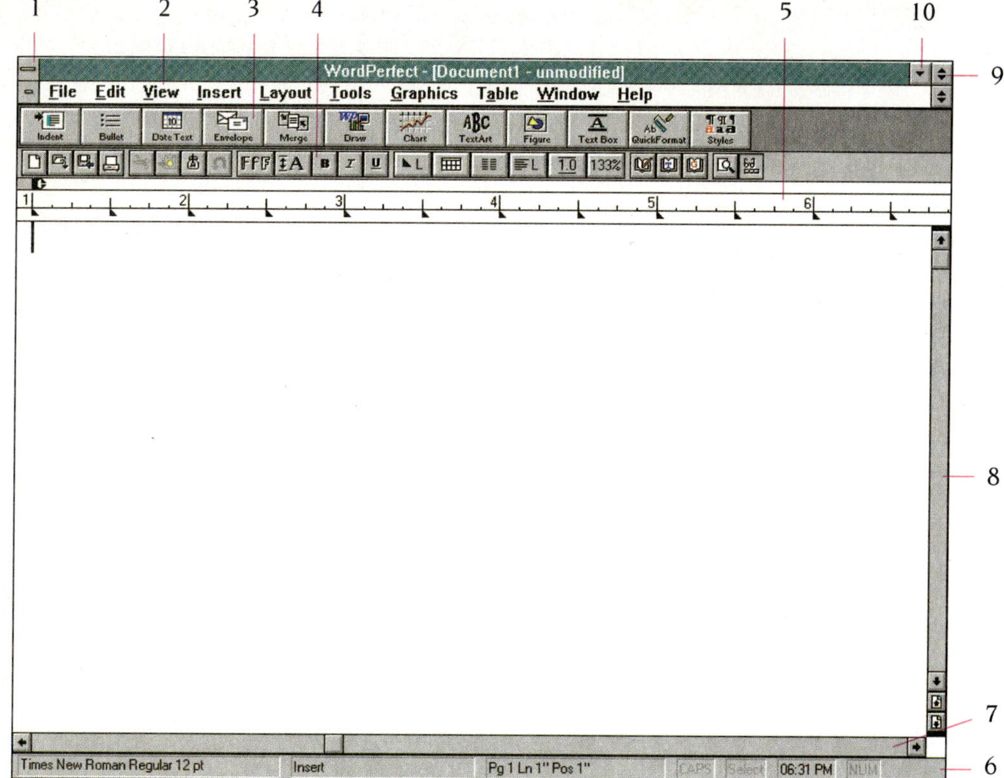

FIGURE 1.12 Screen for Problem 1

2. The Common User interface: Answer the following with respect to Figures 1.2a and 1.2b that appeared earlier in the chapter.
   a. Which pull-down menus are common to both Lotus and WordPerfect?
   b. How do you access the Edit menu in Lotus? in WordPerfect?
   c. How do you open a file in Lotus for Windows? Do you think the same command will work in WordPerfect as well?
   d. Which icons correspond to the Open and Save commands in Lotus? Which icons correspond to these commands in WordPerfect?
   e. What do your answers to parts a through d tell you about the advantages of a common user interface? What do the answers imply about applications from different vendors?

3. What is the difference between:
   a. The insertion and replacement (typeover) modes?
   b. Deleting a character using the Backspace and Del keys?
   c. Typing when text is selected versus typing when no text has been selected?
   d. The I-beam and the insertion point?
   e. A hard and soft carriage return?

4. Trouble shooting: The informational messages in Figure 1.13 appeared (or could have appeared) in response to various commands issued during the chapter.
   a. Which command produced the message in Figure 1.13a? What action is necessary to correct the indicated problem?
   b. Which command produced the message in Figure 1.13b? When would No be an appropriate response to this message?

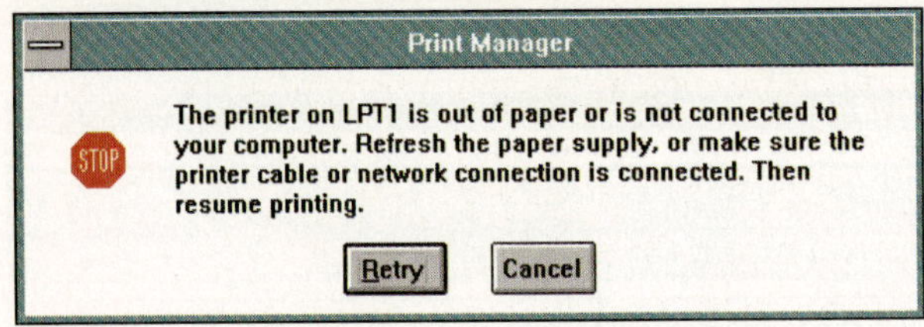

(a) Informational Message 1

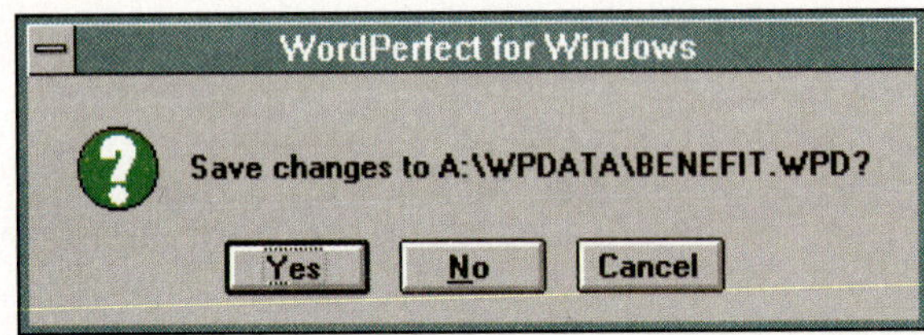

(b) Informational Message 2

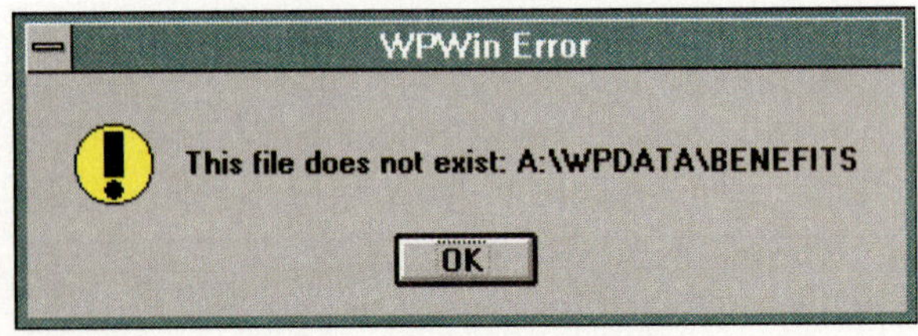

(c) Informational Message 3

FIGURE 1.13 Informational Messages for Problem 4

c. The message in Figure 1.13c appeared in response to a File Open command in conjunction with the file shown earlier in Figure 1.13b. What is the most likely corrective action?

5. Answer the following with respect to the dialog box in Figure 1.14.
   a. Which command produced the dialog box?
   b. Can the Document and Show ¶ options be on at the same time?
   c. Can the Table Gridlines and Comments boxes both be checked?
   d. Are there any text boxes within the figure?
   e. What happens if you click the arrows in the Units of Measure list box?
   f. What happens when you click the OK command button?

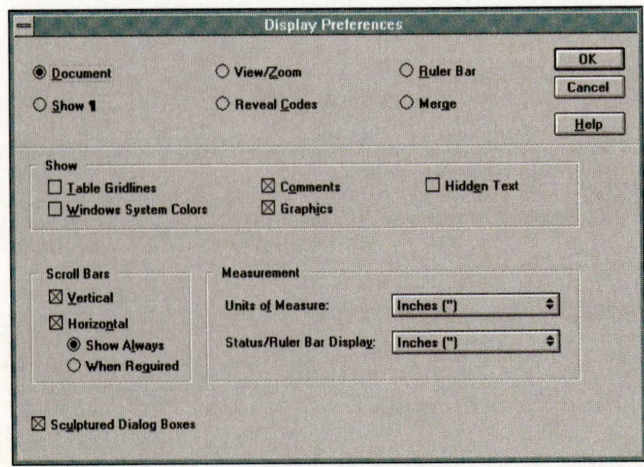

FIGURE 1.14 Dialog Box for Problem 5

6. Exploring help: Answer the following with respect to Figure 1.15.
   a. Which command is discussed? Is this a command that might be useful to you?
   b. What is the equivalent icon on the Power Bar?
   c. Is there any benefit to maximizing the window?
   d. Is there any benefit to minimizing the window?
   e. How do you print the information displayed in the screen?
   f. How do you access the glossary?

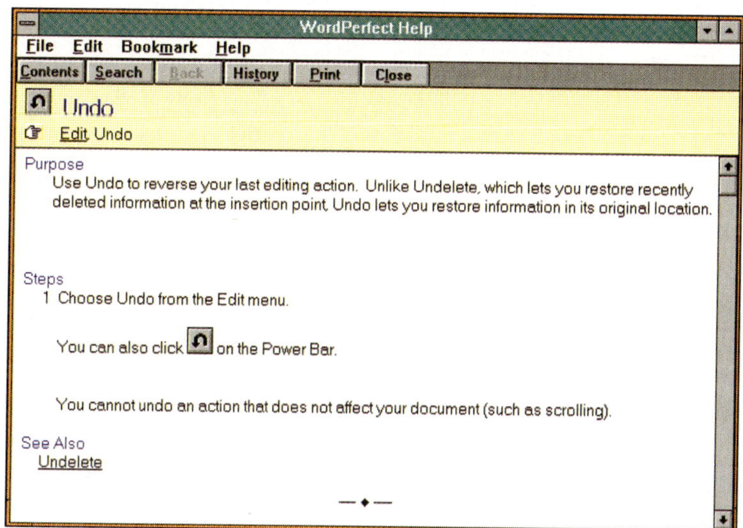

FIGURE 1.15 Help Screen for Problem 6

7. Answer the following with respect to Figure 1.16:
   a. What is the name of the document currently being edited?
   b. What is the position of the insertion point?
   c. Is the ruler present? a Button Bar? the Power Bar? How do you cause the missing elements (if any) to reappear?
   d. Which mode is active, insertion or typeover? How do you switch from one mode to the other?
   e. How do you display (hide) the hard carriage returns? Are the hard returns displayed in the figure?
   f. Has the application window for WordPerfect been maximized? Has the document window within WordPerfect been maximized?
   g. Add your name at the top of the document, then create and print the entire document. Submit the completed document to your instructor.

8. Using the data disk: The document in Figure 1.17 is contained on the data disk as PROB0108.WPD. Open the document, then make the following changes:
   a. Select the text *Your name* and replace it with your name.
   b. Replace *June 1, 1993* with the current date
   c. Insert the phrase *one or* in line 2 so that the text reads . . . *one or more characters than currently exist.*
   d. Delete the word *And* from sentence 4 in line 5, then change the w in *when* to a capital letter to begin the sentence.

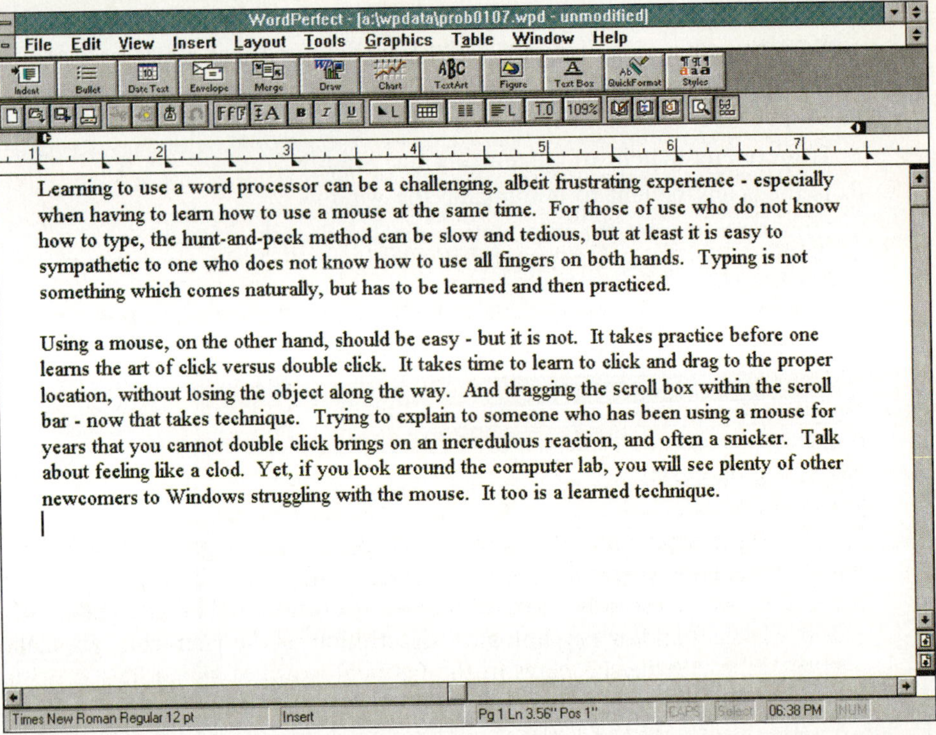

FIGURE 1.16 Screen for Problem 7

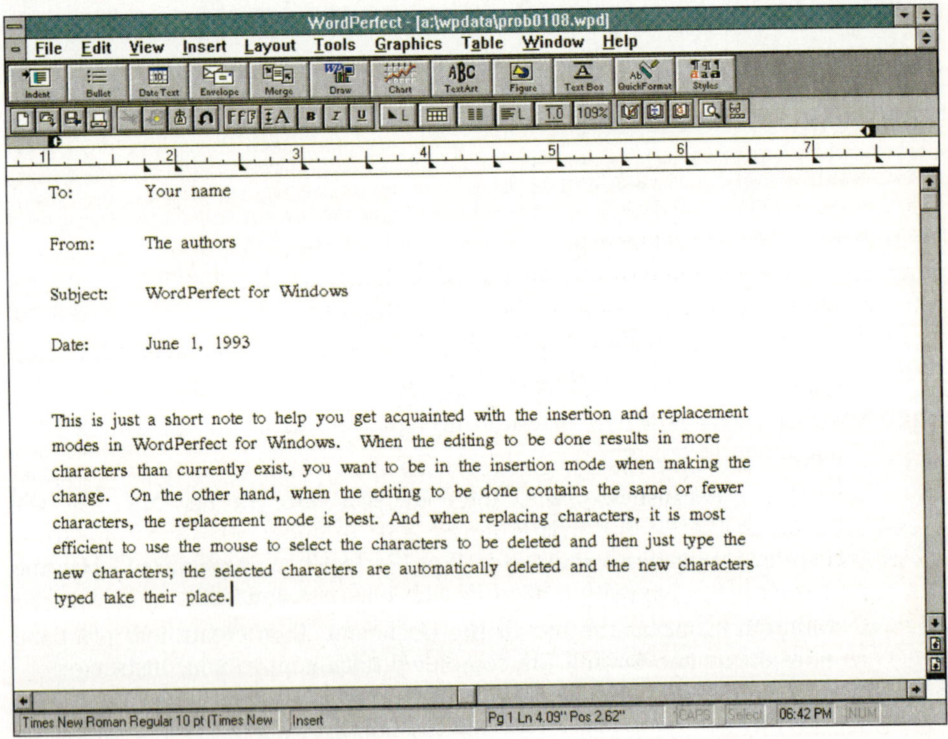

FIGURE 1.17 Screen for Problem 8

e. Change the phrase *most efficient* to *best*.

f. Place the insertion point at the end of sentence 2, make sure you are in the insertion mode, then add the following sentence: *The insertion mode adds characters at the insertion point while moving existing text to the right in order to make room for the new text.*

g. Place the insertion point at the end of the last sentence, press the enter key twice in a row, then enter the following text: *There are several keys that function as toggle switches of which you should be aware. The Ins key switches between the insertion and replacement modes, the Caps Lock key toggles between upper- and lower-case letters, and the Num Lock key alternates between typing numbers and using the cursor control keys.*

h. Save the revised document, then print it and submit it to your instructor.

9. Prepare a one-page memo (approximately 250 words) from student to instructor detailing your background; include any previous knowledge of computers you may have, prior computer courses you have taken, your objectives for the course, and so on. Also, indicate whether you own a PC, whether you have access to one at work, and/or whether you are considering purchase. Include any other information about yourself and/or your computer-related background. Your one page of text should consist of at least two paragraphs. After you have created your memo, print it and submit it to your instructor.

10. Write a short essay (three to four paragraphs) describing your favorite fictional character—whether it be a character from a cherished novel or short story, a classic or recently released movie, or even a mythological tale. Give a brief physical and/or psychological description of the character, an explanation of the role he/she plays in the fictional world in which he/she exists, and the reasons why this character has inspired you to feel as you do. When you have completed the essay, proofread it for errors, make any corrections necessary, then print it and submit it to your instructor for a grade.

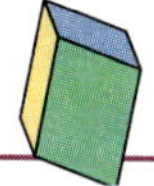

Case Studies

It's a Mess

Newcomers to word processing quickly learn the concept of word wrap and the distinction between hard and soft returns. This lesson was lost, however, on your friend who created the document HELPME.WPD on the data disk. The first several sentences were entered without any hard returns at all, whereas the opposite problem exists toward the end of the document. This is a good friend and her paper is due in one hour. Please help.

Planning for Disaster

Do you have a backup strategy? Do you even know what a backup strategy is? You should learn, because sooner or later you will wish you had one. You will erase a file, be unable to read from a floppy disk, or suffer a hardware failure in which you are unable to access the hard drive. The problem always seems to occur the night before an assignment is due. The ultimate disaster is the disappearance of your computer, by theft or natural disaster (e.g., Hurricane Andrew or the Los Angeles earthquake). Describe in 250 words or fewer the backup strategy you plan to implement in conjunction with your work in this class.

A Letter Home

You really like this course and want very much to have your own computer, but you're strapped for cash and have decided to ask your parents for help. Write a one-page letter describing the advantages of having your own system and how it will help you in school. Tell your parents what the system will cost, and that you can save money by buying through the mail. Describe the configuration you intend to buy (don't forget to include the price of software) and then provide prices from at least three different companies. Cut out the advertisements and include them in your letter. Bring your material to class and compare your research with that of your classmates.

Computer Magazines

A subscription to a computer magazine should be given serious consideration if you intend to stay abreast in a rapidly changing field. The reviews on new products are especially helpful, and you will appreciate the advertisements should you need to buy. Go to the library or a newsstand and obtain a magazine that appeals to you, then write a brief review of the magazine for class. Describe the features you like and don't like. Devote at least one paragraph to an article or other item you find useful.

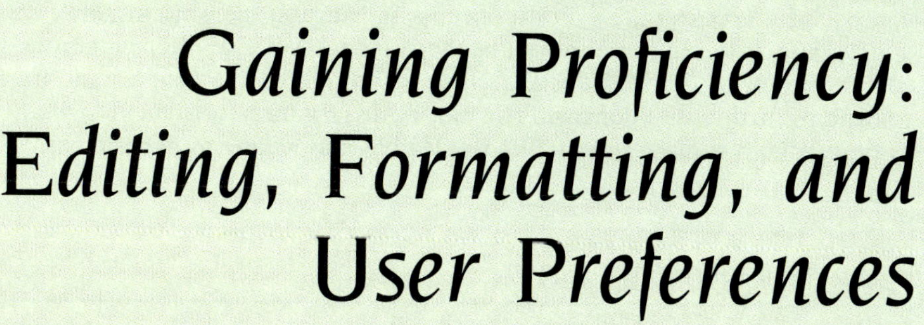

2

Gaining Proficiency: Editing, Formatting, and User Preferences

CHAPTER OBJECTIVES

After reading this chapter you will be able to:

1. Define the select-then-do methodology; describe various ways to select text within a document.
2. Use the clipboard and/or the drag-and-drop capability to move and copy text within a document.
3. Use the Find and Replace commands to substitute one character string for another; describe several options associated with each command.
4. Differentiate between the Save and Save As commands; describe various backup options that can be selected.
5. Define scrolling; scroll to the beginning and end of a document.
6. Distinguish between a serif and a sans serif typeface; change the typeface, style, and/or type size within a document.
7. Reformat a document by changing line spacing, margins, and/or justification; change the tab stops and/or indentation.
8. Establish page breaks within a document; describe the different views available within WordPerfect and the advantages of each.
9. Explain the use of Reveal Codes in editing a document.
10. Customize the WordPerfect environment to your personal preference.

OVERVIEW

The previous chapter taught you the basics of WordPerfect for Windows and enabled you to create and print a simple document. The present chapter significantly extends your capabilities, by presenting a variety of commands that let you change the contents and appearance of a document. These operations are known as editing and formatting, respectively.

You will learn how to move and/or copy text within a document, how to find and replace one character string with another, and how to implement various backup options. You will also learn the basics of typography and be able to switch among the different fonts included within Windows. You will be able to change the justification and/or line spacing within a document, to use tabs and indents, to establish page breaks, and to preview the document before printing. You will also learn how to customize the WordPerfect environment to your personal preferences. All of these commands are implemented in the hands-on exercises, which require your participation at the computer, and which are the very essence of the chapter.

As you read the chapter, realize that there are many different ways to accomplish the same task and that it would be impossible to cover them all. Our approach is to present the overall concepts and suggest the ways we think are most appropriate at the time we introduce the material. We also offer numerous shortcuts in the form of boxed tips that appear throughout the chapter and urge you to explore further on your own. It is not necessary for you to memorize anything as on-line help is always available. Be flexible and willing to experiment.

WRITE NOW, EDIT LATER

You write a sentence, then change it, and change it again, and one hour later you've produced a single paragraph. It happens to every writer—you stare at a blank screen and flashing cursor and are unable to write. The best solution is to brainstorm and write down anything that pops into your head, and to keep on writing. Don't worry about typos or spelling errors because you can fix them later. Above all, resist the temptation to continually edit the few words you've written because overediting will drain the life out of what you are writing. The important thing is to get your ideas on paper.

SELECT-THEN-DO

Most operations in WordPerfect take place within the context of ***select-then-do;*** that is, you select a block of text, then you execute the command to operate on that text. The most basic way to select text is by dragging the mouse; that is, click at the beginning of the selection, press and hold the left mouse button and move to the end of the selection, then release the mouse.

There are, however, many shortcuts to facilitate the process. You can, for example, double click within a word to select the word, triple-click within a sentence to select the sentence, or quadruple-click within a paragraph to select the paragraph. Additional shortcuts are presented in the hands-on exercises, at which point you will have an opportunity to practice.

Selected text is affected by any subsequent operation; for example, clicking the boldface or italics icon changes the selected text to boldface or italics, respectively. You can also drag the selected text to a new location, press the Del key to erase the selected text, or execute any other editing or formatting command. The selected text remains highlighted until you click elsewhere in the document.

SELECT A VARIABLE AMOUNT OF TEXT

Most shortcuts for selecting text focus on a specific unit—a word, a paragraph, a sentence, or the entire document. To select a variable amount of text, click at the beginning of the block, then press and hold the Shift key as you click at the end of the selection.

MOVING AND COPYING TEXT

The ability to move and/or copy text is essential in order to develop any degree of proficiency in editing. A move operation removes the text from its current location and places it elsewhere in the same (or even a different) document. A copy operation retains the text in its present location and places a duplicate elsewhere. Either operation can be accomplished using the Windows clipboard and a combination of the ***Cut, Copy,*** and ***Paste commands.*** (A shortcut, using the mouse to ***drag-and-drop*** text from one location to another, is described in step 8 in the first hands-on exercise.)

The ***clipboard*** is a temporary storage area available to any Windows application. Selected text is cut or copied from a document and placed into the clipboard from where it can be pasted to one or more locations. A move requires that you select the text, execute a Cut command to remove the text from its current location in the document and place it in the clipboard. You then move the insertion point to the new location, and finally paste the text from the clipboard into the new location. A copy operation necessitates the same steps except that the selected text is copied to the clipboard rather than cut.

The Cut, Copy, and Paste commands are found in the Edit menu, or alternatively, can be executed by clicking the appropriate icons on the Power Bar. The contents of the clipboard are replaced by each subsequent Cut or Copy command, but are unaffected by the Paste command; that is, the contents of the clipboard can be pasted into multiple locations in the same or a different document.

DELETE WITH CAUTION

You work too hard developing your thoughts to see them disappear in a flash. Hence, instead of deleting large blocks of text, try moving them to the end of your document where they can be recalled later if you change your mind. A related practice is to remain in the insert mode (as opposed to typeover) to prevent the inadvertent deletion of existing text as new ideas are added.

UNDO COMMAND

The ***Undo command*** reverses the effect of the latest command and is invaluable at any time, but especially when you are learning. The command is executed from within the Edit menu or by clicking the Undo icon on the Power Bar. You can use the command whenever something happens to a document that is different from what you intended, but you must execute the command before any other commands are executed. Some commands, however, cannot be undone; for example, you cannot undo a Save command.

UNDO VERSUS UNDELETE

Undo and Undelete are different commands. The Undo command reverses the effect of the latest command and can restore deleted text, but only if the command is executed immediately after the deletion. The Undelete command can restore any of the last three deleted entries, and further, can be executed after other actions have taken place.

FIND AND REPLACE COMMANDS

The ***Find command*** lets you search for a specific occurrence of a character string in order to perform a subsequent editing or formatting operation. The ***Replace command*** incorporates the Find command and allows you to search for and optionally replace (one or more occurrences of) a designated character string with a different character string.

The two strings are known as the find and replacement strings, respectively, and may consist of a single letter, a word, a sentence, or any combination of text. The two strings do *not* have to be the same length. Either (or both) may include formatting; for example, you could search for a word or phrase in boldface, and replace it with the same (or different) phrase in italics. The Find and Replace commands are illustrated in Figure 2.1.

The search may or may not be ***case sensitive.*** A case-sensitive search matches not only the characters, but the use of upper- and lower-case letters; that is, *There* is different from *there,* and a case-sensitive search on one will not identify the other. A ***case-insensitive*** search is just the opposite and finds both occurrences. The search may also specify a match on the ***whole word only,*** which will identify *there,* but not *therefore* or *thereby*. The dialog box in Figure 2.1a indicates that both options are in effect. (The options were specified by pulling down the Match menu and clicking on the appropriate commands.)

Perhaps the most important distinction is between ***selective replacement,*** whereby you identify each occurrence of the character string, examine it in con-

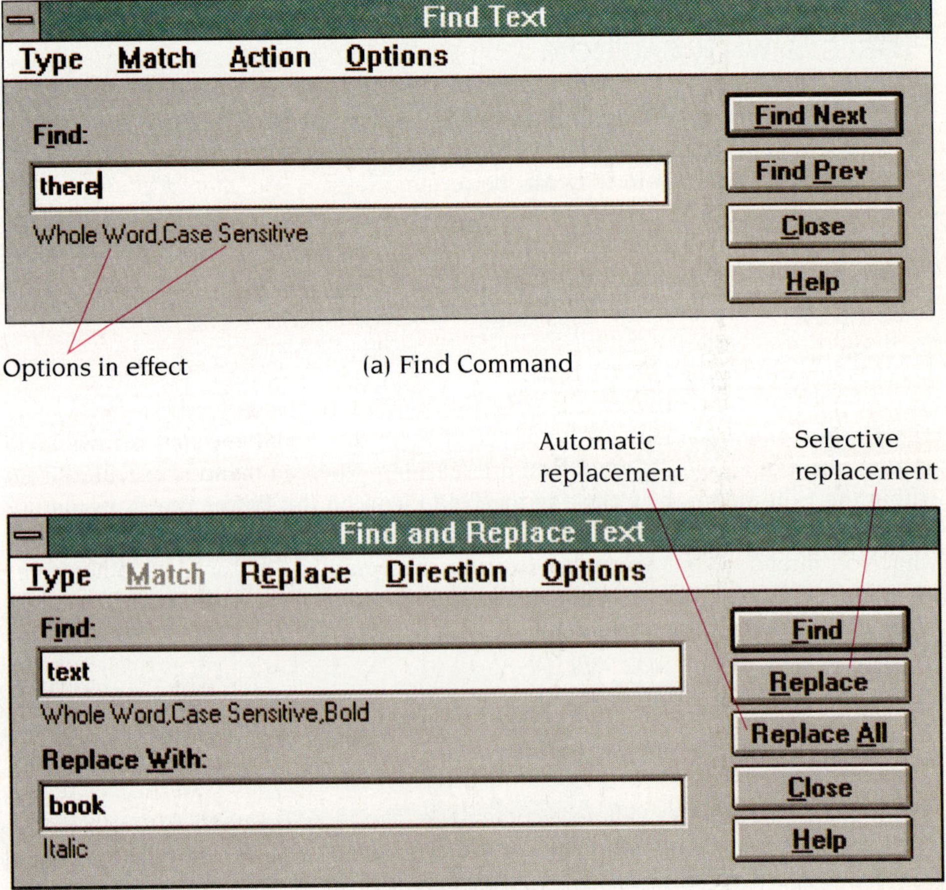

FIGURE 2.1 The Find and Replace Command

text and decide whether to replace it, versus ***global replacement,*** where the substitution is made automatically. The latter often produces unintended consequences and is generally not recommended; for example, if you substitute the word *text* for *book*, the phrase *text book* would become *text text*, which is not what you had in mind.

Selective replacement is implemented in Figure 2.1b by clicking the Find command button, then clicking (or not clicking) the Replace button to make (or not make) the substitution. Automatic replacement is implemented by clicking the Replace All button.

SAVE COMMAND

The ***Save command*** copies the document currently being edited (the document in memory) to a permanent storage medium, that is, to disk. The initial execution of the command requires you to enter a file name (from one to eight characters) and automatically assigns the extension WPD to the document. All subsequent executions of the Save command will save the document under the name you selected, replacing the previously saved version with the new one. The ***Save As command*** saves the existing document under a different name, and is useful when you want to create a second copy of the document before making additional changes.

We cannot overemphasize the importance of periodically saving a document, so that if something does go wrong, you won't lose all of your work. Nothing is more frustrating than to lose hours of effort, due to an unexpected problem in Windows or to a temporary loss of power. Save your work frequently, at least once every 15 minutes. Pull down the File menu and click Save, or click the save icon on the Power Bar. Do it!

QUIT WITHOUT SAVING

There will be times when you do not want to save the changes to a document—for example, when you have edited it beyond recognition and wish you had never started. The Undo command, useful as it is, reverses only the last operation and is of no use if you need to cancel all changes. Pull down the **File menu** and click the **Close command,** then click **No** in response to the message asking whether you want to save the changes to the document. Pull down the **File menu,** click **Open** to reopen the file, then start over from the beginning.

Backup Options

WordPerfect offers several different ***backup*** options. It is up to you to choose the options for your system. We think it important to select the option that creates a backup copy in conjunction with every Save command as illustrated in Figure 2.2. (See step 2 in the ensuing hands-on exercise for instructions on how to establish this option.)

Assume, for example, that you have created the one-line document, *The fox jumped over the fence,* and saved it under the name FOX.WPD. Assume further that you edit the document to read, *The quick brown fox jumped over the fence,* and that you saved it a second time. The second Save command changes the name of the original document from FOX.WPD to FOX.BK!, then saves the current contents of memory as FOX.WPD. In other words, the disk now contains two versions of the document: the current version (FOX.WPD) and the most recent previous version (FOX.BK!).

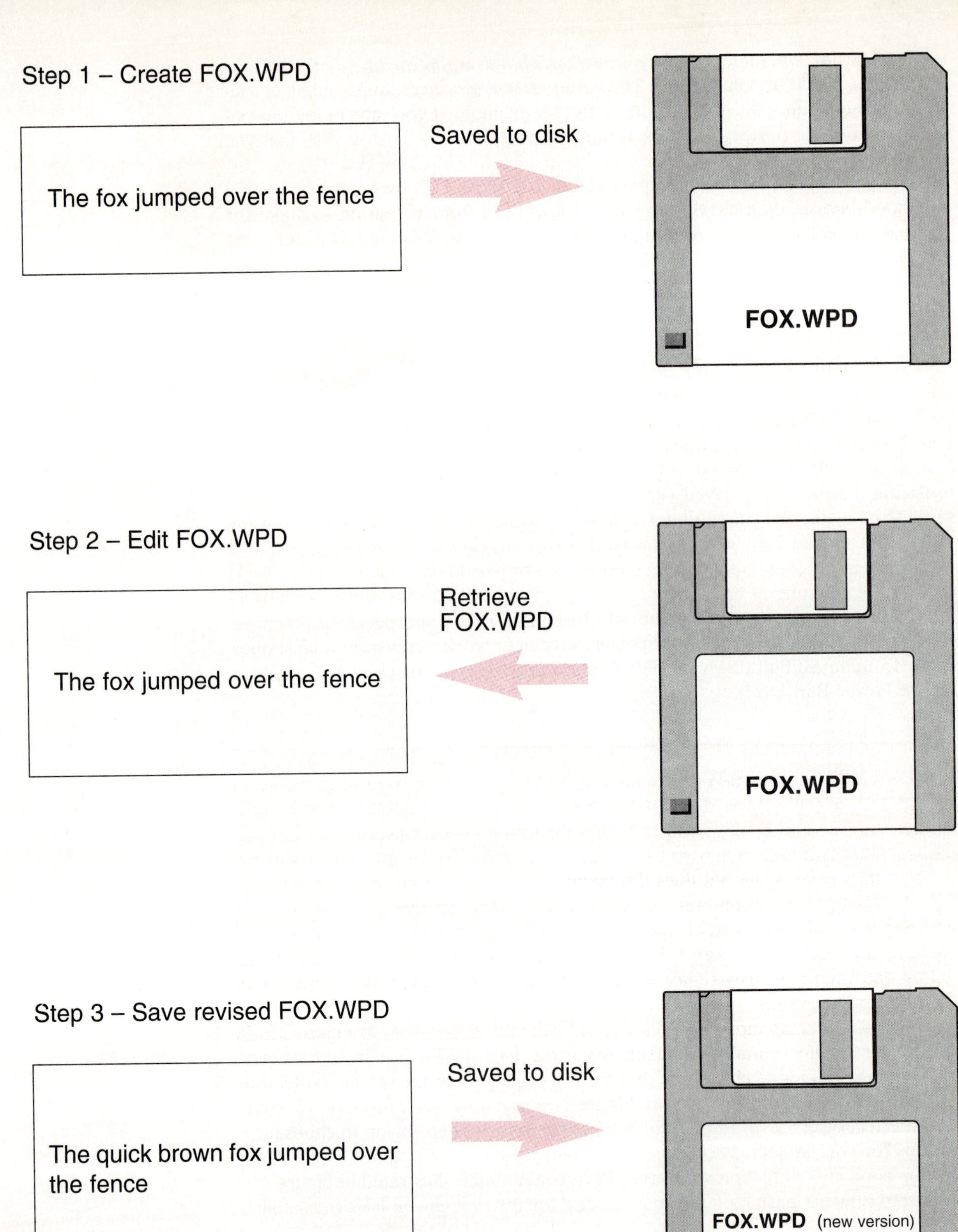

FIGURE 2.2 Backup Procedures

The cycle goes on indefinitely, with FOX.WPD always containing the current version, and FOX.BK! the most recent previous version. If you were to revise and save the document a third time, FOX.WPD would contain the latest revision while FOX.BK! would contain the previous version alluding to the quick brown fox. The original (first) version of the document disappears entirely since only the two latest versions are kept.

The contents of FOX.WPD and FOX.BK! are different, but the existence of the latter enables you to retrieve the previous version if you inadvertently edit beyond repair or accidentally erase the current FOX.WPD version. Should this occur (and it will), you can always retrieve its predecessor and at least salvage your work prior to the last save operation.

TIMED DOCUMENT BACKUP

WordPerfect will automatically save a file at regular intervals (e.g., every ten minutes), provided Timed Document Backup is in effect. The feature is invaluable in the event of a system crash because you can subsequently retrieve the timed backup and resume working. The backup file contains all the formatting and editing changes that were made to a document prior to the last timed backup. Thus if you set timed backup to every ten minutes, you will never lose more than this amount of work. The only disadvantage is a momentary pause every ten minutes while the backup is made.

SCROLLING

Scrolling is necessary when a document is too large to be viewed in its entirety. Figure 2.3a, for example, displays the top portion of a document as it would appear on the monitor. Figure 2.3b shows the entire (printed) document. To see the document in the monitor, you need to scroll, whereby new lines will be brought into view as the old lines disappear.

Scrolling comes about automatically as you reach the bottom of the screen. Entering a new line of text, clicking on the down arrow within the scroll bar, or pressing the down arrow key brings a new line into view at the bottom of the screen and simultaneously removes a line at the top. (The process is reversed at the top of the screen.)

Scrolling occurs most often in a vertical direction as shown in Figure 2.3. It can also occur horizontally, however, when the length of a line in a document exceeds the number of characters that can be displayed on the screen. Note, too, the position of the insertion point in Figure 2.3a and how this information is communicated on the Status Bar.

SCROLLING TIP

Scroll quickly through a document by clicking above or below the scroll box to scroll up or down an entire screen. Move to the top, bottom, or an approximate position within a document by dragging the scroll box to the corresponding position in the scroll bar; for example, dragging the scroll box to the middle of the bar changes the display to the middle of the document. It does not, however, change the insertion point; that is, you must click in the document after scrolling to move the insertion point.

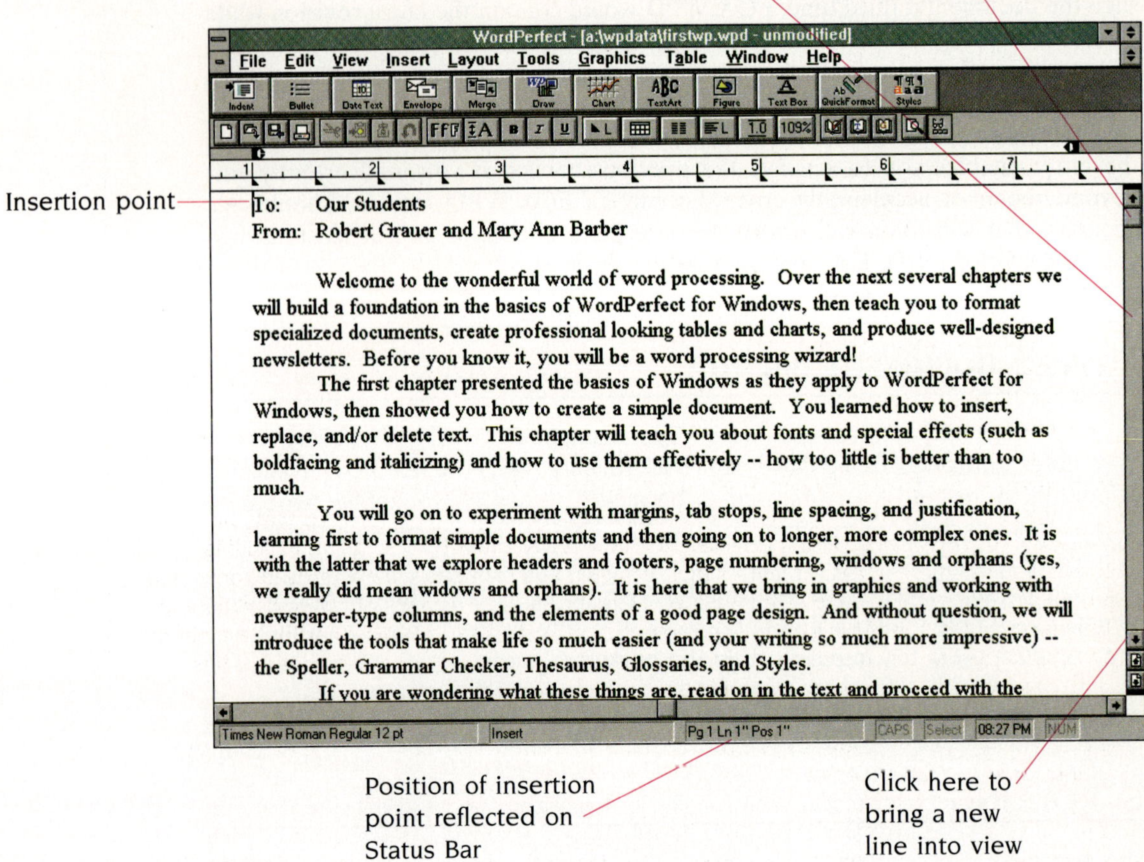

(a) Screen Display

FIGURE 2.3 Scrolling

Hands-On Exercise 1:

Editing

Objective To edit an existing document; to demonstrate scrolling, the Find and Replace, and Save As commands; to move and copy text using the clipboard and the drag-and-drop facility. Use Figures 2.3 and 2.4 as a guide.

Step 1: Load the practice document

- Load WordPerfect as described in the hands-on exercises from Chapter 1.
- Pull down the **File menu.**
- Click **Open** (or click the **File Open icon** on the Power Bar). Click drive C or drive A, depending on whether or not you copied the data disk to your hard drive.
- Scroll through the directory list box until you come to the **WPDATA** directory.
- Double click this directory.
- Double click **FIRSTWP.WPD** to open the document.

To: Our Students
From: Robert Grauer and Mary Ann Barber

Welcome to the wonderful world of word processing. Over the next several chapters we will build a foundation in the basics of WordPerfect for Windows, then teach you to format specialized documents, create professional looking tables and charts, and produce well-designed newsletters. Before you know it, you will be a word processing wizard!

The first chapter presented the basics of Windows as they apply to WordPerfect for Windows, then showed you how to create a simple document. You learned how to insert, replace, and/or delete text. This chapter will teach you about fonts and special effects (such as boldfacing and italicizing) and how to use them effectively — how too little is better than too much.

You will go on to experiment with margins, tab stops, line spacing, and justification, learning first to format simple documents and then advancing to longer, more complex ones. It is with the latter that we explore headers and footers, page numbering, windows and orphans (yes, we really did mean widows and orphans). It is here that we bring in graphics and working with newspaper-type columns, and the elements of a good page design. And without question, we will introduce the tools that make life so much easier (and your writing so much more impressive) — the Speller, Grammar Checker, Thesaurus, Glossaries, and Styles.

If you are wondering what these things are, read on in the text and proceed with the hands-on exercises. Create a simple newsletter, then really knock their socks off by adding graphics, fonts, and TextArt. Create a simple calendar and then create more intricate forms that no one will believe were done by little old you. Create a résumé with your beginner's skills and then make it look like so much more with your intermediate (even advanced) skills. Last, but not least, run a mail merge to produce the cover letters that will accompany your résumé as it is mailed to companies across the United States (and even the world).

It is up to you to practice, for it is only through working at the computer that you will learn what you need to know. Experiment and don't be afraid to make mistakes. Practice and practice some more.

Our goal is for you to learn and to enjoy what you are learning. We have great confidence in you, and in our ability to help you discover what you can do. And to prove us right, we'd love to have you mail us copies of documents that you have created. Write to us at the following address:

Dr. Robert Grauer/Ms. Mary Ann Barber
University of Miami
421 Jenkins Building
Coral Gables, Florida 33124

We look forward to hearing from you and hope that you will like our book. You are about to embark on a wonderful journey toward computer literacy. Be patient, be inquisitive, and enjoy.

(b) Printed Document

FIGURE 2.3 Scrolling (continued)

Step 2: Establish automatic backup (the BK! file)

- Pull down the **File menu**. Click **Preferences.**
- Double click the **File icon** to produce the dialog box of Figure 2.4a. Check the backup options you want—for example, Timed Document Backup every 10 minutes and Original Document Backup to create a BK! file in conjunction with every save operation.
- Click **OK** to close the File Preferences dialog box. Click **Close** to exit the Preferences dialog box and return to the document.

Creates a BK! file

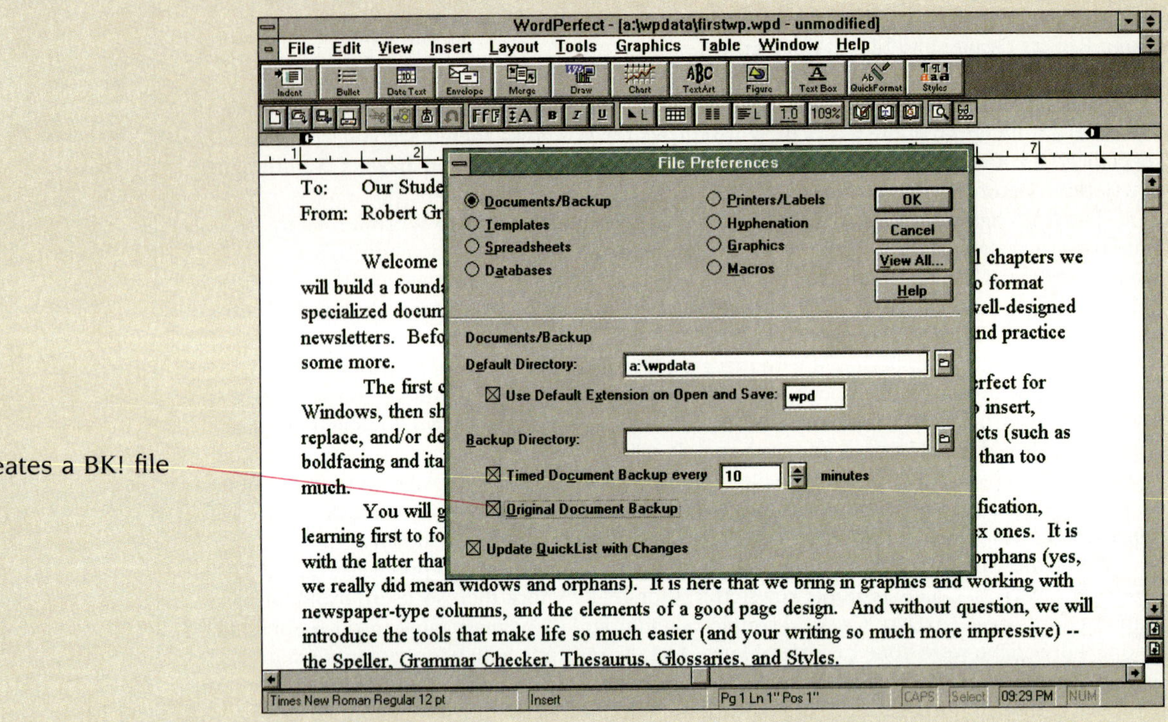

(a) Establishing the Backup Options (step 2)

FIGURE 2.4 Hands-on Exercise 1

CHANGE THE DEFAULT DIRECTORY

The ***default directory*** is where WordPerfect retrieves (saves) documents unless it is otherwise instructed. To change the default directory, pull down the File menu, click Preferences, then double click the File icon to open a dialog box. Enter the name of the new default directory—for example, C:\WPDATA—click OK, then click the Close command button to return to your document. The next time you access the File menu the default directory will reflect these changes.

Step 3: The Save As command

- Pull down the **File menu.**
- Click **Save As** to produce a dialog box requesting the new name of the file.
- Enter a file name from one to eight characters—for example, **PRACTICE** (the WPD extension is added automatically)—and press **enter.** There are now two identical copies of the file on disk: FIRSTWP.WPD, which we supplied, and PRACTICE.WPD, which you just created. The title bar of the document window shows the latter name.

Step 4: Scrolling

- Click the **down arrow** at the bottom of the scroll bar to move down in the document, causing the top line to disappear and be replaced with a new line at the bottom.
- Click the **down arrow** several times to move through the document, then click the **up arrow key** to scroll in the other direction.

- Drag the **scroll box** to the bottom of the scroll bar, to the top of the scroll bar, then to the middle of the scroll bar, noting that in every instance the insertion point does *not* follow the scrolling; that is, you must **click the mouse** to move the insertion point after scrolling with the mouse.

KEYBOARD SHORTCUTS: MOVING WITHIN A DOCUMENT

Press **Ctrl+Home** and **Ctrl+End** to move to the beginning and end of a document. Press **Home** and **End** to move to the beginning and end of a line. Press **PgUp** or **PgDn** to scroll one screen in the indicated direction. Press **Alt+PgUp** or **Alt+PgDn** to scroll to the previous or next page in the document. The advantage to scrolling via the keyboard (instead of the mouse) is that the insertion point moves as you scroll.

Step 5: Insertion versus typeover

- Press the **Ins key** once or twice until you see Typeover in the Status Bar at the bottom of the screen.
- Press the **Ins key** once more so that Typeover disappears and you see Insert in the Status Bar. You are now in the insert mode.
- Press **Ctrl+Home** to move to the beginning of the document, click immediately before the period ending the first sentence, press the **space bar,** then add the phrase **and desktop publishing.**
- Drag the **scroll box** to scroll to the bottom of the document, and click immediately before the first M in Ms. Mary Ann Barber.
- Press the **Ins key** (Typeover should appear in the Status Bar) to toggle to the replacement mode, then type **Dr** to replace Ms.
- Press **Ctrl+Home** to move to the beginning of the document, click and drag the mouse to select the phrase **Our Students,** then type your name to replace the highlighted text.
- Pull down the **File menu** and click **Save** (or click the save icon) to save the changes.

KEEP DUPLICATE COPIES OF IMPORTANT FILES

It is absolutely critical to maintain duplicate copies of important files on a separate disk stored away from the computer. In addition, you should print each new document at the end of every session, saving it before printing (power failures happen when least expected, for example, during the print operation). Hard copy is not as good as a duplicate disk, but it is better than nothing.

Step 6: Find and Replace

- Press **Ctrl+Home** to move to the beginning of the document.
- Pull down the **Edit menu.** Click **Replace** to produce the dialog box of Figure 2.4b. Type **text** in the Find text box.
- Pull down the **Match menu.** Click **Whole Word** to search for whole words only.

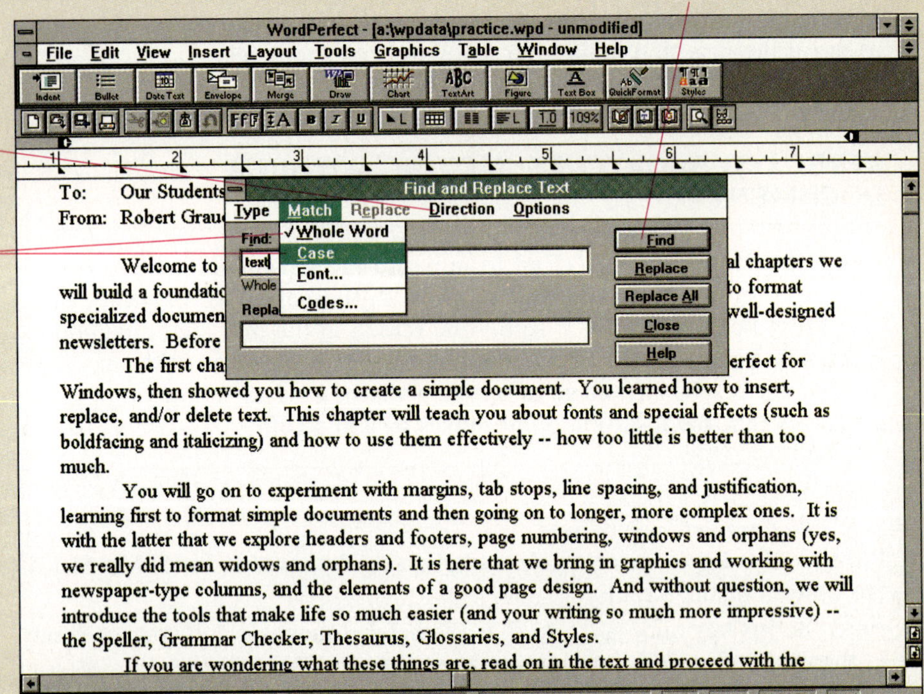

(b) The Find and Replace Command (step 6)

FIGURE 2.4 Hands-on Exercise 1 (continued)

- Pull down the **Match menu** a second time. Click **Case** to make the search case sensitive.
- Press the **Tab key.** Type **book** in the Replace With text box.
- Click the **Find button** to find the first occurrence of the word "text". The dialog box remains on the screen and the first occurrence of "text" is highlighted. This is *not* an appropriate substitution; that is, you should not substitute book for text at this point.
- Click the **Find button** to move to the next occurrence, where the substitution is appropriate. Click **Replace** to make the change and continue searching for the next occurrence.
- Click **OK** to acknowledge the message indicating that the search string (text) can no longer be found.
- Pull down the **Direction menu.** Click **Backward;** that is, you are currently at the end of the document and must search in a reverse direction. (Alternatively, you could press Ctrl+Home to move to the beginning of the document and continue to search in a forward direction.)
- Change the Find and Replace strings to **Mary Ann** and **Maryann,** respectively.
- Click the **Replace All button** to make the substitution automatically throughout the document.
- Click the **Close command button** to close the dialog box.
- Save the document.

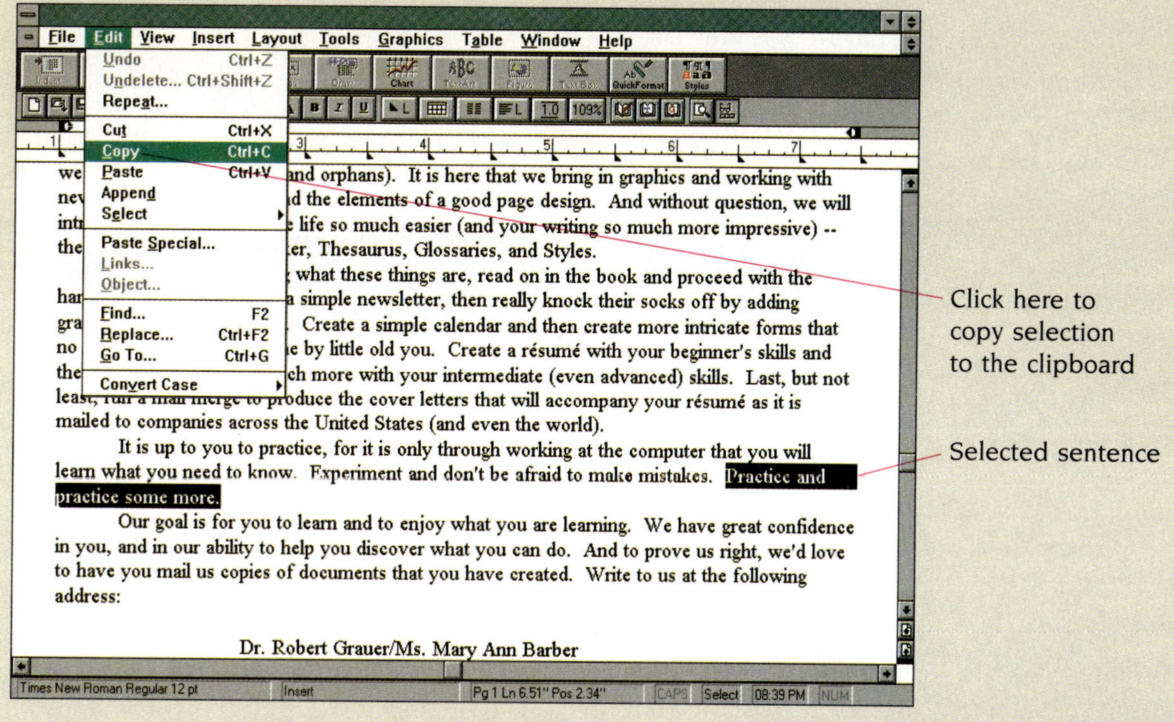

(c) The Copy Command (step 7)

FIGURE 2.4 Hands-on Exercise 1 (continued)

Step 7: The clipboard

- Press **PgDn** to scroll toward the end of the document until you come to the paragraph beginning **It is up to you . . .**
- Select the sentence **Practice and practice some more** by dragging the mouse over the sentence. The sentence will be highlighted as in Figure 2.4c.
- Pull down the **Edit menu.** Click **Copy** to copy the selected text to the clipboard.
- Scroll to the end of the document.
- **Click the mouse** to change the insertion point. Press the **enter** key twice.
- Pull down the **Edit menu.** Click **Paste** to copy the selected sentence.
- Move the insertion point to the right of the exclamation point at the end of the first paragraph (ending with the word *wizard*). Press the **space bar** twice.
- Pull down the **Edit menu.** Click **Paste** to copy the sentence a second time.
- Save the document.

> **KEYBOARD SHORTCUTS: CUT, COPY, AND PASTE**
>
> **Ctrl+X, Ctrl+C,** and **Ctrl+V,** are shortcuts to cut, copy, and paste respectively. The shortcuts are easier to remember when you realize that the operative letters—X, C, and V—are next to each other at the bottom left side of the keyboard.

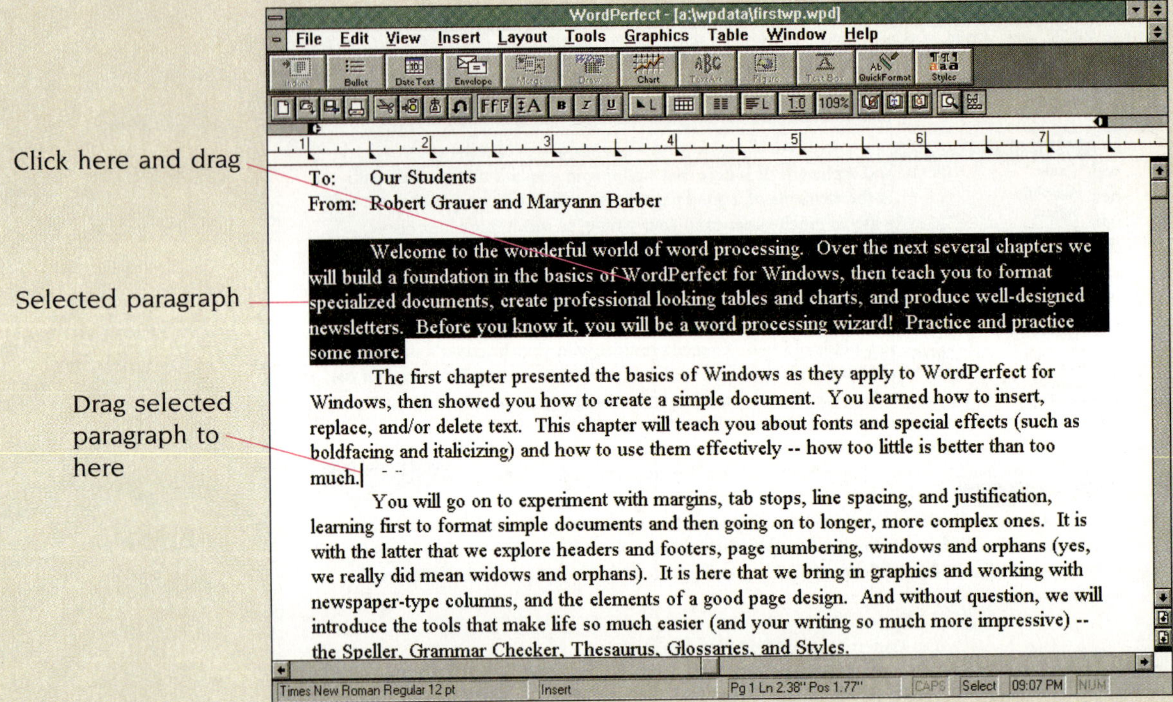

(d) Drag and Drop

FIGURE 2.4 Hands-on Exercise 1 (continued)

Step 8: Drag and drop

- This step takes a little practice, but it is well worth it.
- Click anywhere in the first paragraph. Pull down the **Edit menu.** Click **Select.** Click **Paragraph** to select the first paragraph as shown in Figure 2.4d.
- To move the paragraph, click anywhere in the paragraph and **drag** it to a new location (for example, to the end of the second paragraph), then release the mouse button to complete the move. (A dotted vertical bar appears as you drag the text to indicate its new destination.)
- Pull down the **Edit menu.**
- Click **Undo** (or click the **Undo icon** on the Power Bar) to reverse the move and return the paragraph to its initial position.
- Click anywhere in the first paragraph. Pull down the **Edit menu.** Click **Select.** Click **Paragraph** to select the first paragraph.
- To copy the paragraph, press and hold the **Ctrl key** as you **click and drag** the paragraph to its new location.
- Click the **Undo icon** to undo the Copy command. Practice the drag-and-drop procedure several times until you are confident you can move and copy with precision.

SELECT TEXT THROUGH A QUICKMENU

Point to the left margin, next to the sentence or paragraph you want to select. Click the **right mouse button** to produce a **QuickMenu.** Click Select Sentence, Select Paragraph, Select Page, or Select All as appropriate.

Step 9: Print the completed document

- Pull down the **File Menu.**
- Click **Save** (or click the **Save icon**) to save the document a final time.
- Pull down the **File menu.**
- Click **Print.** Click the **Print command button** to print the completed document.
- Pull down the **File menu** and click **Exit** (or double click the control-menu box) to quit WordPerfect and return to Program Manager.

TYPOGRAPHY

Typography is the process of selecting typefaces, type styles, and type sizes. The importance of these decisions is obvious, for the ultimate success of any document depends greatly on its appearance. Type should reinforce your message without calling attention to itself and should be consistent with the information you want to convey. The ensuing sections define various terms in typography.

Typeface

A ***typeface*** is a complete set of characters (upper- and lower-case letters, numbers, punctuation marks, and special symbols). Figure 2.5 illustrates two typefaces, ***Times New Roman*** and ***Arial,*** that are supplied with Windows, and which in turn are accessible from WordPerfect or any other Windows application.

One definitive characteristic of any typeface is the presence or absence of tiny cross lines that end the main stroke of each letter. A ***serif*** typeface has these lines; a ***sans-serif*** type face (*sans* from the French for *without*) does not. Times New Roman is a serif typeface; Arial is a sans-serif typeface.

Serifs help the eye connect one letter with the next and are generally used with large amounts of text. This book, for example, is set in a serif typeface. A sans-serif typeface is more effective with smaller amounts of text and appears in headlines, corporate logos, airport signs, and so on. Serif typefaces are thought to be easier to read and to convey a sense of authority; sans-serif typefaces produce a more informal result.

The type you choose should be consistent with the message you want to convey, neither too large nor too small, neither too bold nor too reserved. A serif typeface has tiny cross strokes that end the main strokes of each letter; a sans-serif typeface does not.

(a) Times New Roman

The type you choose should be consistent with the message you want to convey, neither too large nor too small, neither too bold nor too reserved. A serif typeface has tiny cross strokes that end the main strokes of each letter; a sans-serif typeface does not.

(b) Arial

FIGURE 2.5 Typefaces

Any typeface can be set in different ***type styles,*** such as regular, boldface, or italics. A ***font*** (as the term is used in Windows) is a specific typeface in a specific style—for example, **Arial bold** or *Times New Roman italic.*

Type Size

Type size is a vertical measurement and is specified in points, where one ***point*** is equal to 1/72 of an inch; that is, there are 72 points to the inch. The measurement is made from the top of the tallest letter in a character set (e.g., an upper-case T) to the bottom of the lowest letter (e.g., a lower-case y). Most documents are set in 10 or 12 point type; newspaper columns may be set as small as 8 point type. Type sizes of 14 points or higher are ineffective for large amounts of text. Figure 2.6 shows the same phrase set in varying type sizes.

Some typefaces appear larger (smaller) than others even though they may be set in the same point size. The type in Figure 2.5a, for example, looks smaller than the corresponding type in Figure 2.5b even though both are set in the same point size. This is because the Arial typeface users longer ascenders (strokes that climb upward from the baseline) and longer descenders (strokes that reach downward) than the Times New Roman design.

This is Arial 8 point type

This is Arial 10 point type

This is Arial 12 point type

This is Arial 18 point type

This is Arial 24 point type

This is Times New Roman 8 point type

This is Times New Roman 10 point type

This is Times New Roman 12 point type

This is Times New Roman 18 point type

This is Times New Roman 24 point type

FIGURE 2.6 Type Size

TrueType

Windows 3.1 supports a new type of font technology known as ***TrueType,*** which ensures that the fonts you see on the monitor match those used in the printed document. Equally important, TrueType fonts are scalable, meaning that you can select any type size from 4 to 127 points. TrueType fonts are accessible from any Windows application

The basic Windows installation includes a total of 14 TrueType fonts: *Times New Roman* (in regular, bold, italic, and bold italic styles), *Arial* (in regular, bold, italic, and bold italic styles) *Courier New* (in regular, bold, italic, and bold italic styles), and two special fonts: *Symbol* and *Wingdings*. WordPerfect includes several additional fonts, giving you a great deal of flexibility in the documents you create.

All fonts are classified as either monospaced or proportional. A ***monospaced font,*** such as Courier New, has a fixed pitch (uniform character width). Monospaced fonts are used in tables and financial projections, where items must be precisely lined up, one beneath the other. A ***proportional font,*** such as Times New Roman or Arial, allocates a different amount of space for each character according to the width of the character. Proportional fonts create a more professional appearance and are appropriate for most documents.

POINT VERSUS PITCH

Character pitch specifies the number of characters per inch (cpi) and is used exclusively with monospaced fonts. The larger the cpi number, the smaller the characters and the smaller the corresponding point size. To convert pitch to points, divide 120 by the pitch; for example, a pitch of 12 characters per inch is equivalent to 10 point type (120/12).

FORMATTING

A change in typography is only one way to alter the appearance of a document; indeed, one of the most appealing features of WordPerfect is the ease with which various designs are implemented. You can change the fonts or margins in a document, go from single spacing to double spacing (or vice versa), or change the ***alignment*** (justification), all with a mouse click or two. The procedure of changing a document's appearance is known as ***formatting*** and is covered in the remainder of the chapter.

Alignment

Text can be aligned in four different ways as shown in Figure 2.7. It may be fully justified (flush-left/flush-right), left-aligned (flush-left with a ragged-right margin), right-aligned (flush-right with a ragged-left margin), or centered within the margins (ragged left and right).

Most studies indicate that left-aligned text is easiest to read. The first letters of each line align with each other, making it easy for the eye to find the beginning of the line. The lines themselves are of irregular length. There is uniform spacing between words, and the ragged margin on the right adds white space to the text, giving it a lighter and more informal look.

We, the people of the United States, in order to form a more perfect Union, establish justice, insure domestic tranquility, provide for the common defense, promote the general welfare, and secure the blessings of liberty to ourselves and our posterity, do ordain and establish this Constitution for the United States of America.

(a) Fully Justified (flush-left/flush-right)

We, the people of the United States, in order to form a more perfect Union, establish justice, insure domestic tranquility, provide for the common defense, promote the general welfare, and secure the blessings of liberty to ourselves and our posterity, do ordain and establish this Constitution for the United States of America.

(b) Left Aligned (flush-left/ragged-right)

We, the people of the United States, in order to form a more perfect Union, establish justice, insure domestic tranquility, provide for the common defense, promote the general welfare, and secure the blessings of liberty to ourselves and our posterity, do ordain and establish this Constitution for the United States of America.

(c) Right Aligned (flush-right/ragged-left)

We, the people of the United States, in order to form a more perfect Union, establish justice, insure domestic tranquility, provide for the common defense, promote the general welfare, and secure the blessings of liberty to ourselves and our posterity, do ordain and establish this Constitution for the United States of America.

(d) Centered (ragged-left/ragged-right)

FIGURE 2.7 Alignment

Fully justified text produces lines of equal length with adjusted word spacing. It may be more difficult to read than text that is left-aligned because of the *uneven* (sometimes excessive) word spacing and/or the greater number of hyphenated words needed to justify the lines. Nevertheless, fully justified type is used by magazines, newspapers, and books, because the word density is higher; that is, less space is required for the same amount of text, resulting in fewer pages and cost reduction.

Type that is centered or right justified is restricted to limited amounts of text where the effect is more important than the ease of reading. Centered text, for example, appears frequently on wedding invitations or formal announcements. Right-justified text is used with figure captions and short headlines.

Tabs and Indents

Anyone who has used a typewriter is familiar with the function of the Tab key; that is, press Tab and the insertion point moves to the next ***tab stop*** (a measured position to align text at a specific place.) The Tab key functions identically within WordPerfect except it is much more powerful because you can choose from four different types of tab stops (left, center, right, and decimal). You can also specify a ***leader character,*** typically dots or hyphens, to draw the reader's eye across the page. Tabs are often used to create tables within a document.

The default tab stops are set every 1/2 inch and are left-aligned, but you can change the ***alignment*** and/or position with the Tab Set command in Figure 2.8a. Four types of alignment are possible:

- ***Left alignment,*** where the text *begins* at the tab stop and corresponds exactly to the Tab key on a typewriter
- ***Right alignment,*** where the text *ends* at the tab stop; right alignment is used to align page numbers in a table of contents
- ***Center alignment,*** where text centers over the tab stop
- ***Decimal alignment,*** which lines up numeric values in a column on the decimal point

The use of a dot leader together with a right tab is illustrated in Figure 2.8b. The default tab stops have been cleared in favor of a single right tab at 5.5 inches, which has been specified with a dot leader. The resulting document is shown in Figure 2.8b.

Different types of indentation are possible as can be seen from the examples in Figure 2.9. The amount of indentation is controlled by the tab stop (.5 inch is the default), but the type of indentation is determined by the ***Paragraph command*** in the Layout menu. There is no indentation in Figure 2.9a in order that the paragraph provide a basis of comparison for the other examples.

The Tab key provides the simplest indentation and is used in Figure 2.9b to indent the first line of a paragraph. A tab affects only one line, whereas an indent affects the entire paragraph.

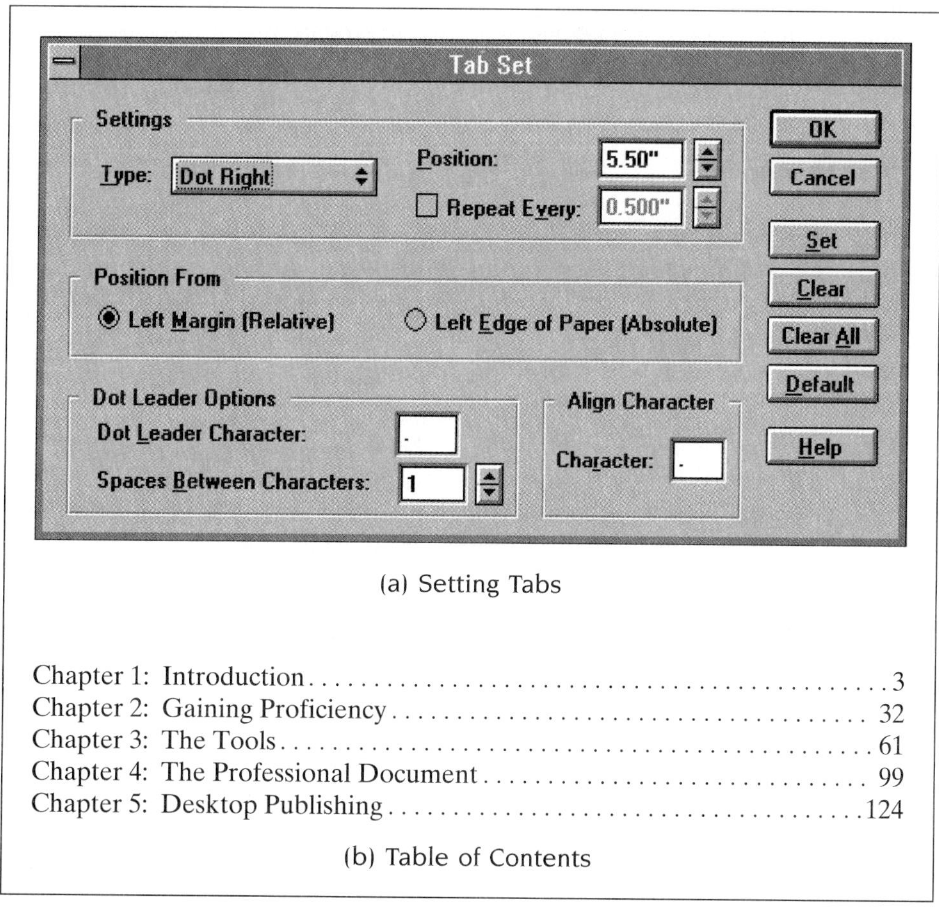

(a) Setting Tabs

Chapter 1: Introduction...3
Chapter 2: Gaining Proficiency......................................32
Chapter 3: The Tools...61
Chapter 4: The Professional Document.............................99
Chapter 5: Desktop Publishing......................................124

(b) Table of Contents

FIGURE 2.8 Tabs

This paragraph is set with full justification and no indentation, and thus the entire paragraph aligns vertically with the left and right margins. The paragraph provides a basis for comparison with the other examples in the figure.

(a) No Indentation

This paragraph uses the Tab key to indent the first line to the first tab stop. The Tab key should always be used instead of the space bar. The remaining lines in the paragraph align vertically with the left and right margins.

(b) Tab

This paragraph illustrates the Paragraph Indent command, which indents the entire paragraph to the first tab stop. Every line in the paragraph aligns with the right margin.

(c) Indent

This paragraph illustrates the Paragraph Double Indent command to indent the paragraph on both sides. This type of indentation is very effective to highlight a paragraph within a document.

(d) Double Indent

This paragraph illustrates the Paragraph Hanging Indent Command in which the first line begins to the left of the remaining lines of the paragraph. This type of indentation is often used with bulleted or numbered lists.

(e) Hanging Indent

FIGURE 2.9 Indents

The Paragraph ***Indent command*** in Figure 2.9c indents the entire paragraph from the left. The ***Double Indent command*** in Figure 2.9d indents the paragraph on both the left and right. The ***Hanging Indent command*** in Figure 2.9e causes the first line of the paragraph to begin to the left of the remaining lines in the paragraph.

Page Breaks

One of the first concepts you learned was that of word wrap, whereby WordPerfect inserts a soft carriage return at the end of a line in order to begin a new line. The carriage returns inserted by WordPerfect are described as "soft" returns because their number and location will change as you add or delete text within the document. They are very different from the hard returns inserted by the user whose number and location remain constant.

In much the same way, WordPerfect automatically goes to the top of a new page when text no longer fits on the current page, producing a ***soft page break.*** These page breaks are "soft" because their number and location will change as you edit the document. And just as you can insert a hard return to start a new paragraph, you can insert a ***hard page break*** to force any part of a document to begin on a new page. (Press **Ctrl+Enter** or pull down the ***Insert menu*** and click ***Page Break.***)

In determining the location of the soft page breaks, WordPerfect can prevent the occurrence of isolated lines of text known as ***widows*** and ***orphans.*** The last line of a paragraph appearing by itself at the top of a new page is called a widow; the first line of a paragraph appearing at the bottom of a page is called an orphan.

WordPerfect enables you to further control pagination by specifying that a designated block of text should not be split over two pages. It might not matter, for example, whether a list of items appears at the bottom of one page or at the top of the next, only that the entire list appear on the same page. The ***Page command*** in the ***Layout menu*** lets you specify that the lines be kept together.

PORTRAIT VERSUS LANDSCAPE ORIENTATION

A document may be printed in one of two ways, ***portrait orientation*** (the default) or ***landscape orientation***; the latter flips the page 90 degrees so that its dimensions are 11 x 8½ rather than the other way around. To change the orientation of a document (or page within a document), pull down the **Layout menu**, click **Page**, then click **Paper Size.** Click on the Paper Definition you want, then click the **Select command button.**

VIEW MENU

WordPerfect provides three different views of a document: Draft, Page, and Two Page. All three views are WYSIWYG (What You See Is What You Get) in that fonts and associated formatting (italics, bold, underlining, and so on) appear on the monitor as they will on the printed page. The difference between the ***Draft view*** and ***Page view*** is that the latter more closely resembles the printed document. Page View displays the top and bottom margins, headers, footers, footnotes, and other features that do not appear in the Draft view. The Draft view, however, is faster because WordPerfect spends less time formatting the display. The ***Two Page view*** is similar to the Page view except that it displays consecutive pages side by side.

The ***Zoom command*** is available within the Draft and Page views to display the document at magnifications from 25% to 400%. (The Zoom command does not affect the size of the text on the printed page.) A Zoom percentage (magnification) of 100% displays the document in the approximate size of the text on the printed page. You can magnify the percentage—for example, 150% to make the characters larger on the screen to facilitate editing—or reduce it—for example, 50% to see more of the document at one time. Alternatively, you can let WordPerfect determine the magnification for you, by selecting one of three additional Zoom options—Page Width, Margin Width, or Full Page. ***Page Width*** displays the text with left and right margins, whereas ***Margin Width*** displays the text with a minimum of space to the left and right. Full Page displays a complete page.

The various views and associated magnifications are useful at different times within the editing process. Figure 2.10a displays a document in Draft View, the suggested mode for creating the document and initial editing. The zoom is set to Margin Width, which increases the size of the characters by minimizing the amount of white space to the left and right of the text. Figure 2.10b displays the same document in Page View with Zoom set to Full Page to see the document as it will appear on the printed page.

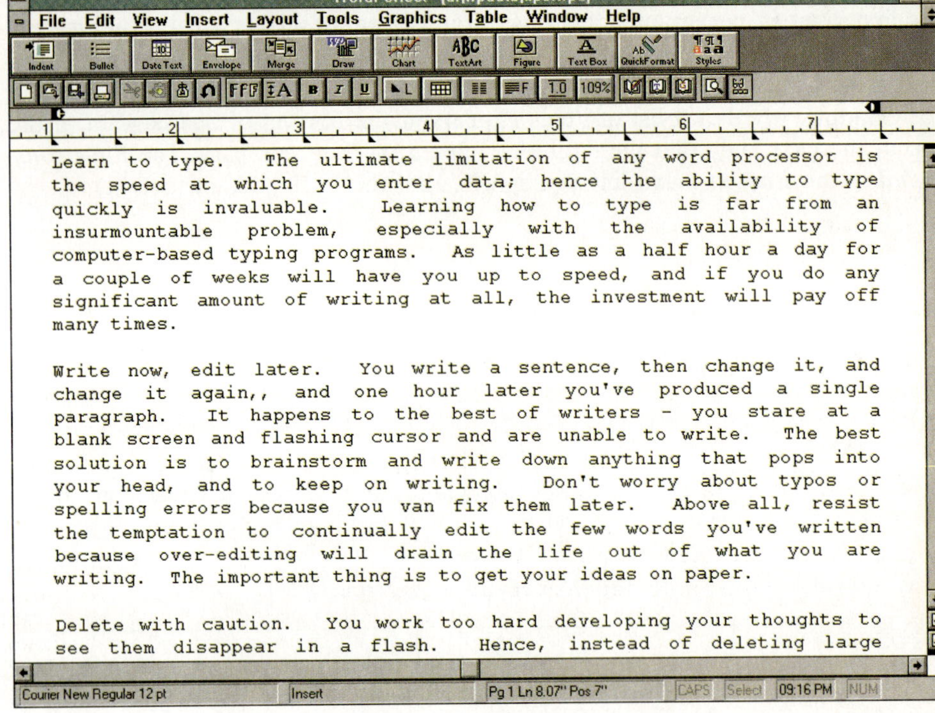

(a) Draft View (Zoom—Margin Width)

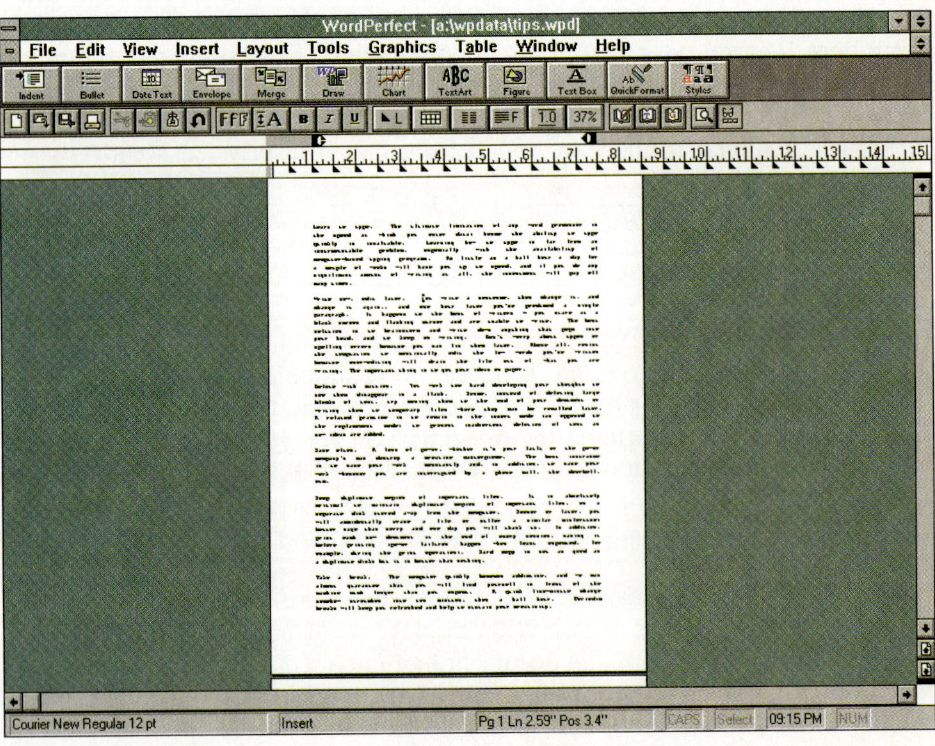

(b) Page View (Zoom—Full Page)

FIGURE 2.10 The View Menu

AN EXERCISE IN DESIGN

The following exercise has you retrieve the document shown in Figure 2.11, then experiment with the various formatting options discussed in the chapter. The original document uses a typewriter-style font (Courier New), without boldface or italics, and you are asked to improve its appearance. The first step in the exercise directs you to save the document under a new name so that you can always return to the original if necessary.

Learn to type. The ultimate limitation of any word processor is the speed at which you enter data; hence the ability to type quickly is invaluable. Learning how to type is far from an insurmountable problem, especially with the availability of computer-based typing programs. As little as a half hour a day for a couple of weeks will have you up to speed, and if you do any significant amount of writing at all, the investment will pay off many times.

Write now, edit later. You write a sentence, then change it, and change it again, and one hour later you've produced a single paragraph. It happens to the best of writers - you stare at a blank screen and flashing cursor and are unable to write. The best solution is to brainstorm and write down anything that pops into your head, and to keep on writing. Don't worry about typos or spelling errors because you can fix them later. Above all, resist the temptation to continually edit the few words you've written because over-editing will drain the life out of what you are writing. The important thing is to get your ideas on paper.

Delete with caution. You work too hard developing your thoughts to see them disappear in a flash. Hence, instead of deleting large blocks of text, try moving them to the end of your document or writing them to temporary files where they can be recalled later. A related practice is to remain in the insert mode (as opposed to the replacement mode) to prevent inadvertent deletion of text as new ideas are added.

Save often. A loss of power, whether it's your fault or the power company's, can destroy a creative masterpiece. The best insurance is to save your work constantly and, in addition, to save your work whenever you are interrupted by a phone call, the doorbell, etc.

Keep duplicate copies of important files. It is absolutely critical to maintain duplicate copies of important files, on a separate disk stored away from the computer. Sooner or later, you will accidentally erase a file or suffer a similar misfortune; better safe than sorry and one day you will thank us. In addition, print each new document at the end of every session, saving it before printing (power failures happen when least expected, for example, during the print operation). Hard copy is not as good as a duplicate disk but it is better than nothing.

Take a break. The computer quickly becomes addictive, and we can almost guarantee that you will find yourself in front of the machine much longer than you expect. A quick five-minute change somehow stretches into ten minutes, then a half hour. Periodic breaks will keep you refreshed and help to sustain your creativity.

Impose a time limit. A word processor is supposed to save time and make you more productive. It will do exactly that provided you use the word processor for its primary purpose - writing and editing. It is all too easy, however, to lose sight of that objective and spend inordinate amounts of time on formatting, which is often counter-productive. Concentrate on the content of your document rather than its appearance. Impose a time limit on the amount of time spent on formatting and end the session when the limit is reached.

FIGURE 2.11 An Exercise in Design

There is no right and wrong with respect to design, and you are free to choose any combination of fonts that appeal to you. The exercise takes you through various formatting options but lets you make the final decision. It ends by asking you to print the final document and submit it to your instructor.

IMPOSE A TIME LIMIT

A word processor is supposed to save time and make you more productive. It will do exactly that provided you use the word processor for its primary purpose—writing and editing. It is all too easy, however, to lose sight of that objective and spend too much time formatting the document. Concentrate on the content of your document rather than its appearance. Impose a time limit on the amount of time you will spend on formatting. End the session when the limit is reached.

HANDS-ON EXERCISE 2:

Formatting

Objective: To experiment with different formatting; to change fonts, line spacing, margins, alignments, and justification; to implement widow and orphan protection and a page break; to display a document in different views and magnification. Use Figure 2.12 as a guide in the exercise.

Step 1: Load the practice document.

- Load WordPerfect.
- Pull down the **File menu.** Click **Open** (or click the **Open icon** on the Power Bar).
- If you have not yet changed the default directory:
  - — Click the appropriate drive.
  - — Scroll through the directory list box until you come to the **WPDATA** directory.
  - — Double click the **WPDATA** directory.
- Scroll through the file list box until you come to the TIPS.WPD file. Double click **TIPS.WPD** to open the document.
- Pull down the **File menu.** Click **Save As** to save the file as **MYTIPS.WPD.** The title bar reflects MYTIPS.WPD, but you can always return to the original TIPS.WPD document if you edit the duplicated file beyond repair.

Step 2: The View menu

- Pull down the **View menu.** Click **Draft.**
- Pull down the **View menu** a second time. Click **Zoom.**
- Click **Margin Width.** Click **OK** so that the view in your document matches Figure 2.12a.

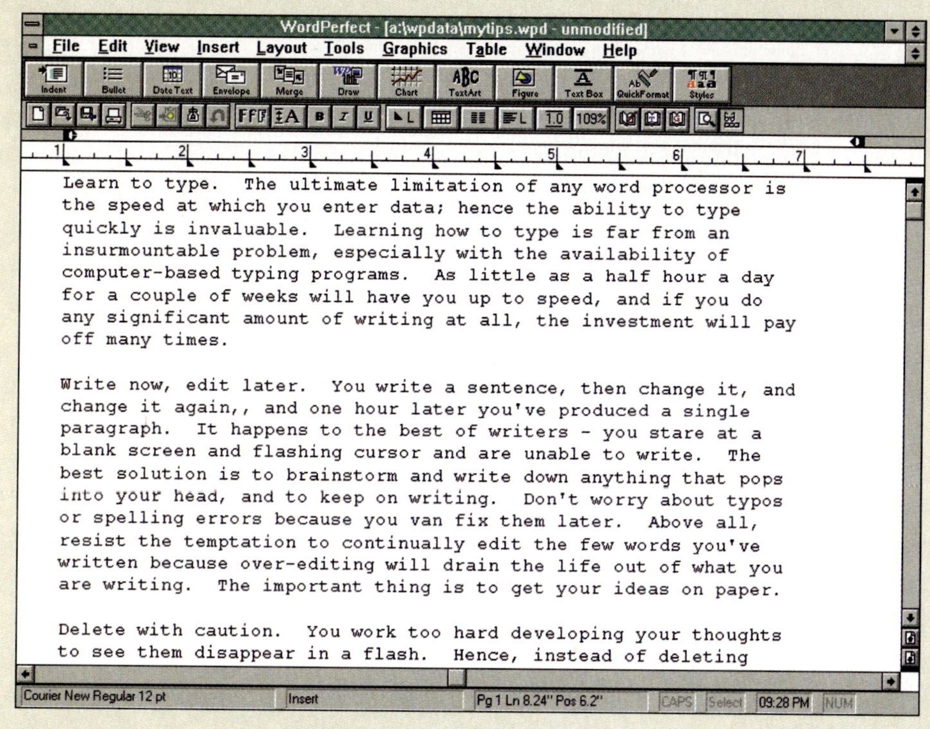

(a) The Original Document (steps 1 and 2)

FIGURE 2.12 Hands-on Exercise 2

Step 3: Changing fonts

- Press **Ctrl+Home** to move to the beginning of the document.
- Pull down the **Layout menu**. Click **Font** to produce the dialog box in Figure 2.12b.
- Click the **down arrow** on the **Font Face list box** to scroll through the list of available fonts. Click a different typeface—for example, **Times New Roman.**
- Click the **down arrow** on the **Font Size list box** to scroll through different point sizes. Click the desired point size—for example, **12** point as in the figure.
- Click **OK** to change the font and return to the document. The font change affects the entire document because no text was selected prior to executing the command, and because the insertion point was at the beginning of the document when the command was issued.

> **TYPOGRAPHY TIP: USE RESTRAINT**
>
> More is not better, especially in the case of too many typefaces and styles, which produce cluttered documents that impress no one. Try to limit yourself to a maximum of two typefaces per document, but choose multiple sizes and/or styles within those typefaces. Use boldface or italics for emphasis, but do so in moderation, because if you emphasize too many elements, the effect is lost.

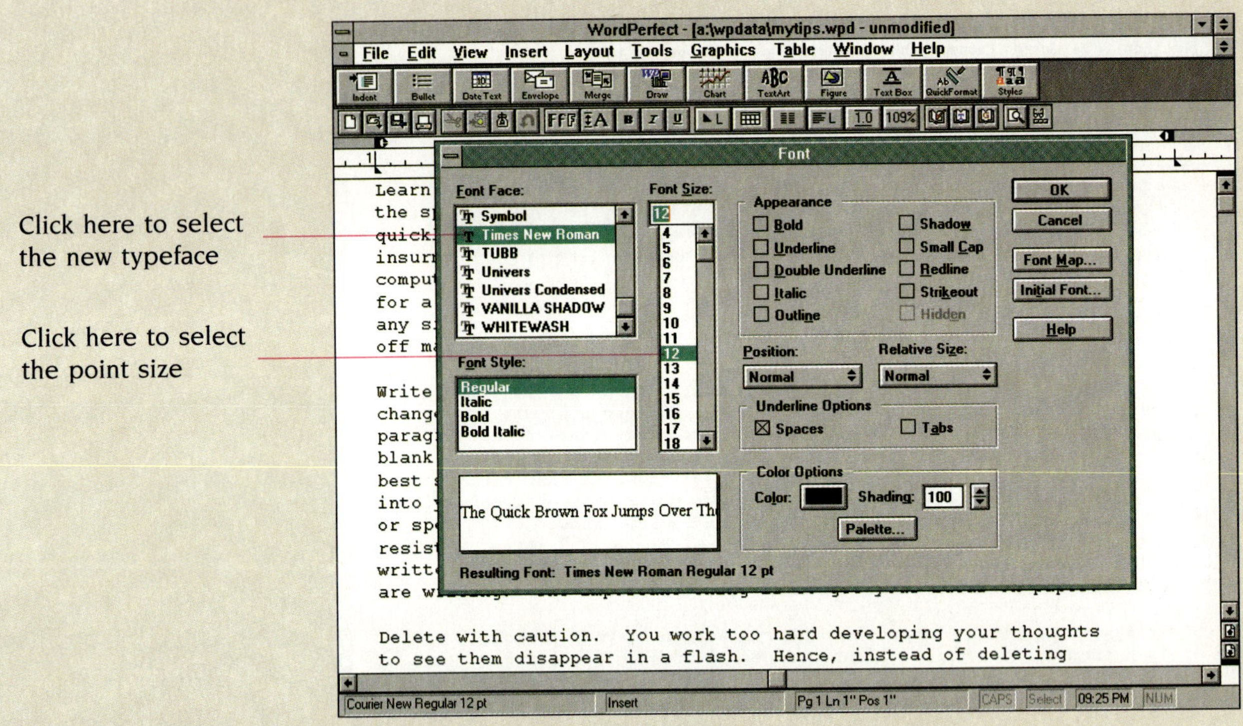

(b) Changing Fonts (step 4)

FIGURE 2.12 Hands on Exercise 2 (continued)

Step 4: Select then do

- Select the title of the first tip, **Learn to type,** which appears at the beginning of the document.
- Pull down the **Layout menu.** Click **Font.** Choose a different typeface—for example, **Arial**—and click **OK.** This time the font change affected only the selected text (Learn to type) because the text was selected prior to changing the font.
- Pull down the **Edit menu** and click **Undo** (or click the **Undo icon** on the Power Bar) to cancel the effect of the last command.
- Experiment with different fonts and/or different point sizes until you are satisfied with the design of your document. We have chosen Times New Roman, 12 point, for the entire document.
- Save the document.

SELECTING TEXT FROM THE LEFT MARGIN

Point to the left margin, next to the sentence or paragraph you want to select. Click once to select the sentence. Double click to select the paragraph.

Step 5: Boldface and Italics

- Select the title of the first tip, **Learn to Type.**
- Click the **Italics icon** on the Power Bar to italicize the selected text. The text

remains highlighted to indicate it is still selected and will be affected by the next command(s).

- Click the **Boldface** icon to set the phrase in boldface italics.
- Choose the combination you like best (boldface, italics, or boldface italics) and use it for the titles of all the tips in the document. You must, however, do one tip at a time, because only one block can be selected at a time. We have chosen boldface italics as shown in Figure 2.12c. Note, too, that the italics and boldface icons function as toggle switches; that is, clicking the italics icon when text is already italicized returns the text to normal.
- Pull down the **File menu.** Click **Save** (or click the **Save icon**) to save the changes.

QUICK FORMAT

The ***QuickFormat*** command copies the current fonts and/or attributes from one place in a document to another. Select the text containing the desired formatting, then click the QuickFormat icon on the Button Bar. The mouse pointer changes to a roller to indicate that you can paint other areas in the document with the current attributes; just drag the mouse over the additional areas, which will assume the identical formatting characteristics as the original text. Click the QuickFormat icon a second time to return to normal editing.

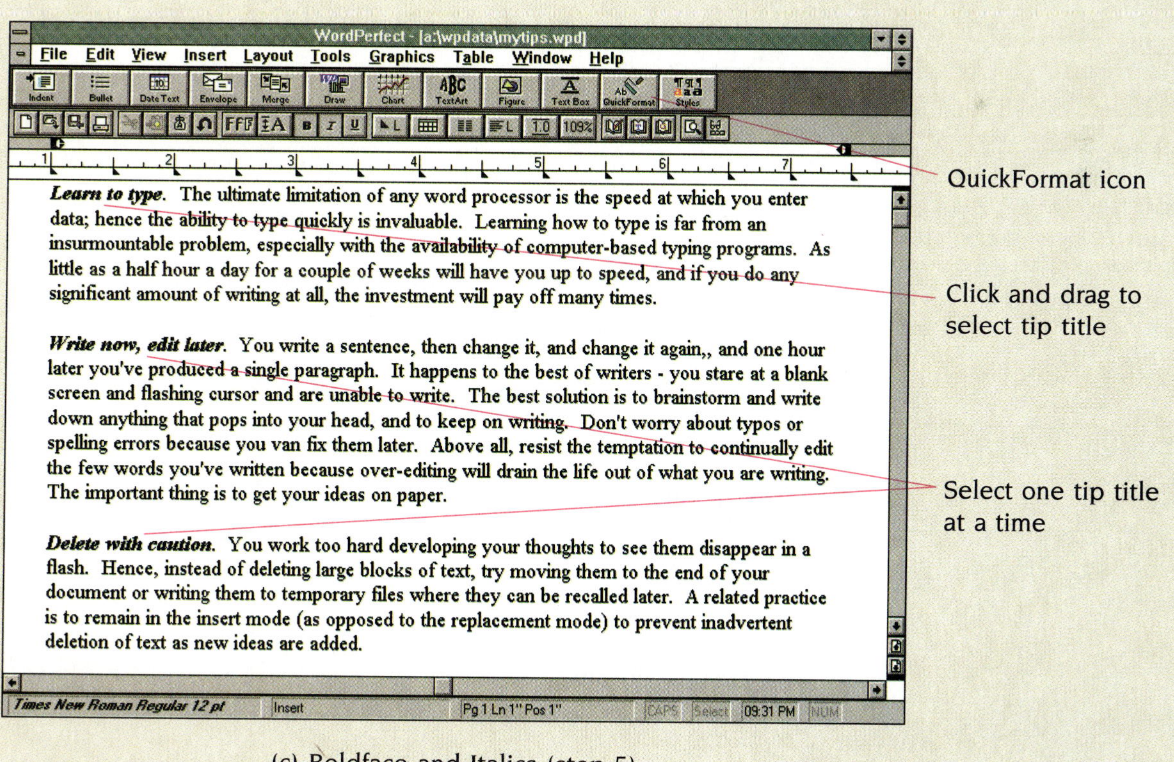

(c) Boldface and Italics (step 5)

FIGURE 2.12 Hands-on Exercise 2 (continued)

Step 6: Justification and Line Spacing

- Press **Ctrl+Home** to move to the beginning of the document.
- Pull down the **Layout menu.** Click **Justification** to pull down the cascade menu in Figure 2.12d.
- A check mark appears next to the word Left to indicate that the document is currently left-justified. Click **Full** to change to full justification.
- Pull down the **Layout menu** a second time. Click **Line.** Click **Spacing.**
- Click the **up arrow** box in the list box to select a different line spacing (or type the desired line spacing in the text box). Click **OK** to accept the new spacing and return to the document.
- We elected to keep the original (single) spacing and clicked the **Cancel** command button to exit the dialog box without changing the spacing.
- Save the document.

THE POWER BAR

Many formatting commands can be implemented more quickly from the Power Bar than from the pull-down menu. Some commands, such as boldface and italics, are executed simply by clicking the icon. Other icons have multiple options and require an additional action. To change justification, for example, click the justification icon on the Power Bar, drag the pointer to the desired choice (left, center, right, or full) in the menu that appears, then release the mouse button.

Insertion point is at beginning of document and no text is selected

Change to full justification

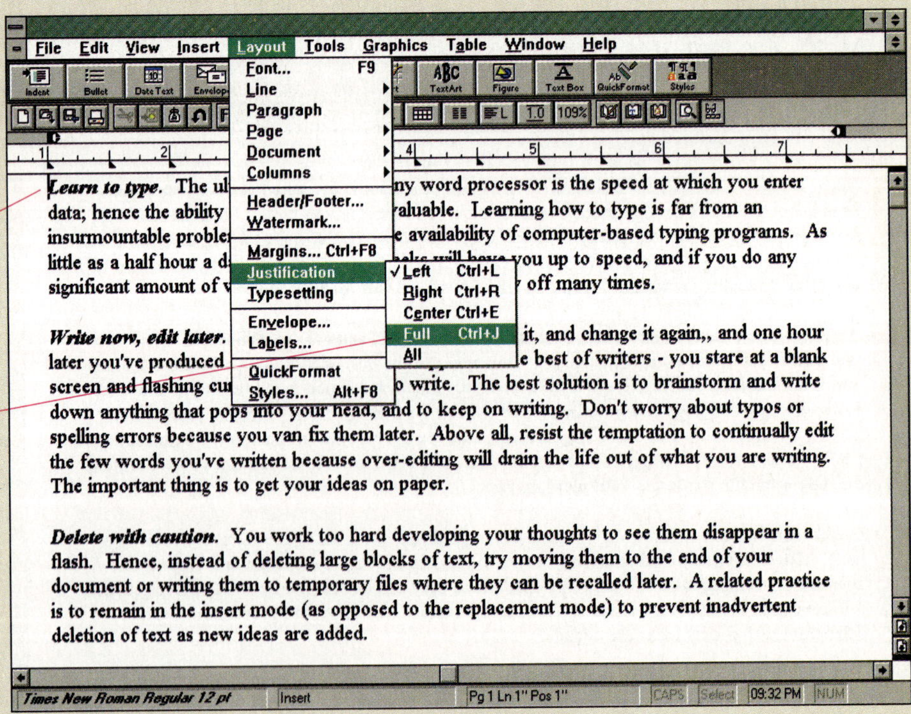

(d) Justification

FIGURE 2.12 Hands-on Exercise 2 (continued)

Step 7: Tabs

- Press **Ctrl+Home** to move to the beginning of the document.
- Press the **Tab key**. The paragraph is indented .5 inch (the default amount).
- Pull down the **Layout menu**. Click **Line**. Click **Tab Set** to produce the dialog box in Figure 2.12e.
- Change the entry in the **Position Text Box** to .25 inch. Click **OK**. The indentation changes automatically to .25 inch.
- Decide whether or not you want to keep the indentation but maintain a uniform look throughout the document. Press the **backspace key** to delete the Tab from this paragraph, or alternatively, insert a Tab at the beginning of every other paragraph.
- Save the document.

Step 8: Margins

- Press **Ctrl+Home** to move to the beginning of the document.
- Pull down the **Layout menu.** Click **Margins.**
- Enter **1.25** in the text boxes for the left, right, top, and bottom margins as shown in Figure 2.12f. Press the **Tab key** to move from one text box to the next.
- Click **OK** to return to the document. The change affects the entire document because the insertion point was at the beginning of the document and no text was selected.
- Save the document.

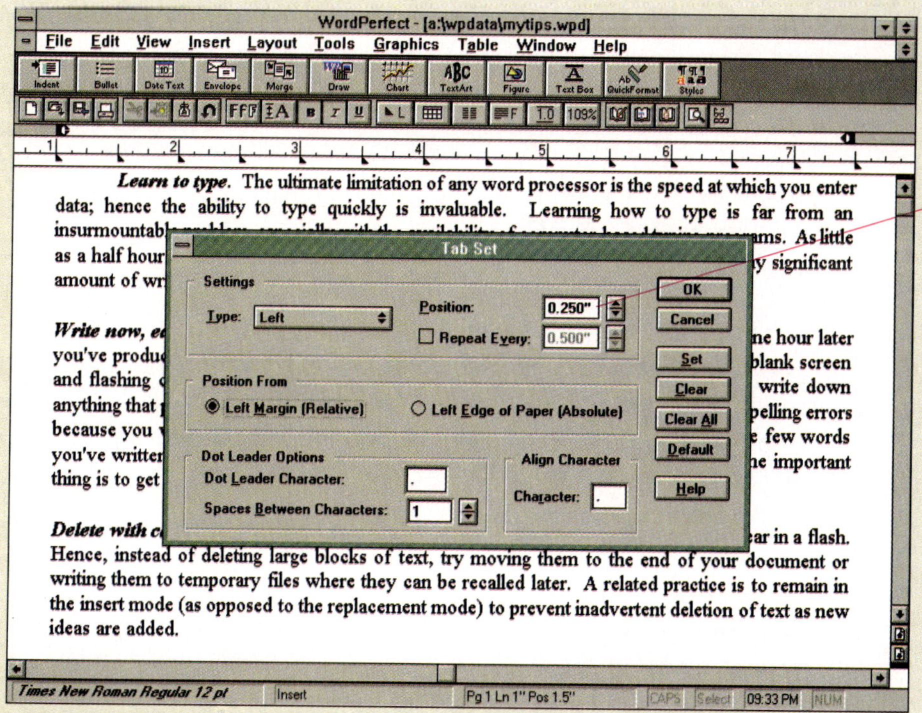

(e) Setting Tabs (step 7)

FIGURE 2.12 Hands-on Exercise 2 (continued)

Insertion point is at beginning of document and no text is selected

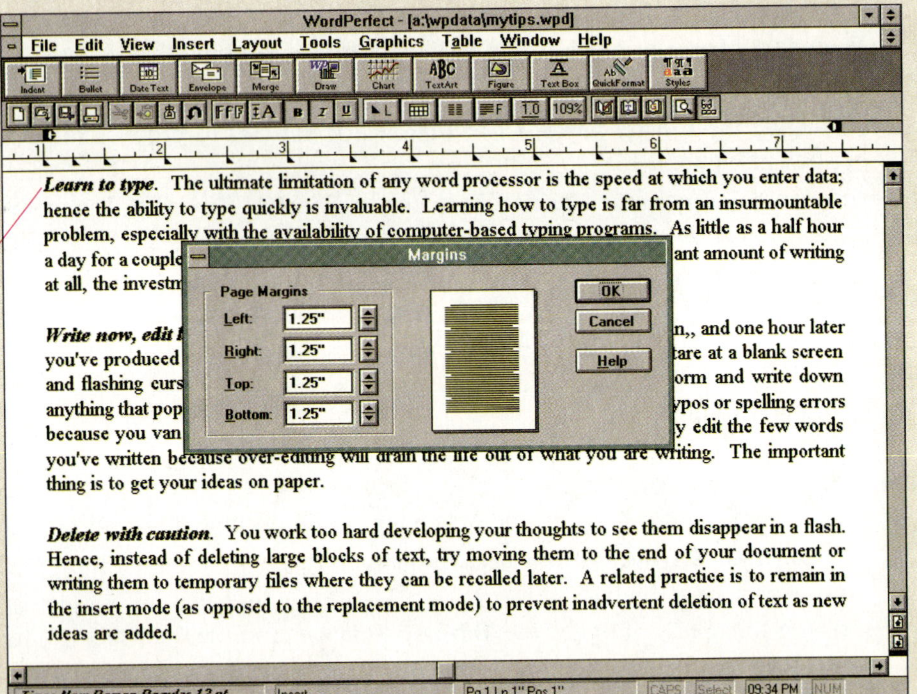

(f) Changing Margins (step 8)

FIGURE 2.12 Hands-on Exercise 2 (continued)

DIALOG BOX SHORTCUTS

You can use the mouse to click on an option box, to mark a check box on or off, or to pull down a drop-down list box and select an option. You can also use a keyboard shortcut for each of these actions.

- Press **Tab (Shift+Tab)** to move forward (backward) from one field or command button to the next.
- Press **Alt** plus the underlined letter to move directly to a field or command button.
- Press **Enter** to activate the highlighted command button.
- Press **Esc** to exit the dialog box without taking action.
- Press the **Space Bar** to toggle check boxes on or off.
- Press the **down arrow** to open a list box once the list has been accessed; press the **up** or **down arrow** to move between options in a list box.

Step 9: Widow and orphan protection

- Press **Ctrl+Home** to move to beginning of the document.
- Pull down the **Layout menu.** Click **Page.** Click **Keep Text Together** to produce the dialog box in Figure 2.12g.
- Check the box for **Widow/Orphan** to prevent single lines of text from being separated from the rest of the paragraph. Click **OK.**
- Save the document.

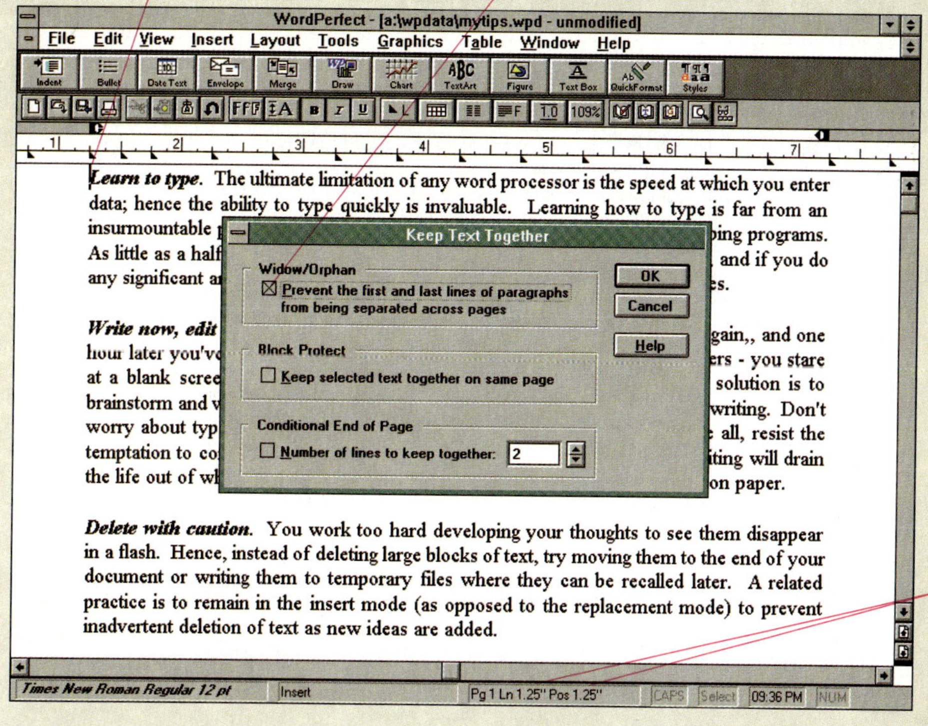

(g) Widow and Orphan Protection (step 9)

FIGURE 2.12 Hands-on Exercise 2 (continued)

Step 10: Create a title page

- Press **Ctrl+Home** to move to the beginning of the document.
- Press **Ctrl+Enter** to insert a hard page break, creating a new page before the list of tips.
- Press the **up arrow key** to move to the newly created page. Create a title page as shown in Figure 2.12h, containing the title, **Word Processing Tips,** on one line and your name on the next.
- Select both lines, then pull down the **Justification icon** on the Power Bar and click **Center.**
- Select the first line of the title, then click the **Font Size icon** on the Power Bar as shown in Figure 2.12h. Click **36.**
- Click outside the selection to deselect it.
- Save the document.

DESELECTING TEXT

The effects of a formatting change are often difficult to see when text is selected, and thus it may be necessary to deselect the text in order to view the change. Even if this is not the case, selected text is affected by the next command, and thus you must deselect it unless you want to continue editing the selected text. Click anywhere in the document to deselect text.

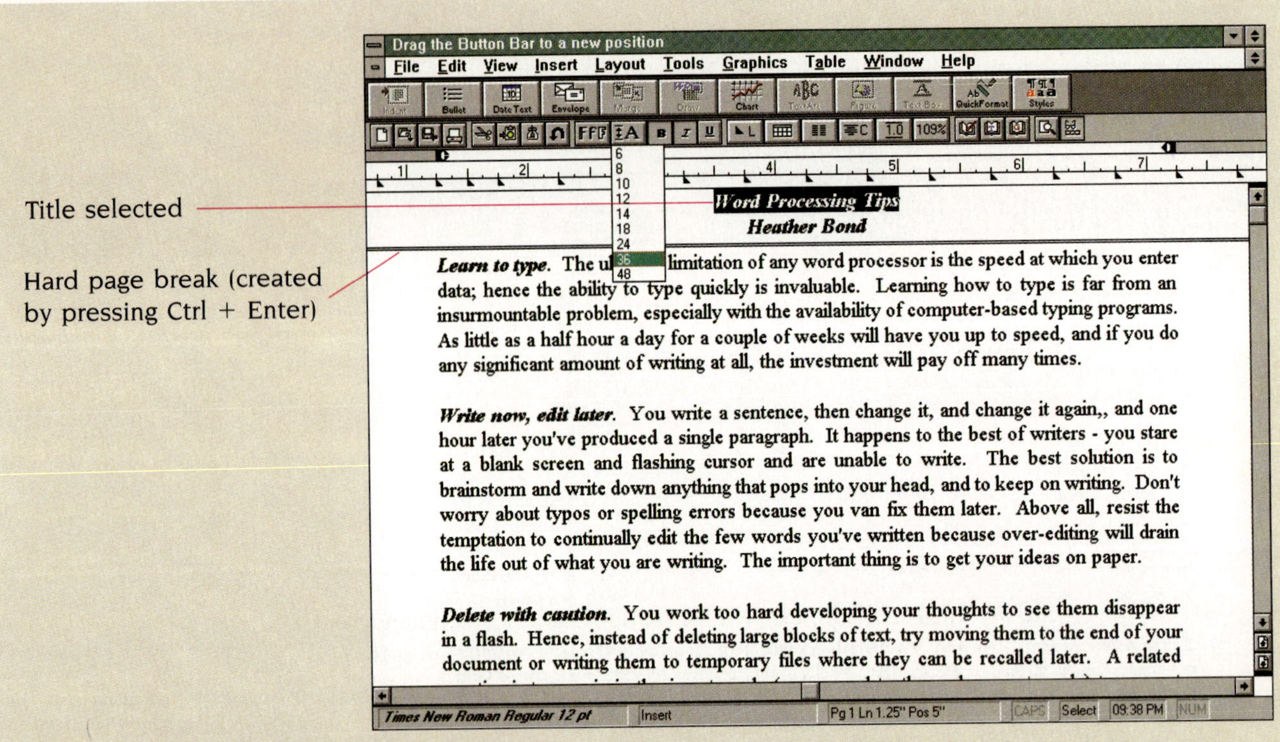

(h) Creating a Title Page (step 10)

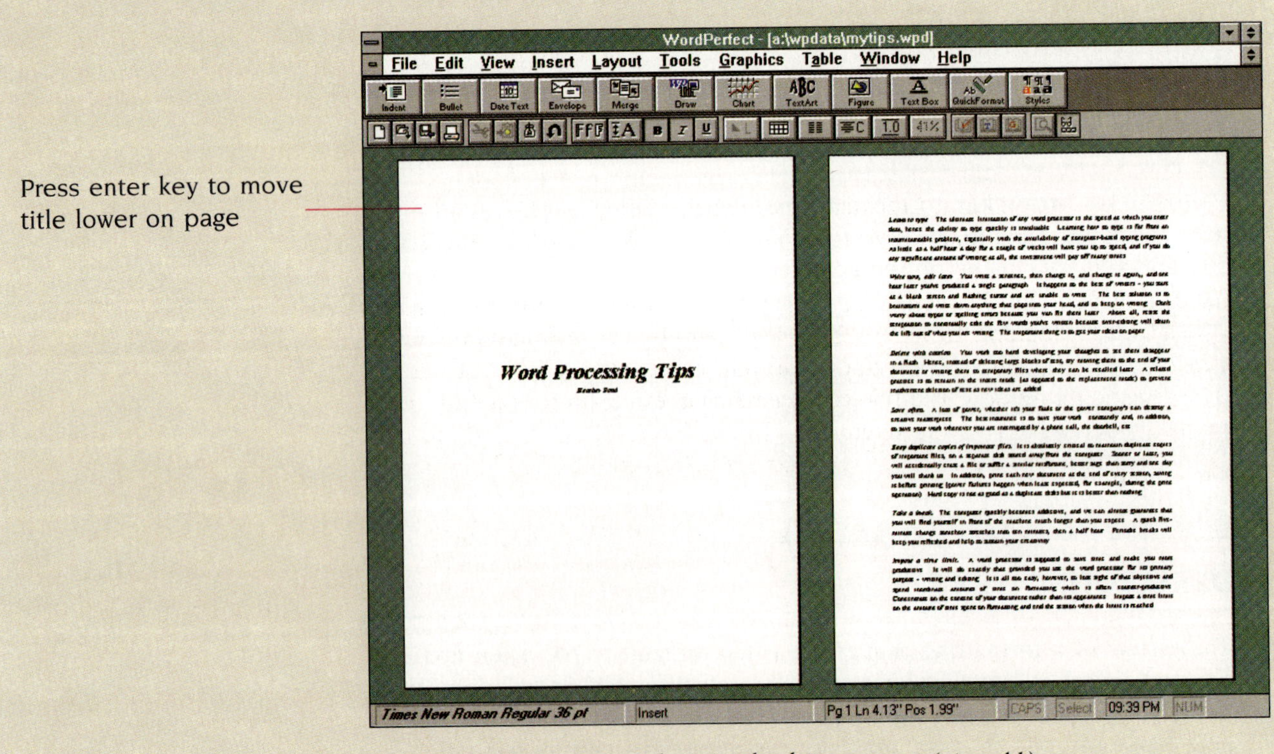

(i) The Finished Document (step 11)

FIGURE 2.12 Hands-on Exercise 2 (continued)

Step 11: The Finished Document

- Pull down the **View menu.** Click **Two Page** to view the facing pages as shown in Figure 2.12i.
- Click in front of the title, then press the **enter key** several times to move the title lower on the page.
- Save the completed document.
- Pull down the **File menu.**
- Click **Print,** then click the **Print command button** to print the completed document.
- Exit WordPerfect. Congratulations on a job well done.

REVEAL CODES

WordPerfect inserts a code into a document with every formatting command you execute. There are codes for virtually everything—for example, hard and soft returns, hard and soft page breaks, line spacing, margins, justification, fonts, and so on. The codes are not visible in the normal editing window, but they are important, because they determine how a document will look on the printed page.

The effect of a formatting command depends on whether or not text was selected when the command was executed. Any command that is executed after text has been selected applies only to the selected text and places a pair of formatting codes in the document. Any command that is executed without previously selecting text places a single code into the document and applies from that point forward (or until another formatting command is issued).

The ***Reveal Codes command*** in the ***View menu*** displays the text and codes in a second window as shown in Figure 2.13. The Reveal Codes window contains the identical text as in the regular window, but with the formatting codes visible. Anything contained within a box is a hidden code; for example, HRt and SRt denote a hard and soft return, respectively. The meaning of most codes is intuitive; for example, Just:Full and LnSpacing:1.00 denote full justification and single spacing, respectively. (The function of the Open Style code is explained in Chapter 4.)

Different values can be associated with the same formatting code in different portions of a document. In Figure 2.13, for example, the left margin is set at 1.25 inches at the beginning of the document and changed to 1.75 inches at the start of the second paragraph. The first code remains in effect until a second (overriding) code appears later in the document. In similar fashion, the line spacing changes from double spacing in the first paragraph to single spacing in the second paragraph. Other codes occur in pairs that point to each other—for example, the italic codes before and after the words *full justification*. The first of the paired italic codes points to the right and turns on the effect; the second points to the left and turns the effect off.

The Reveal Codes window is very helpful in solving problems related to the appearance of a document as it shows the precise formatting in effect. You can edit a document within the Reveal Codes window just as you do in the regular window. You can use the mouse or arrow keys to move the insertion point and the Del key to remove a hidden code. You can also double click a code to open the associated dialog box; for example, double clicking on the Times New Roman code at the beginning of the document will open the Font dialog box.

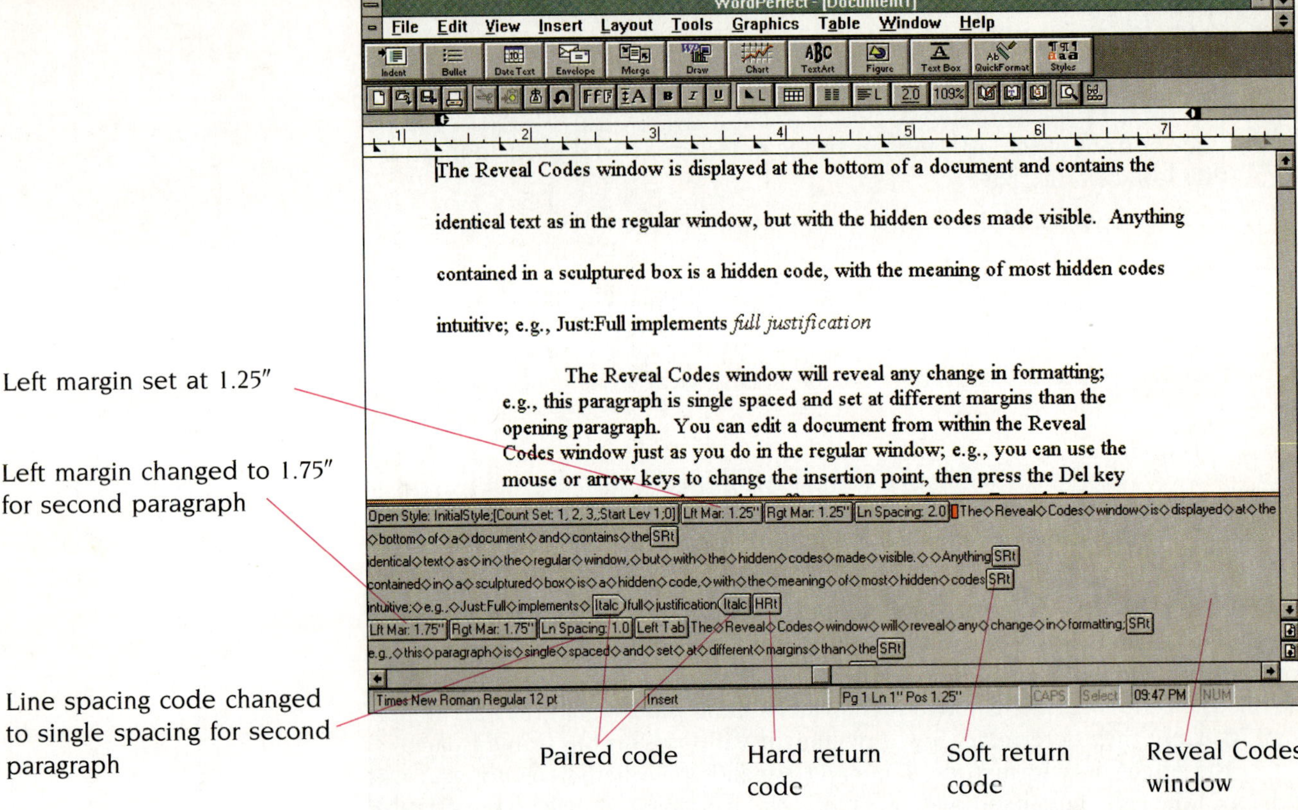

FIGURE 2.13 Reveal Codes

> ## AUTO CODE PLACEMENT
>
> Certain codes (left and right margins, justification, and line spacing) are always placed at the beginning of a paragraph regardless of the insertion point. Other codes (top and bottom margins and page numbering) are placed at the beginning of the page. Pull down the View menu and click Reveal Codes to determine the precise formatting in a document.

File Preferences

WordPerfect provides the ultimate in flexibility by allowing you to customize every aspect of its environment to suit your personal preference. In the beginning you will be content to use the default settings built into the program, but as you become more proficient, you will want to change WordPerfect to match the way you work. Indeed we have already seen several examples in which we altered the default settings to better suit our needs—for example, changing the backup options in the first hands-on exercise.

Changes to the WordPerfect environment are implemented through the ***File Preferences command*** as shown in Figure 2.14. Pull down the File menu, click Preferences, then double click the icon containing the items you want to change. Double click the Display icon in Figure 2.14a, then select the Reveal Codes option, to produce the dialog box in Figure 2.14b.

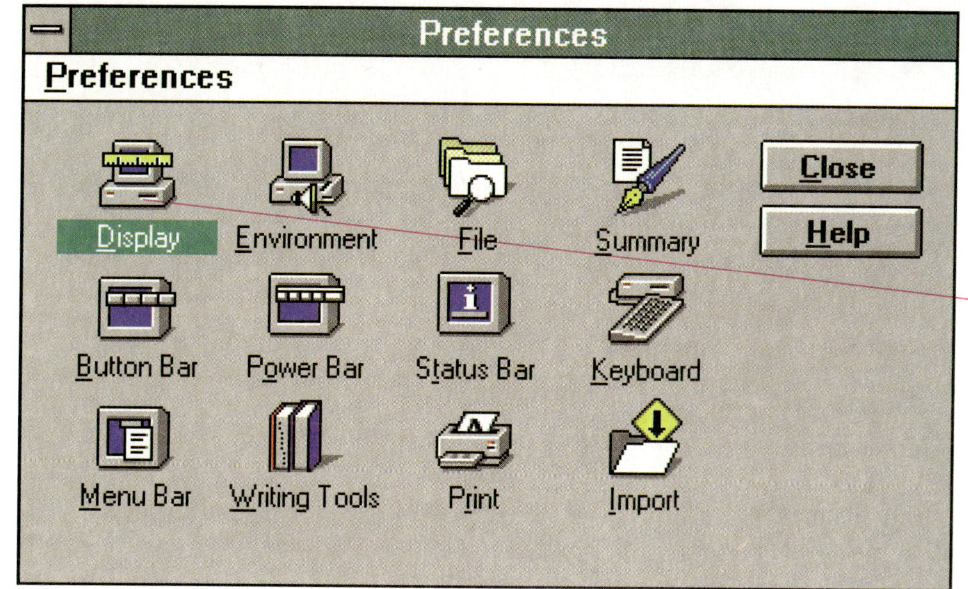

(a) File Preferences Command

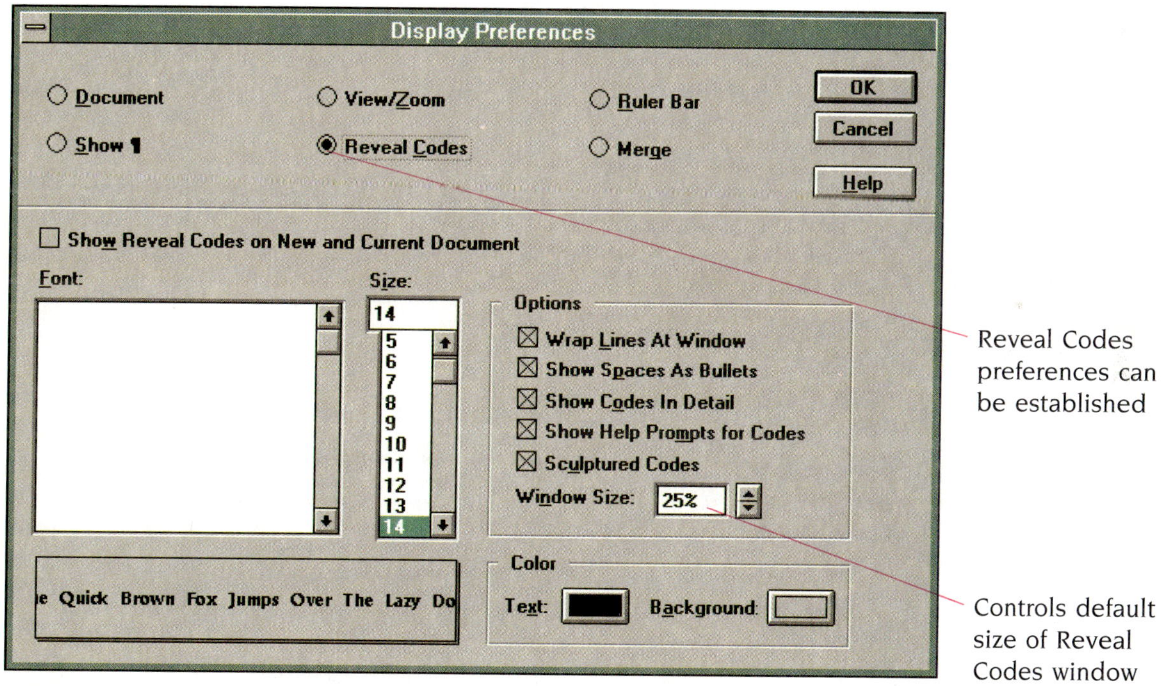

(b) Display Preferences (Reveal Codes)

FIGURE 2.14 Customizing WordPerfect

The Reveal Codes option button is selected in Figure 2.14b. (You can establish preferences for other features by clicking the appropriate buttons.) We have checked all of the option boxes in order to display the maximum amount of information in the Reveal Codes Window. Note, too, that you can control the size of the Reveal Codes window through the Window Size text box.

Hands-On Exercise 3:

Reveal Codes

Objective Use the Reveal Codes command to display the hidden codes in order to edit the document. Use the File Preferences command to customize WordPerfect.

Step 1: File Preferences

- Pull down the **File menu.** Click **Preferences** to produce the dialog box in Figure 2.15a.
- Double click the **Status Bar icon** to produce the dialog box to set Status Bar preferences.
- Click the arrows in the Status Bar Items list box to scroll through the available options. (A description of the selected item appears at the bottom of the dialog box.) Check the individual options on or off according to your personal preference.
- The indicators are placed on the Status Bar in the order they are selected, but you can drag an indicator from one position to another. You can also change the size of an indicator by dragging the edge.
- Click **OK** when you are satisfied with the appearance of the Status Bar.
- Click **Close** to exit the Preferences dialog box and return to your document. The Status Bar will retain the new settings for all future documents.

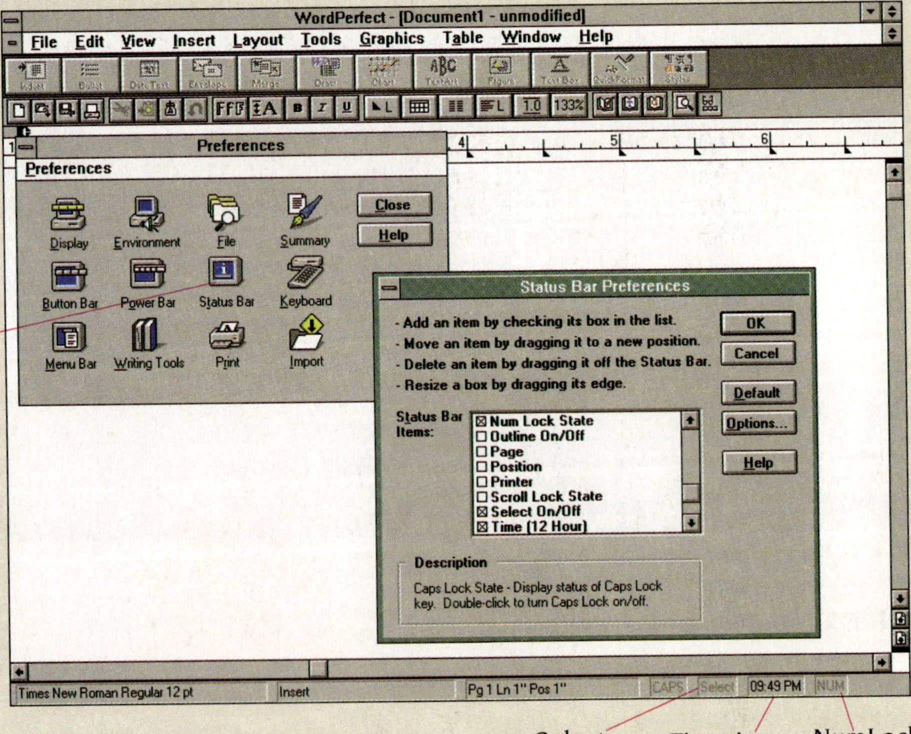

(a) The File Preferences Command (step 1)

FIGURE 2.15 Hands-on Exercise 3

DOUBLE CLICK THE STATUS BAR

Double click different areas of the Status Bar to change the indicated settings; for example, double clicking the CAPS or NUM indicators toggles the corresponding keys on or off. Double clicking on the Ins/Typ indicator toggles from insertion to typeover mode. Double clicking the font indicator produces the Font dialog box. And finally, double clicking the box containing the position of the insertion point (the page and line indicator) produces a dialog box to move to any page within the document.

Step 2: Open the Reveal Codes window

- Pull down the **File menu.** Open the **MYTIPS.WPD** document from the previous exercise.
- Pull down the **View menu.**
- Click **Reveal Codes** to open the Reveal Codes window as shown in Figure 2.15b. Do not be concerned if the size of your Reveal Codes Window, the codes themselves, or the amount of text you see are different from ours. (You may not see any text at all, depending on how many hard returns are at the top of your document.)
- Pull down the **View menu** a second time; a check appears next to the Reveal Codes command. Click **Reveal Codes** to remove the check and close the Reveal Codes window.

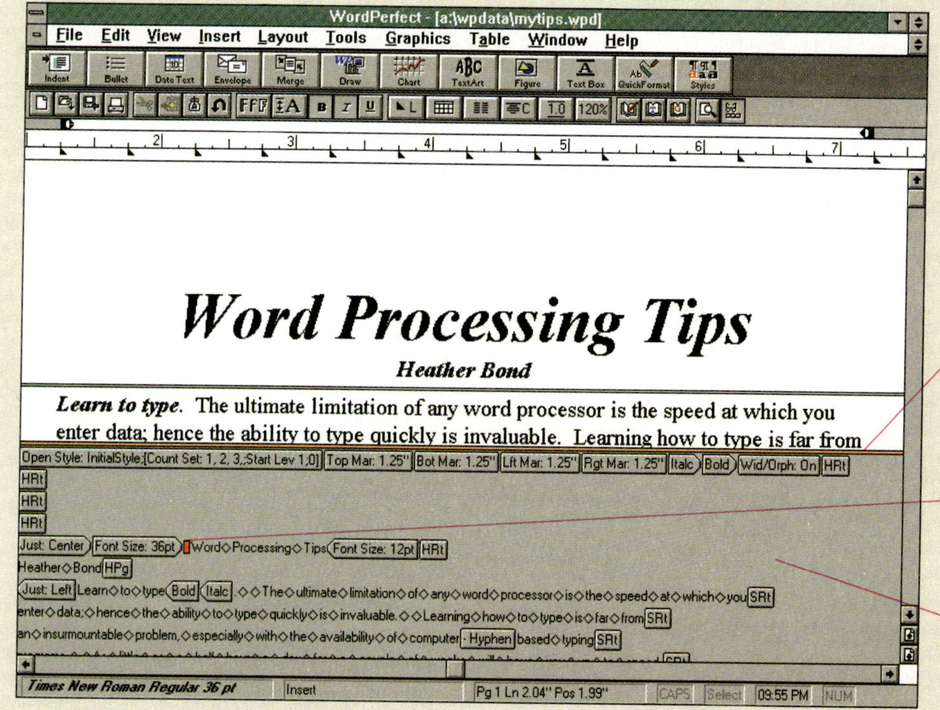

(b) The Reveal Codes Window (step 2)

FIGURE 2.15 Hands-on Exercise 3 (continued)

- The Reveal Codes command functions as a toggle switch; that is, click it once and you open the Reveal Codes window; click it a second time and you close the window.

Step 3: Size the Reveal Codes window

- Press **Alt+F3** to open the Reveal Codes window.
- Point to the **border** separating the document window from the Reveal Codes window. The mouse pointer changes to a double arrow.
- Drag the **border up** (down) to increase (decrease) the size of the Reveal Codes window.

TOGGLE REVEAL CODES ON AND OFF

Press **Alt+F3** to toggle Reveal Codes on or off. Alternatively, you can reveal the codes and size the window at the same time, by dragging the thick line at the bottom of the scroll bar toward the top of the document.

Step 4: Edit the Reveal Codes

- Scroll with the **down arrow key** until you can see the Font Size code that appears to the left of the title.
- Click in the **Reveal Codes window** immediately to the right of the **Font Size code** as shown in Figure 2.15b. (It doesn't matter if your document has one or more hard returns between the Font Size code and the title; just click immediately after the code.)
- Press the **backspace key** to delete the Font Size code, which changes the size of the title (back to the default size) in the editing window.
- Pull down the **Edit menu** and click **Undo** as shown in Figure 2.15c (or click the **Undo icon** on the Power Bar). The title is restored to 36 point type in the Editing window and the File Size code reappears in the Reveal Codes window.
- Scroll through the document and experiment with deleting (and restoring) various hidden codes.

EDITING WITH REVEAL CODES

Use the backspace key to delete the code to the *left* of the insertion point. Use the Del key to delete the code to the *right*. Use the Undo command immediately after deleting a code to restore the deleted code (the Undelete command will not work). Double click a reveal code to open the associated dialog box; for example, double click any code containing a font or font attribute to display the Font dialog box.

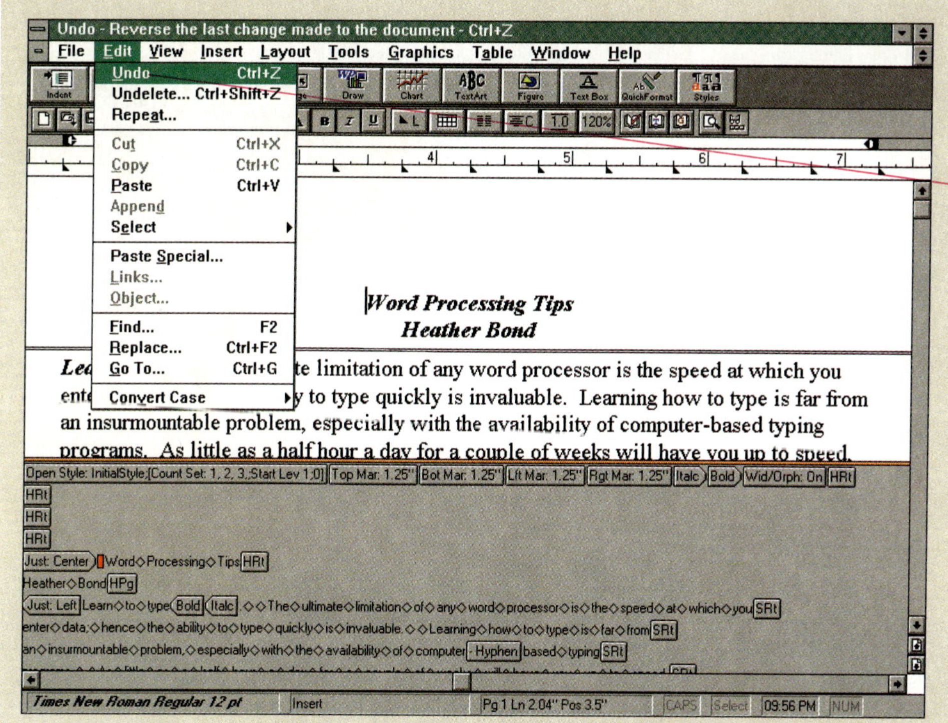

(c) Editing Reveal Codes (step 4)

FIGURE 2.15 Hands-on Exercise 3 (continued)

Step 5: Quick Format

- Press **Ctrl+Home** to move to the beginning of the document, then scroll with the **down arrow key** to the first tip. Select the title of the first tip, **Learn to Type.**
- Click the **Font icon** on the Power Bar. Click **Arial.** The title should be in Arial, and in boldface italics, since the bold and italics styles were applied in the previous exercise. (If this is not the case, edit the Reveal Codes as necessary.)
- Click anywhere in the tip title. Click the **QuickFormat icon** on the Button Bar. Click the **Fonts and Attributes** button, then click **OK.**
- The mouse pointer changes to a roller as shown in Figure 2.15d to indicate that you can paint other areas in the document with the current attributes.
- Drag the mouse over the other tip titles in the document to copy the formatting (Arial boldface italics) from the first tip. When you are finished, click the **QuickFormat icon** a second time to return to normal editing.
- The title of every tip should now be in Arial boldface italics, which can be verified by looking in the Reveal Codes window. Note the paired codes for bold and italics that surround the title of each tip. Observe also the switch in typeface, from Arial at the beginning of the tip title to Times New Roman at the end.
- Close the Reveal Codes window.
- Save the document.
- Exit WordPerfect.

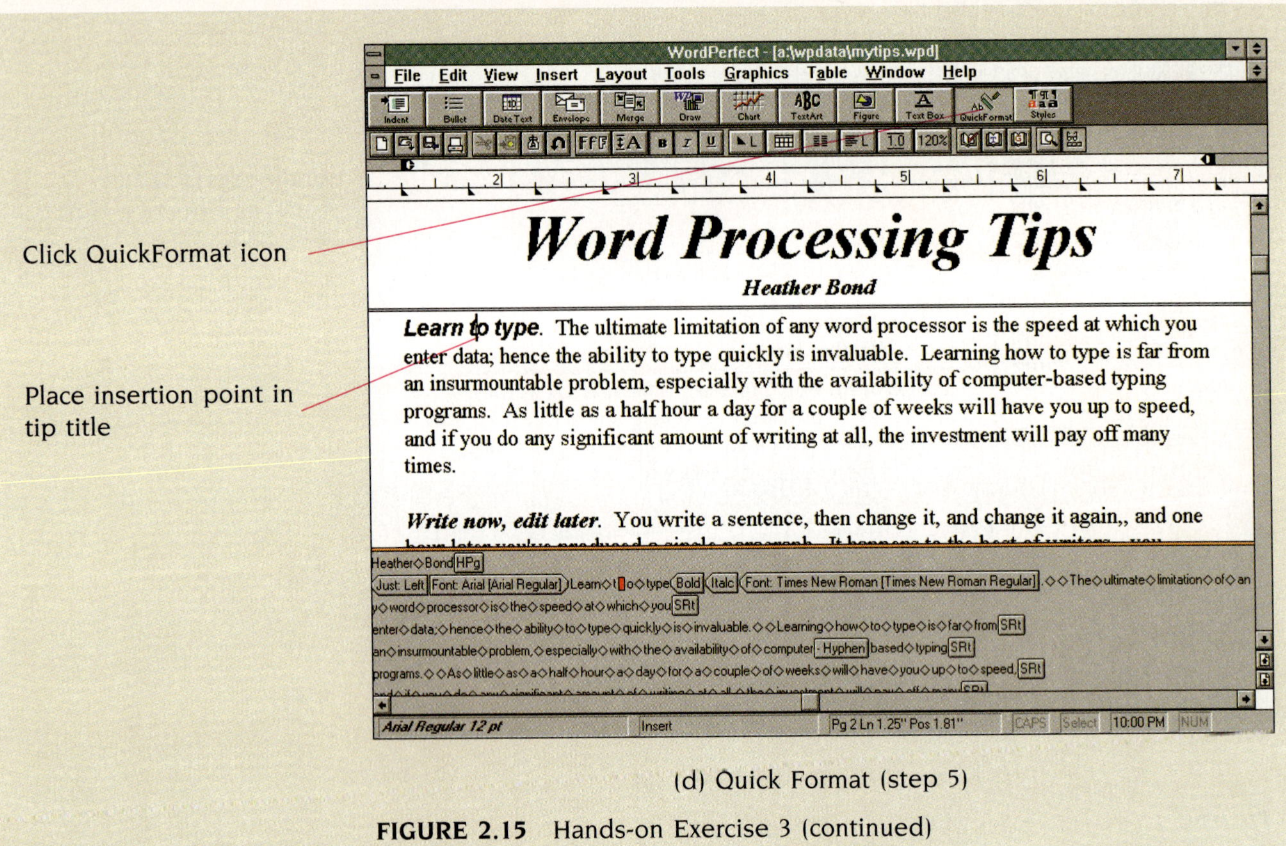

(d) Quick Format (step 5)

FIGURE 2.15 Hands-on Exercise 3 (continued)

SUMMARY

Many operations in WordPerfect are done within the context of select-then-do; that is, select the text, then execute the necessary command. Text may be selected by dragging the mouse, by accessing the Select command in the Edit menu, by using the ***selection area*** to the left of a document, or by clicking the right mouse button to produce a QuickMenu. Text is deselected by clicking outside the selected text.

The Find and Replace commands locate a designated character string and optionally replace one or more occurrences of that string with a different character string. The search may be case sensitive and/or restricted to whole words. It may also include specific fonts and/or attributes such as boldface or italics.

Text is moved or copied through a combination of the Cut, Copy, and Paste commands and/or the drag-and-drop facility. The contents of the clipboard are replaced by any subsequent Cut or Copy command, but are unaffected by the Paste command; that is, the same text can be pasted into multiple locations. The Undo command reverses the effect of the latest command. The Undelete command restores any of the last three deletions.

Scrolling occurs when a document is too large to be seen in its entirety. Scrolling with the mouse changes the display on the screen, but does not change the location of the insertion point; that is, you must click in the document to move the insertion point. Scrolling via the keyboard (for example, PgUp and PgDn) changes what is seen on the screen as well as the location of the insertion point.

The Save command copies the document in memory to disk under its existing name. The Save As command saves the document under a different name and is useful when you want to retain both a copy of the current document prior to any changes as well as a copy of the modified document.

Windows 3.1 includes 14 TrueType fonts. WordPerfect provides additional fonts. All TrueType fonts are scalable and available to any Windows application. A serif typeface (for example, Times New Roman) has tiny cross lines that end the main strokes of each letter. A sans-serif typeface (e.g., Arial) does not have these cross lines.

Indentation is used to offset different parts of a document to lend emphasis. The amount of indentation is controlled by the tab stop (.5 inch is the default), but the type of indentation is determined by the Paragraph command in the Layout menu.

A soft page break occurs as text flows from the bottom of one page to the top of the next. A hard page break is inserted by the user to force text to begin on a new page.

The View menu offers three views of a document: Draft, Page, and Two Page. The first two views may be displayed at magnifications ranging from 25% to 400%.

The Reveal Codes window contains the identical text as in the regular window, but with the hidden codes made visible.

The File Preferences command enables you to customize the WordPerfect environment.

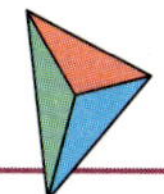

Key Words and Concepts

Alignment
Arial
Automatic replacement
Backup
BK! extension
Case sensitive
Case insensitive
Center alignment
Clipboard
Copy command
Cut command
Decimal tab
Default directory
Double Indent command
Draft view
Drag-and-drop
File Preferences command
Find command
Font
Formatting
Global replacement
Hanging Indent command
Hard page break
Indent command
Insert menu
Landscape orientation
Layout menu
Leader character
Left tab
Margin Width
Orphan
Page break
Page command
Page view
Page Width
Paragraph command
Paste command
Point size
Portrait orientation
QuickFormat command
QuickMenu
Replace command
Reveal Codes command
Right tab
Sans-serif typeface
Save As command
Save command
Scrolling
Select-then-do
Selection area
Selective replacement
Serif typeface
Soft page break
Tab stop
Times New Roman
TrueType
Two Page View
Type style
Typeface
Undo command
View menu
Whole word only
Widow
Zoom command

Multiple Choice

1. Which of the following commands does *not* place data onto the clipboard?
   (a) Cut
   (b) Copy
   (c) Paste
   (d) All of the above

2. What happens if you select a block of text, copy it, move to the beginning of the document, paste it, move to the end of the document, and paste the text again?
   (a) The selected text will appear in three places: at the original location, and at the beginning and end of the document
   (b) The selected text will appear in two places: at the beginning and end of the document
   (c) The selected text will appear in just the original location
   (d) The situation is not possible; that is, you cannot paste twice in a row without an intervening cut or copy operation

3. What happens if you select a block of text, cut it, move to the beginning of the document, paste it, move to the end of the document, and paste the text again?
   (a) The selected text will appear in three places: at the original location and at the beginning and end of the document
   (b) The selected text will appear in two places: at the beginning and end of the document
   (c) The selected text will appear in just the original location
   (d) The situation is not possible; that is, you cannot paste twice in a row without an intervening cut or copy operation

4. The default tab stops are set to:
   (a) Left tabs every ½ inch
   (b) Left tabs every ¼ inch
   (c) Right tabs every ½ inch
   (d) Right tabs every ¼ inch

5. How do you change the font for *existing* text within a document?
   (a) Select the text, then choose the new font
   (b) Choose the new font then select the text
   (c) Either (a) or (b)
   (d) Neither (a) nor (b)

6. Which of the following is true regarding the Undo and Undelete commands?
   (a) The Undo command can restore only the most recently deleted character string, and further, it must be executed immediately after the deletion has taken place
   (b) The Undelete command can restore the last three character strings that were deleted, and further, it can be executed at any time
   (c) Both (a) and (b)
   (d) Neither (a) nor (b)

7. Which menu contains the Preferences command to customize WordPerfect?
   (a) File menu

(b) Edit menu
(c) Layout menu
(d) Tools menu

8. The spacing in an existing multipage document is changed from single spacing to double spacing. What can you say about the number of hard and soft page breaks before and after the formatting change?
(a) The number of soft page breaks is the same but the number and/or position of the hard page breaks is different
(b) The number of hard page breaks is the same, but the number and/or position of the soft page breaks is different
(c) The number and position of both hard and soft page breaks are the same
(d) The number and position of both hard and soft page breaks are different

9. Which of the following deselects a selected block of text?
(a) Clicking outside the selected text
(b) Clicking any alignment icon on the Power Bar
(c) Clicking the boldface or italics icons
(d) All of the above

10. Which of the following describes the Arial and Times New Roman fonts?
(a) Arial is a sans-serif font, Times New Roman is a serif font
(b) Arial is a serif font, Times New Roman is a sans-serif font
(c) Both are serif fonts
(d) Both are sans-serif fonts

11. The find and replacement strings must be
(a) The same length
(b) The same case, either upper or lower
(c) The same length and the same case
(d) Neither the same length nor the same case

12. Assume that you are in the middle of a multipage document. How do you scroll to the beginning of the document and simultaneously move the insertion point?
(a) Press Ctrl+Home
(b) Drag the scroll bar to the top of the scroll box
(c) Both (a) and (b)
(d) Neither (a) nor (b)

13. Orphans and widows are:
(a) WordPerfect documents that are somehow lost on a hard drive
(b) Individual commands executed without a pull-down menu
(c) The first (last) line of a paragraph that is isolated at the bottom (top) of a page
(d) Isolated words set in a different typeface than the rest of a document

14. Which of the following will select a paragraph?
(a) Double clicking in the left margin next to the paragraph
(b) Pointing to the left margin, clicking the right mouse button, then clicking Select Paragraph in the resulting menu
(c) Both (a) and (b)
(d) Neither (a) nor (b)

15. Which command saves the document in memory and creates a backup copy with the BK! extension?
    (a) The Save command provided the proper backup option has been set
    (b) The Save As command provided the proper backup option has been set
    (c) The Save command irrespective of the backup options in effect
    (d) The Save As command irrespective of the backup options in effect.

ANSWERS

1. c	**6.** c	**11.** d
2. a	**7.** a	**12.** a
3. b	**8.** b	**13.** c
4. a	**9.** a	**14.** c
5. a	**10.** a	**15.** a

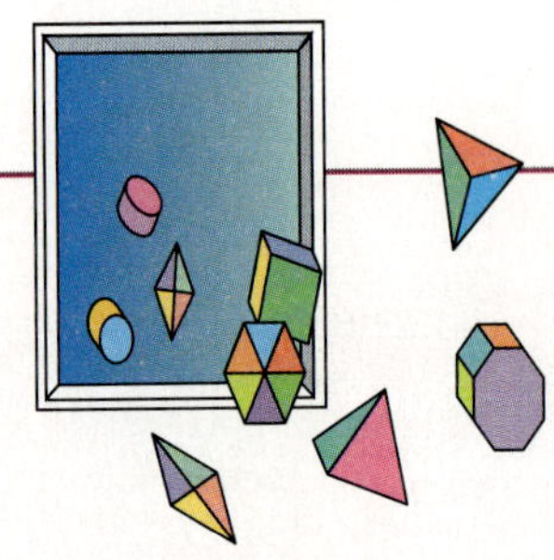

EXPLORING WORDPERFECT

1. Use Figure 2.16 to match each action with its result; a given action may be used more than once.

Action		**Result**
a. Click at 1	___	Change the typeface of the selected text
b. Click at 2	___	Boldface the selected text
c. Click at 3	___	Save the edited document
d. Click at 4	___	Change all occurrences of *write* to *type*
e. Click at 5	___	Establish widow/orphan protection
f. Click at 6	___	Change the Zoom to Page Width
g. Click at 7	___	Italicize the selected text
h. Click at 8	___	Copy the selected text to the clipboard
i. Click at 9	___	Preview the document prior to printing
j. Click at 10	___	Display the Reveal Codes window

2. Use the Preamble to the Constitution as the basis for the following exercise, which you are to complete and submit to your instructor. Enter the text as shown below:

> *We, the people of the United States, in order to form a more perfect Union, establish justice, insure domestic tranquility, provide for the common defense, promote the general welfare, and secure the blessings of liberty to ourselves and our posterity, do ordain and establish this Constitution for the United States of America.*

   a. Choose any typeface you like, but specify italic as the style, and 10 points as the size. Use single spacing and left justification.
   b. Copy the preamble to a new page, then change the specifications for the copied text to double spacing and full justification. Use the same typeface as before, but choose regular rather than italic for the style.

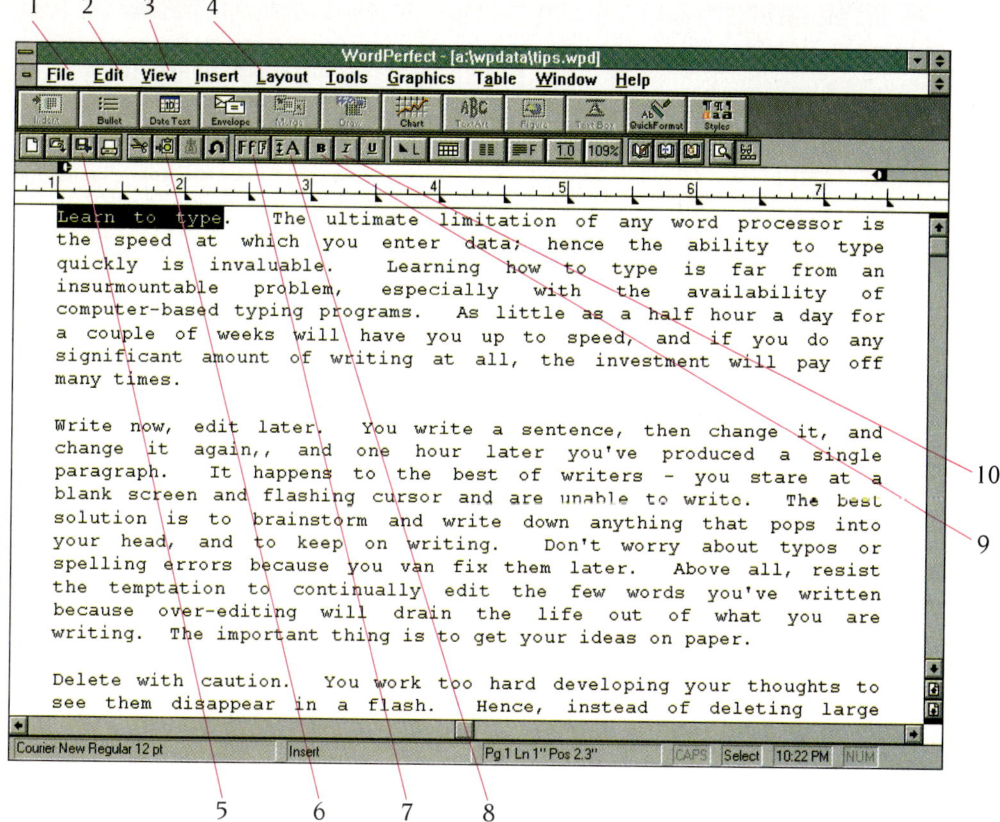

FIGURE 2.16 Screen for Problem 1

c. Create a title page for your assignment, containing your name, the course name, and an appropriate title. Use a different typeface for the title page than in the rest of the document, and set the title in at least 24 points. Submit all three pages to your instructor.

3. Figure 2.17 displays an additional practice document on the data disk.

a. Open the document PROB0203.WPD on the data disk.

b. Copy the sentence, *Discretion is the better part of valor,* to the beginning of the first paragraph.

c. Move the second paragraph to the end of the document.

d. Change the typeface of the entire document to 12 point Arial.

e. Change all whole word occurrences of *feel* to *think*.

f. Change the spacing of the entire document from the single spacing to 1.5. Change the justification of the entire document to fully justified.

g. Set the phrases *Layout Justification* and *Layout Line Spacing* in italics.

h. Create a title page that precedes the document. Set the title, *Discretion in Design,* in 24 point Arial bold and center it approximately two inches from the top of the page. Right justify your name toward the bottom of the document in 12 point Arial regular.

i. Save the modified document as SOLUTION.WPD.

j. Print the revised document and submit it to your instructor.

4. Prepare a personal ad for placement in a newspaper that could be distributed to the class at large. Any writing style is acceptable, but try to make it creative. A poem or limerick would be fine. The only requirement is to

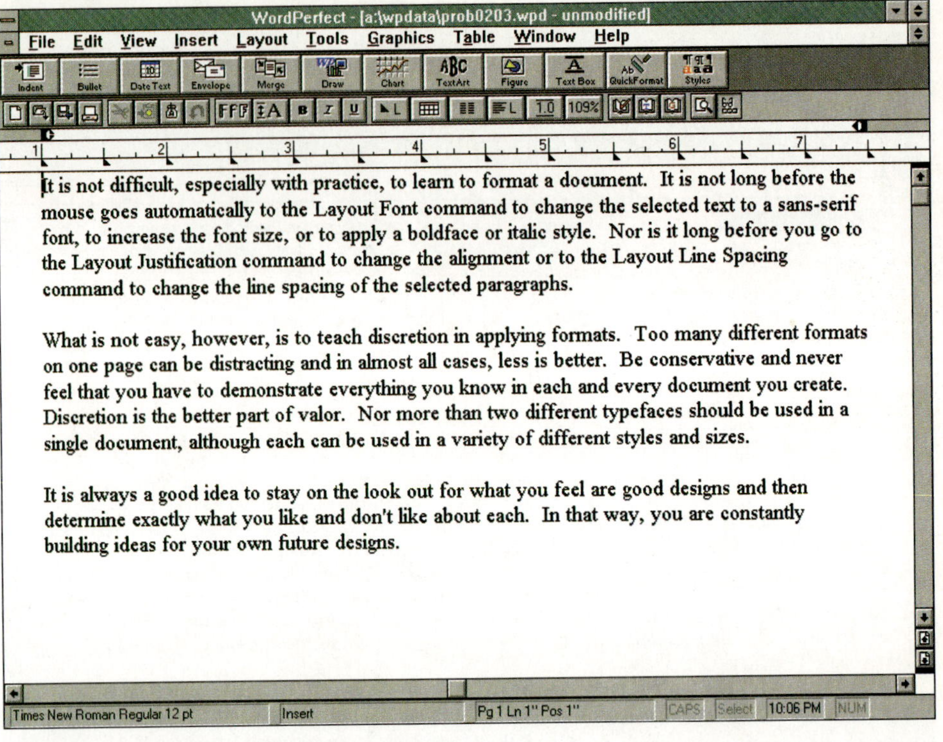

FIGURE 2.17 Screen for Problem 3

demonstrate proficiency in the use of a word processor, with adherence to the following specifications:

a. Fully justified text
b. A line length of 4 inches
c. Boldface the information on how to reply (centered on the last line), which should be a box number consisting of the last four digits of your social security number and the first two characters of your last name.
d. A sample appears below:

Dynamic professor seeks motivated students for exciting course in Windows applications. Presentation of Windows concepts, WordPerfect, Lotus, and Presentation graphics. Approximately 10 home-work assignments, two tests, and a final. No previous knowledge of computers is required.

Respond to 1234GR

5. What is the fastest way (using the mouse or keyboard, whichever you prefer) to:

a. Scroll to the beginning or end of a document? Does this action also move the insertion point?
b. Copy formatting from one place in a document to another?
c. Select a word? a sentence? a paragraph? the entire document?
d. Copy a block of text to multiple destinations within the same document?
e. Change the selected text to boldface or italics?
f. Save the document being edited?
g. Change the line spacing?
h. Change the alignment (justification)?
i. Change the font for selected text?

6. WordPerfect can be used to prepare any kind of document, not only one that is limited to traditional text—for example, the set of dots below. Recreate the figure below consisting of 12 rows of 15 dots each. (To make life really interesting, you might try doing this with the fewest number of commands possible. Compare your solution to that of your neighbor.)

```
.   .   .   .   .   .   .   .   .   .   .   .   .   .   .
.   .   .   .   .   .   .   .   .   .   .   .   .   .   .
.   .   .   .   .   .   .   .   .   .   .   .   .   .   .
.   .   .   .   .   .   .   .   .   .   .   .   .   .   .
.   .   .   .   .   .   .   .   .   .   .   .   .   .   .
.   .   .   .   .   .   .   .   .   .   .   .   .   .   .
.   .   .   .   .   .   .   .   .   .   .   .   .   .   .
.   .   .   .   .   .   .   .   .   .   .   .   .   .   .
.   .   .   .   .   .   .   .   .   .   .   .   .   .   .
.   .   .   .   .   .   .   .   .   .   .   .   .   .   .
.   .   .   .   .   .   .   .   .   .   .   .   .   .   .
.   .   .   .   .   .   .   .   .   .   .   .   .   .   .
```

The figure represents the children's game of *dots,* in which the players take turns connecting two adjacent dots. Each player is allowed one line per turn, except in the event that the last line drawn completes a box. In that case, the player puts his or her initial in the box and goes again. The player with the most boxes at the end of the game wins. Most of the action takes place at the end of the game, at which time runs of 10, 20, or 30 boxes are possible.

7. Exploring File Preferences: Answer the following with respect to the Preferences command and associated dialog box in Figure 2.18.
   a. Which menu contains the Preferences command?
   b. What other action was taken after executing the Preferences command to produce the dialog box in the figure?.
   c. How many checked boxes are visible in the figure? Identify the icon on the Power Bar that corresponds to each of the visible checked boxes.
   d. How do you remove an icon from the Power Bar? Remove the Underline icon from your Power Bar to make sure of your answer.
   e. How do you add an icon to the Power Bar? Add the Edit Undelete icon to your Power Bar to make sure of your answer.
   f. How can you change the position of an existing icon on the Power Bar?
   g. How can you separate one icon from another?
8. The document in Figure 2.19 exists on the data disk but with no formatting. Open the file PROB0208.WPD, then implement the changes below so that your file matches the document in the figure.
   a. Set top and bottom margins of 2 inches each.
   b. Set left and right margins of 1 inch each.

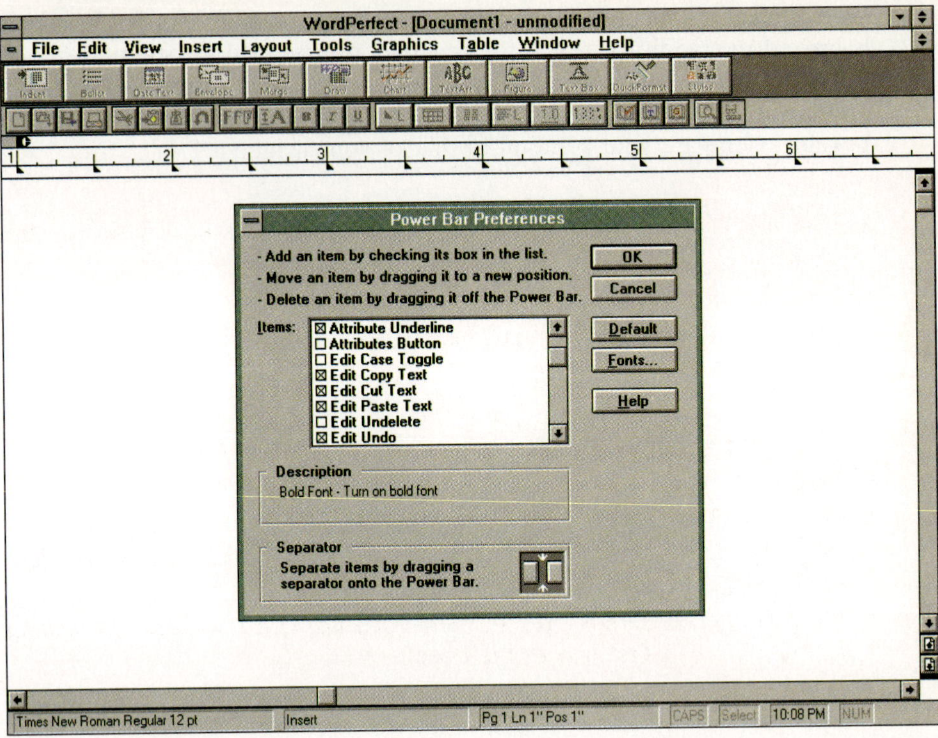

FIGURE 2.18 Power Bar Preferences

TYPOGRAPHY

The art of formatting a document is more than just knowing definitions, but knowing the definitions is definitely a starting point. A ***typeface*** is a complete set of characters with the same general appearance, and can be *serif* (cross lines at the end of the main strokes of each letter) or *sans serif* (without the cross lines). A ***type size*** is a vertical measurement, made from the top of the tallest letter in the character set to the bottom of the lowest letter in the character set. ***Type style*** refers to variations in the typeface, such as boldface and italics.

Several typefaces are shipped with Windows, including *Times New Roman*, a serif typeface, and *Arial*, a sans serif typeface. Additional typefaces are included in WordPerfect for Windows. A serif typeface should be used for large amounts of text whereas sans-serif is best used for titles and subtitles. It is best not to use too many different typefaces in the same document, but rather to use only one or two and then make the document interesting by varying their size and style.

FIGURE 2.19 Document for Problem 8

c. Establish 1.5 line spacing for the document. Leave an extra line between the paragraphs.

d. Change the typeface for the body of the document to 12 point Times New Roman.

e. Find the word Arial within the document, then change its typeface to 12 point Arial.

f. Use italics and boldface italics on the highlighted terms as shown in the figure.

g. Set the title of the document in 18 point Arial bold. Center the title.

h. Justify the document (flush left/flush right).

9. Exploring Reveal Codes: Answer the following with respect to the screen in Figure 2.20.

a. Which keystroke combination toggles Reveal Codes on and off?

b. How do you change the size of the Reveal Codes window?

c. How do you combine the two paragraphs into a single paragraph?

d. Why are there two hidden codes for Bold, each pointing in a different direction?

e. How would you remove the italics associated with the words *formatting command* in the first line of the document?

f. What are the left and right margin settings in effect for the document? What are the top and bottom margins?

g. Which font, and which characteristics, are in effect for the first paragraph? Which font is in effect for the second paragraph?

h. What happens if you delete a hidden code? if you double click on a hidden code?

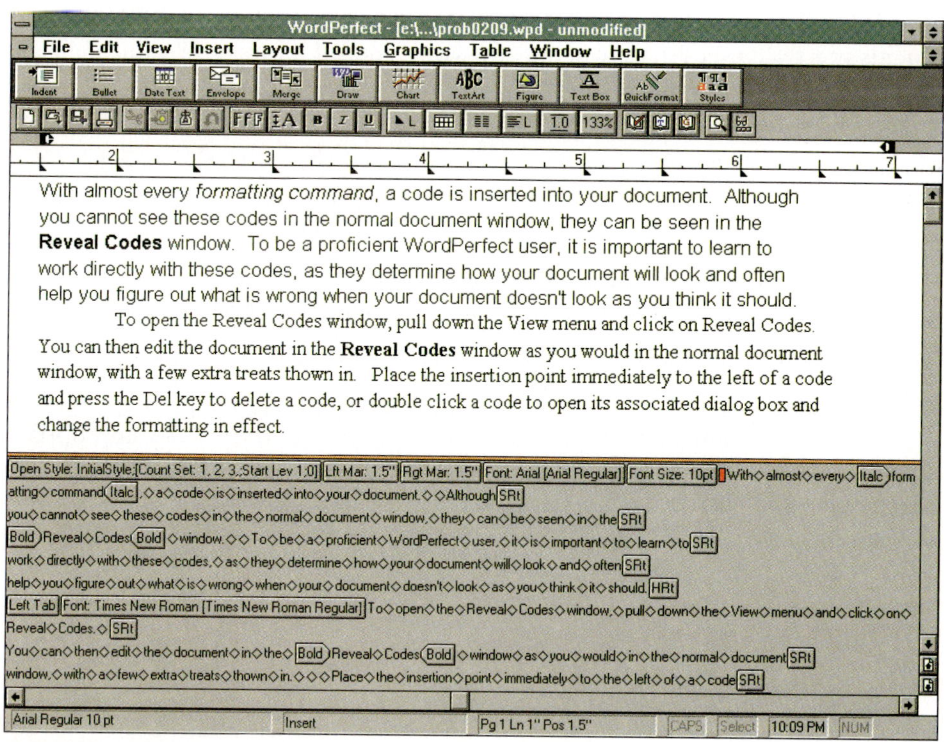

FIGURE 2.20 Screen for Problem 9

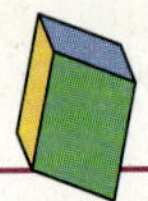

Case Studies

Computers Past and Present

The ENIAC was the scientific marvel of its day and the world's first operational electronic computer. It could perform 5,000 additions per second, weighed 30 tons and took 1500 square feet of floor space. The price was a modest $486,000 in 1946 dollars. The story of the ENIAC and other influential computers of the authors' choosing is found in the file HISTORY.WPD, which we failed to format, so we are asking you to do it for us. Be sure to use appropriate emphasis to highlight the names of the various computers.

Your Own Reference Manual

The clipboard is a temporary storage area available to all Windows applications. Selected text is cut or copied from one document into the clipboard from where it can be pasted into another document altogether. Use on-line help to obtain detailed information on several topics within WordPerfect for Windows, then use the Edit Copy command to copy the information to the clipboard, and paste it into a new document, which will become your personal reference manual. To do an outstanding job, you will have to format the reference manual after the information has been copied from the clipboard. Be sure to include a title page.

Fonts, Fonts, and More Fonts

In the beginning fonts were expensive and Courier was good enough. Then came TrueType and all of a sudden font packages that used to cost hundreds of dollars were sold for almost nothing. The problem is that fonts have gotten out of hand and most of us have many more than we use. Do you really need all of the fonts on your system? Do you have any idea how much disk space the fonts require? Which fonts are your favorites and where did you get them? In what type of documents are they used? Can you suggest some type of strategy for font management and selection? Answer these questions in a nicely formatted report of one to two pages.

Your First Consultant's Job

Go to a real installation—for example, a doctor's or an attorney's office, the company where you work, or the computer lab at school. Determine the backup procedures that are in effect, then write a one-page report indicating whether the policy is adequate and, if necessary, offering suggestions for improvement. Your report should be addressed to the individual in charge of the business and it should cover all aspects of the backup strategy; that is, which files are backed up and how often, and what software is used for the backup operation. Use appropriate emphasis (e.g., bold italics) to identify any potential problems. This is a professional document (it is your first consultant's job) and its appearance must be perfect in every way.

3

The Tools: Preparing a Résumé and Cover Letter

CHAPTER OBJECTIVES

After reading this chapter you will be able to:

1. Implement a spell check; describe the function of the supplementary dictionary in checking the spelling in a document.
2. Use the thesaurus to look up synonyms and antonyms.
3. Explain the objectives and limitations of a program to check grammar.
4. Insert the current date into a document; distinguish between a date code and date text.
5. Distinguish between the form file and data file used in a mail merge; create and print a set of form letters.
6. Include a subset of records from a data file in the mail merge operation; print the records in a sequence other than the order in which they appear in the data file.
7. View multiple documents at the same time; change the size and or position of the window in which each document is displayed.
8. Use one or more ExpressDocs to create predefined documents.

OVERVIEW

Is graduation coming close and the pressure for a job getting to you? Would you like to prepare a professional résumé and associated cover letter, and be able to mail it to multiple employers? In this chapter we tell you how as we present the tools to add the finishing touches to a document and make it as error free as possible. We show you how to use a spelling checker and introduce the thesaurus as a means of adding precision to your writing. We present the grammar checker as a convenient way of finding a variety of errors, but remind you there is no substitute for carefully proofreading the final document.

The chapter is built around a résumé and the associated cover letter to a potential employer, then extends the example to a mail merge that takes the tedium out of sending form letters. The chapter also introduces the ExpressDocs feature in WordPerfect, which helps you create predefined documents quickly and easily. We believe this to be a very enjoyable chapter that will add significantly to your capability in WordPerfect. As always, learning is best accomplished by doing, and the hands-on exercises are essential to master the material.

THE SPELLING CHECKER

The ***spelling checker*** is an integral part of any full-featured word processor. You are well advised to use it because spelling errors make your work look sloppy and discourage the reader before he or she has read what you had to say. Errors can cost you a job, a grade, a lucrative contract, or an award you deserve.

The spelling checker can be used to check an individual word, a block of selected text, or the document as a whole. The word(s) in question are checked against a built-in dictionary, with any mismatch (a word found in the document but not in the built-in dictionary) flagged as an error.

The dictionary included with WordPerfect is limited to standard English. It does not include many proper names, acronyms, abbreviations, or specialized terms. Hence, the use of any such item is considered a misspelling. You can, however, add such words to a ***supplementary dictionary*** so that they will not be flagged in the future. You can also purchase specialized dictionaries containing medical or legal terminology or even a foreign language. The spelling checker will inform you of repeated words and irregular capitalization, but it cannot flag properly spelled words that are used improperly; for example, *two bee or knot too be* is not the answer.

The spelling checker is called from the ***Tools menu*** or by clicking the ***Spell Check icon*** on the Power Bar. Its capabilities are illustrated in conjunction with the text in Figure 3.1a. The spelling checker goes through the document and returns the errors one at a time, offering several options for each mistake. You can change the misspelled word to one of the alternatives suggested by WordPerfect, leave the word as is, or add the word to the supplementary dictionary.

The first error is *embarassing* with the program's suggestion(s) for correction displayed in the list box in Figure 3.1b. To accept the highlighted suggestion, click the Replace command button; the substitution will be made automatically in the existing document. To accept an alternate suggestion, click the desired word, then click the Replace command button. The spelling checker detects both irregular capitalization and duplicated words as shown in Figures 3.1c and 3.1d, respectively.

The error in Figure 3.1e, *Grauer,* is not a misspelling, but a proper noun not found in the standard ***main dictionary.*** No correction is required and the appropriate action is either to skip the word (taking no further action) or, better yet, add it to the supplementary dictionary so that it will not be flagged in future sessions.

THE SUPPLEMENTARY DICTIONARY

It's easy to add a word to the supplementary dictionary, but how do you delete a word if you've added it incorrectly? Pull down the Tools menu and click Speller, then pull down the Dictionaries menu. Click Supplementary, then click WPSPELUS.SUP, the name of the default supplementary dictionary. Click the Edit command button, then find the word(s) you want to delete and click the Delete command button. Close the dialog box and return to your document.

A spelling checker will catch embarassing mistakes, iRegular capitalization and duplicate words words. It will also flag proper nouns, for example Robert Grauer, but you can add terms to an auxiliary dictionary so that they will not be flagged in the future. It will not, however, notice properly spelled words that are used incorrectly; for example, Two bee or knot too be is not the answer.

(a) The Text

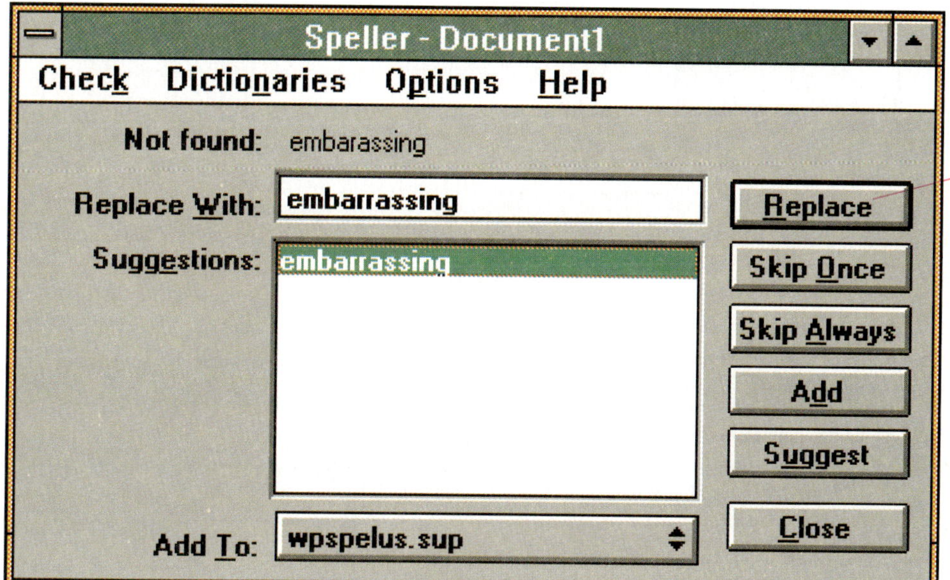

(b) Ordinary Misspelling

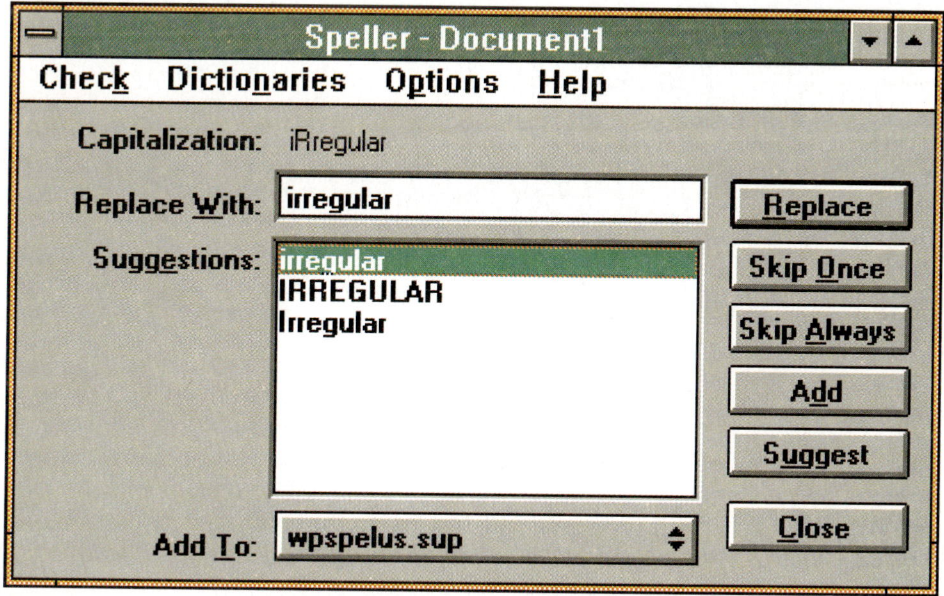

(c) Irregular Capitalization

FIGURE 3.1 The Spelling Checker

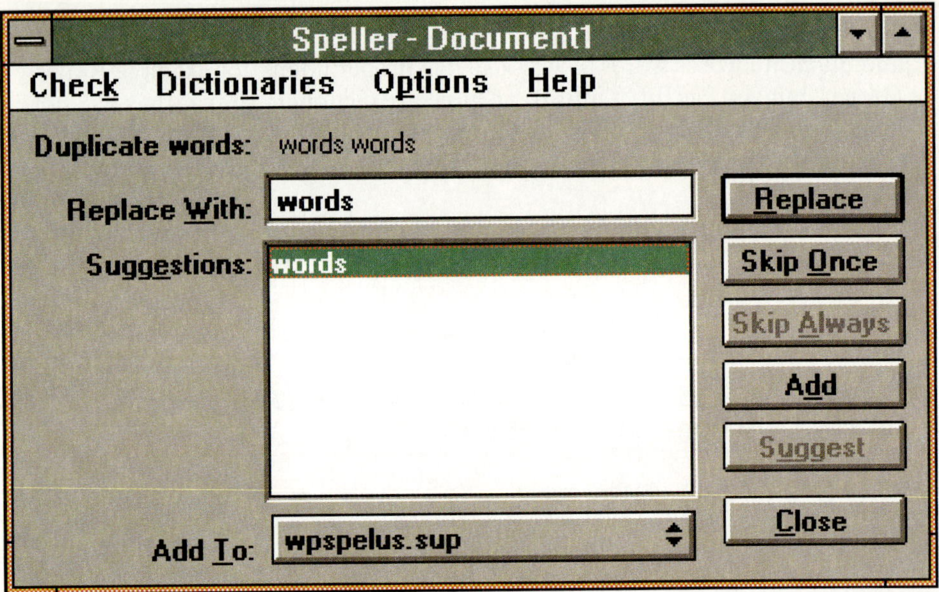

(d) Duplicated Word

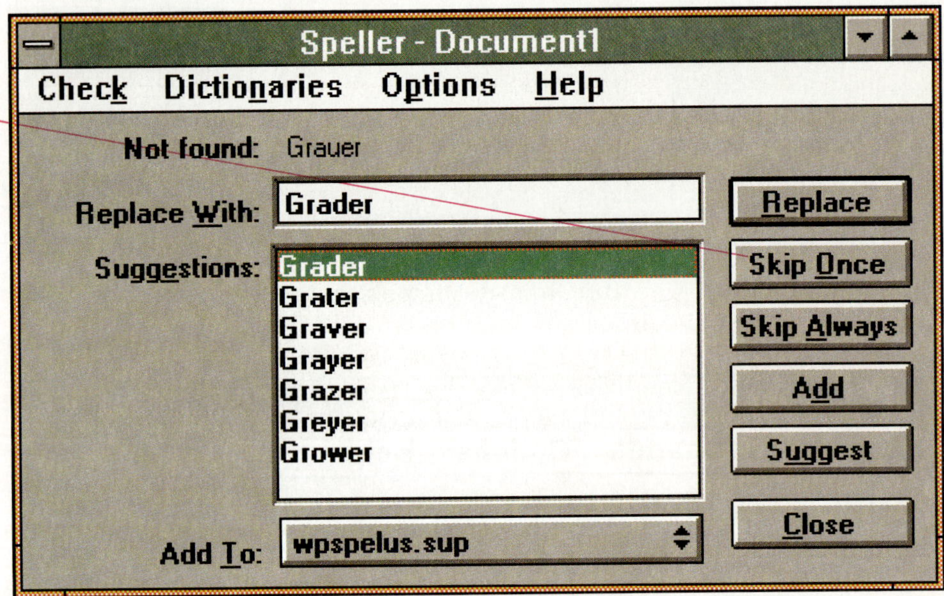

(e) Proper Noun

FIGURE 3.1 The Spelling Checker (continued)

THESAURUS

Mark Twain said the difference between the right word and almost the right word is the difference between a lightning bug and lightning. The ***thesaurus*** is the second major tool in a word processor and, to our way of thinking, is as essential as a spelling checker. The thesaurus is both fun and educational. It helps you to avoid repetition, and it polishes your writing.

The thesaurus is called from the Tools menu or by clicking its icon on the Power Bar. You click anywhere within the word you want to look up, then invoke the thesaurus and follow your instincts. The thesaurus offers suggestions for different forms of a word (e.g., noun, adjective, and verb) as in Figure 3.2a, and (by double clicking any bulleted word in the suggestion list) provides additional suggestions as in Figure 3.2b. Substitutions (in the document) are made automatically by selecting the desired ***synonym*** (or ***antonym***) and clicking the Replace button.

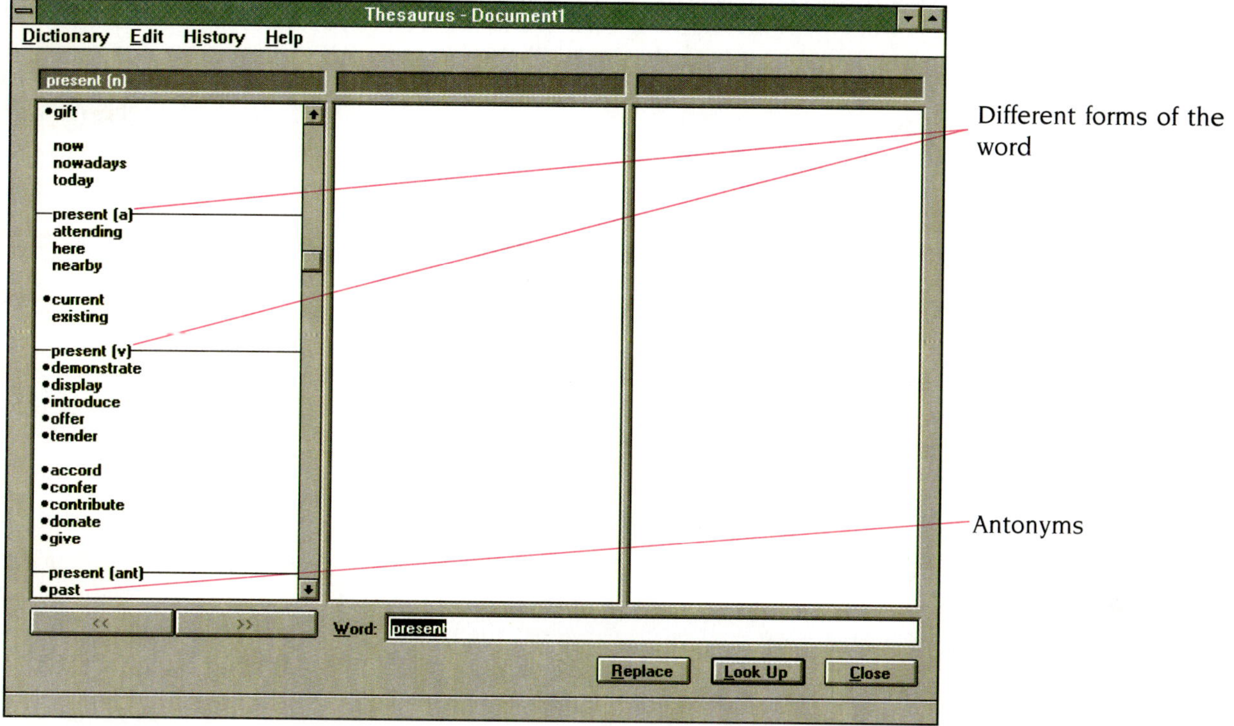

(a) Different Forms of the Word

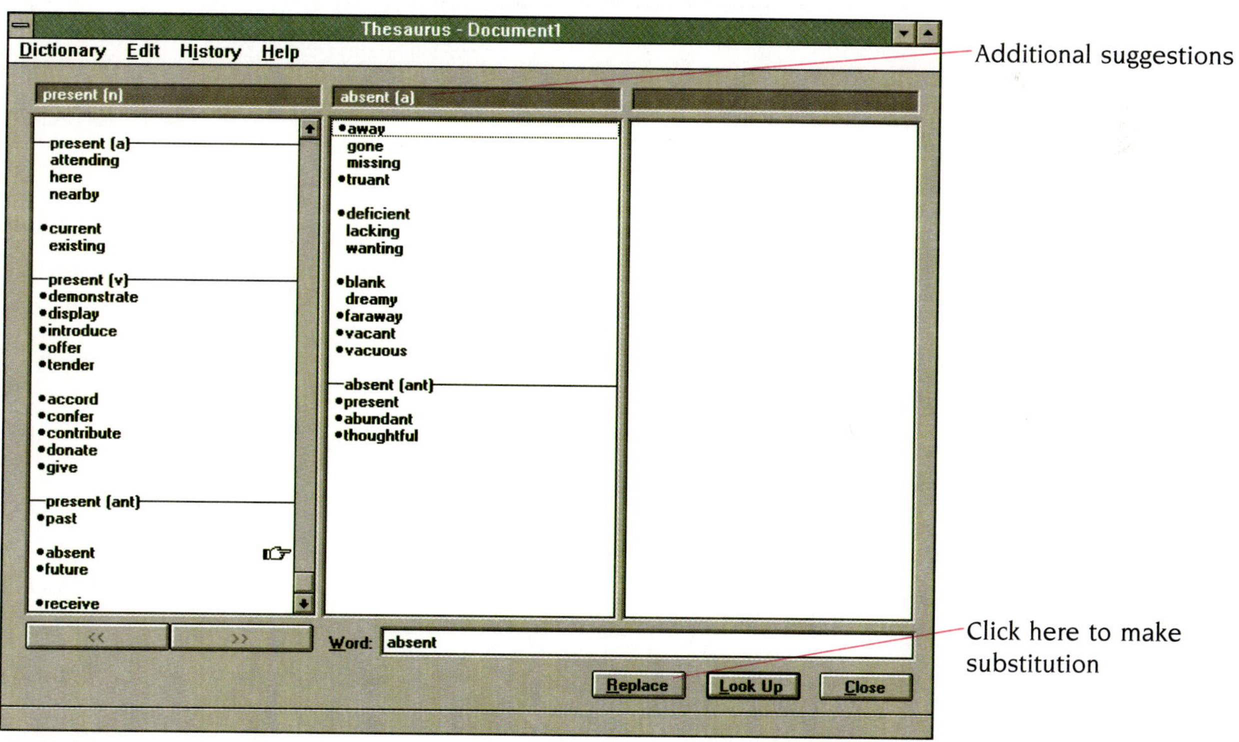

(b) Antonyms

FIGURE 3.2 The Thesaurus

The ***grammar checker*** attempts to catch mistakes in punctuation, writing style, and word usage by comparing strings of text within a document to a series of predefined rules. As with the spelling checker, errors are brought to the screen where you can accept the suggestion and make the replacement automatically in the document, or more often, edit the highlighted text to make changes.

Unlike a spelling checker, the grammar checker is subjective, and what seems appropriate to you may be objectionable to someone else. More significantly, the English language is just too complicated for the grammar checker to detect every error or even most of them. Nevertheless the program has much to offer; several examples are presented in Figure 3.3.

The grammar checker detects the inconsistency between subject and verb in Figure 3.3a and suggests the appropriate correction (catch instead of catches). It also detects the superfluous comma in Figure 3.3b. These examples show the gram-

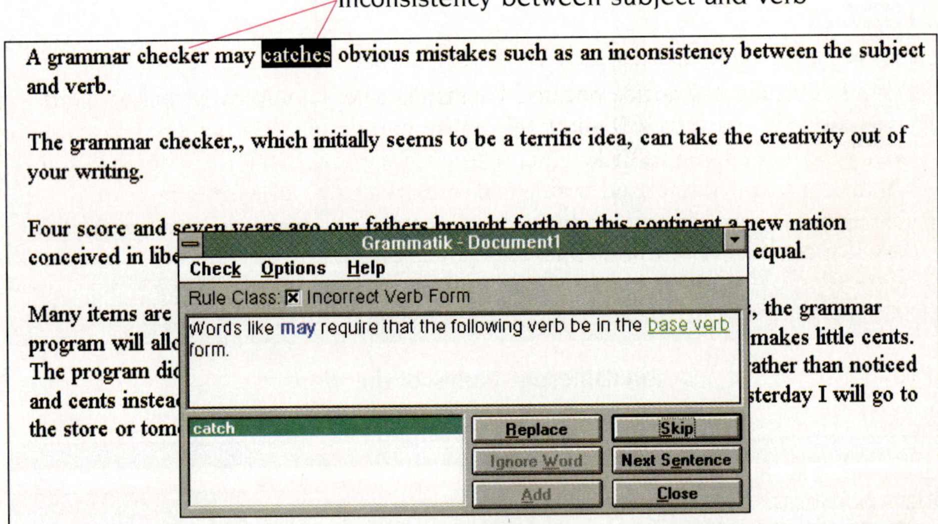

(a) Inconsistent Verb

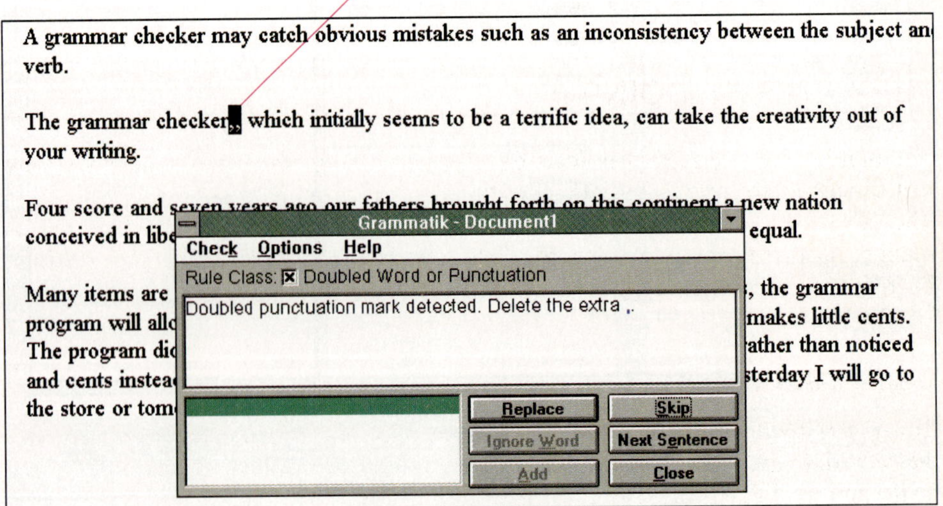

(b) Doubled Punctuation

FIGURE 3.3 The Grammar Checker

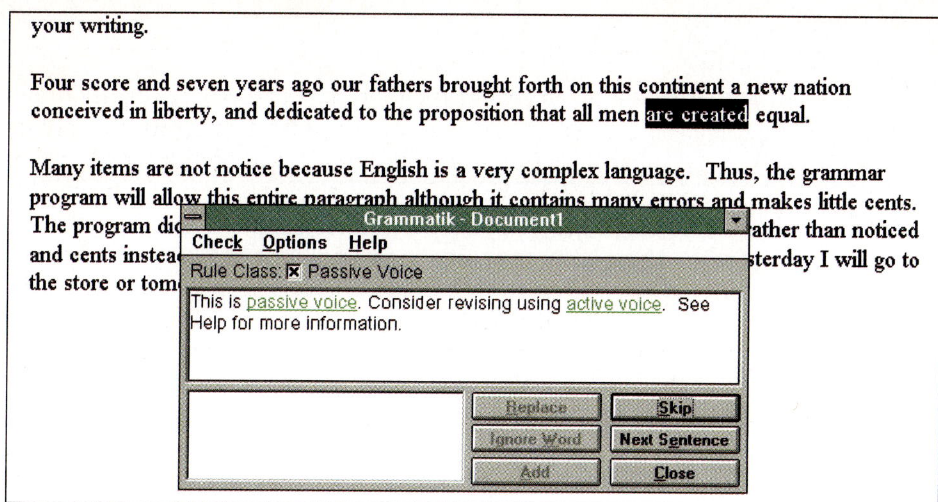

(c) Subjective Rules

Many items are not notice because English is a very complex language. Thus, the grammar program will allow this entire paragraph although it contains many errors and makes little cents. The program did not find any mistakes in the next sentence that used notice rather than noticed and cents instead of sense. It does not object to misplaced tenses such as yesterday I will go to the store or tomorrow I went to the store.

(d) Paragraph

FIGURE 3.3 The Grammar Checker (continued)

mar checker at its absolute best, but much of the time it is more subjective and less efficient. It objects, for example, to the phrase *all men are created equal* in Figure 3.3c, citing excessive use of the passive voice. It also accepts the entire paragraph in Figure 3.3d without error. Suffice it to say that there is no substitute for carefully proofreading every document you create.

LEARNING BY DOING

The hands-on exercise that follows develops a unified example in which the tools just discussed are used to create a cover letter and résumé as shown in Figure 3.4. The cover letter includes the date and requires an envelope in which it can be mailed. Both requirements are used to introduce additional capabilities within WordPerfect for Windows.

Insert Date Command

The ***Insert Date command*** puts the current date into a document in one of two ways, as date text or as a date code. ***Date text*** always displays the same date; that is, if you insert date text into a document on September 1 and open the document one month later, it will still display September 1. The ***date code*** is updated each time you open the document. If you insert the date code on September 1 and open the document one month later, the displayed date will be October 1.

ELVIS PRESLEY

Graceland Mansion • Memphis, TN 38116 • (901) 332-3322 •

OBJECTIVE

To emerge from hiding and perform once more before live audiences at major Las Vegas night clubs. To appear on late night television.

EDUCATION

1953 – Graduated from Humes High School, Memphis, Tennessee.

EXPERIENCE

1954 – 1977, Featured Singer, Concert Circuit
Traveled extensively on the concert circuit, including 22 club appearances in Las Vegas and Lake Tahoe

1956 – 1977, Recording Artist
Recorded 72 albums, including *Loving You, Elvis' Christmas Album, Elvis Is Back, G.I. Blues, Blue Hawaii, Elvis for Everyone, How Great Thou Art, Worldwide 50 Gold Award Hits, Moody Blues*

1956 – 1972, Recording Artist
Recorded 38 Top Ten hits, 18 of which climbed to #1 on the chart, including *Heartbreak Hotel, Hound Dog, Don't Be Cruel, Love Me Tender, All Shook Up, Teddy Bear, Jailhouse Rock, Hard Headed Woman, Stuck on You, It's Now or Never, Are You Lonesome Tonight, Good Luck Charm,* and *Suspicious Minds.*

1956 – 1972, Movie and Television Star
Performed in 38 feature-length movies, including *Love Me Tender, Jailhouse Rock, Blue Hawaii, Viva Las Vegas, The Trouble with Girls,* and *Elvis on Tour.* Featured on 15 television shows, including *The Milton Berle Show, The Steve Allen Show, Ed Sullivan's Toast of the Town,* and the *Today Show.*

HONORS

Picture placed on United States Postage Stamp
3 Grammy Awards
Male Entertainer of the Year

(a) Résumé

FIGURE 3.4 The Presley Comeback

ELVIS PRESLEY

GRACELAND MANSION • MEMPHIS, TN 38116 • (901) 332-3322 •

November 28, 1993

Mr. David Letterman
1697 Broadway
New York, NY 10019

Dear Mr. Letterman:

I am seeking an engagement as the lead act at a Las Vegas night club. I have extensive experience both in private clubs and road tours throughout the United States, and have enclosed my résumé for your review.

It has been some time since I have been in the public eye, but I have never stopped singing or living my music. I am well aware of current trends and have many new songs that will, without question, catch the public's imagination. Everyone needs a gimmick in today's market and I have several extraordinary concepts in mind.

I would welcome the opportunity to meet you to discuss my ideas and audition my new act. An appearance on your show would help to launch my comeback. Please contact me at the above address or call me at 1-800-HOUND-DOG. I look forward to hearing from you.

Sincerely,

Elvis

(b) Cover Letter

FIGURE 3.4 The Presley Comeback (continued)

The difference between the two can be seen by examining the Reveal Codes window in Figure 3.5a. The date text is displayed as regular text, whereas the date code is enclosed in a sculptured box indicative of a formatting code. When WordPerfect encounters the date code in a document, it retrieves the current date and time from the computer's internal clock and calendar, thus saving you the trouble of manually updating the document.

The Date Format command is illustrated in Figure 3.5b and gives you the flexibility of choosing from one of several predefined formats. Alternatively, you can click the Custom command button and create your own format.

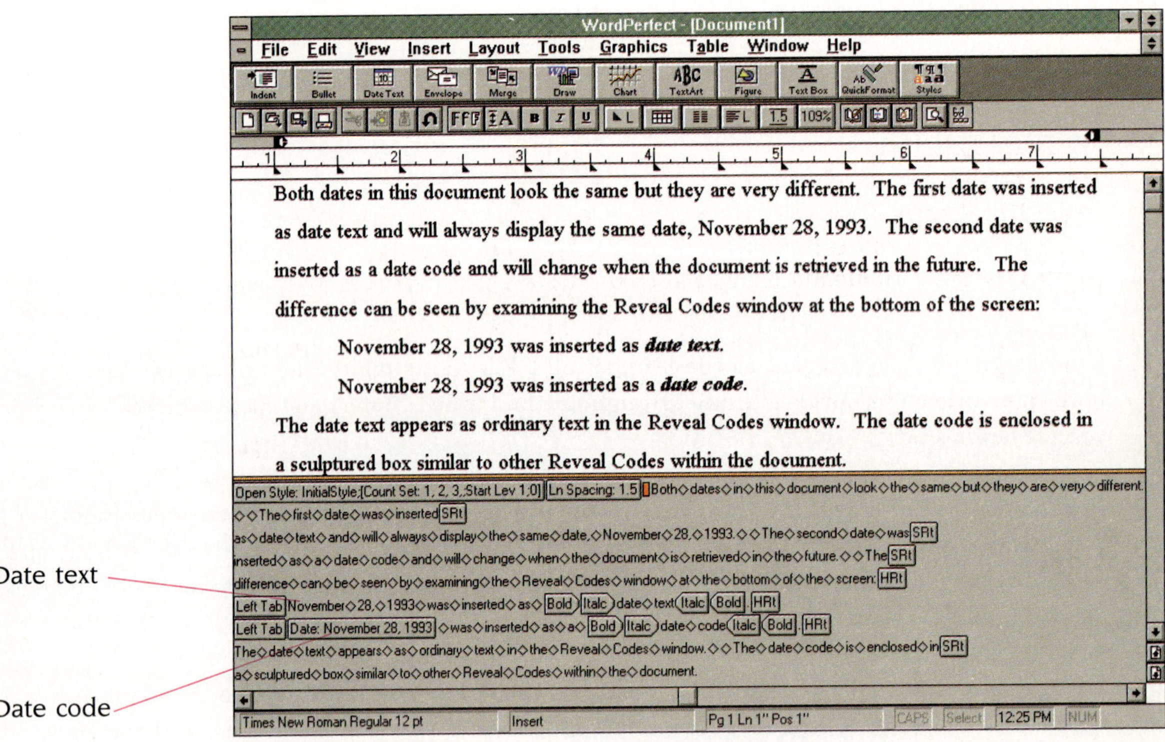

(a) Date Code versus Date Text

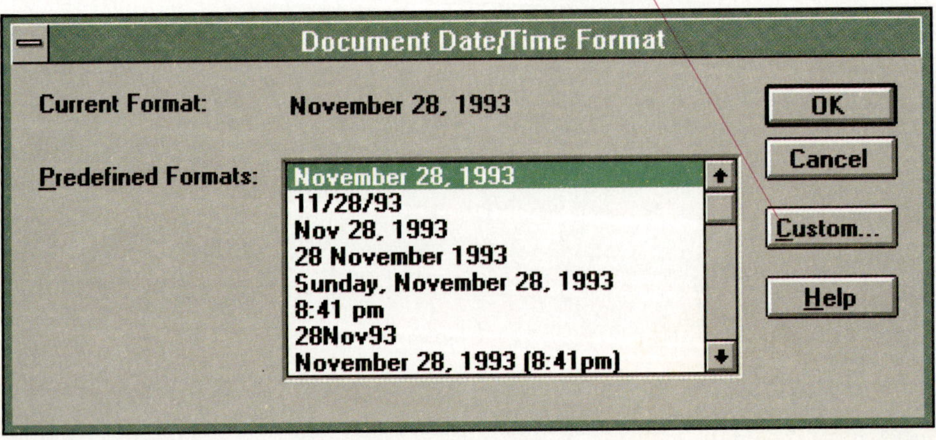

(b) Changing the Date Format

FIGURE 3.5 The Insert Date Command

THIRTY SECONDS IS ALL YOU HAVE . . .

Thirty seconds is the average amount of time a personnel manager spends skimming your résumé and deciding whether or not to call you for an interview. It doesn't matter how much training you've had or how good you are if your résumé and cover letter fail to project a professional image. Know your audience and use the vocabulary of your targeted field. Be positive and describe your experience from an accomplishment point of view. Maintain a separate list of references and have it available on request. Be sure that all information is accurate. Be conscientious about the design of your résumé and proofread the final documents very carefully.

The Insert Character Command

One characteristic that distinguishes the professional document (from that of the would-be professional) is the use of true typographic characters; for example, ½ and ¼ rather than 1/2 and 1/4; ™ rather than TM, © rather than (C), and so on. The ***Insert Character command*** enables you to access these characters as shown in Figure 3.6.

WordPerfect groups the special characters into sets. You place the insertion point where you want the character to appear in the document, choose the set containing the desired character (Typographic Symbols in Figure 3.6), then click the Insert (or Insert and Close) command button. All characters are scalable from 4 to 127 points and you can produce some truly unusual documents.

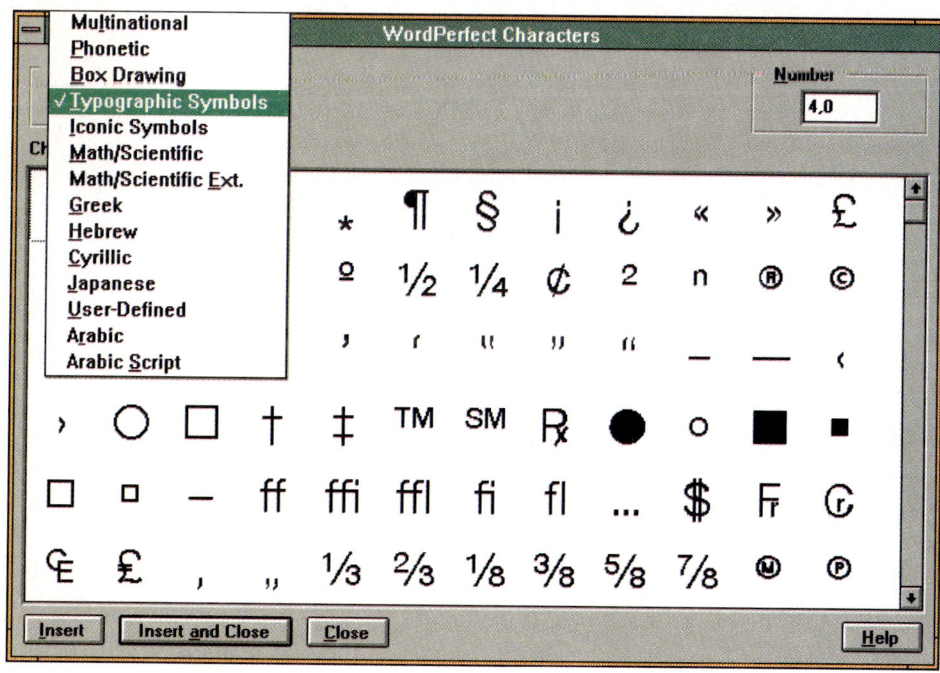

FIGURE 3.6 The Insert Character Command

Creating an Envelope

Anyone who has used a word processor knows that printing an envelope poses potential problems in that the physical document (the envelope) is a different size than the letter it contains, and hence the margins and orientation must change accordingly. It is trivial, however, in WordPerfect and is accomplished by clicking the ***Envelope icon*** on the default Button Bar. This in turn produces a dialog box where you supply or edit the necessary addresses.

The addressee's information is taken directly from the cover letter as described in step 7 of the following exercise. The return address can be entered in the dialog box, or it can be obtained from a set of previously stored addresses. WordPerfect also lets you choose different-sized envelopes.

HANDS-ON EXERCISE 1:

Proofing a Document

Objective To use the spelling checker, thesaurus, and grammar checker; to insert a date code and special characters into a document; to create (and print) an envelope. Use Figure 3.7 as a guide for the exercise.

Step 1: Load the practice document.

- Pull down the **File menu.** Click **Open** (or click the **File Open icon** on the Power Bar).
- If you have not yet changed the default directory:
  - Click the appropriate drive.
  - Scroll through the directory list box until you come to the **WPDATA** directory.
  - Double click the **WPDATA** directory.
- Double click **ELVISBEF.WPD** to open the document.
- Pull down the **File menu.**
- Click the **Save As** command to save the document as **ELVISAFT.WPD.** The title bar reflects **ELVISAFT.WPD,** but you can always return to the original document if you edit the duplicated file beyond redemption.

Step 2: Today's date

- The document displays the current (system) date rather than the date in our letter. It's not magic and works because we created the letter using a date code rather than date text.
- Press **Alt+F3** to open the Reveal Codes window.
- Scroll through the document until you see the date code displayed in the Reveal Codes window.
- Press **Alt+F3** to close the Reveal Codes window and begin working on the document.

THERE IS A DIFFERENCE

Date code and date text are easily confused, but they represent different concepts and have different uses. The date code reflects the current date (the date the document is retrieved), whereas date text indicates the date the document was created; the date code changes daily, whereas date text does not.

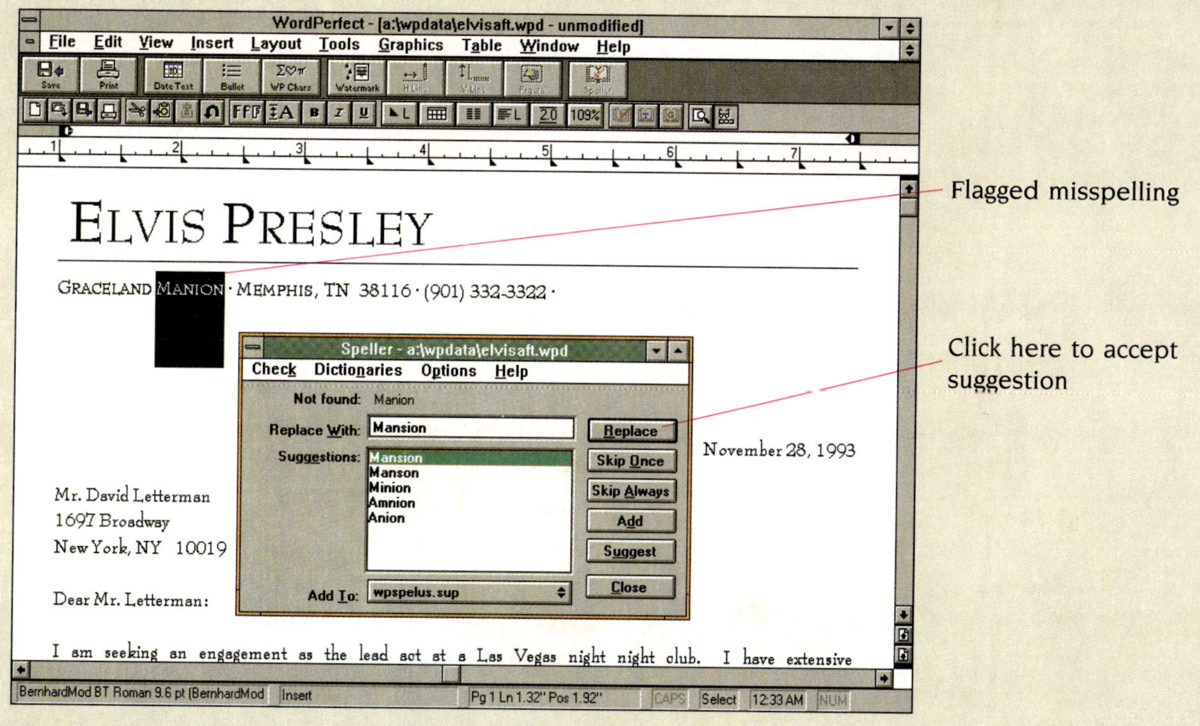

(a) The Spell Check (step 3)

FIGURE 3.7 Hands-on Exercise 1

Step 3: The spelling checker

- Pull down the **Tools menu** and click **Speller** (or click the **Spell Check icon** on the Power Bar). Click the **Start command button** to begin checking the document.
- *Graceland* is flagged as the first misspelling (unless a previous user added it to the supplementary dictionary). Click the **Skip Always command button** to accept Graceland as written or the **Add command button** if you want to add Graceland to the supplementary dictionary.
- The spell check next flags *manion* as shown in Figure 3.7a. Click the correct spelling (if it is not already highlighted), then click the **Replace command button** to correct the spelling in the document.
- The program will find several other spelling errors in the document. In addition to misspellings it will detect duplicate words (night night) and irregular capitalization (EVeryone) and suggest alternatives for each.

OPTIONS IN THE SPELLING CHECKER

If WordPerfect fails to check the entire document and/or fails to detect the duplicated word or irregular capitalization, it may be because the options have not been properly set. Click the Spell Check icon on the Power Bar, pull down the Check menu, and click Document to check the entire document. Pull down the Options menu and check Duplicate Words and Irregular Capitalization.

- Choose the appropriate corrections and click the ***Replace command button*** as needed.
- Click **Yes** when the spell check is complete to return to the document.
- Save the file.

Step 4: The thesaurus

- Click anywhere within the word you want to change; e.g, click *magnificent* in Figure 3.7b.
- Pull down the **Tools menu** and click **Thesaurus** (or click the **Thesaurus icon** on the Power Bar).
- Click **extraordinary** in the list of alternate words. Click the **Replace command button** to make the substitution in your document.
- Change other words as you see fit; for example, we changed **chance** to opportunity. (You can request additional suggestions by double clicking any word preceded by a bullet within the thesaurus dialog box.)
- Save the document.

Step 5: The grammar checker

- Press **Ctrl+Home** to move to the beginning of the document.
- Pull down the **Tools menu.** Click **Grammatik.**
- Pull down the **Options menu,** and if necessary, remove the check next to **Show spelling errors.** Click **OK** if you see a message indicating that Grammatik uses a different supplemental dictionary than WordPerfect.
- Click the **Start command button** to begin checking the document. The suggestions are subjective and you may use them or not as you see fit. Click the **Skip command button** in Figure 3.7c so as not to replace Letterman with varsity athlete.

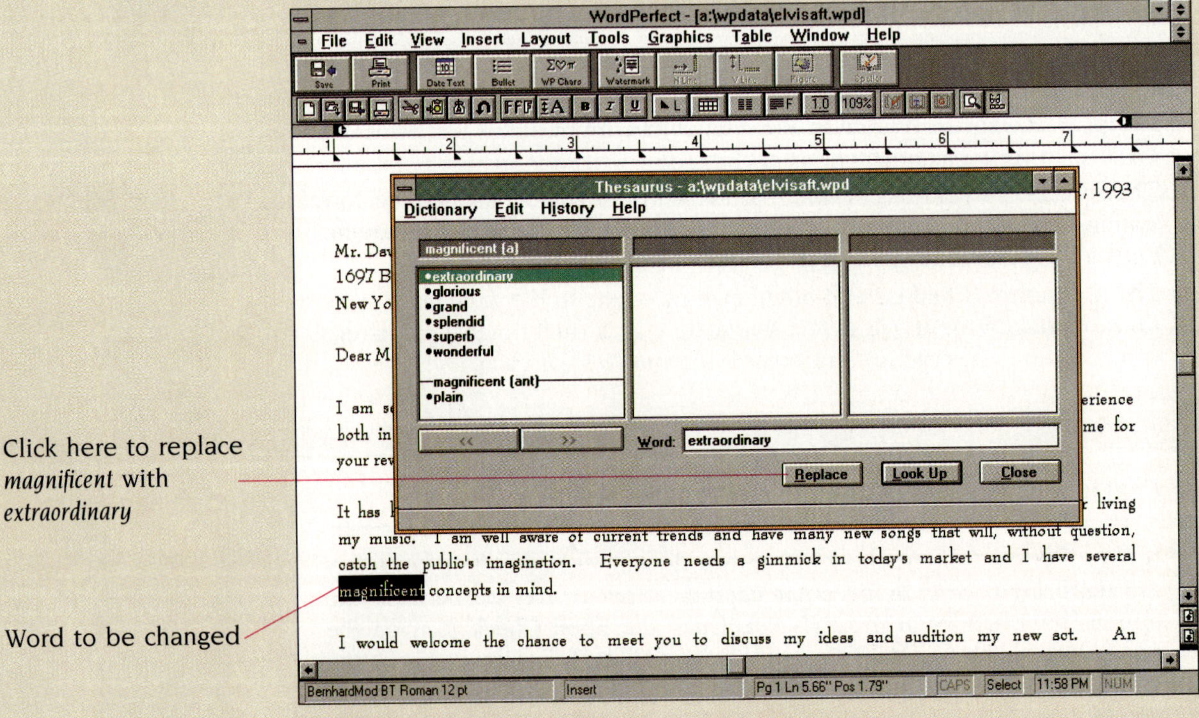

(b) The Thesaurus (step 4)

FIGURE 3.7 Hands-on Exercise 1 (continued)

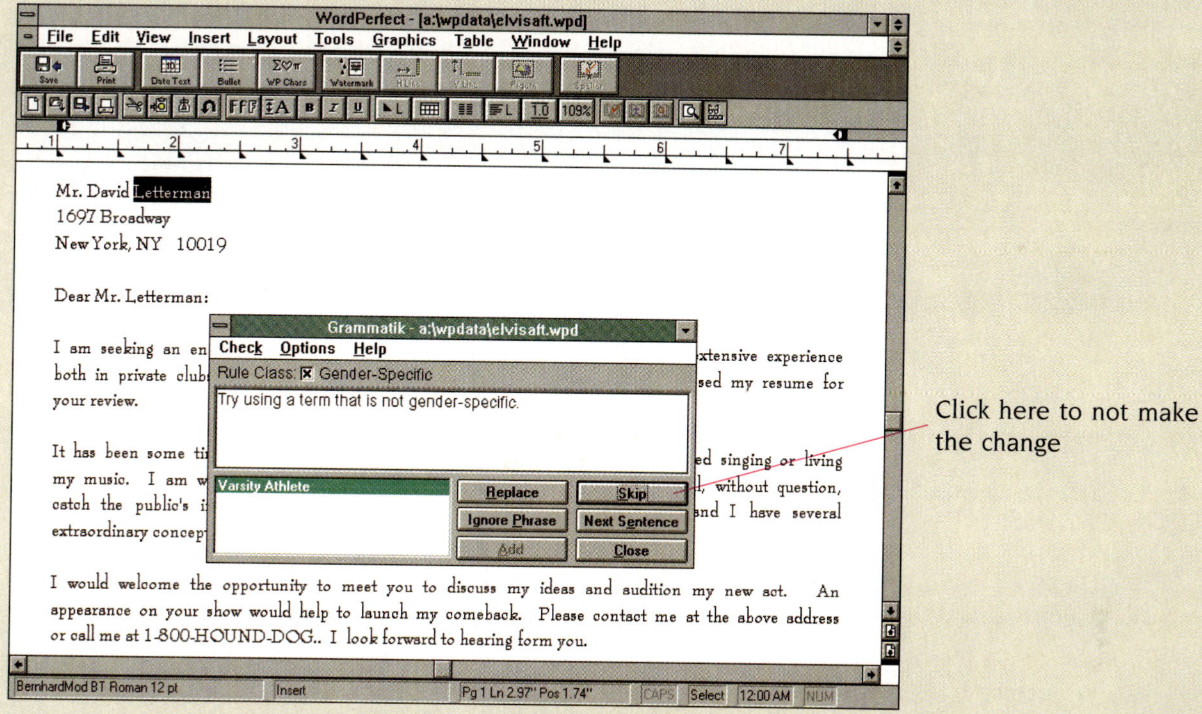

(c) The Grammar Check (step 5)

FIGURE 3.7 Hands-on Exercise 1 (continued)

- Go through the entire document and accept the suggestions that make sense to you. The grammar checker is not perfect, but it does catch two genuine errors; the double period after HOUND-DOG and the word *form* rather than *from* in the last sentence.
- Click **Yes** to close Grammatik and return to your document.
- Save the document.

THE DICTIONARIES ARE DIFFERENT

The ***Grammatik*** grammar checker uses a different dictionary from the spell check built into WordPerfect. The results are also different; for example, Presley is accepted by the regular spell check but flagged by the Grammatik program. We suggest that you spell check the document directly and bypass the spell check in Grammatik. Pull down the Tools menu, click Grammatik, pull down the Options menu, and remove the check next to Show spelling errors.

Step 6: Special characters

- The proper spelling of résumé places accents over both letter e's. Click before the first e in resume in the first paragraph of the letter.
- Pull down the **Insert menu.** Click **Character** to produce the dialog box in Figure 3.7d.
- Click the up arrow in the **Character Set list box.** Select the **Multinational Character Set.**

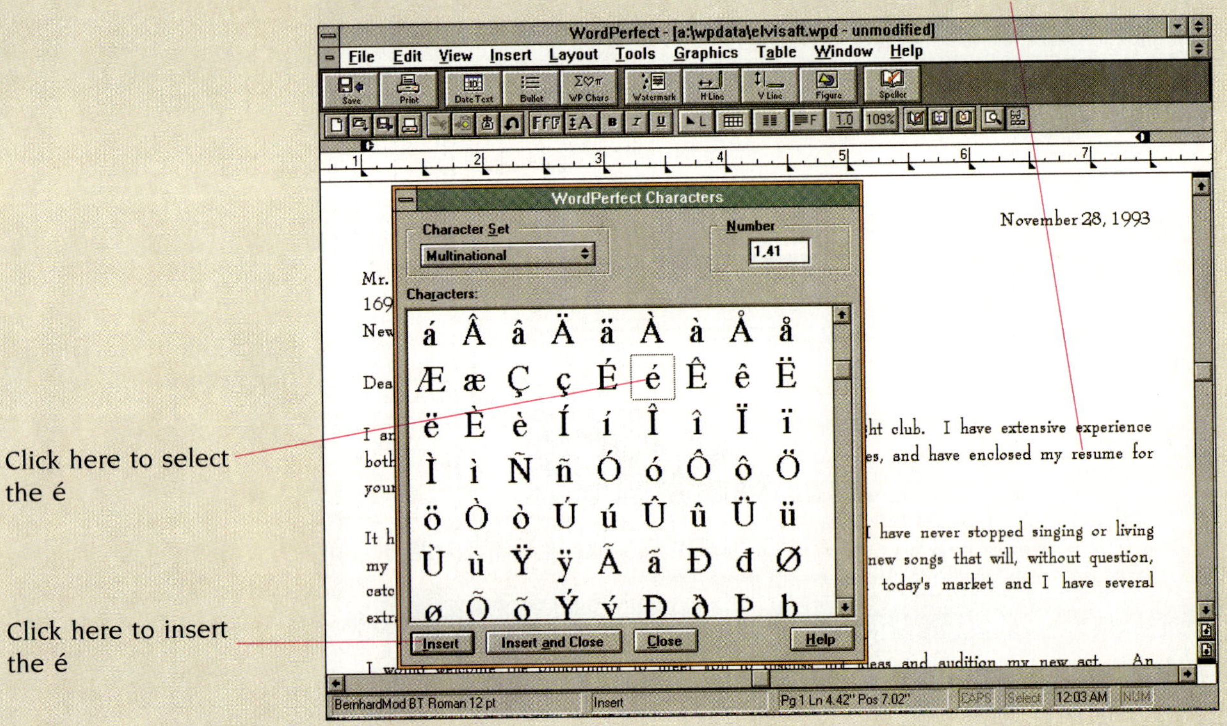

(d) Special Characters (step 6)

FIGURE 3.7 Hands-on Exercise 1 (continued)

- Scroll in the Character list box until you see the **é**. Click the **é** to select it, then click the **Insert command button.**
- Click in the document window before the last e in résumé. (You may need to move the dialog box in order to see the word you are editing.) Click the **Insert and Close command button** in the dialog box. Delete the original unaccented e's.
- Save the document.

Step 7: Create an envelope

- Press **Ctrl+Home** to move to the beginning of the document.
- Click and drag to select the three-line address for David Letterman.
- Pull down the **Layout menu** and click **Envelope** to produce the window of Figure 3.7e.
- David Letterman's address will appear automatically on the envelope because you selected the address prior to executing the command. You may or may not see Elvis' return address, depending on who last used WordPerfect. Type the return address if necessary.
- Click the **Append to doc** command button.
- Save the document.

Step 8: The Completed Document

- Press **Ctrl+Home** to move to the beginning of the document.
- Pull down the **View menu.** Click **Two Page** to produce the view in Figure 3.7f.

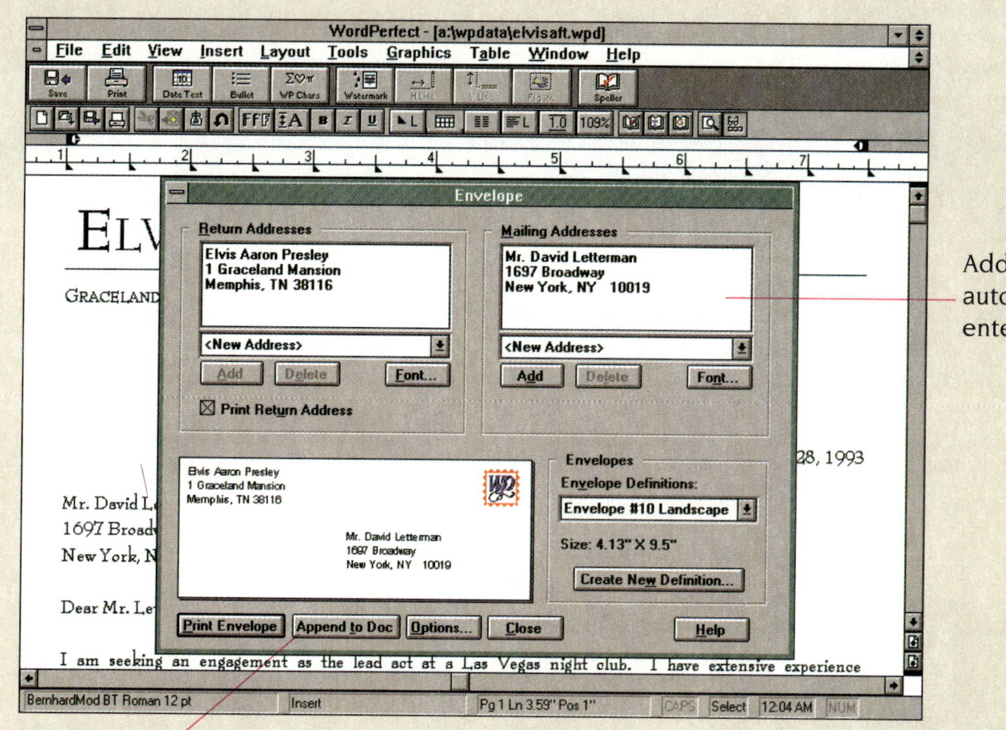

(e) Creating an Envelope (step 7)

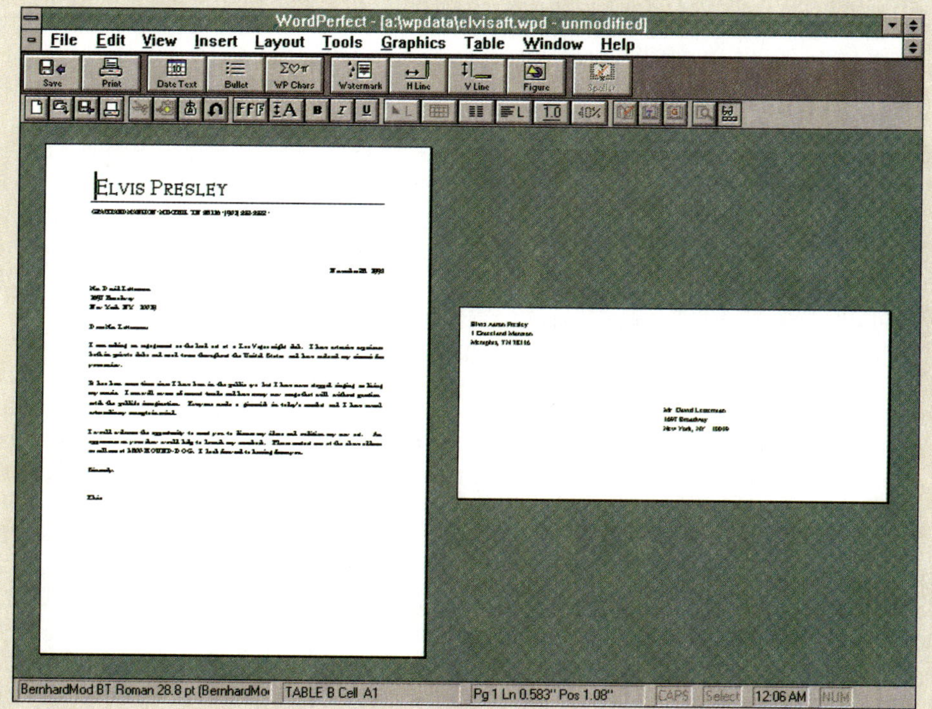

(f) The Completed Document (step 8)

FIGURE 3.7 Hands-on Exercise 1 (continued)

- Do not print the envelope unless you can manually feed an envelope into the printer.
- Click the page containing the letter (page one in our document).
- Pull down the **File menu.** Click **Print.** Click the **Current Page command button.** Click **OK** to print just this page.
- Pull down the **File menu.** Click **Close** to close the document but remain in WordPerfect for the next exercise.

PRINT SELECTED PAGES

Why print an entire document if you want only a few pages? Pull down the File menu and click Print as you usually do to initiate the printing process. Click the Multiple Pages option button, press enter, then enter the page numbers and/or page ranges you want; for example, 3, 6–8 will print page three and pages six through eight.

EXPRESSDOCS

The letter to David Letterman and the accompanying résumé were both based on designs (templates) provided by WordPerfect. Elvis supplied the content but WordPerfect took care of the formatting. That left Elvis free to concentrate on the message he wanted to deliver.

A ***template*** is a partially completed document that contains formatting, text, graphics, and other information. It may be as simple as a memo or as complex as a report or news letter. You can design your own templates or you can use the ones built into WordPerfect; the latter are known as ***ExpressDocs.*** WordPerfect comes with 45 ExpressDocs, four of which are shown in Figure 3.8. You've already seen the cover letter and résumé; the fax and press release are developed in the next exercise.

Each ExpressDoc template contains one or more ***fields.*** A field is a place holder for data and marks the position in a document where the information will go. Some fields are found in many different templates—for example, <address>, <name>, and <telephone> in Figure 3.8. Other fields are specific to the individual template—for example, [Title of Press Release] in Figure 3.7d.

Fields that represent personal data are enclosed in angled brackets. Fields that represent template-specific data are enclosed in square brackets. The personal data (the fields in angled brackets) is supplied once, the first time you use an ExpressDoc template. (WordPerfect prompts you for your name, address, telephone, and other personal information, then stores your responses in a file for use with any other ExpressDoc template. You can update the data if it changes.) The template-specific information is entered each time you use the ExpressDoc in which it is needed.

ExpressDoc templates are accessed from the File menu by clicking on the Template command, then double clicking the specific template from the available list box. WordPerfect will prompt for the information (fields) it needs, then use the ***Autofill macro*** to create a new document. The document will be based on the template, the personal data common to all ExpressDocs, and the template-specific information you supplied. The newly created document can be saved under its own name and treated like any other document.

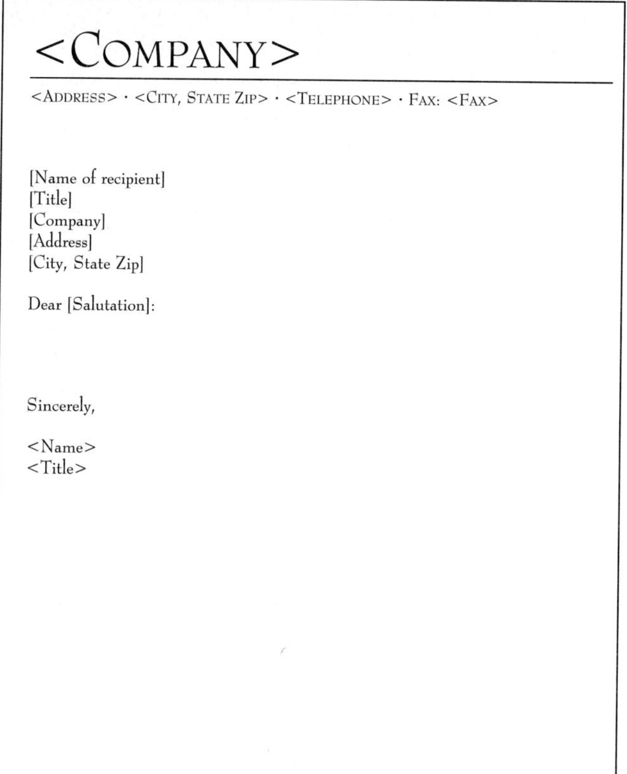

<COMPANY>

<ADDRESS> · <CITY, STATE ZIP> · <TELEPHONE> · FAX: <FAX>

[Name of recipient]
[Title]
[Company]
[Address]
[City, State Zip]

Dear [Salutation]:

Sincerely,

<Name>
<Title>

(a) Letter

<NAME>

<Address> • <City, State Zip> • <Telephone>

OBJECTIVE

Type the work objective here. Keep it simple. Use styles to help the reader distinguish the different topics of your résumé.

SKILLS

Describe any skills you have that may relate to the position you're applying for.

EDUCATION

Type the details of your educational background here, including degree, school name, graduation date, and location of school. Include details such as awards.

EXPERIENCE

Type your work experience here. Starting with your most recent job, include the name, address, phone# and employer's name. Include your job title and the specific duties of the job.

(b) Résumé

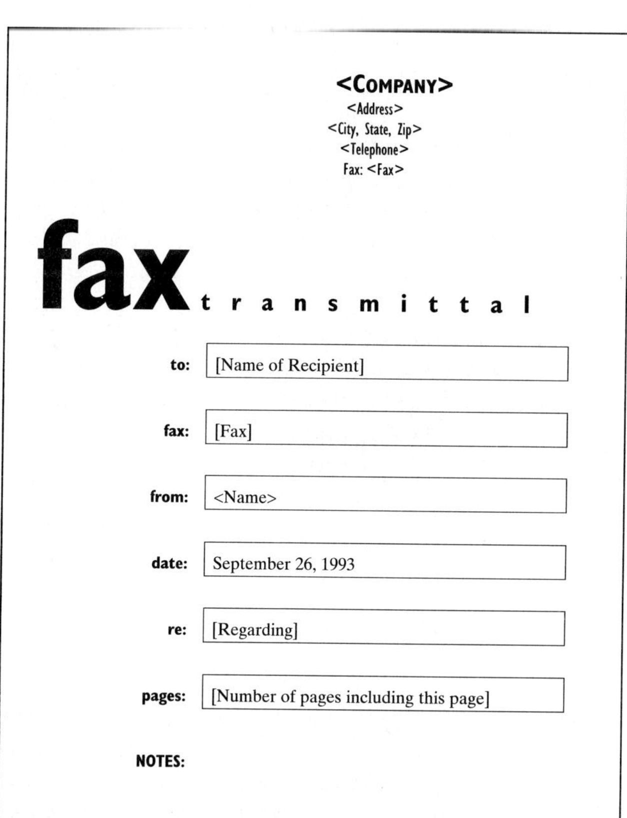

<COMPANY>
<Address>
<City, State, Zip>
<Telephone>
Fax: <Fax>

fax transmittal

to:	[Name of Recipient]
fax:	[Fax]
from:	<Name>
date:	September 26, 1993
re:	[Regarding]
pages:	[Number of pages including this page]

NOTES:

(c) Fax

PRESSRELEASE

<Company> • <Address> • <City, State Zip> • <Telephone> • Fax: <Fax>

For Immediate Release

Date:	September 26, 1993
Contact:	[Name of Contact]
Phone:	[Telephone number of Contact]
Fax:	[Fax number of Contact]

[Title of Press Release]

(d) Press Release

FIGURE 3.8 ExpressDocs

ExpressDocs help you create professionally designed documents with a minimum of time and effort. The content is still up to you. The templates are easy to use and are illustrated in the following exercise. The exercise also shows you how to work with multiple documents at the same time and how you can cascade (tile) the windows within which the documents are contained.

HANDS-ON EXERCISE 2:

ExpressDocs

Objective To use the ExpressDocs feature to create two documents based on existing templates. To view multiple documents at the same time. Use Figure 3.9 as a guide.

Step 1: Open the template

- Pull down the **File menu.** Click **Template** to produce the dialog box in Figure 3.9a.
- Click the arrows in the Document Template scroll bar until you come to fax1, the first of five fax designs.
- Click **fax5** (or whichever fax you prefer). Click **OK** (or press the **enter key**).

Step 2: Enter personal information

- You may or may not be requested to enter personal information:
  - — If this is the first time the ExpressDocs feature is being used, you will see a dialog box requesting the personal information. Click **OK,** then enter the personal information as indicated in Figure 3.9b. Press the **Tab key** to move from one text box to the next as you enter the data.

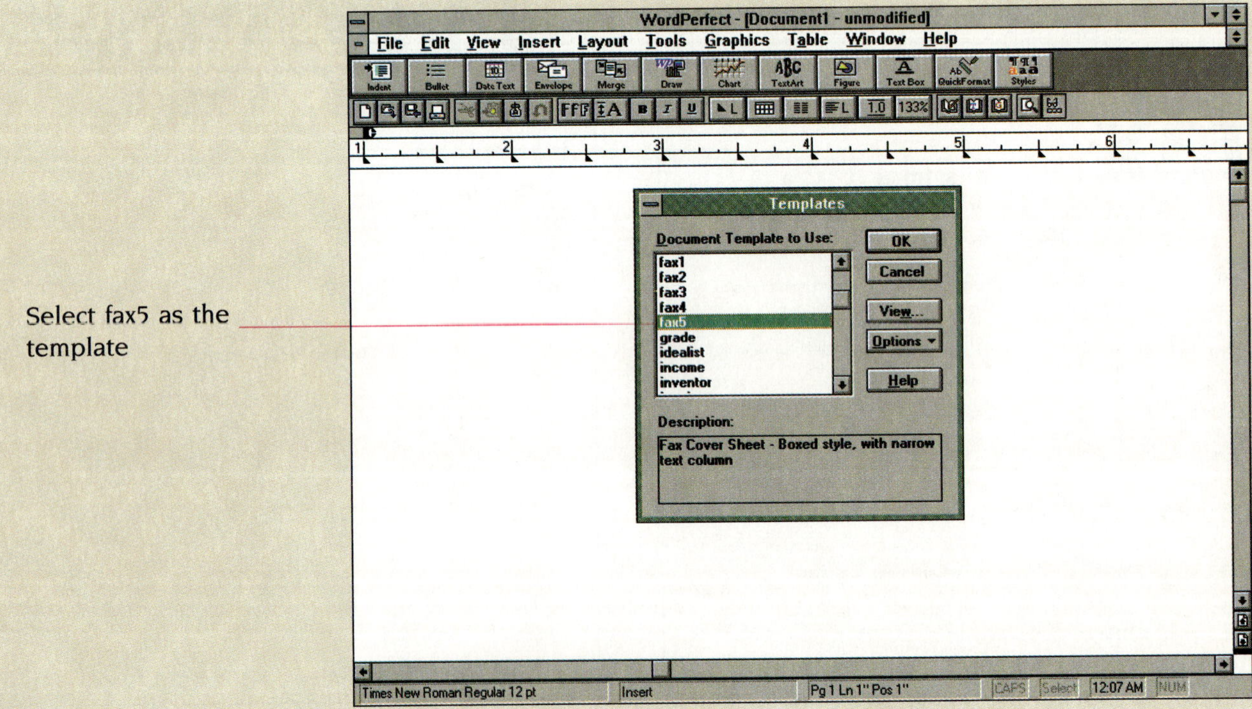

(a) Selecting a Template (step 1)

FIGURE 3.9 Hands-on Exercise 2

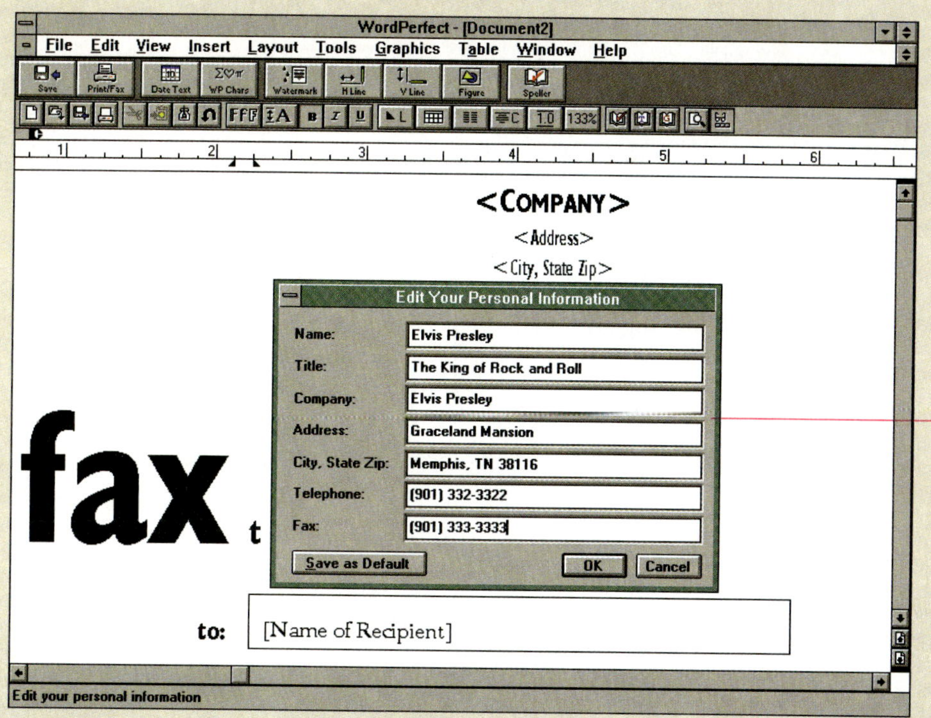

(b) Personal Information (step 2)

FIGURE 3.9 Hands-on Exercise 2 (continued)

— If you (or someone else) has previously entered the personal information, you will see a message box asking you to wait, then you will see the dialog box described in step 3.

➤ You have to enter the personal information only once, after which it will be used for every template in which it is needed.

Step 3: Enter template information

➤ To view or change the personal information, click the **Personal Info command button** shown in Figure 3.9c, which produces a dialog box similar to Figure 3.9b. Click **OK** when you are finished.

➤ Enter the template-specific information shown in Figure 3.9c. Use the **Tab key** to move from one text box to the next.

➤ Click **OK** or press the **enter key** when you have completed the information.

➤ You will see an informational message indicating that the Autofill macro is working to create the template.

➤ After the macro is complete, the insertion point will be positioned at the end of the template where you can add additional comments as necessary.

➤ Pull down the **File menu.** Click **Save.** Type **ELVISFAX** as the name of the document, then press the **enter key.**

Step 4: Open a second template

➤ Pull down the **File menu.** Click **Template.**

➤ Click the arrows in the Document Template scroll bar. Scroll through the available templates until you come to Press1, the first of two designs for a press release.

➤ Click **Press2,** then click **OK** to select the template.

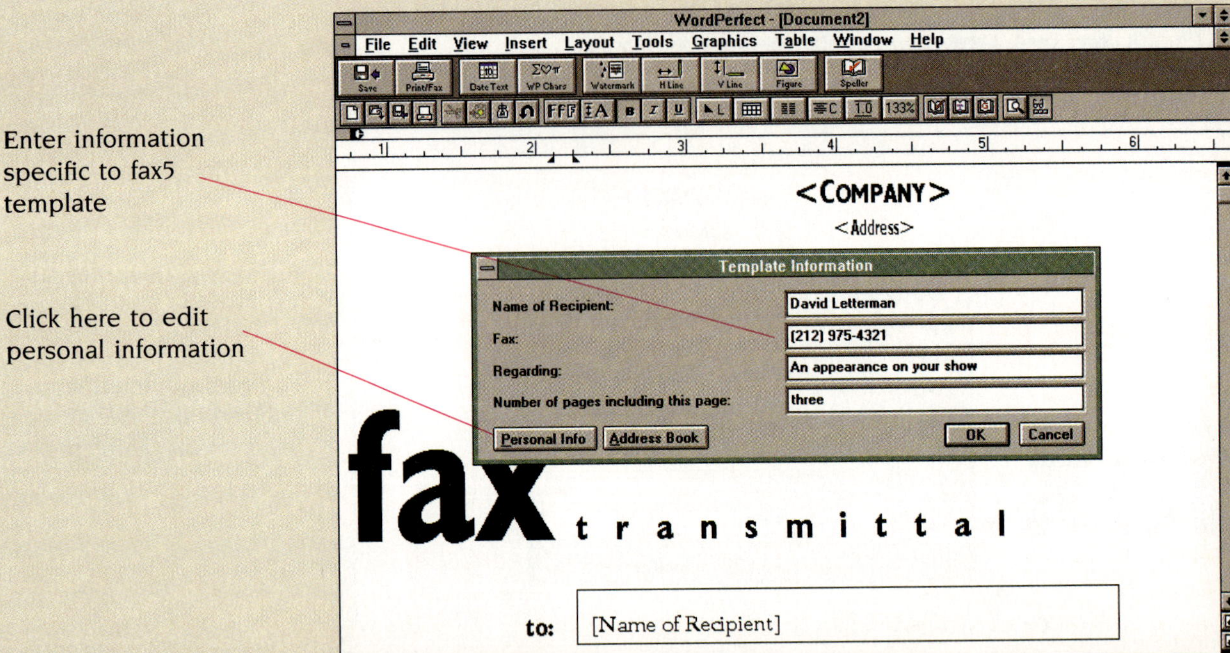

(c) Template Information (step 3)

FIGURE 3.9 Hands-on Exercise 2 (continued)

- There is no need to enter personal information as it was already entered in conjunction with the earlier document. You can, however, click the **Personal Info command button** to change the existing personal data.
- Enter the information in the dialog box of Figure 3.9d. Click **OK** when you have entered all of the information.
- The Autofill macro will take over and generate the first part of the press release.

Step 5: Modify the template

- The Autofill macro ends and positions you at the end of the document. Type the text of the press release as shown in Figure 3.9e.
- Select the Phone and Fax lines as shown in Figure 3.9e. Press the **Del key.**
- Pull down the **File menu.** Click **Save.** Type **ELVISPRS** as the name of the document.

Step 6: View both documents simultaneously

- Pull down the **Window menu** as shown in Figure 3.9f.
- Click **Cascade** to see the open documents, each in its own window, and each with its own title bar: Document1, ELVISFAX.WPD, and ELVISPRS.WPD. The latter is highlighted to indicate that ELVISPRS.WPD is the active document and that it will be affected by all subsequent commands.
- Click anywhere in a window to make it active and move to the front of the cascaded windows.
- Click in the window for Document 1 to make it the active window. Pull down the **File menu** and click **Close** to close the document. (You do not need to save it.)

Enter information specific to Press2 template

Click here to edit personal information

(d) Template Information (step 4)

WordPerfect - [Document2]

File Edit View Insert Layout Tools Graphics Table Window Help

Date: November 28, 1993
Contact: Elvis Presley
Phone: (901) 332-3522
Fax: (901) 333-3333

Elvis Returns

Memphis, TN—Elvis Presley ended almost 20 years of speculation today when he appeared as a surprise guest on the David Letterman show. It was truly the King, although he is much heavier than when he last appeared in public. Presly was unavailable for comment other than to say he was beginning a world tour to make up for lost time.

Arrus BT Roman 12 pt | Insert | Pg 1 Ln 3.82" Pos 1" | CAPS | Select | 12:41 AM | NUM

Select and press Del key to delete these two lines

(e) Deleting Labels (step 5)

FIGURE 3.9 Hands-on Exercise 2 (continued)

(f) The Tile and Cascade Commands

FIGURE 3.9 Hands-on Exercise 2 (continued)

- Move and/or size the windows so that your screen matches Figure 3.9f.
  - — To ***size a window,*** point to any border (the mouse pointer changes to a double arrow), then drag the border in the direction you want to go; that is, inward to shrink the window or outward to enlarge it. You can point to a corner, rather than a border, to change both dimensions at the same time.
  - — To ***move a window,*** point to its title bar, then drag the window to its new position.
- Your screen should now resemble Figure 3.9f.
- Save both documents a final time.
- Pull down the **File menu** and exit WordPerfect.

MAIL MERGE

A ***mail merge*** takes the tedium out of sending form letters, as it creates the same letter many times, changing only the name, address (and other information as appropriate) from letter to letter. You might use the mail merge capability to look for a job upon graduation, when you send essentially the same letter to many different people. The concept is illustrated in Figure 3.10, where Elvis drafts a form letter describing his comeback, then merges that letter with a list of names and addresses to produce the individual letters.

A mail merge requires the creation of two separate documents—the ***form file*** in Figure 3.10a and the ***data file*** in Figure 3.10b. The form file contains standardized text together with one or more fields to indicate where variable data is to be inserted in the form letter. The data file contains the information that varies from letter to letter, such as the recipient's name and address. The information for each individual is called a ***record,*** and there are as many records as there are people who receive the letter. Each record is divided into ***fields*** that describe the data within the record—for example, prefix, firstname, lastname, and street. Every record in the file contains the same record layout—that is, the same fields in the same order. The value of each field varies from record to record.

In order for the mail merge to work, the form letter has to indicate how information is to be extracted from the data file. The form letter and data file are created in conjunction with one another, with merge codes in the form letter corresponding to fields in the data file. The first line in the form letter contains three fields: *Prefix, Firstname,* and *Lastname.* (The field names are not typed into the letter explicitly, but are entered through special commands described in the hands-on exercise.)

The merge process examines each record in the data file and substitutes the appropriate field values for the corresponding merge codes as it creates the individual form letters. For example, the first three fields in the first record produce *Mr. David Letterman,* the fields in the second record, *Mr. Arsenio Hall,* and so on.

In similar fashion, the second line of the form letter contains the *Street* field, and the third line the *City, State,* and *Zipcode* fields. The salutation repeats the *Prefix* and *Lastname* fields. The mail merge prepares the letters one at a time, with one letter created for each record in the data file until the file of names and addresses is exhausted. The individual letters are shown in Figure 3.10c. Each letter begins on a new page.

FILE DESIGN

The zipcode should be defined as a separate field in the data file in order to sort by zipcode and take advantage of bulk mail. A person's first and last name should also be defined separately, so that you have access to either field, perhaps to create a friendly salutation such as Dear Joe or to sort on last name.

Implementation in WordPerfect

The implementation of a merge in WordPerfect is straightforward once you understand the basic concept. The ***Merge command*** is located in the Tools Menu and requires three basic steps:

1. Create and save the data file
2. Create and save the form file
3. Merge the two files and print the form letters

The merge creates a third file containing the individual form letters. This is the file that you will print at the end of the exercise. Realize, too, that in doing the exercise, multiple documents will be open at the same time. This in turn makes it necessary to move and/or size the windows on the desktop, and to switch back and forth between the open windows. It sounds more complicated than it is, and all steps are described in detail in the hands-on exercise. Remember, too, the availability of on-line Help. Just pull down the Help menu and search on the key word, *merge.*

Merge codes reflect which field will be used in that location

ELVIS PRESLEY

GRACELAND MANSION • MEMPHIS, TN 38116 • (901) 332-3322 •

November 28, 1993

FIELD(Prefix) FIELD(Firstname) FIELD(Lastname)
FIELD(Street)
FIELD(City), FIELD(State) FIELD(Zipcode)

Dear FIELD(Prefix) FIELD(Lastname):

I am seeking an engagement as the lead act at a Las Vegas night club. I have extensive experience both in private clubs and road tours throughout the United States, and have enclosed my résumé for your review.

It has been some time since I have been in the public eye, but I have never stopped singing or living my music. I am well aware of current trends and have many new songs that will, without question, catch the public's imagination. Everyone needs a gimmick in today's market and I have several extraordinary concepts in mind.

I would welcome the opportunity to meet you to discuss my ideas and audition my new act. An appearance on your show would help to launch my comeback. Please contact me at the above address or call me at 1-800-HOUND-DOG. I look forward to hearing from you.

Sincerely,

Elvis

(a) The Form File

Prefix	Firstname	Lastname	Street	City	State	Zipcode
Mr.	David	Letterman	1697 Broadway	New York	NY	10019
Mr.	Arsenio	Hall	555 Melrose Avenue	Hollywood	CA	90038
Mr.	Jay	Leno	3000 West Alameda Avenue	Burbank	CA	91523

(b) The Data File

FIGURE 3.10 The Mail (Print) Merge

ELVIS PRESLEY

Graceland Mansion • Memphis, TN 38116 • (901) 332-3322 •

Mr. Jay Leno
3000 West Alameda Aven
Burbank, CA 91523

Dear Mr. Leno:

I am seeking an engageme
both in private clubs and r
for your review.

It has been some time since
my music. I am well aware
catch the public's imaginat
extraordinary concepts in r

I would welcome the oppo
appearance on your show
address or call me at 1-800

Sincerely,

Elvis

ELVIS PRESLEY

Graceland Mansion • Memphis, TN 38116 • (901) 332-3322 •

Mr. Arsenio Hall
5555 Melrose Avenue
Hollywood, CA 10019

Dear Mr. Hall:

I am seeking an engageme
both in private clubs and r
for your review.

It has been some time since
my music. I am well aware
catch the public's imagina
extraordinary concepts in r

I would welcome the oppo
appearance on your show
address or call me at 1-800

Sincerely,

Elvis

ELVIS PRESLEY

Graceland Mansion • Memphis, TN 38116 • (901) 332-3322 •

November 28, 1993

Mr. David Letterman
1697 Broadway
New York, NY 10019

Dear Mr. Letterman:

I am seeking an engagement as the lead act at a Las Vegas night club. I have extensive experience both in private clubs and road tours throughout the United States, and have enclosed my résumé for your review.

It has been some time since I have been in the public eye, but I have never stopped singing or living my music. I am well aware of current trends and have many new songs that will, without question, catch the public's imagination. Everyone needs a gimmick in today's market and I have several extraordinary concepts in mind.

I would welcome the opportunity to meet you to discuss my ideas and audition my new act. An appearance on your show would help to launch my comeback. Please contact me at the above address or call me at 1-800-HOUND-DOG. I look forward to hearing from you.

Sincerely,

Elvis

Data from data file merged into form letter

(c) The Printed Letters

FIGURE 3.10 The Mail (Print) Merge (continued)

HELP TIPS

Click the maximize button to maximize the Help window and increase the amount of information displayed on the screen, then press the restore button to reduce Help to its previous size. Press the Tab key to jump from one highlighted topic to the next. Press the enter key to display the highlighted topic. Click the minimize button to reduce the Help window to an icon, then press Alt+Tab to move between open applications and retrieve the Help window at a later time.

Hands-On Exercise 3:

Mail Merge

Objective To create a form file and associated data file in conjunction with the merge facility in WordPerfect; to view multiple documents at the same time. The exercise uses the completed letter from the first exercise.

Step 1: Retrieve the cover letter

- Pull down the **File menu.** Click **Open.**
- Double click **ELVISAFT.WPD** to open the edited version of the cover letter from the previous exercise.
- Pull down the **File menu** and save the document as **FORMLET.WPD.**
- The merge could be developed to print envelopes as well as form letters, but we will omit the envelope from the exercise. Scroll through the letter until you come to Elvis' signature. Click after the signature, then delete the remainder of the document; that is, delete the envelope.
- Save the revised letter.

> **DAYLIGHT SAVINGS TIME**
>
> The date field uses the computer's internal clock and calendar to obtain the current time and date. But what if your computer has the wrong information? Open the Main group in Program Manager, double click the Control Panel icon, then double click the Date/Time icon to open a dialog box. Enter the correct time and date, click OK to accept the new settings, then close the Control Panel application.

Step 2: The Merge command

- Pull down the **Tools menu.** Click **Merge** to produce the dialog box in Figure 3.11a.
- Check the box to place records in a table as indicated in the figure.
- Click the **Data command button.**
- Click the option button for **New Document Window.**
- Click **OK** to begin creating the data file as shown in Figure 3.11b.

Step 3: Enter the field names

- Type **Prefix** as the name of the first field. Press the **enter key** (or click the **Add command button**) to move to the second field.
- Type **Firstname,** then continue to add the remaining fields shown in the figure.
- Click the **OK command button** after you have entered the last field (Zipcode).
- The data file has been defined. You should see the Quick Data Entry box of Figure 3.11c.

Step 4: Enter the data

- Enter data for the first record. Type **Mr.** in the Prefix field.
- Press the **enter key** to move to the next (firstname) field and type **David.**

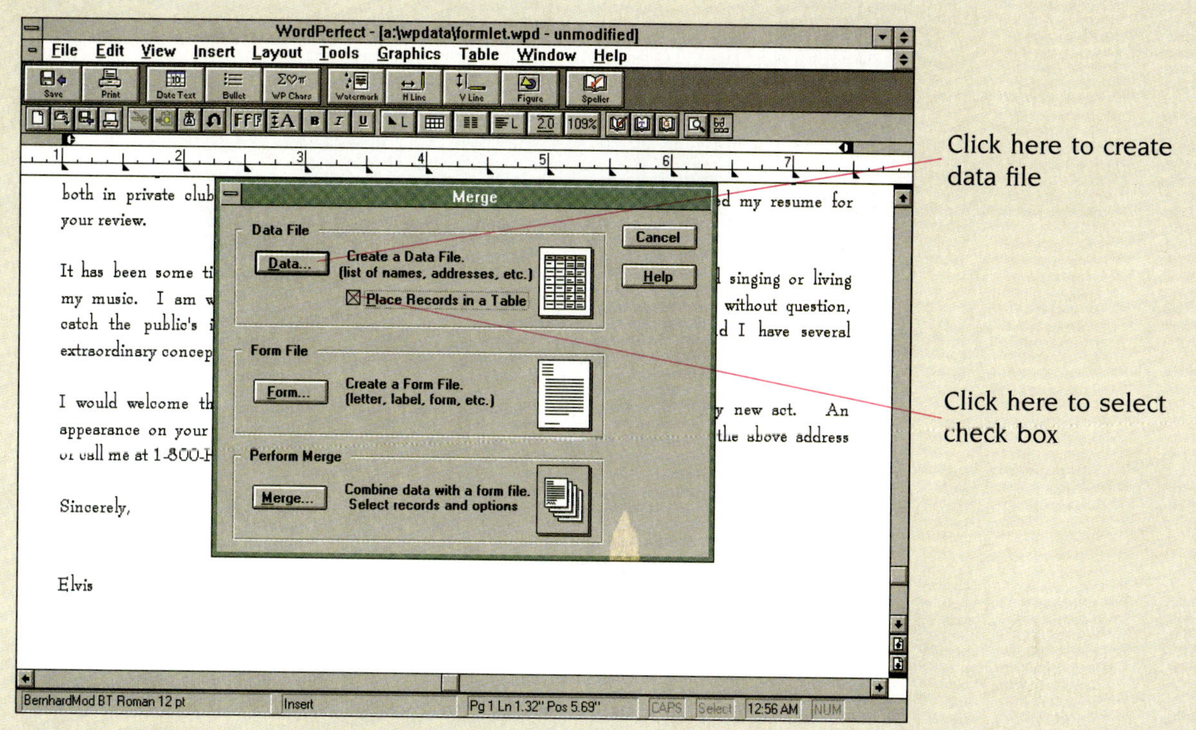

(a) The Merge Command (step 2)

Enter field names here one at a time

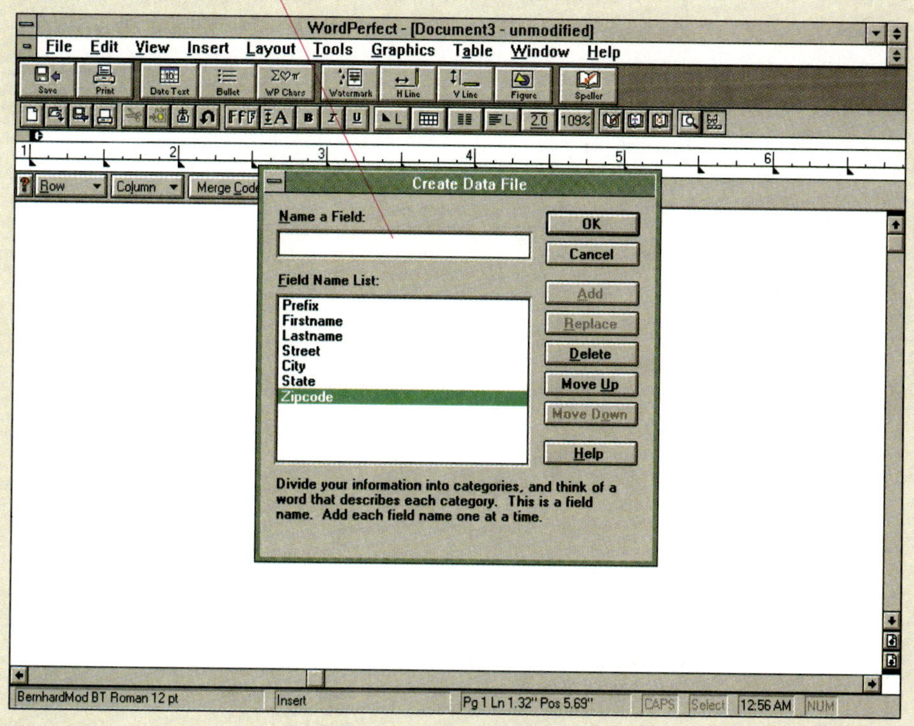

(b) Define the Fields (step 3)

FIGURE 3.11 Hands-on Exercise 3

Enter data for first record one field at a time

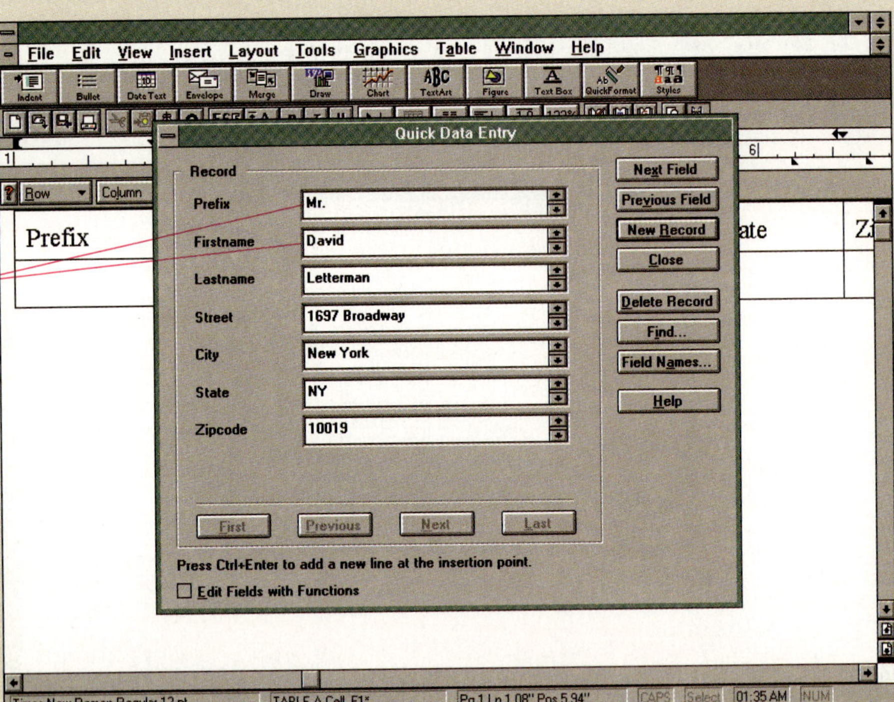

(c) Quick Data Entry (step 4)

FIGURE 3.11 Hands-on Exercise 3 (continued)

- Continue in this fashion until you have entered all fields for the first record.
- Press the **enter key** to move to the first field in the next record. Complete the records for Arsenio Hall and Jay Leno using the data in Figure 3.11d.
- Click the **Close command button** when you have completed entering the data.
- Click **Yes** when asked whether to save the file on disk.
- Type **Names** as the file name. Click **OK.**

COLUMN WIDTH

Do not be concerned if the field names and/or values wrap within a column as that has no effect on the merge. Nevertheless, you can eliminate some or all of the wrapping by changing to a smaller type size. Press Ctrl+Home+Home to move to the beginning of the document *before* the table. Click the Font Size icon on the Power Bar, then click a smaller type size—for example, 10 point, or if necessary, 8 point.

Step 5: Associate the form file

- Click the **Go to Form command button** on the Feature Bar as shown in Figure 3.11d. Do not be concerned with the message No Associated File as you have not yet linked the Names file to the form letter.
- Click the **Select Command Button** as shown in the figure.
- Double click the **FORMLET.WPD** file (created in step 1) in the list box of file names.
- Click **Yes** when asked whether to change to a Merge Form File.

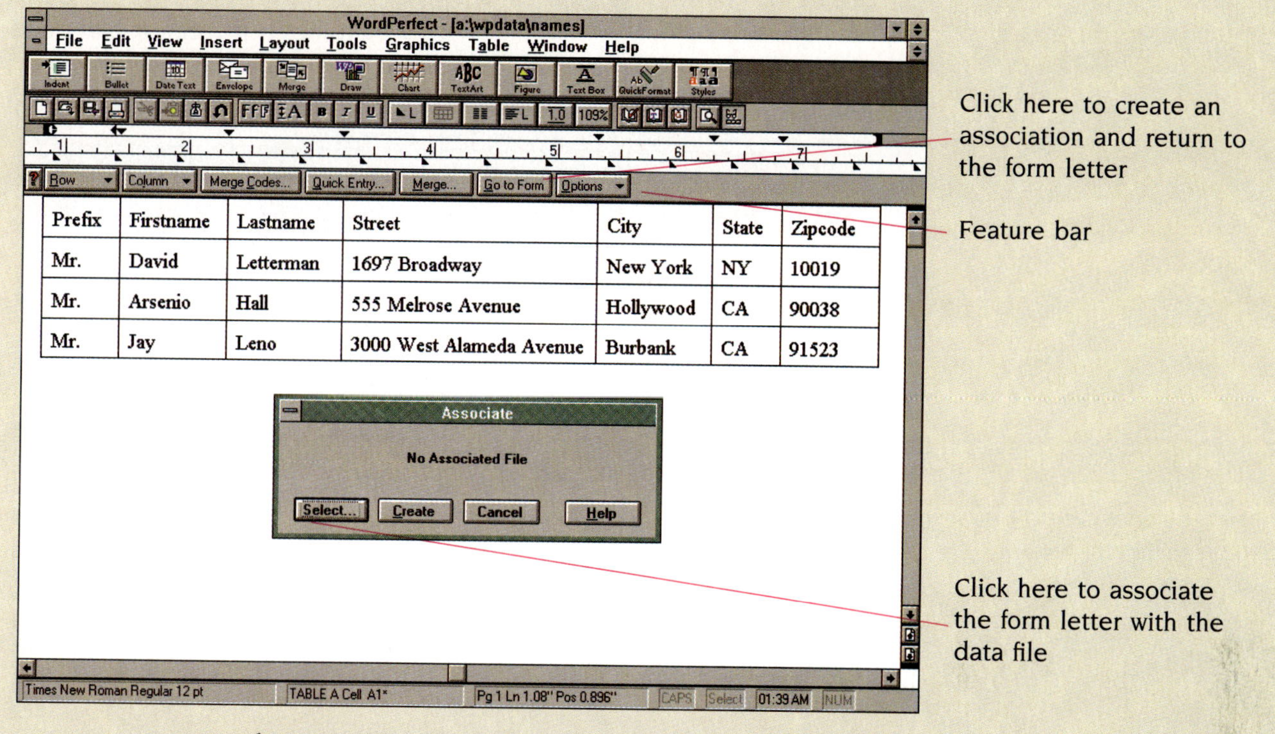

Prefix	Firstname	Lastname	Street	City	State	Zipcode
Mr.	David	Letterman	1697 Broadway	New York	NY	10019
Mr.	Arsenio	Hall	555 Melrose Avenue	Hollywood	CA	90038
Mr.	Jay	Leno	3000 West Alameda Avenue	Burbank	CA	91523

(d) Associating with a Form File (step 5)

FIGURE 3.11 Hands-on Exercise 3 (continued)

Step 6: Modify the form letter

- If necessary, press **Ctrl+Home** to move to the beginning of the document.
- Delete the three-line address at the beginning of the letter as well as Mr. Letterman's name in the salutation. Move the insertion point above the salutation.
- Click the **Insert Field button** on the Feature Bar to display the window of Figure 3.11e. It contains the field names in the NAMES file.
- Click the **Prefix field** if it is not already highlighted. Click the **Insert command button** to insert the field into the form letter. The word FIELD will appear in red, followed by the word Prefix enclosed in red braces to indicate a merge field.
- Press the **space bar** to leave a space between the prefix and the first name.
- Click **Firstname** to select the next field. Click the **Insert command button** to add this field to the form letter. Press the **space bar.**
- Click **Lastname** to select the next field. Click the **Insert command button** to add this field.
- Press the **enter key** to move to the next line and insert the **Street** field.
- Continue in this fashion, entering the fields, spaces, hard returns, and commas as needed, until you have modified the form letter to match Figure 3.11e. Type a colon after the Lastname field in the salutation.
- Click the **Close command button.**
- Save the completed form letter.

Step 7: View both documents simultaneously

- Pull down the **Window menu.** Click **Cascade** to see both documents at the same time. Each document is in its own window, and each has its own title bar, FORMLET.WPD and NAMES. The title bar of the latter is highlighted

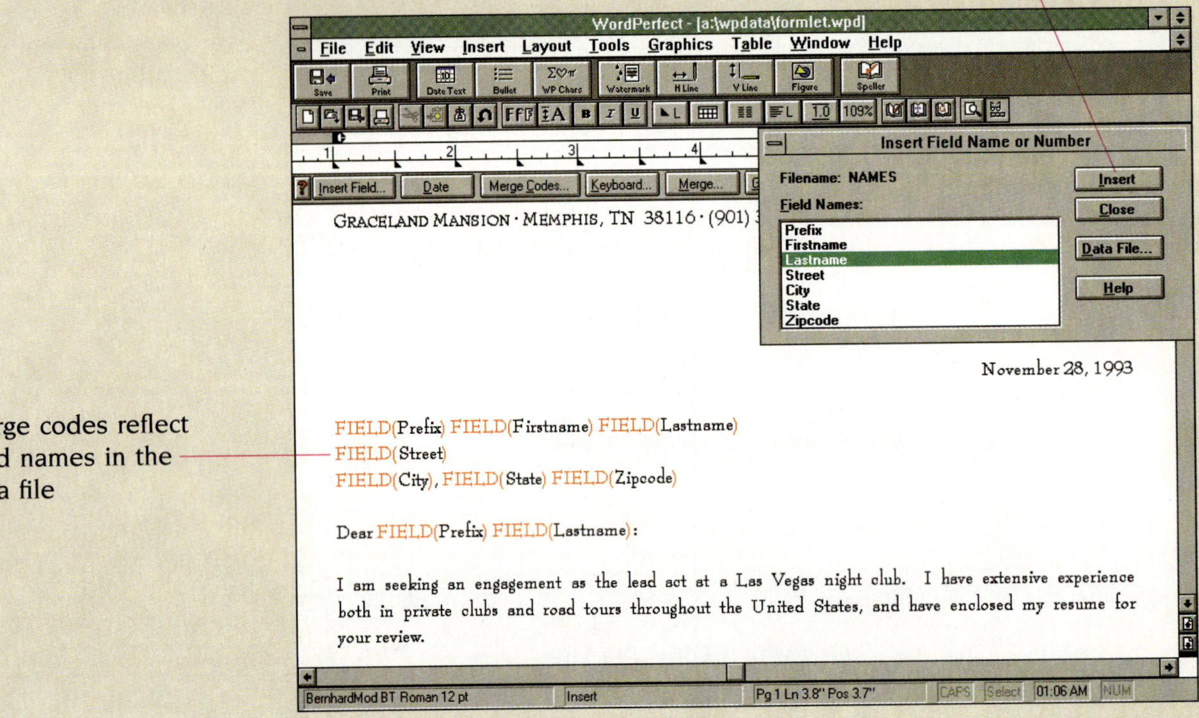

(e) Inserting Field Names (step 6)

FIGURE 3.11 Hands-on Exercise 3 (continued)

to indicate that it is the active document and will be affected by all subsequent commands.

- You may want to move and/or size the windows so that your screen matches Figure 3.11f.
  - Click anywhere in a window to make it active. Alternatively, you can also click the Go To Form and Go To Data buttons on the Feature Bars to transfer back and forth between the windows.
  - To size a window, point to any border (the mouse pointer changes to a double arrow), then drag the border in the direction you want to go—inward to shrink the window or outward to enlarge it. Drag a corner, rather than a border, to change both dimensions at the same time.
  - To move a window, point to its title bar, then drag the window to its new position.
- Your screen should now resemble Figure 3.11f.

Step 8: Merge

- Click anywhere in the FORMLET.WPD window to make it active as shown in Figure 3.11f.
- Click the **Merge button** on the Feature Bar. Click **Merge** in the dialog box to produce a second dialog box as shown in Figure 3.11g.
- Click **OK** to perform the merge. You will see a message displayed on the monitor as the letters are being created.
- Pull down the **Window menu.** Three windows are open: NAMES, FORMLET.WPD, and Document1 (the document containing the form letters).

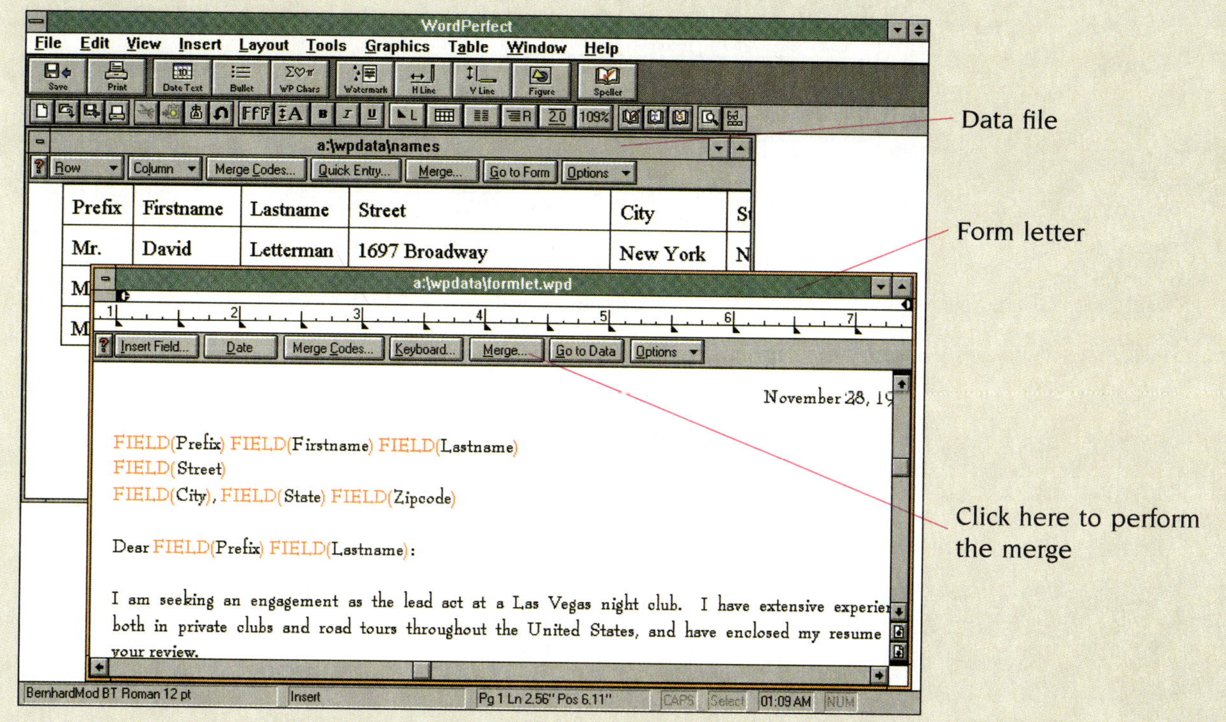

(f) Cascaded Windows (step 7)

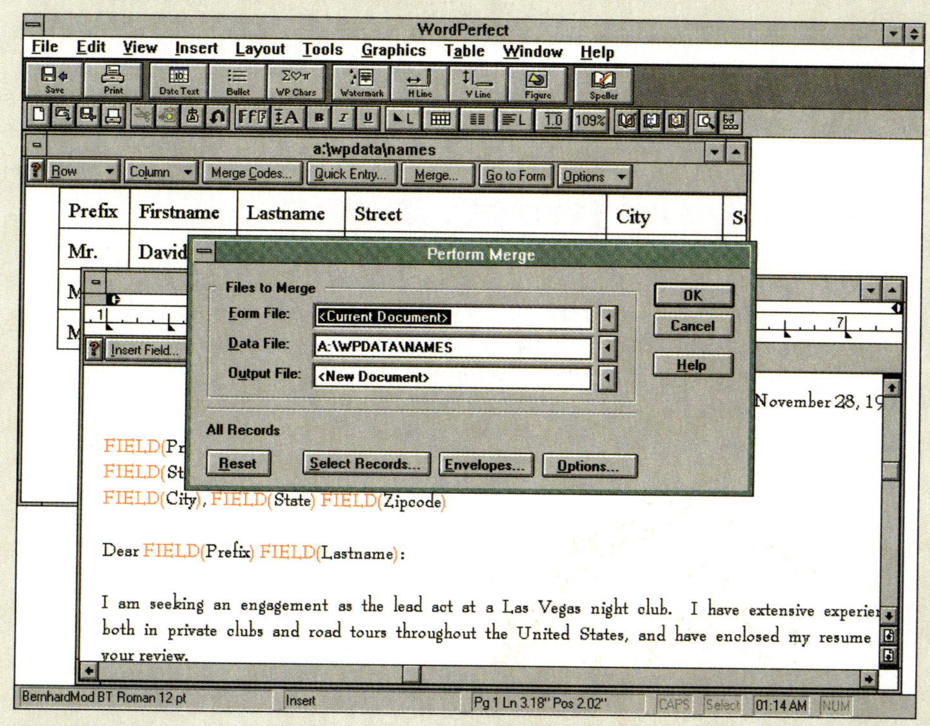

(g) Merge the Files (step 8)

FIGURE 3.11 Hands-on Exercise 3 (continued)

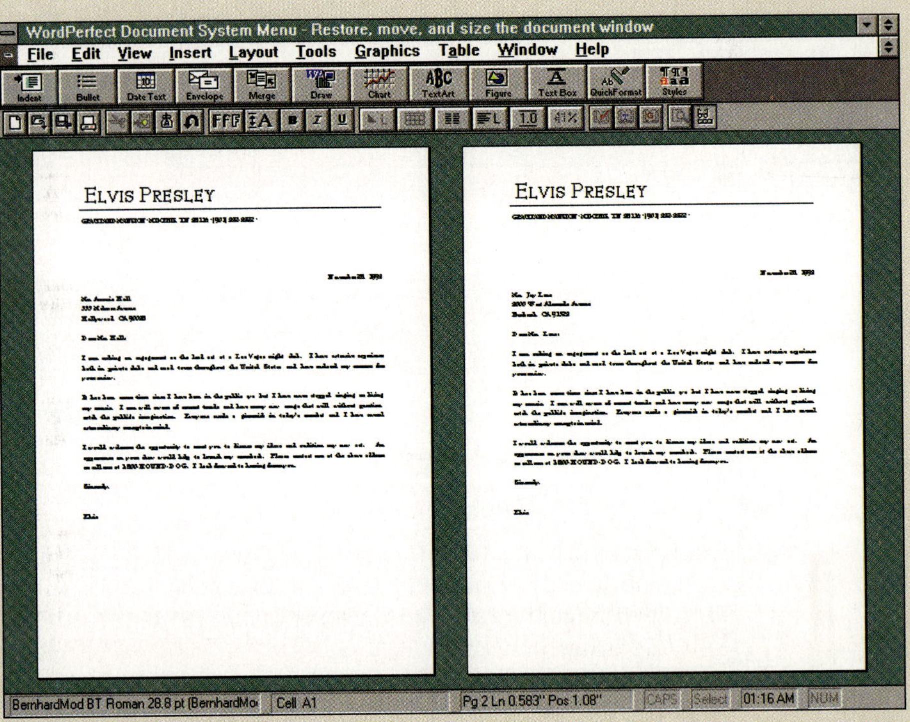

(h) The Merged Letters (step 8)

FIGURE 3.11 Hands-on Exercise 3 (continued)

- Click **Document1.** Maximize the window.
- Press **Ctrl+End** to move to the end of the document. The Status Bar should indicate that you are on page 3, which corresponds to the third form letter.
- Pull down the **View menu.** Click **Two Page** to display the form letters side by side as shown in Figure 3.11h. (Press Alt+PgUp or Alt+PgDn as necessary to view the different letters.)

MERGE SELECTED LETTERS

The merge can be restricted to designated records and/or records meeting specific criteria; that is, a letter does not have to be created for every record in the data file. Click the Select Records command button from the Perform Merge dialog box, then click the option button to Mark Records or Specify Conditions. Select the records to be included, then perform the merge as usual.

Step 9: Exit WordPerfect

- Double click the **control-menu box** in the application window for WordPerfect to exit the program, but pay close attention to the informational messages that ask whether to save the modified file(s).
- There is no need to save the file containing the individual letters because you can always recreate the merged letters provided you have the form letter and data file.
- Save FORMLET.WPD and NAMES if you are prompted to do so.

SUMMARY

The spelling checker compares the words in a document to those in a standard and/or supplementary dictionary. It will detect misspellings, duplicated words, and/or irregular capitalization, but will not flag properly spelled words that are used incorrectly. The thesaurus suggests alternative forms of a word, such as nouns and verbs, and generally offers antonyms as well as synonyms. A grammar checker attempts to catch mistakes in punctuation, writing style, and word usage by comparing strings of text within a document to a series of predefined rules.

A date is inserted into a document as date text or as a date code. Date text remains constant, whereas a date code is updated each time the document is opened.

Envelopes are printed (and/or inserted into a document) with the Envelope command in the Layout menu.

A template is a partially completed document that contains formatting, text, graphics, and other information. WordPerfect provides 45 professionally designed templates known as ExpressDocs.

A mail merge creates the same letter many times, changing only the variable data—for example, the addressee's name and address as appropriate—from letter to letter. It is performed in conjunction with a form file and a data file, both of which exist as separate documents.

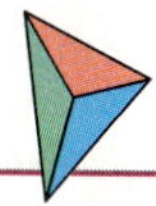

Key Words and Concepts

Antonym
Autofill macro
Data file
Date code
Date text
Envelope icon
ExpressDocs
Feature Bar
Field
Form file
Global replacement
Grammar checker
Grammatik
Insert Character command
Insert Date command
Mail merge
Main dictionary
Merge command
Moving a window
Record
Selective replacement
Sizing a window
Spell Check icon
Spelling checker
Supplementary dictionary
Synonym
Template
Thesaurus
Tools menu

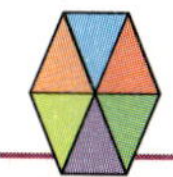

Multiple Choice

1. Which of the following can be detected by the spelling checker?
   (a) Duplicate words
   (b) Irregular capitalization
   (c) Both (a) and (b)
   (d) Neither (a) nor (b)
2. Which of the following is true about the thesaurus?
   (a) It will recognize different forms of the same word—for example, a noun and a verb
   (b) It will generally offer antonyms as well as synonyms
   (c) Both (a) and (b)
   (d) Neither (a) nor (b)

3. Which of the following are unlikely to be found in a supplementary dictionary?
   (a) Proper names
   (b) Words related to the user's particular application
   (c) Acronyms created by the user for his or her application
   (d) Standard words of English usage

4. Ted and Sally both use WordPerfect but on different computers. Both have written a letter to Dr. Joel Stutz and have run a spelling check on their respective documents. Ted's program flags *Stutz* as a misspelling, whereas Sally's accepts it as written. Why?
   (a) The situation is impossible; if they use identical word processing programs, they should get identical results
   (b) Ted has added *Stutz* to the supplementary dictionary
   (c) Sally has added *Stutz* to the supplementary dictionary
   (d) All of the above reasons are equally likely as a cause of the problem

5. A spelling checker will do all of the following except:
   (a) Flag properly spelled words used incorrectly
   (b) Locate misspelled words
   (c) Accept (as correctly spelled) words that are found in the supplementary dictionary
   (d) Suggest alternatives to misspellings it identifies

6. Which of the following best describes how files are saved and printed within the merge operation?
   (a) The form file and data file are printed but not saved
   (b) The merged file is saved but not printed
   (c) Both (a) and (b)
   (d) Neither (a) nor (b)

7. The names and addresses of the individuals slated to receive a form letter are contained in:
   (a) The form file and the data file
   (b) The form file only
   (c) The data file only
   (d) The program file for WordPerfect

8. Which of the following best describes a person's first name, last name, and street address as they would be entered in the form file?
   (a) Characters
   (b) Fields
   (c) Records
   (d) Files

9. Which of the following is the first step in changing the position of a window?
   (a) Point to the title bar
   (b) Point to any corner or border
   (c) Point to the menu bar
   (d) Minimize or maximize the window

10. Which of the following is the first step in changing the size of a window?
    (a) Point to the title bar
    (b) Point to any corner or border
    (c) Point to the menu bar
    (d) Point to the control-menu box

11. Which of the following is correct?
    (a) The date code reflects a specific date and does not change if the document is opened on a different day
    (b) Date text is updated automatically when a document is opened
    (c) Both (a) and (b)
    (d) Neither (a) nor (b)

12. Which of the following is true of the ExpressDocs supplied within WordPerfect?
    (a) Exactly one template is supplied for every type of document
    (b) The same personal information may be used in different templates
    (c) Both (a) and (b)
    (d) Neither (a) nor (b)

13. Which of the following is true regarding the fields used in an ExpressDoc template?
    (a) Angled brackets (< >) denote a field with personal information
    (b) Square brackets ([ ]) indicate a field specific to the template in use
    (c) Both (a) and (b)
    (d) Neither (a) nor (b)

14. Which of the following is accurate with respect to the Feature Bars presented in the chapter?
    (a) The Go to Form command button is found on the Feature Bar for the data file
    (b) The Go to Data command button is found on the Feature Bar for the form file
    (c) Both (a) and (b)
    (d) Neither (a) nor (b)

15. Which of the following is true regarding the form letter and data file associated with the mail merge operation?
    (a) They are stored in the same document
    (b) They are stored in separate documents, but only one can be open at a time
    (c) They are stored in separate documents, both can be open at the same time, but only one document can be visible
    (d) They are stored in separate documents, both can be open at the same time, and both can be visible at the same time

ANSWERS

1. c	**6.** d	**11.** d
2. c	**7.** c	**12.** b
3. d	**8.** b	**13.** c
4. c	**9.** a	**14.** c
5. a	**10.** b	**15.** d

EXPLORING WORDPERFECT

1. Use Figure 3.12 to match each action with its result; a given action may be used more than once.

Action		Result
a. Click at 1, then click at 2	___	Save the current document
b. Click at 3	___	Format the date
c. Click at 4	___	Grammar check the document
d. Click at 5	___	Create an envelope
e. Click at 6, then click at 2	___	Spell check the document
f. Click at 7	___	Change the e in resume to é
g. Click at 8	___	Open a template
h. Double click at 1; click at 9	___	Select a word and find a synonym
i. Click at 10	___	Create a data file for a mail merge
j. Click at 11	___	Change to a Two Page view of the document

2. Prepare a résumé for Benjamin Franklin, who was one of the most versatile geniuses in history. Franklin was born penniless, the fifteenth child of a candle maker, yet he went on to distinguished careers in four diverse areas (business, science, literature, and politics). Two of his inventions (bifocal lenses and the lightning rod) are still in use today. He was the only person to sign four of our country's most important documents (the Declaration of

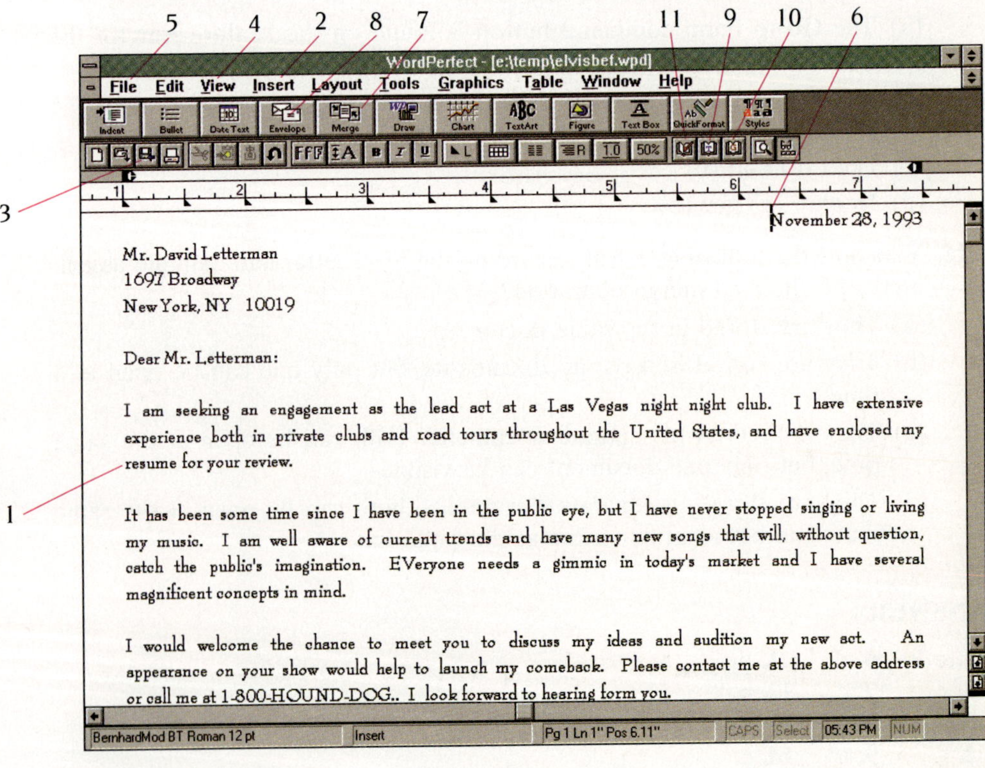

FIGURE 3.12 Screen for Problem 1

Independence, the Constitution, the treaty of alliance with France, and the peace treaty ending the American Revolution). Franklin was also the essence of the public-spirited citizen and organized the first fire department in Philadelphia, helped organize the first hospital in America, founded the first library in America, and presided over the first anti-slavery society in America. He spoke four foreign languages and, incidentally, was quite a ladies' man. You can use your imagination for Franklin's address (e.g., c/o the Continental Congress) and telephone (e.g., not yet invented), but the résumé must be otherwise accurate.

3. Troubleshooting: The messages in Figure 3.13 appeared (or could have appeared) in conjunction with the exercises in the chapter. Indicate which command produced the individual messages and the necessary corrective action (if any).

(a) Informational Message 1

WordPerfect for Windows

Save changes to A:\WPDATA\ELVISPRS.WPD?

Yes No Cancel

(b) Informational Message 2

(c) Informational Message 3

FIGURE 3.13 Informational Messages for Problem 3

4. Figure 3.14 contains the draft version of the PROB0304.WPD document contained on the data disk.

   a. Proofread the document and circle any mistakes in spelling, grammar, capitalization, or punctuation.

All documents should be thoroughly proofed before they be printed and distributed. This means that documents, at a minimum should be spell cheked,, grammar cheked, and proof read by the author. A documents that has spelling errors and/or grammatical errors makes the Author look unprofessional and illiterate and their is nothing worse than allowing a first impression too be won that makes you appear slopy and disinterested, and a document full or of misteakes will do exactly that. Alot of people do not not realize how damaging a bad first impression could be, and documents full of misteaks has cost people oppurtunities that they trained and prepared many years for.

FIGURE 3.14 Screen for Problem 4

b. Load the document into WordPerfect and run the spelling checker. Did WordPerfect catch any mistakes you missed? Did you find any errors that were missed by the program?

c. Use the thesaurus to come up with alternative words for *document,* which appears entirely too often within the paragraph.

d. Run the grammar checker on the revised document. Did the program catch any grammatical errors you missed? Did you find any mistakes that were missed by the program?

e. Correct the document as best you can. Add a second paragraph with your impressions of the grammar checker.

f. Add your name to the revised document, save it, print it, and submit the completed document to your instructor.

5. Time Management: One of the keys to being successful is to manage your time effectively. Make a schedule, then stick to it. The ExpressDoc template in Figure 3.15 is an ideal tool to help you plan your activities.

a. Which template produced the document in Figure 3.15?

b. What is the significance of the text that appears in angled brackets in the upper left portion of the figure?

c. What other templates could be used as the basis for documents to help you manage your time efficiently?

d. Choose the template you believe most useful, then create a real schedule for yourself based on the template you select. Print the document and submit it to your instructor.

6. Exploring ExpressDocs: WordPerfect comes with 45 ExpressDoc templates, which serve as the basis for a variety of documents.

a. How many different templates are provided for a letterhead? Choose the design you like best and create your own letterhead.

b. How many different templates are provided for a fax transmittal? Choose the design you like best and create your own fax cover sheet.

c. How many different templates are provided for a sign (flyer)? Choose a real or imaginary event and create a sign to publicize that event.

d. Explore the list of available templates and choose a completely different category from those in parts (a), (b), or (c).

Print each of the documents and submit them to your instructor.

Weekly Planner

<Name>
<Address>
<City, State, Zip>
<Telephone>
Fax:<Fax>

Monday	Tuesday
8:00	8:00
9:00	9:00
10:00	10:00
11:00	11:00
12:00	12:00
1:00	1:00
2:00	2:00
3:00	3:00
4:00	4:00
5:00	5:00

Things To Do This Week

Wednesday	Thursday
8:00	8:00
9:00	9:00
10:00	10:00
11:00	11:00
12:00	12:00
1:00	1:00
2:00	2:00
3:00	3:00
4:00	4:00
5:00	5:00

Notes

Friday	Saturday
8:00	8:00
9:00	9:00
10:00	10:00
11:00	11:00
12:00	12:00
1:00	1:00
2:00	2:00
3:00	3:00
4:00	4:00
5:00	5:00

FIGURE 3.15 Weekly Planner

7. Exploring Character Sets: The Insert Character command was used in the first hands-on exercise to insert an accented e (from the multinational character set) into the word résumé. There are several additional character sets from which you can choose—for example, the Iconic character set shown in Figure 3.16a.

   Use your imagination, and the fact that all characters are scalable from 4 to 127 points, to recreate the document in Figure 3.16. Better yet, use your imagination to create your own documents.

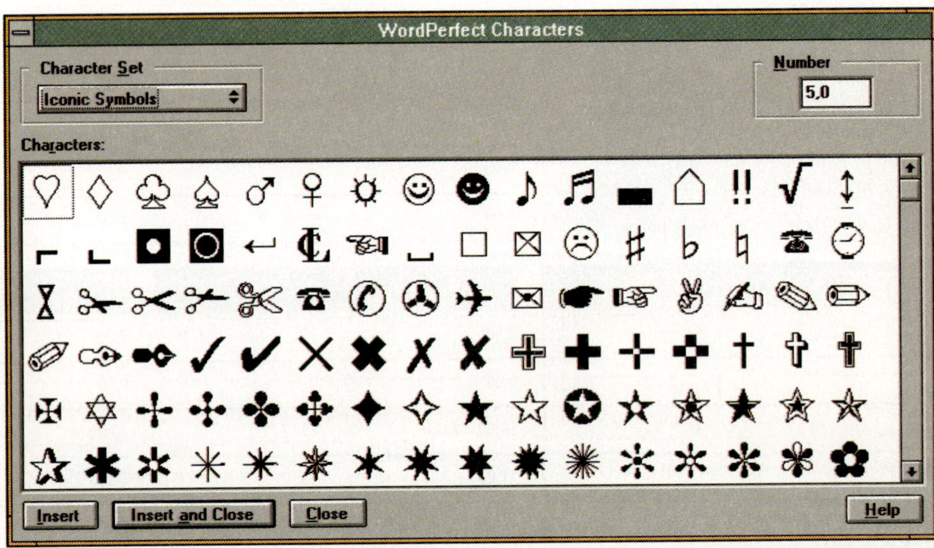

(a) The Iconic Character Set

Valentine's Day

We'll serenade your sweetheart

Call 284–LOVE

(b) A Valentine's Message

FIGURE 3.16 Screen and Document for Problem 7

8. Exploring Mail merge: The Data File in Figure 3.17 is to be used in a mail merge welcoming the members of the ΦΔΓ sorority for the Fall semester. The text of the cover letter is up to you, but you have to modify the data file to reflect recent changes in the membership:
   a. Add Anne Green to the file PROB0308.WPD on the data disk, as she has decided to return to school after all. Anne is a junior. Her permanent address is 567 West Flagler Street, Tampa, FL 33020.
   b. Delete Jackie St. Clair from the file, as she has become inactive.
   c. Use the Insert Character command and the Greek Character Set to include the name of the sorority (in Greek) within the letter.

firstname	lastname	street	city	state	zipcode	year
Andrea	Lalji	1234 Delaware Avenue	Ft. Lauderdale	FL	33312	Sr
Francine	Blum	278 West 77 Terrace	Chicago	IL	60620	Jr
Lien	Le	9807 S.W. 152 Street	Miami	FL	33156	So
Sylvia	Gudat	426 Savona Avenue	Minneapolis	MN	55346	Sr
Debbie	Rowe	8900 W. Jamaica Avenue	New York	NY	10020	So
Tiffany	Bost	900 Hurricane Drive	Miami	FL	33124	Jr
Kim	Zimmerman	8344 N.W. 74 Street	Gainesville	FL	32601	Sr
Jackie	St. Clair	456 Ryder Road	Boston	MA	02190	Jr
Beth Ann	King	900 Mahoney Drive	Buffalo	NY	14203	So
Joan	Rhyne	2500 Freshman Way	Miami	FL	33157	Sr
Carol	Villar	234 Rivo Alto	Miami Beach	FL	33155	Jr
Lori	Pryor	8976 S.W. 75 Street	San Francisco	CA	94114	So
Claudia	Moore	3456 Robertson Way	Denver	CO	80228	Sr
Jessica	Kinzer	7177 Lewis Way	Atlanta	GA	30316	Jr
Jennie	Lee	897 Best Street	Charleston	SC	29410	So
Bianca	Costo	8765 S.W. 79 Court	Miami	FL	33176	Sr
Jamie	Metzger	5660 N.W. 175 Terrace	Baltimore	MD	21224	So
Jennifer	Vedo	8765 Jackson Manor	Santa Rosa	CA	95405	Jr
Cori	Rice	2980 S.W. 75 Street	Coral Gables	FL	33124	Sr
Lynda	Black	7500 Reno Road	Houston	TX	77090	So

FIGURE 3.17 Data File for Problem 8

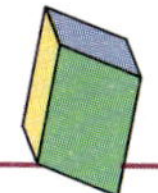

Case Studies

What Else Can Go Wrong?

You don't know how it happened, but your secretary used an old version of both the form letter and data file for the most important mail merge of your career. The good news is that it was only a trial effort (only four letters were created) and the real mailing did not go out. There are so many problems that it's hard to describe them all, but there were mistakes in both the form letter and data file.

You won't even be able to read the form letter unless you change the font size. Give this your immediate attention as the mailing is already late; your instructor needs to see the four letters first thing in the morning. Start with the OLDLETER.WPD and OLDDATA.WPD files on the data disk.

A Junior Year Abroad

How lucky can you get? You are spending the second half of your junior year in Paris. The problem is you will have to submit your work in French, and the English version of WordPerfect won't do. Is there a foreign language version available? What about the dictionary and thesaurus? How do you enter the accented characters that occur so frequently? You are leaving in two months, so you need to get busy. What are your options? Bon voyage.

A Better Printer

The 200 cps dot matrix printer that has served you (and your brother before you) so well is on its last legs, and it's just as well. It's too slow, too noisy, and the output is nowhere as crisp as that of your classmates. You are considering a laser printer, and your parents have agreed to help, provided you keep the price down. What are the most important factors in the purchase of a laser printer? How important are speed, resolution, and memory? Are there other types of printers you should consider beside the dot matrix and laser? Summarize your findings in a one-page document to share with your classmates.

Looking for Business

Every business needs customers and one way of finding customers is through the mail. The mechanics of a mail merge are easy. The hard part is obtaining and then maintaining a suitable mailing list. Mailing lists are for sale, however, just like anything else. The tricky part is knowing where to look and you are on your own, other than our suggestion to start with the yellow pages. Obtain genuine prices and descriptions for lists that you think will be suitable for your business.

4

The Professional Document: Styles and Tables

CHAPTER OBJECTIVES

After reading this chapter you will be able to:

1. Create a header and a footer; establish different headers or footers for the odd and even pages in the same document.
2. Insert page numbers into a document.
3. Create a bulleted or numbered list.
4. Create and change a style; apply an existing style to multiple paragraphs within a document.
5. Explain in general terms the tables feature in WordPerfect; create a table and insert it into a document.
6. Modify an existing table by adding or deleting rows and columns; merge multiple cells into a single cell.
7. Change the borders and shading for cells in a table; change the formatting characteristics of text within a cell.
8. Use one or more ExpressDoc templates to create a predefined table.

OVERVIEW

This chapter presents a series of features to give a document a professional look. We begin with page numbers, headers, and footers—elements that are essential in documents that extend beyond a page or two. We discuss the concept of a style, or set of formatting instructions that provide a consistent appearance to similar elements within a document.

The second half of the chapter introduces the tables feature, one of the most powerful capabilities within WordPerfect. Tables provide an easy way to arrange text, numbers, and/or graphics. We show you how to create and modify a table. We also use several ExpressDoc templates to create additional tables for a variety of applications.

The hands-on exercises are essential to your mastery of the material. This chapter contains three exercises, each of which creates one or more documents of which you will be justifiably proud.

PAGE NUMBERS

The ***Page Numbering command*** inserts page numbers into a document. The page numbers can appear at the top or bottom of a page, and can be left justified, centered, or right justified. The position is selected from the drop-down list box shown in Figure 4.1a. The sample pages in the dialog box show how the page numbers will appear in the printed document.

The command buttons provide additional flexibility. The Value command button changes the starting page number; that is, you need not start at page one. The Font command button changes the typeface, type style, and/or point size for the page numbers. The Options command button produces the dialog box of Figure 4.1b that lets you add text before or after the page number. You can also change the style of the page numbers and/or include Chapter and Volume numbers in addition to the page number. The sample pages in the dialog box show the options in effect—for example, lowercase roman numbers, preceded by the word Preface, centered across the bottom of each page.

The Go To Command

The ***Go To command*** in the Edit menu moves the insertion point to the top of a specific page and is very useful in long documents. Execution of the command produces a dialog box in which you enter the desired page number. Alternatively, the command will let you move to the top or bottom of the current page, or return to the previous position prior to moving the insertion point.

The Go To command also recognizes a ***bookmark,*** a unique location that you define within the document. You can create as many bookmarks as you like—for example, a bookmark for each major topic in a term paper. Each new bookmark is automatically added to a list that is presented when the Go To Bookmark command is executed.

Moving to a bookmark is easier than moving to a specific page because you do not have to know the page number. Moreover, the bookmarks will adjust automatically for the subsequent insertion or deletion of text; that is, going to a bookmark named "conclusion" will always move to this section in a document, independent of whether its page number changes or not.

HEADERS AND FOOTERS

Headers and footers give a professional appearance to a document. A ***header*** consists of one or more lines that are printed at the top of every page. A ***footer*** is printed at the bottom of every page. A given document may contain headers but not footers, footers but not headers, or both headers and footers.

The advantage of using a header or footer (over typing the text yourself at the top or bottom of every page) is that you type the text only once, when you create the header or footer. WordPerfect then inserts the header or footer at the appropriate location on every page. Headers and footers adjust automatically for changes in page breaks caused by the insertion or deletion of text in the body of the document. They will appear on every page until they are discontinued or replaced by another header or footer.

The ***Header/Footer command*** in the Layout menu creates either element as shown in Figure 4.2. A document can have two headers, Header A and Header B, or two footers, Footer A and Footer B. You indicate the element you want to create and its position—for example, Header A on every page. Alternatively, you might want to create one header for the even pages and a different header for

Page Numbering
Placement
Position:
Bottom Center
Sample Facing Pages
2
3
OK
Cancel
Font...
Options...
Value...
Help
Click here to change typeface and/or size of page number
Click here to add text before or after page number
Page numbers are bottom center

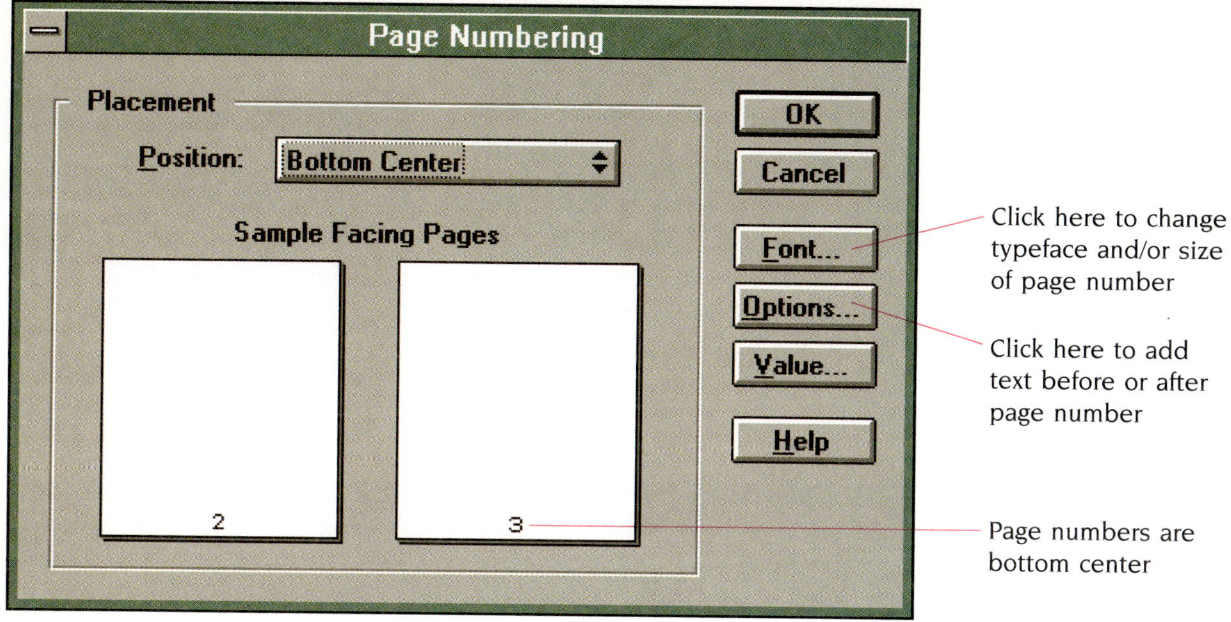

(a) Position

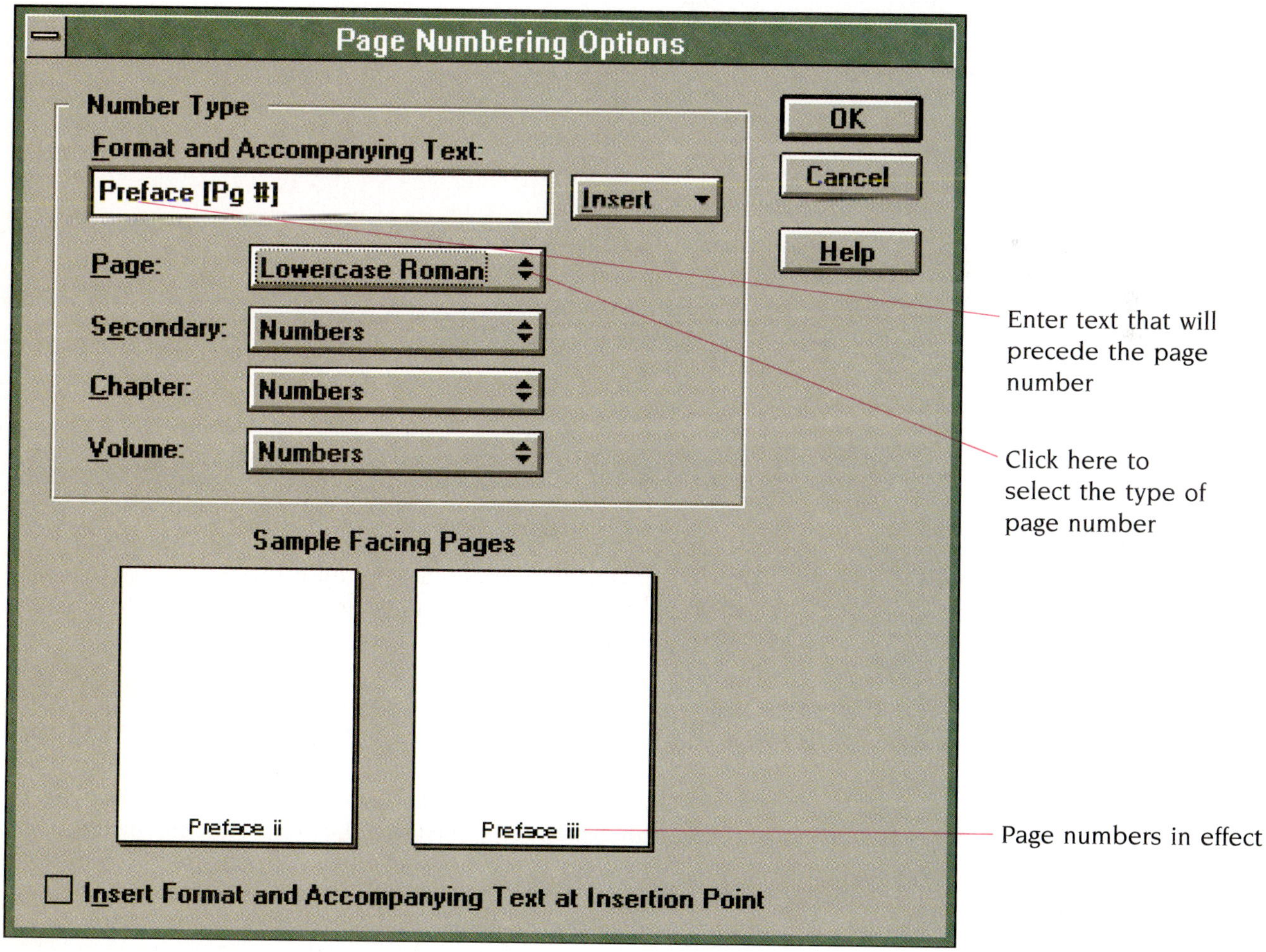

Page Numbering Options
Number Type
Format and Accompanying Text:
Preface [Pg #]
Insert
Page:
Lowercase Roman
Secondary:
Numbers
Chapter:
Numbers
Volume:
Numbers
Sample Facing Pages
Preface ii
Preface iii
Insert Format and Accompanying Text at Insertion Point
OK
Cancel
Help
Enter text that will precede the page number
Click here to select the type of page number
Page numbers in effect

(b) Options

FIGURE 4.1 Page Numbering

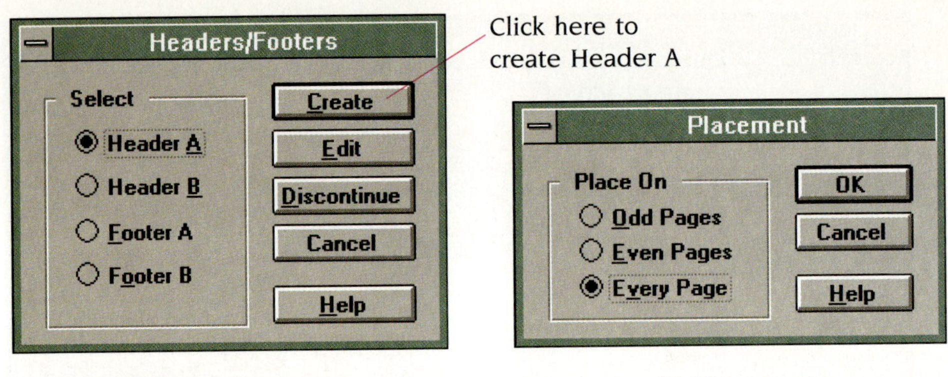

(a) Choosing a Header or Footer

(b) Placement

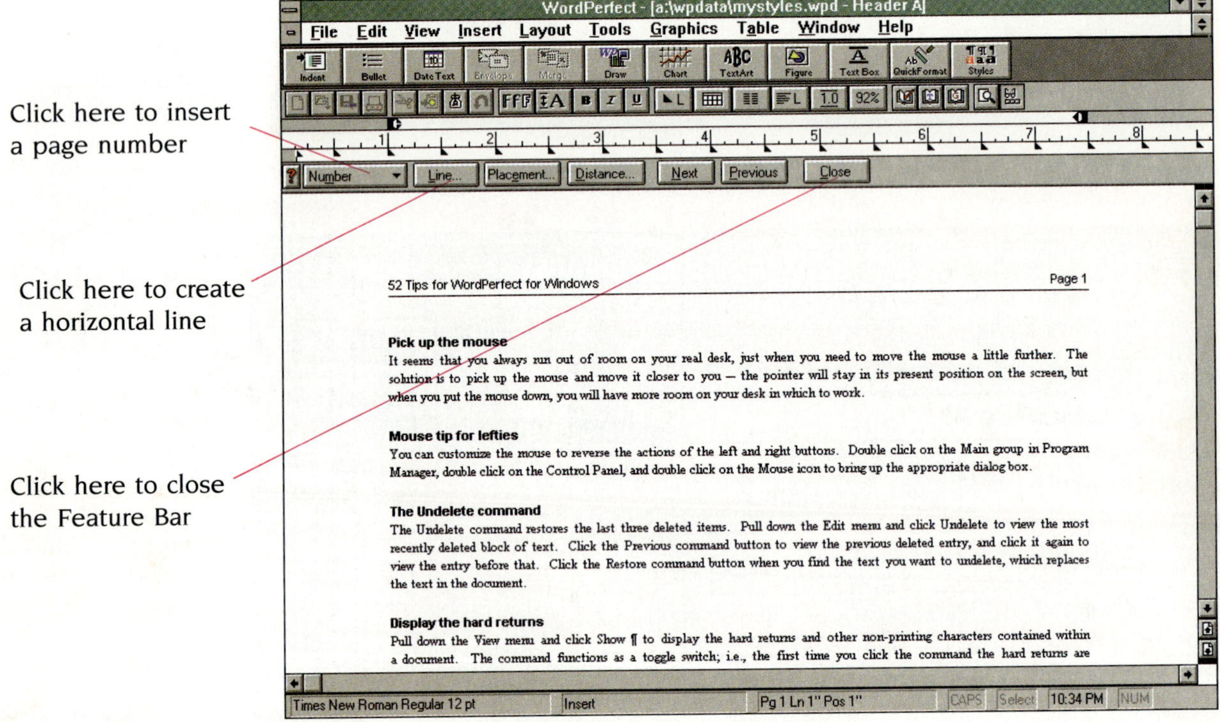

(c) The Feature Bar

FIGURE 4.2 Headers and Footers

the odd pages. The use of alternating headers or footers is quite common; for example, the text you are reading uses different footers for the odd and even pages.

Headers and footers are formatted like any other paragraph. They can be centered, left or right justified, and set in any available font. They can include page numbers and/or horizontal lines to offset them from the main part of the page. Execution of the Header/Footer command displays the Feature Bar shown in Figure 4.2c, which contains the following command buttons:

Number — Inserts a page number in the header or footer; the command button also enables you to change the type of page number and/or the starting page number

Line	Creates a horizontal line
Placement	Determines the placement of the header/footer and on which pages (odd, even, or every page)
Distance	Controls the distance between the header/footer and the body of the text
Next/Previous	Moves to the next/previous header or footer
Close	Exits the header/footer area and closes the feature bar

HEADERS, FOOTERS, AND THE VIEW MENU

If you do not see the headers or footers on the screen, it is because you are working in the Draft view as opposed to the Page or Two Page view. Many people prefer to work in the Draft view because it is faster since WordPerfect spends less time formatting the display. The other views more closely resemble the printed document and show top and bottom margins, headers, footers, and footnotes.

LISTS

The ***Bullets & Numbers command*** in the Insert menu creates a list according to the options in Figure 4.3. A ***bulleted list*** emphasizes (and separates) the items in a list. A ***numbered list*** sequences (and prioritizes) the items. You can choose any of the indicated bullet types or any of the numbering schemes. Numbered lists enable you to change the starting value as shown in the figure. Lists are easy to implement and are illustrated in the hands-on exercise.

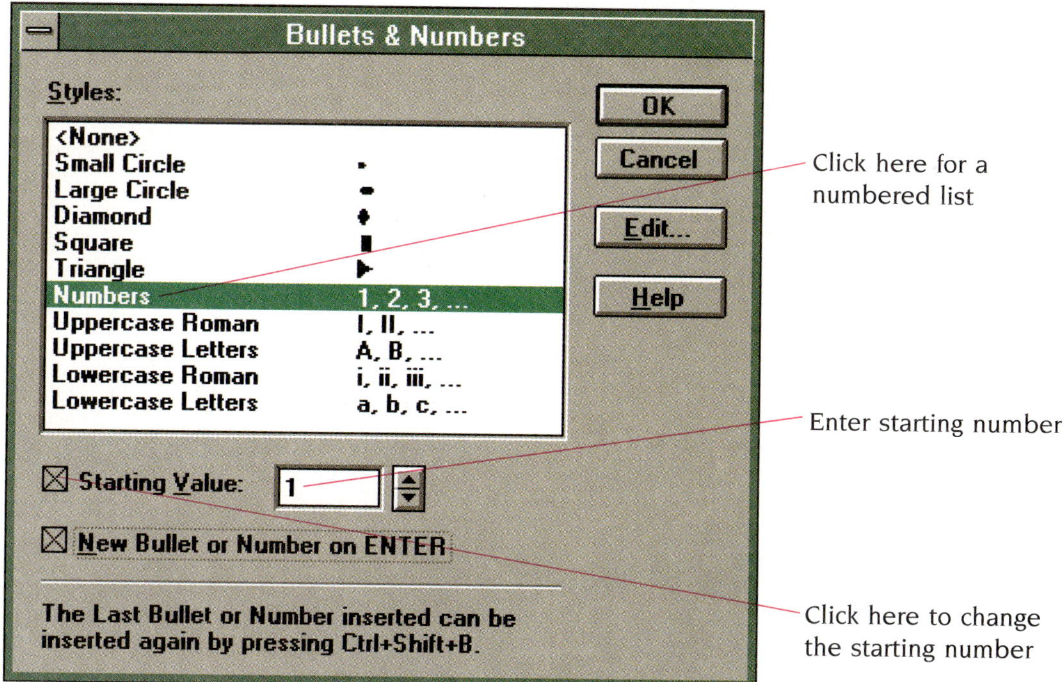

FIGURE 4.3 Bullets and Numbers

THE COACH

The Coach is a series of interactive lessons within the Help facility that provides step-by-step instructions for various features in WordPerfect. Pull down the Help menu, click Coach, then double click Bullets, and let Coach guide you through the process of creating a bulleted list.

STYLES

A characteristic of professional documents is the use of uniform formatting for each element. Different elements can have different formatting. Headings may be set in one font and the text under those headings in a different font. You may want the headings centered and the text fully justified.

If you are like most people, you will change your mind several times before arriving at a satisfactory design, after which you will want consistent formatting for each element in the document. You can use the QuickFormat command (see page 63) to copy the formatting from one element to another, but it still requires you to select the individual elements and paint each one whenever formatting changes.

A much easier way to achieve uniformity is to store the formatting information as a ***style,*** then apply that style to multiple occurrences of the same element within the document. Change the style, and you automatically change all text defined by that style.

Styles are created on the character, paragraph, or document level. A ***character style*** affects only the selected text, a ***paragraph style*** affects the current paragraph, and a ***document style*** affects all subsequent text. The way to apply a style depends on the type of style. To apply a character style, select the text; to apply a paragraph style, click anywhere in the paragraph; and to apply a document style, click at the point in the document where the style is to take effect.

The ***Styles command*** in the Layout menu creates and/or modifies a style, then applies that style within a document. Execution of the command displays the Style List shown in Figure 4.4a, which lists the styles that have been defined in a document. Styles are modified or defined through the Edit and Create command

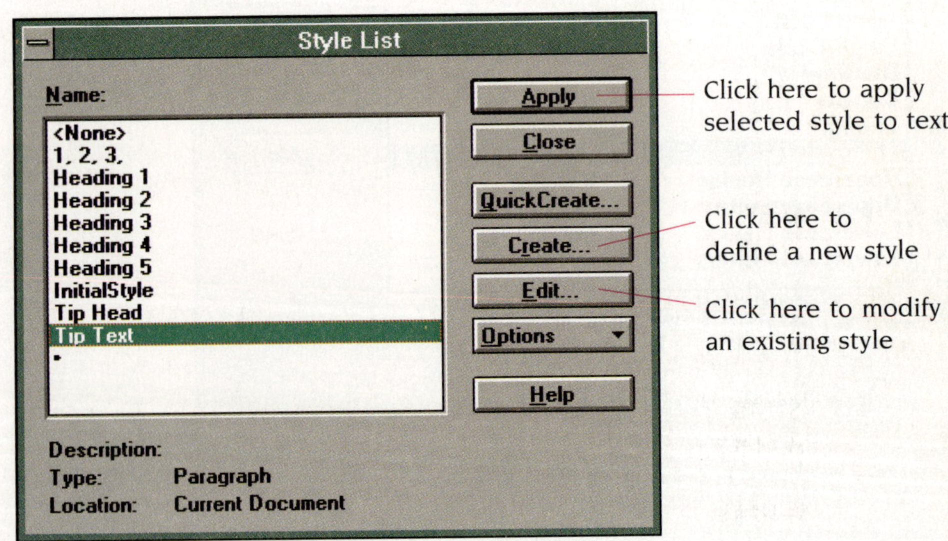

(a) Style List

FIGURE 4.4 Styles

buttons in Figure 4.4a, respectively. These commands invoke the Styles Editor in Figure 4.4b, which contains the formatting commands to create or modify a style.

The concept of a style is further illustrated by viewing the Reveal Codes window in Figure 4.4c. The title of each tip in the document is enclosed in paired

Styles Editor
Edit Insert Layout Tools Graphics Table
Style Name: Tip Text
Description:
Type: Paragraph (paired)
Enter Key will Chain to: <Same Style>
OK
Cancel
Help
Contents
Font: Times New Roman [Times New Roman Regular] Font Size: 10pt Just: Full
Reveal Codes
Show 'Off Codes'

Click here to select a font for the style or to select alignment

Codes for style being defined

(b) Styles Editor

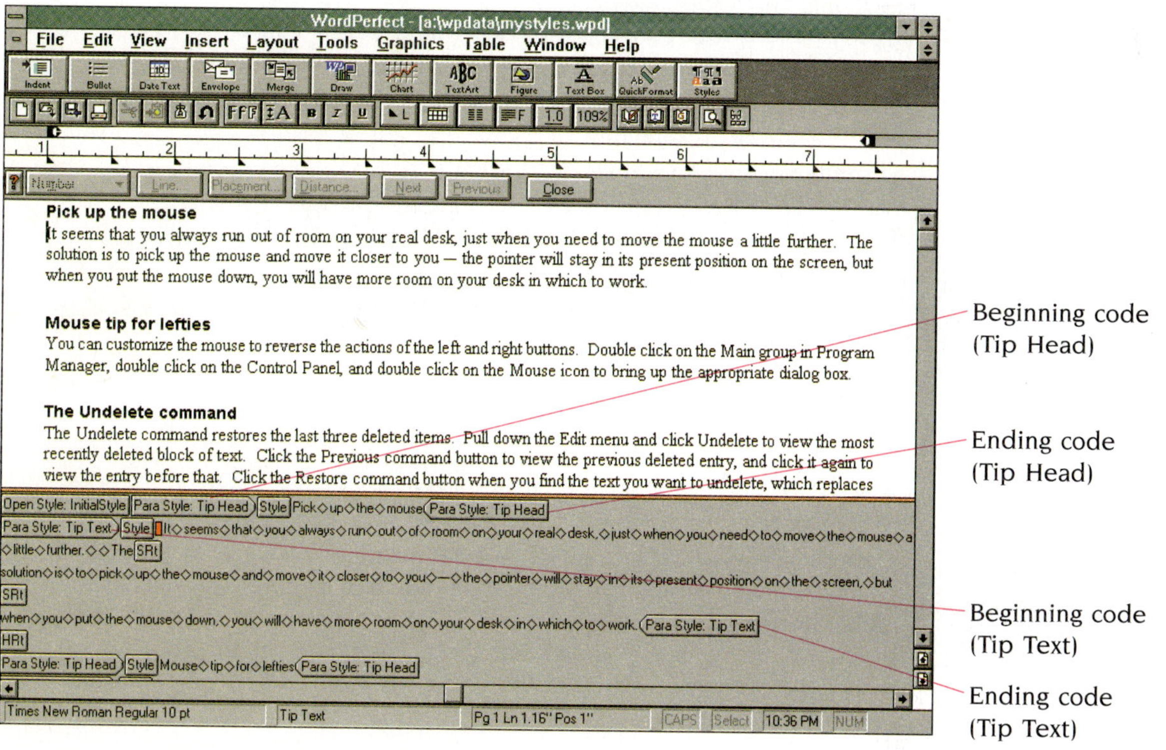

(c) Reveal Codes

FIGURE 4.4 Styles (continued)

codes that begin and end the Tip Head style. In similar fashion the text of each tip is enclosed in paired codes that begin and end the Tip Text style. No other formatting codes are shown, yet the document window displays the title in boldface Arial and the text in Times Roman. The formatting is produced through the previously defined styles, such as the Tip Text style defined in Figure 4.4b.

Styles automate the formatting process and provide a consistent appearance to a document. Any type of formatting information can be stored within a style. Once a style has been defined, it can be applied to multiple elements within a document to produce identical formatting.

STYLES AND THE STATUS BAR

The Status Bar displays the style in effect at the insertion point, provided the General Status option has been selected for display. Double clicking the style name produces the Style List dialog box and is equivalent to executing the Style command from the Layout menu.

HANDS-ON EXERCISE 1:

Headers, Lists, and Styles

Objective To create a numbered list; to demonstrate the use of styles within a document; to create a header that includes page numbers. Use Figure 4.5 as a guide for the exercise.

Step 1: The Go To command

- Load WordPerfect. Pull down the **File menu.** Click **Open.**
- Double click **WPTIPS.WPD** to retrieve the unformatted document we will use throughout the exercise. The document consists of 52 tips for WordPerfect that appear throughout the text.
- Save the document as **MYSTYLES.WPD** so that you can return to the original WPTIPS.WPD if necessary.
- Pull down the **View menu.** Click **Page.** Pull down the **View menu** a second time. Zoom to **Page Width.**
- Pull down the **Edit menu.** Click **Go To** to produce the dialog box in Figure 4.5a.
- Click **Page Number.** Type **11** (the last page in the document). Click **OK.**

THE GO TO COMMAND AND THE STATUS BAR

The fastest way to execute the Go To command is to double click the Page Number on the Status Bar. If the page number is not displayed on the Status Bar, pull down the File menu, click Preferences, then double click the Status Bar icon. Check the box for Combined Position. Click OK to accept the changes, then close the File Preferences dialog box to return to your document.

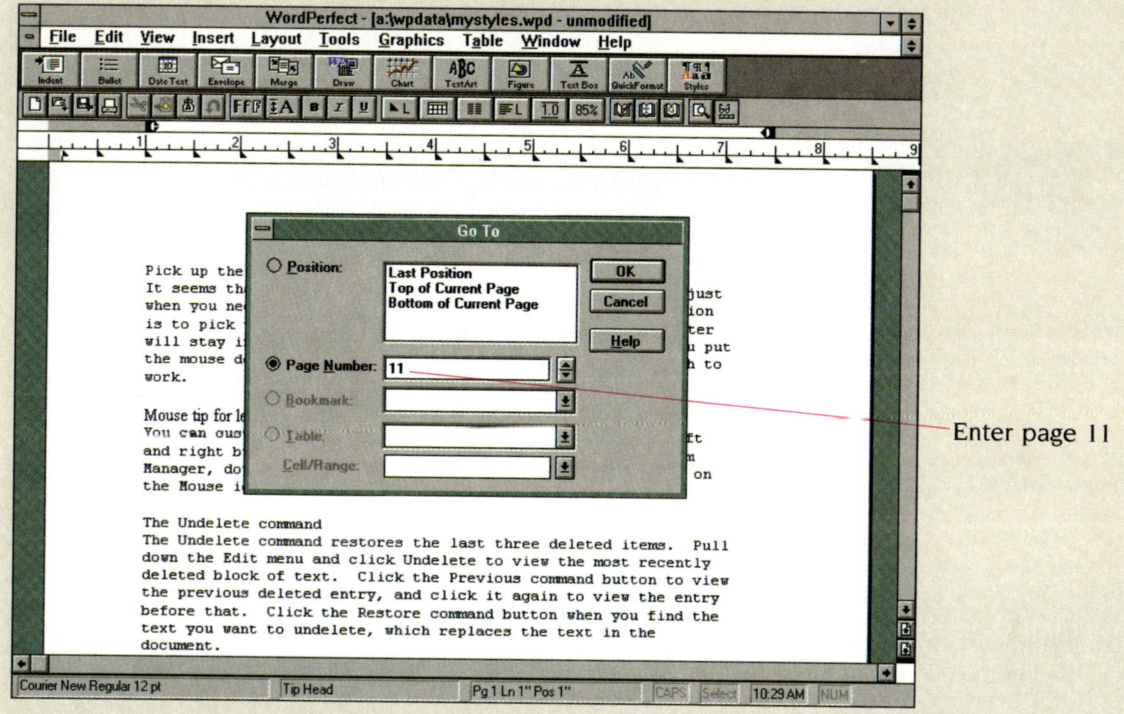

(a) Edit Go To Command (step 1)

FIGURE 4.5 Hands-on Exercise 1

Step 2: Bulleted and numbered lists

- Point to the left margin and click the **right mouse button** to produce a QuickMenu.
- Click **Select Page** to select the entire last page, which contains the list of tips.
- Pull down the **Insert menu.** Click **Bullets & Numbers** to produce the dialog box in Figure 4.5b.
- Click **Numbers** from the list of Styles.
- Click the **Starting Value box.** Be sure that the number 1 appears in the associated text box.
- Click **OK** to produce the numbered list; the tips should be numbered from 1 to 52.
- Click outside the list to deselect the text. Save the document.

BOOKMARKS

Establish your own place markers (known as bookmarks) that enable you to go directly to any place in a document. Place the cursor where you want the bookmark, pull down the **Insert menu,** and click **Bookmark.** Enter a short name (20 characters or fewer consisting of letters, numbers, and/or the underscore) and click **OK.** To return to the bookmark when editing the document, pull down the **Edit menu,** click **Go To,** click the **Bookmark option button,** then select the name of the bookmark.

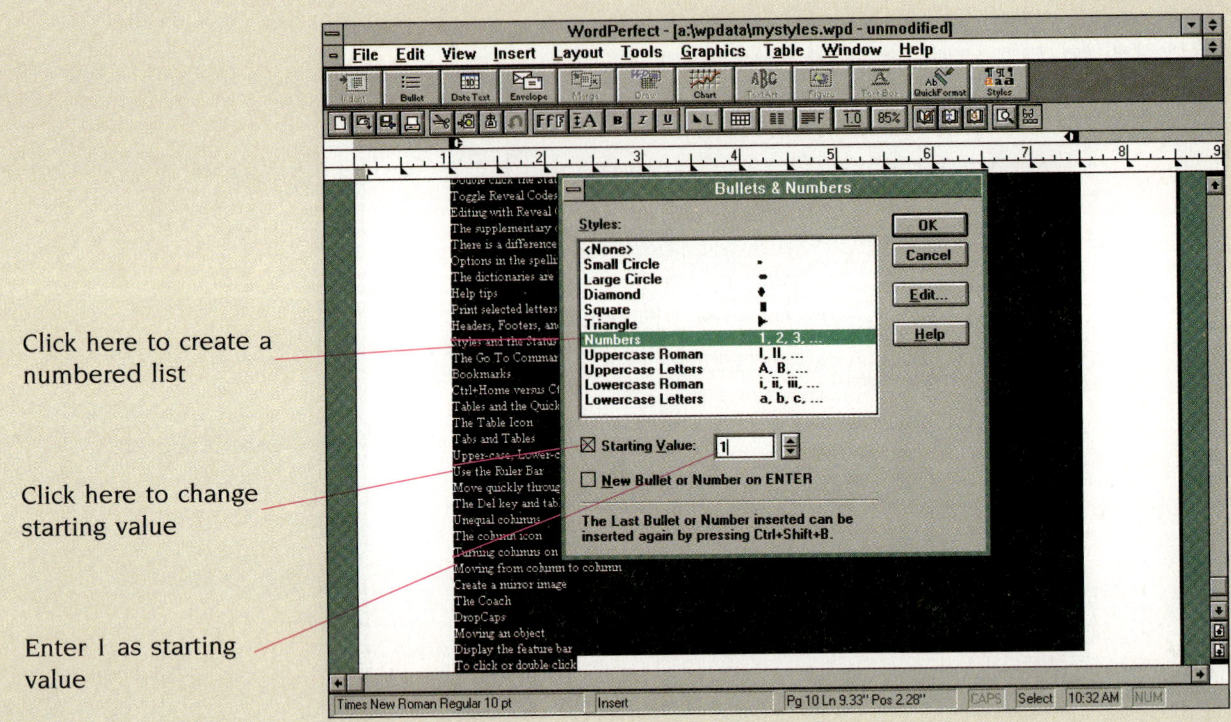

(b) Bullets and Numbers Command (step 2)

FIGURE 4.5 Hands-on Exercise 1 (continued)

Step 3: Global formatting

- Pull down the **Edit menu** and click **Go To** (or press **Ctrl+G**). Type **1** and press **enter** to return to the first page of the document.
- Press **Alt+F3** to open the Reveal Codes window as shown in Figure 4.5c.
- Press the **left arrow key** until you are immediately to the right of the Open Style code. (You cannot move to the left of the Open Style code.)
- Pull down the **Layout menu.** Click **Page.** Click **Keep Text Together** to produce the dialog box in Figure 4.5c. Check the box to implement **Widow/Orphan** protection. Click **OK.**
- Pull down the **Layout menu.** Click **Margins.** Change the **Top margin** to **.75** inch. Click **OK.**
- Save the document.

CTRL+HOME VERSUS CTRL+HOME+HOME

Ctrl+Home moves you to the beginning of a document and places the insertion point *after* any hidden codes that may exist. Ctrl+Home+Home also moves to the beginning of the document but sets the insertion point *before* the hidden codes. The difference is significant.

Step 4: The Reveal Codes Window

- All headings in the document have been assigned the same style (Tip Head). The text for each tip has been assigned a second style (Tip Text).

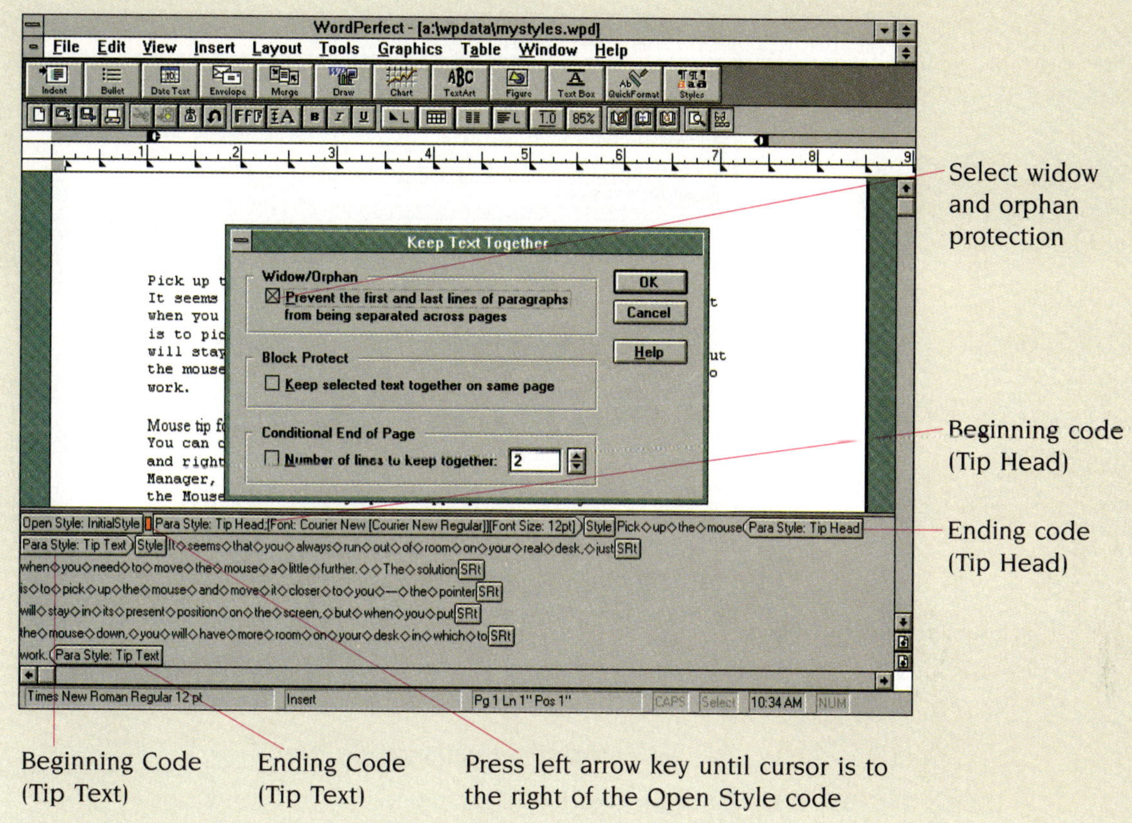

(c) Reveal Codes (step 3)

FIGURE 4.5 Hands-on Exercise 1 (continued)

- Look carefully at the Reveal Codes window in Figure 4.5c.
  - You will see an open paired code for the paragraph style Tip Head immediately before the title of the first tip (Pick Up the Mouse). You will see the closing paired code after the title.
  - In similar fashion you will see an open paired code for the paragraph style Tip Text before the first sentence in the text and a closing code at the end of the tip.
- Press **Alt+F3** to close the Reveal Codes window.

Step 5: Change the heading style

- Pull down the **Layout menu.** Click **Styles.**
- Click **Tip Head** in the Name List box. Click the **Edit command button** to produce the dialog box in Figure 4.5d.
- Click in the **Contents** area. Press the **Del key** to delete the hidden codes, which presently define the style (12 point Courier New).
- Pull down the **Layout menu.** Click **Font.** Choose **10 point Arial bold.** Click **OK.**
- Click **OK** to accept the revised style and exit the Styles Editor dialog box. Click **Close** to exit the Style List dialog box.
- The formatting of the tip headings (except for Mouse Tip for Lefties) has been changed to reflect the new definition of the Tip Head style.
- Save the document.

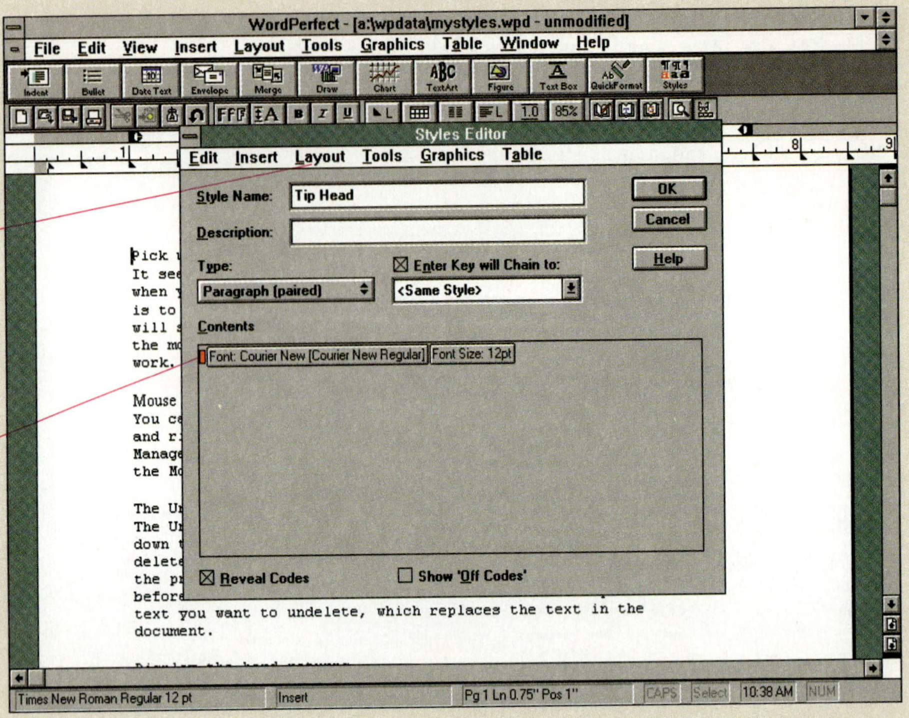

Click here to select a new font for the style

Click here and press Del key to delete existing codes

(d) Change the Heading Style (step 5)

FIGURE 4.5 Hands-on Exercise 1 (continued)

THE QUICKCREATE COMMAND

Create a character or paragraph style from existing text that has already been formatted. Place the insertion point within the formatted text, pull down the Layout menu, click Styles, and click **QuickCreate.** Enter a name for the style (and optionally a description). Choose Paragraph or Character, then click OK.

Step 6: Apply a paragraph style

- The Mouse Tip for Lefties has not been formatted because it is not yet associated with the Tip Head style.
- Click anywhere in the tip heading, Mouse Tip for Lefties.
- Pull down the **Layout menu.** Click **Styles.**
- Click **Tip Head** in the Name List in Figure 4.5e.
- Click **Apply** to apply this style to the current paragraph. The formatting matches that of the other headings.

Step 7: Change the text style

- Pull down the **Layout menu.** Click **Styles.**
- Click **Tip Text** from the Name List box. Click the **Edit command button.**
- Click in the **Contents** area. Press the **Del key** to delete the hidden codes which presently define the style (12 point Courier New, left justification).

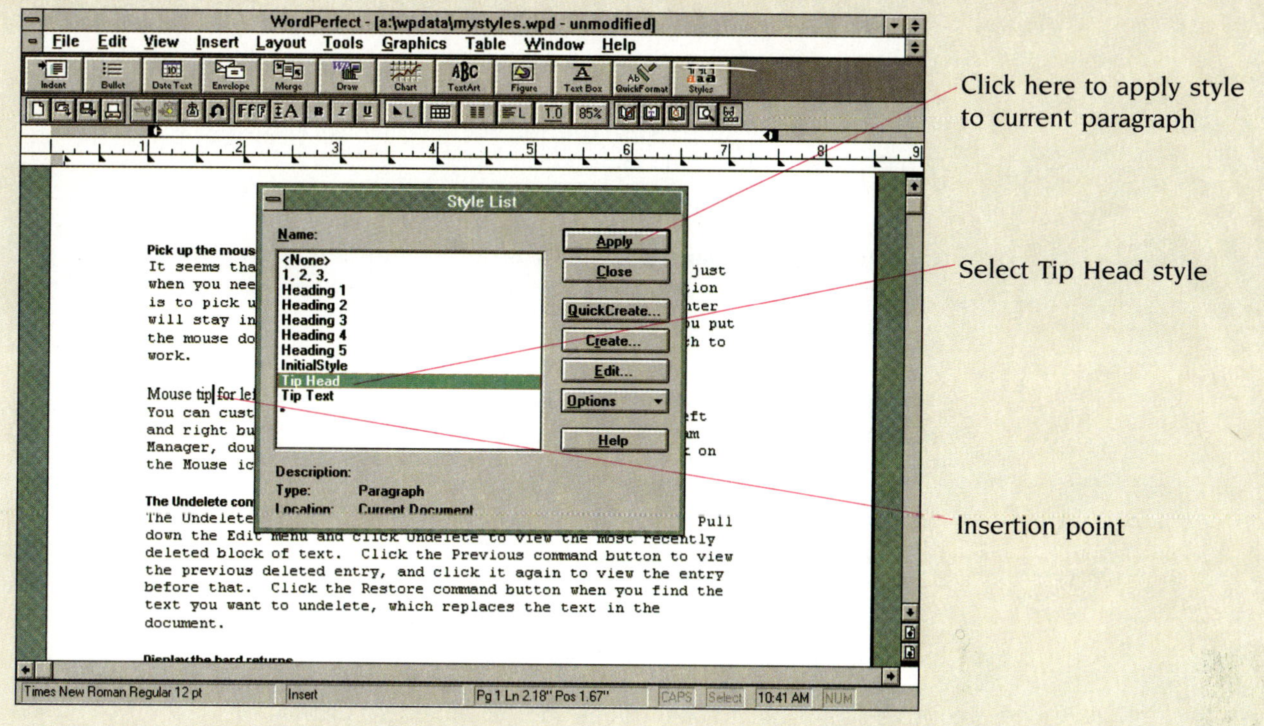

(e) Change the Text Style (step 6)

FIGURE 4.5 Hands-on Exercise 1 (continued)

- Pull down the **Layout menu.** Click **Font.** Specify **10 point Times New Roman.** Click **OK.**
- Pull down the **Layout menu.** Click **Justification.** Click **Full.**
- Click **OK** to exit the Styles Editor dialog box.
- Click the **Close command button** to close the Style List dialog box and return to your document.
- Save the document.

VARIETY IS THE SPICE OF LIFE

We have restricted our design to the Arial and Times New Roman fonts because they are supplied with Windows and hence are always available. WordPerfect for Windows supplies several additional fonts that you can specify within the styles for the Tip Head and/or Tip Text.

Step 8: Add the header

- Pull down the **View menu** and check that you are in the **Page view.**
- Pull down the **Layout menu.** Click **Header/Footer.** Click **Create.**
- Click the **Font button** on the Power Bar. Click **Arial.**
- Click the **Font Size button** on the Power Bar. Click **8** (for 8 point type).
- Type the text of the header, **52 Tips for WordPerfect for Windows.**

➤ Pull down the **Layout menu.** Click **Line.** Click **Flush Right.** Type the word **Page.** Do *not* press the enter key.

➤ Click the **Number button** on the Header Feature Bar. Click **Page Number** as shown in Figure 4.5f. You will see the number 1 entered to the right of the header. Press the **enter key.**

Step 9: Add a line to the header

➤ Click the **Line button** on the Header Feature Bar. Click **OK** to accept the single line as shown in Figure 4.5g.

➤ Click the **Close command button** on the Header Feature Bar.

➤ Click the **Page down icon** on the scroll bar to scroll to the next page. You will see the header you just created, but the page number will show page 2.

➤ Save the document.

> **DISPLAY THE FEATURE BAR**
>
> It's easy to create a header or footer, but how do you change it once the item has been closed and the Feature Bar disappears? Point to the header or footer, then click the right mouse button to display a QuickMenu. Click Feature Bar to open the header or footer for editing.

Click here to select Flush Right for page number

Click here to change the font

Click here to change the size

Click here to create a line

Click here to place a page number in the header

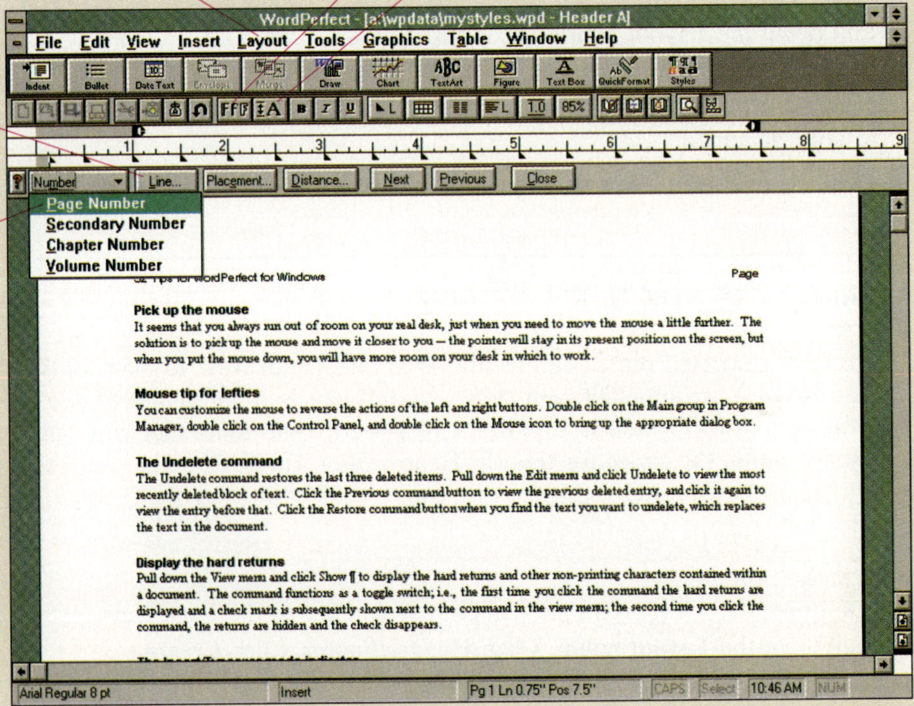

(f) Create the Header (step 7)

FIGURE 4.5 Hands-on Exercise 1 (continued)

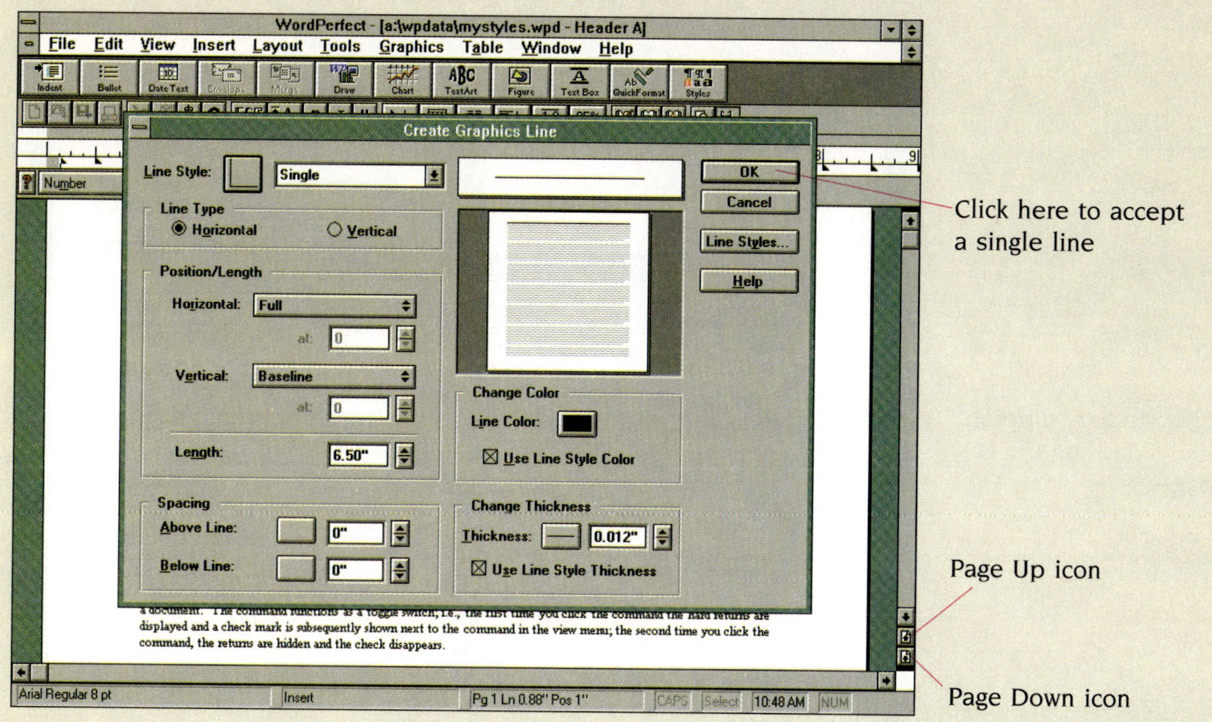

(g) Adding a Line to the Header (step 9)

FIGURE 4.5 Hands-on Exercise 1 (continued)

Step 10: Create the title page

- Press **Ctrl+Home** to move to the beginning of the document. Press **Ctrl+Enter** to create a page break for the title page. Press the **up arrow** to move to the newly created page.
- Pull down the **View menu.** Click **Two Page** to view the pages as shown in Figure 4.5h.
- Press **enter** several times to move to an appropriate position for the title. (Do not be concerned if you see the header on the title page as we will remove it shortly.)
- Center the title, **52 Tips for WordPerfect for Windows** in **24 Point Arial Bold.** Deselect the text.
- Press **enter** several additional times to move further down the page.
- Change to **14 point type.**
- Add **by Robert Grauer and Maryann Barber** on one line, then **Prepared for** followed by your name on the next line.
- Pull down the **Layout menu.** Click **Page.** Click **Suppress.** Check the box for **Header A.** Click **OK** to suppress the header on the title page only.
- Save the document.

Step 11: Adjust the page numbers

- The page numbers should be changed so that the tips begin on page number 1. (The title page is physically the first page of the document, but that page is not numbered.)
- Pull down the **View menu.** Click **Page.** Pull down the **View menu** a second time. Zoom to **Page Width.**

Click here to suppress the header on the title page

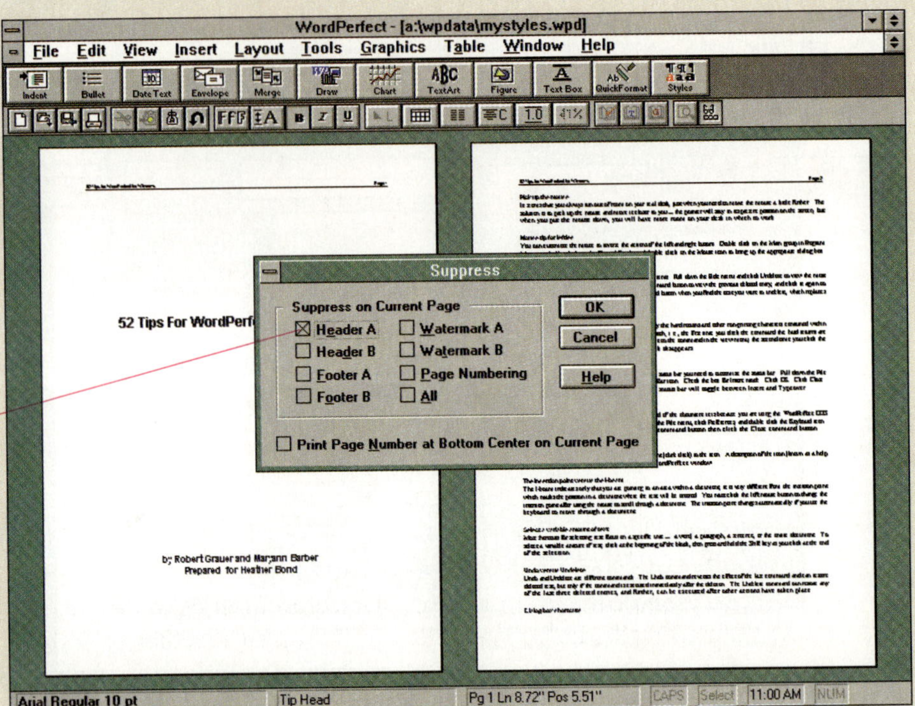

(h) Creating a Title Page (step 10)

Enter 1 as the new page number

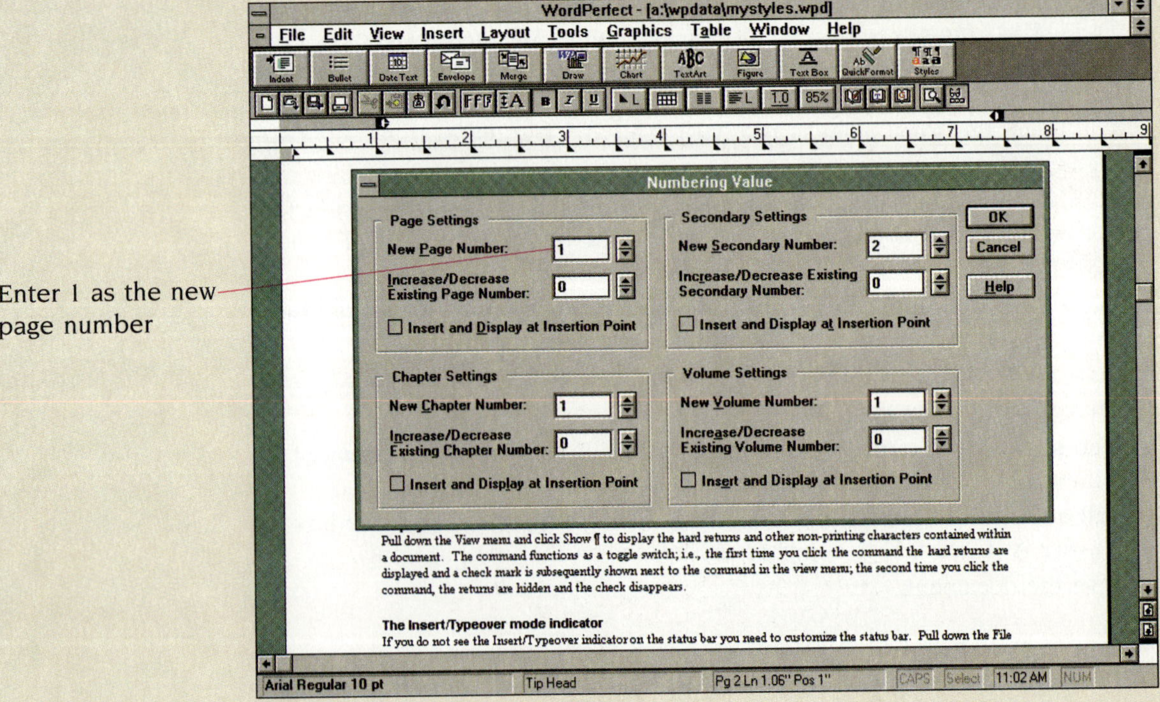

(i) Adjusting the Page Numbers (step 11)

FIGURE 4.5 Hands-on Exercise 1 (continued)

- Pull down the **Edit menu.** Click **Go To.** Type **2** in the dialog box for page number and press the **enter key.**
- Pull down the **Layout menu.** Click **Page.** Click **Numbering.**
- Click the **Value command button** to produce the dialog box in Figure 4.5i. Type **1** as the New Page Number. Click **OK.** Click **Close.**
- Save the document. Print the completed document and review the tips at your leisure. Exit WordPerfect.

TABLES

The ***tables feature*** is one of the most powerful in WordPerfect and enables you to create an almost limitless variety of documents. The study schedule in Figure 4.6a, for example, is actually a 12 × 8 (12 rows and 8 columns) table as can be seen from the underlying structure in Figure 4.6b.

Tables such as the study schedule are created through commands in the Tables menu. The rows and columns in a table intersect to form ***cells.*** Commands operate on one or more cells. Individual cells can be joined together to form a larger cell as was done in the first and last rows of Figure 4.6. The rows within a table can be different heights, and each row may contain a different number of columns.

TABLES AND THE STATUS BAR

The cells in a table are identified by a column letter and a row number (identical to the convention used in a spreadsheet). Cell B4, for example, corresponds to the cell in column B, row 4. The Status Bar displays the location of the insertion point by showing the cell coordinates, provided the General Status option has been selected for display on the Status Bar.

Creating a Table

Invoking the ***Create command*** in the Table menu is the first step in creating a table. Execution of the command produces a dialog box in which you select the number of rows and columns—for example, 12 and 8—respectively, for the table in Figure 4.6.

Once a table has been defined, you enter text in individual cells. Text wraps as it is entered within a cell, so that you can add or delete text in a cell without affecting the text in other cells. You can format the contents of an individual cell the same way you format an ordinary paragraph. You can change the font, use boldface or italics, change the justification, or apply any other formatting command. You can also select multiple cells and apply the formatting to all selected cells.

The ***Insert and Delete commands*** in the Table menu enable you to add new rows or columns, or delete existing rows or columns. You can invoke other commands to shade and/or border selected cells or the entire table. You can also change formatting in a single cell, a range of selected cells, or the entire table. You can join cells together or split cells apart. It's easy, and as you may have guessed, it's time for another hands-on exercise.

Weekly Class and Study Schedule							
	Monday	Tuesday	Wednesday	Thursday	Friday	Saturday	Sunday
8:00AM							
9:00AM							
10:00AM							
11:00AM							
12:00PM							
1:00PM							
2:00PM							
3:00PM							
4:00PM							
Notes							

(a) The Completed Table

(b) Underlying Structure

FIGURE 4.6 The Tables Feature

TABLES AND THE QUICKMENU

Point to any cell in a table, then click the right mouse button to produce a QuickMenu listing available commands from the Table menu.

HANDS-ON EXERCISE 2:

Creating a Table

Objective To create a table; to change row heights and column widths; to join cells together; to apply borders and shading to selected cells. Use Figure 4.7 as a guide.

Step 1: Page Setup

- Pull down the **Layout menu.** Click **Margins.** Set the left and right margins to **.50** inch. Set the top and bottom margins to **.75** inch. Click **OK.**
- Pull down the **Layout menu** a second time. Click **Page.** Click **Paper Size** to produce the dialog box in Figure 4.7a.
- Scroll through the open list box until you are able to select **Letter Landscape.**

Step 2: Create the table

- Pull down the **View menu.** Click **Page.** Pull down the **View menu** a second time. Zoom to **Page Width.**
- The ruler extends to 11 inches, which is consistent with the landscape orientation. The left and right margins are set at .5 inch each, consistent with the margin commands from step 1.
- Pull down the **Table menu.** Click **Create** to produce the dialog box in Figure 4.7b.
- Enter **8** and **12** as the number of columns and rows, respectively. Click **OK** to create the table shown in Figure 4.7c.
- Save the document as **STUDY.WPD.**

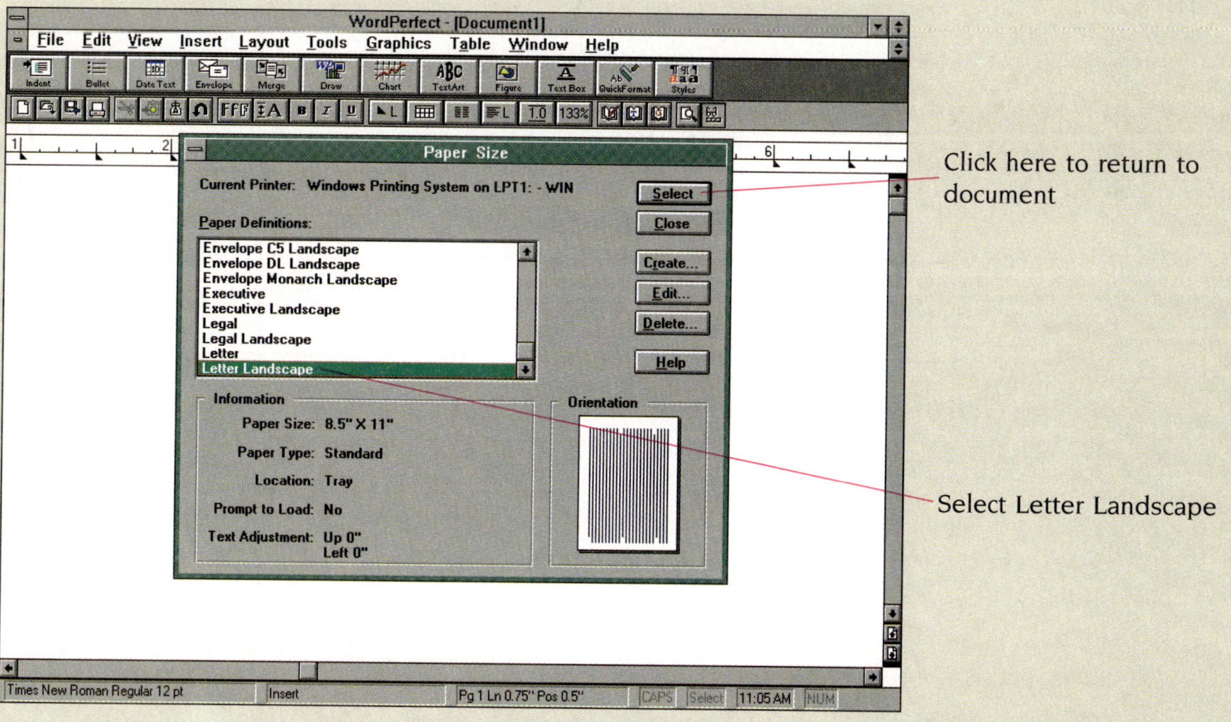

(a) Change the Orientation (step 1)

FIGURE 4.7 Hands-on Exercise 2

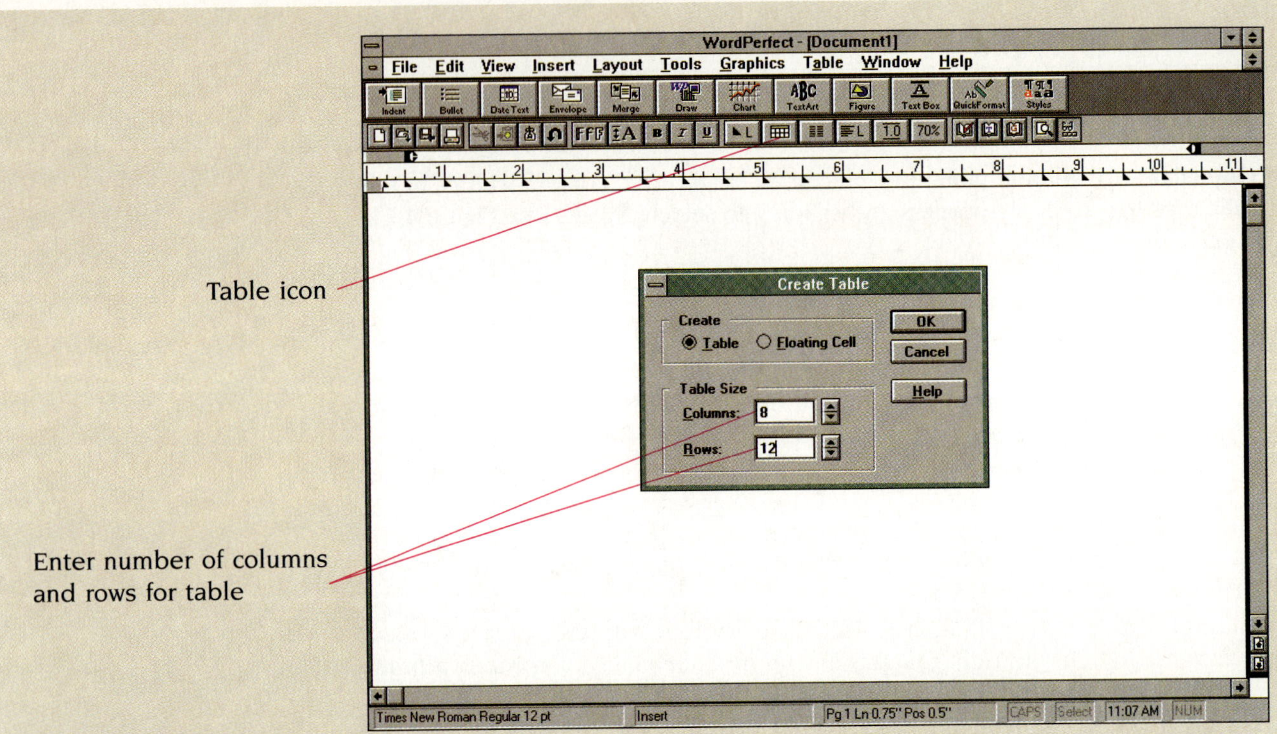

(b) Create the Table (step 2)

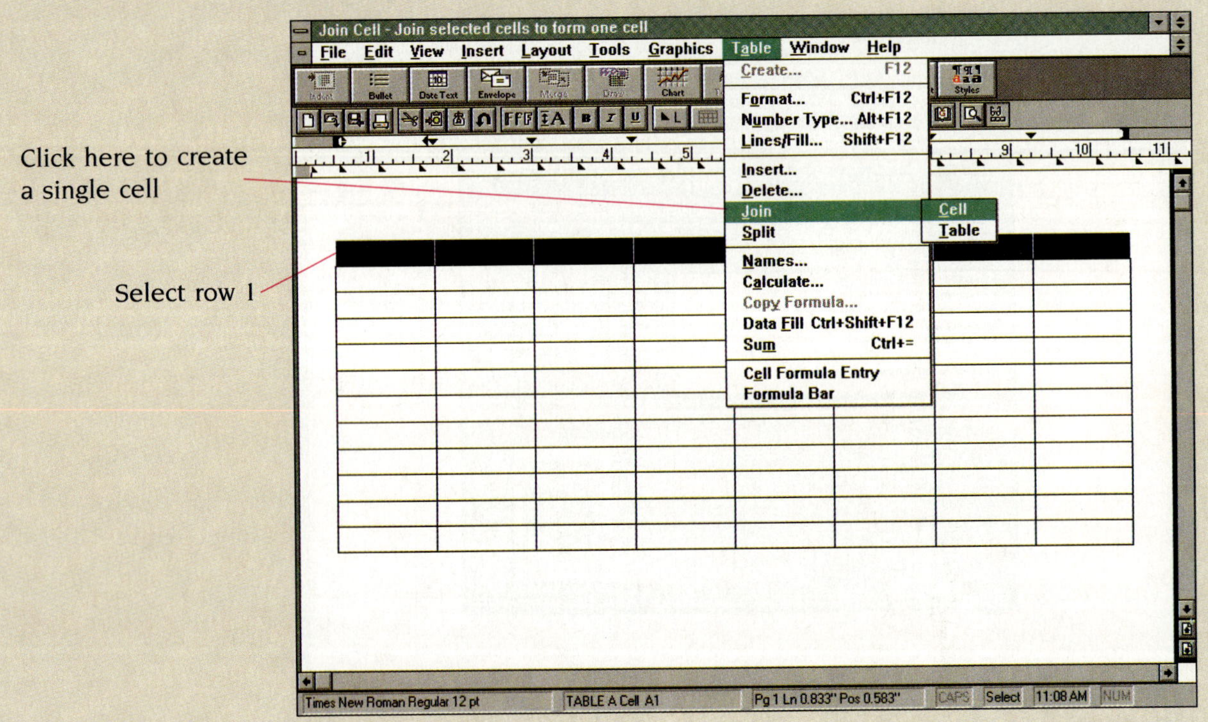

(c) Join the Cells (step 4)

FIGURE 4.7 Hands-on Exercise 2 (continued)

THE TABLE ICON

The fastest way to create a table is to use the Table icon on the Power Bar. Click the Table icon to display a grid, then drag the mouse across and down the grid until you have the desired number of rows and columns. Release the mouse to insert the table into the document.

Step 3: Table basics

- Practice moving within the table:
  - If the cells in the table are empty, press the **left and right arrow keys** to move from column to column. If the cells contain text, press **Tab** and **Shift+Tab.**
  - Press the **up and down arrow keys** to move from row to row.
- Select a cell, row, column, or block of contiguous cells.
  - To select a cell, point to the **left or top border** of the cell (the pointer changes to an arrow) and click.
  - To select a row, point to the **left border** of any cell in the row (the pointer changes to an arrow) and double click.
  - To select a column, point to the **top border** of any cell in that column (the pointer changes to an arrow) and double click.
  - To select adjacent cells or multiple rows and columns, drag the mouse over the cells.

TABS AND TABLES

The Tab key functions differently in a table than in a regular document. Press the **Tab** key to move to the next cell in the current row (or to the first cell in the next row if you are at the end of a row). Press **Shift+Tab** to move to the previous cell in the current row (or to the last cell in the previous row). Press **Ctrl+Tab** to insert a tab character at the insertion point.

Step 4: Join the cells

- Point to the **left border** of any cell in the first row (the mouse pointer changes to an arrow). Double click the mouse to select the entire row as shown in Figure 4.7c.
- Pull down the **Table menu.** Click **Join.** Click **Cell** to create a single cell.
- Type **Weekly Class and Study Schedule.** Use the Power Bar to change the font and justification as follows:
  - Select the text **Weekly Class and Study Schedule.**
  - Click the **Font icon** to choose an appropriate font—for example, **Arial.**
  - Click the **Font size icon** to choose an appropriate size—for example, **24** point.

— Click the **Bold icon** on the Power Bar.

— Click the **Justification icon** and **center** the text.

➤ Click outside the selected text to continue working in the table.

➤ Point to the **left border** of any cell in the last row (the mouse pointer changes to an arrow). Double click the mouse to select the entire row.

➤ Pull down the **Table menu.** Click **Join.** Click **Cell** to create a single cell.

➤ Type **Notes** and format the entry in 12 point Arial Bold.

➤ Save the table.

Step 5: Enter the days and hours

➤ Click the second cell in the second row. Type **Monday.**

➤ Press the **Tab** (or **right arrow**) **key** to move to the next cell. Type **Tuesday.** Continue until the days of the week have been entered.

➤ Use the Power Bar to change the font and justification as follows:

— Select the entire row as shown in Figure 4.7d.

— Click the **Font icon** to choose an appropriate font—for example, **Arial.**

— Click the **Font size icon** to choose an appropriate size—for example, **10** point.

— Click the **Justification icon** and **center** the text.

— Click anywhere in the table to deselect the text and see the effect of the formatting change.

➤ Click the first cell in the third row. Type **8:00AM.** Press the **down arrow key** to move to the first cell in the fourth row. Type **9:00AM.** Continue in this

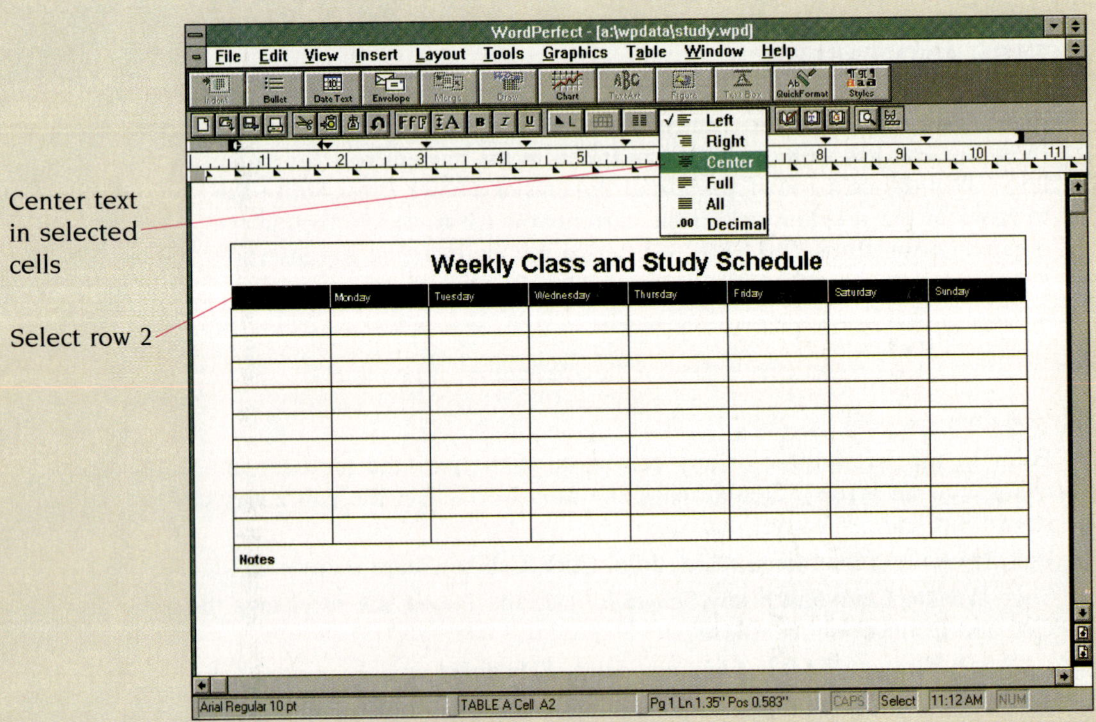

(d) Formatting Table Entries (step 5)

FIGURE 4.7 Hands-on Exercise 2 (continued)

fashion until you have entered the hourly periods up to 4:00PM. Format as appropriate.

- Save the table.

UPPERCASE, LOWERCASE, AND INITIAL CAPS

The Edit Convert Case command is the ideal way to recover from accidentally toggling the Caps Lock key on or off. Select the text you wish to change, pull down the Edit menu, and click Convert Case. Click Uppercase, Lowercase, or Initial Capitals, then deselect the text to continue working in the document.

Step 6: Change the row heights

- Click in the cell for Notes immediately after the letter S. Press the **enter key** five times. The height of the cell increases automatically to accommodate the additional carriage returns.
- Select the cells containing the hours of the day. Pull down the **Table menu.** Click **Format.**
- Click the **Row option button** to produce the dialog box in Figure 4.7e. The dialog box indicates that you are referencing rows 3 to 11.
- Click the option button for **Fixed Row Height.** Type **.5** to set the row height of the selected rows. Click **OK.** Click outside the selected cells to see the new row heights.
- Save the document.

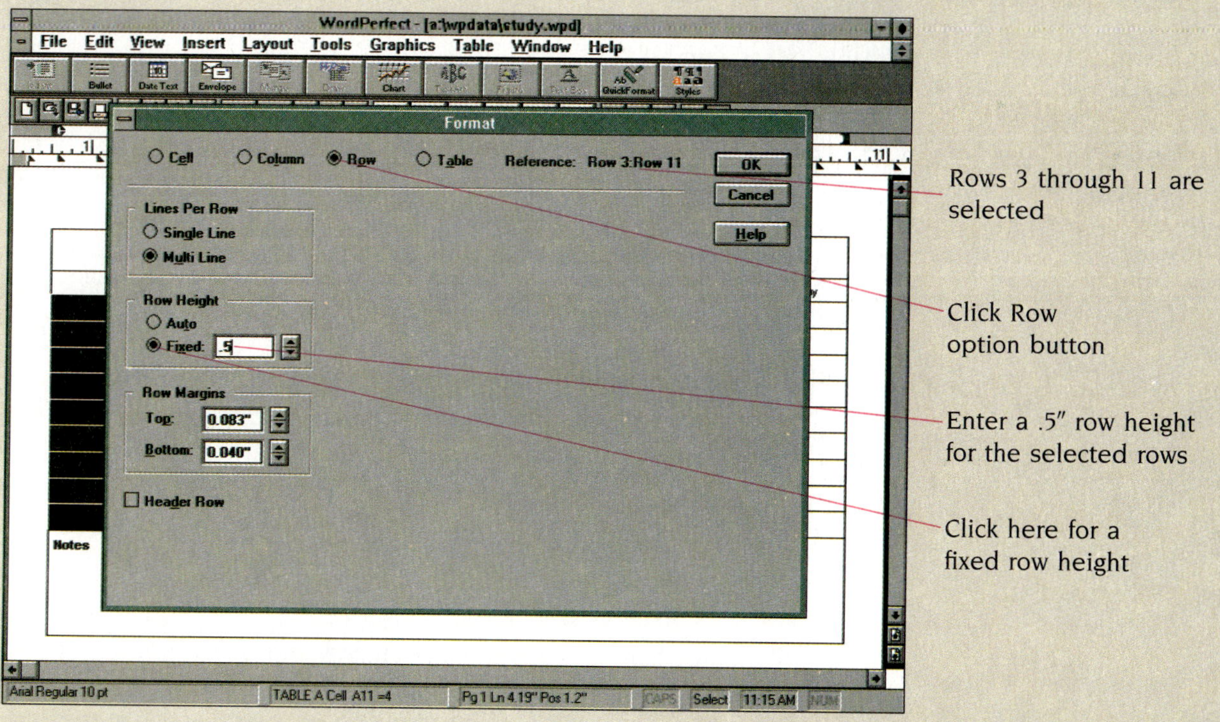

(e) Changing the Row Heights (step 6)

FIGURE 4.7 Hands-on Exercise 2 (continued)

CHANGE THE COLUMN WIDTH

The Ruler Bar is the fastest way to change the column widths in a table. Click anywhere in the column whose width you want to change, then drag the inverted triangle (▼) on the ruler to the right (left) to increase (decrease) the width of the column.

Step 7: Access the QuickMenu

- Zoom to **Full Page** to see the entire table, which should fit on a single page as shown in Figure 4.7f. Delete one or two hard returns from the Notes cell if the table continues to a second page.
- Select the first two rows of the table.
- Click the **right mouse button** to produce the QuickMenu shown in Figure 4.7f.

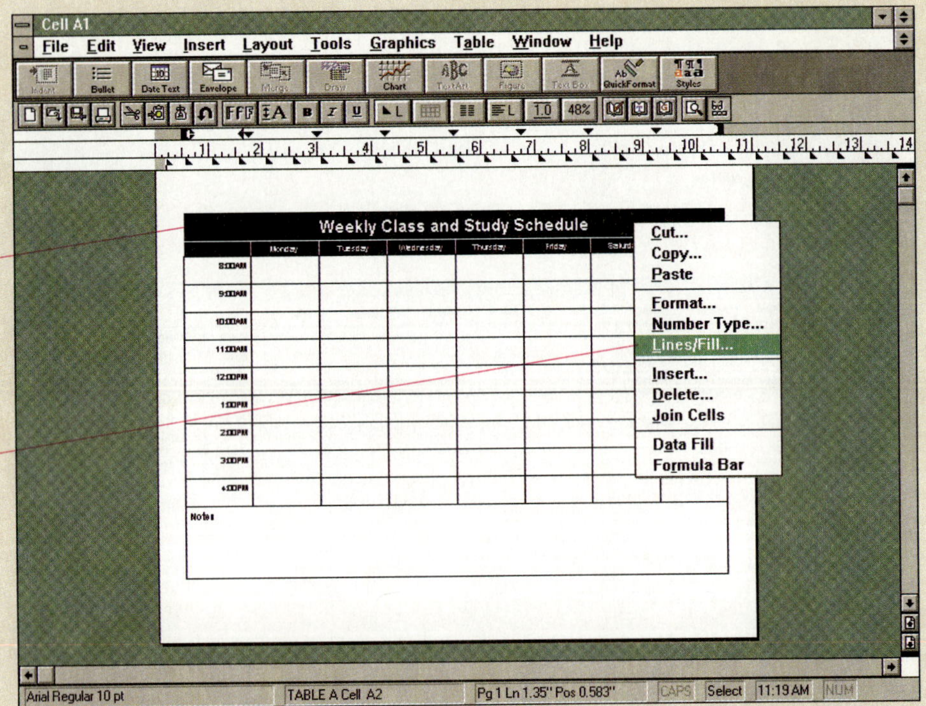

(f) The Table QuickMenu (step 7)

FIGURE 4.7 Hands-on Exercise 2 (continued)

Step 8: The Line/Fill command

- Click the **Lines/Fill** command from the QuickMenu to produce the dialog box in Figure 4.7g.
- Click the arrow in the drop-down list box next to Fill Style. Click **10% Fill** as shown in Figure 4.7g.
- Click **OK** to close the dialog box.
- Click outside the selected rows.

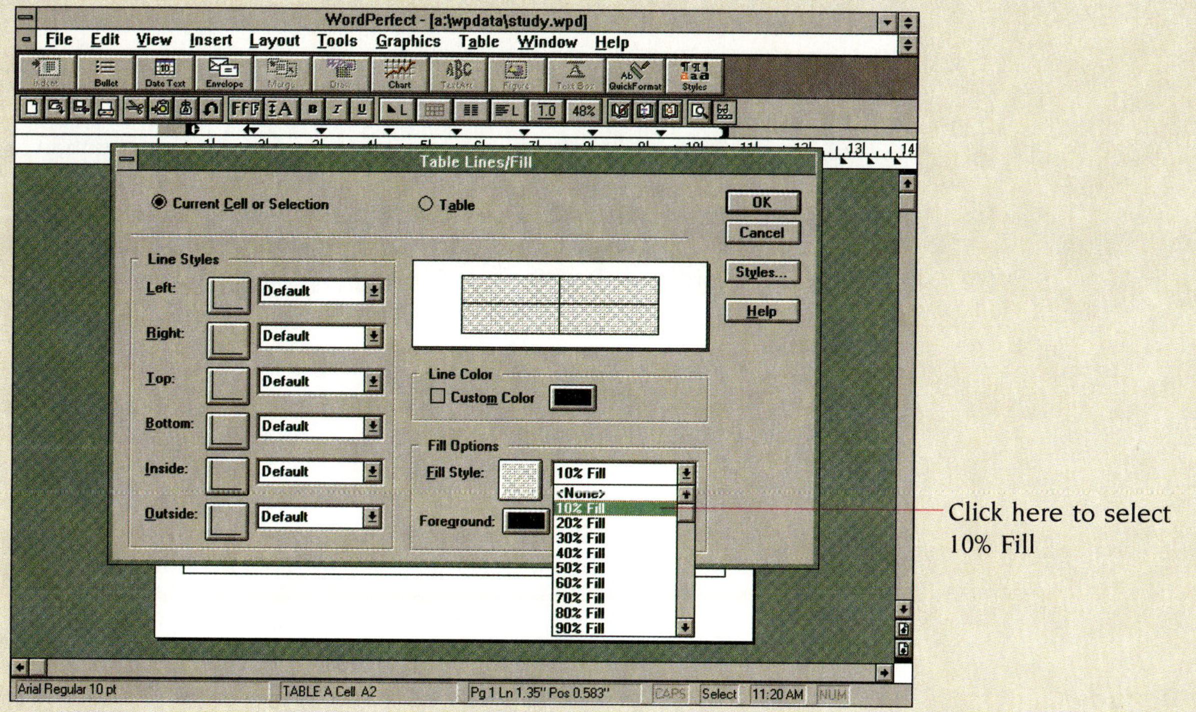

(g) The Lines/Fill Command (step 8)

Step 9: The completed schedule

- ➤ The completed schedule is shown in Figure 4.7h.
- ➤ Save the table. Print the table. Exit WordPerfect.

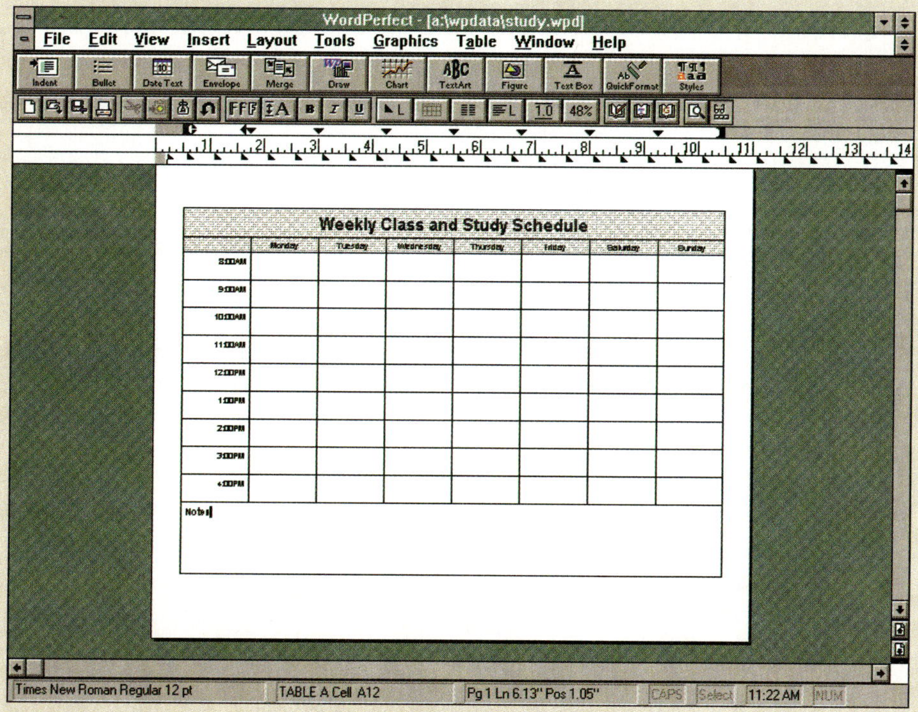

(h) The Completed Table (step 9)

FIGURE 4.7 Hands-on Exercise 2 (continued)

EXPRESSDOCS AND TABLES

The tables feature can be extended to many other examples, and we hope you apply the concepts in the hands-on exercise to tables of your own design. The only limitation is your own imagination.

Figure 4.8 contains three additional examples to further illustrate the tables feature. Unlike the study schedule these tables were not created from scratch, but were based on ***ExpressDoc templates*** included with WordPerfect. Recall from Chapter 3 that a template is a partially completed document that contains text and/or formatting information. The template may also contain one or more fields that require information from outside the template—for example, the user's name or address.

ExpressDoc templates, be they tables or ordinary documents, are accessed from the File menu by executing the Template command, then double clicking the specific template from the available list box. WordPerfect will prompt for any additional information (fields) it might need, then use the ***Autofill macro*** to create a new document based on the template, the personal data common to all ExpressDocs, and the template specific information you supplied. The newly created document can be saved under its own name and treated like any other document.

Modifying a Table

Some ExpressDoc templates need little, if any, modification. The tables in Figure 4.8, for example, were generated almost entirely by the Autofill macro and required little change. Other templates, however, require more substantial modifications in order to be useful.

Figure 4.9 contains two versions of a class schedule: the ExpressDoc template provided by WordPerfect in Figure 4.9a and the completed schedule in Figure 4.9b. At first glance, the only changes appear to be the completed course data. Look closely, however, and note the following:

- The completed schedule contains an additional column for the Instructor's name
- The completed schedule contains an additional row to accommodate a fifth course.

The changes were implemented through the Insert command in the Table menu, which adds rows and columns as necessary. Note, too, that the field names in the template of Figure 4.9a have been replaced by the student's name, semester, and year in the completed schedule in Figure 4.9b. This was done automatically by the Autofill macro, which prompts for the template-specific information when the ExpressDoc template is retrieved initially. Recall, however, the distinction between fields enclosed in angled brackets that represent personal data (e.g., <Name>), versus those in square brackets that pertain to the specific template (e.g., [Semester] and [Year]).

Other modifications can be implemented through the ***Table Format command,*** which lets you fine tune the row height or column width by selecting the

> **BLOCK PROTECT A TABLE**
>
> A table inserted into a multipage document will be broken arbitrarily by ordinary pagination, but you can use the Block Protect feature to keep the table together. Select the entire table, pull down the Layout menu, click Page, and click Keep Text Together. Click Keep Selected Text on Same Page. Click OK.

Daily Planner

Robert Grauer
1718 Vestal Drive
Coral Springs, FL 33071
(305) 753-0345
Fax: (305)753-1752

Morning Appointments	Afternoon Appointments
7:00	1:00
7:30	1:30
8:00	2:00
8:30	2:30
9:00	3:00
9:30	3:30
10:00	4:00
10:30	4:30
11:00	5:00
11:30	5:30
12:00	6:00

✓	Things To Do Today

Daily Record of Events - Notes, Conversations

Today

Daily Expenses

(a) Daily Planner (PLANDAY Template)

Application For Employment

Hurricane HotLine
Student Union - Room 421
Coral Gables, Florida 33124
(305) 284-CALL
Fax: (305)284-FAXX

Personal Information	
Name:	Date:
Social Security Number:	
Home Address:	
City, State, Zip	
Home Phone:	Business Phone:
US Citizen?	If Not Give Visa No. & expiration:

Position Applying For	
Title:	Salary Desired:
Referred By:	Date Available:

Education	
High School (Name, City, State):	
Graduation Date:	
Business or Technical School:	
Dates Attended:	Degree, Major:
Undergraduate College:	
Dates Attended:	Degree, Major:
Graduate School:	
Dates Attended:	Degree, Major:

References

(b) Job Application (JOBAPP Template)

1994 *March* 1994

SUNDAY	MONDAY	TUESDAY	WEDNESDAY	THURSDAY	FRIDAY	SATURDAY
		1	2	3	4	5
6	7	8	9	10	11	12
13	14	15	16 *Jessica's Birthday*	17	18	19
20	21	22	23	24	25	26
27	28	29	30	31		

(c) Calendar (CAL_SIDE Template)

FIGURE 4.8 What You Can Do with Tables

appropriate commands from the Table menu. (Some cells are protected, however, and it is necessary to ***disable cell locks*** to modify the ExpressDoc templates.) The exercise that follows has you retrieve the templates in Figures 4.8 and 4.9 in order to tailor the tables for your personal use.

Class Schedule

<Name>
[Semester]
[Year]

Class	Time	Bldg/Room	Mon	Tue	Wed	Thu	Fri

(a) CLASSCHD Template (original table)

Class Schedule

Heather Bond
Spring
1994

Class	Instructor	Time	Bldg/Room	Mon	Tue	Wed	Thu	Fri
CIS120	Barber	10:50	Jenkins 402		X		X	
ECO211	Foley	12:15	Jenkins 301		X		X	
MAS201	Cuffe	9:00	Jenkins 408	X		X		X
THA330	Plant	10:00	Memorial 215	X		X		X
HIS301	Sacasas	12:00	Memorial 110	X		X		X

(b) Completed Table (at end of exercise)

FIGURE 4.9 Modifying a Table

HANDS-ON EXERCISE 3:

ExpressDocs and Tables

Objective To use the ExpressDocs feature to create and modify a table; to select individual cells, rows, and columns, and change the formatting characteristics; to specify different borders and shading for various cells. Use Figure 4.10 as a guide.

Step 1: Open the CLASSCHD template

- Pull down the **File menu.**
- Click **Template** to produce the dialog box in Figure 4.10a.
- Scroll through the open list box until you can select the **CLASSCHD** template.
- You will see a message indicating that the Autofill macro is executing, after which you will see the table and dialog box in Figure 4.10b.

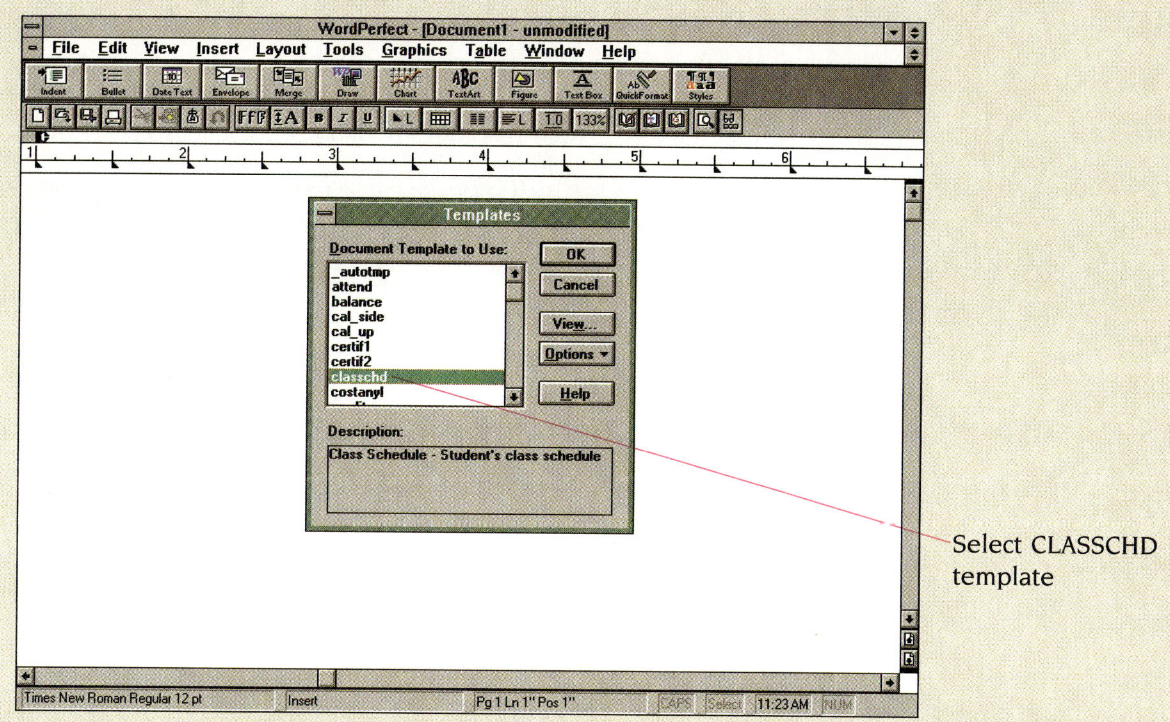

(a) File Template Command (step 1)

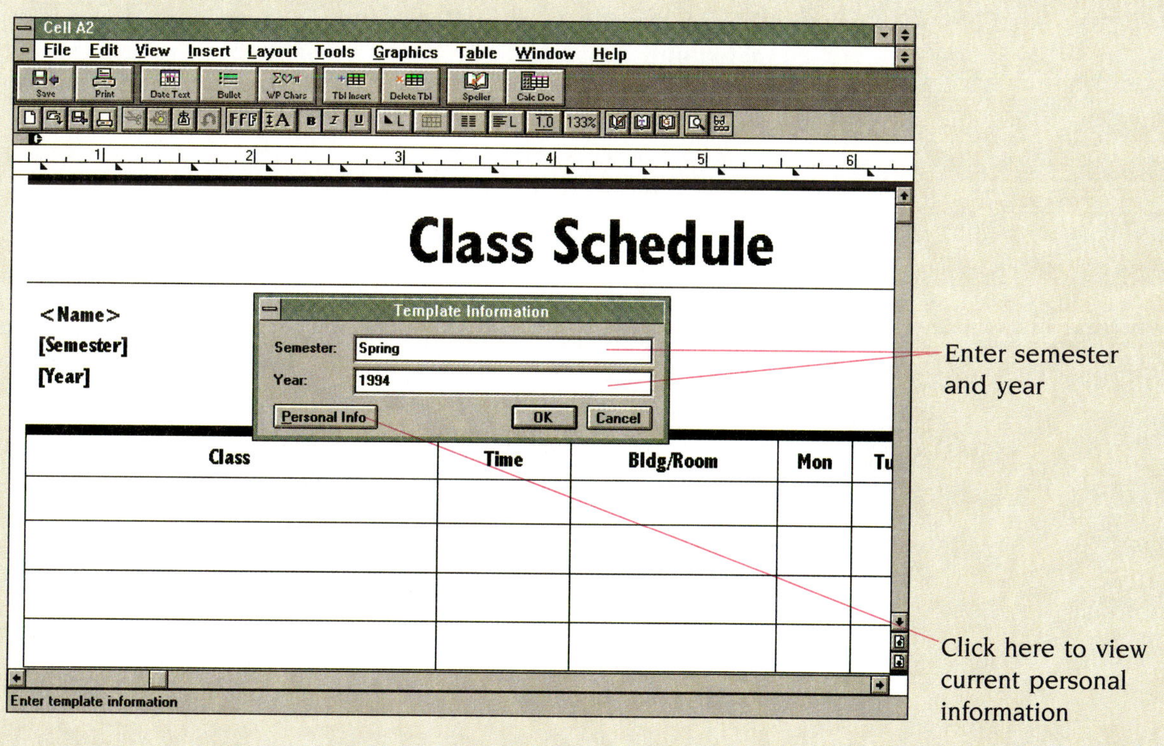

(b) Supply the Template Information (step 2)

FIGURE 4.10 Hands-on Exercise 3

MOVE QUICKLY THROUGH A LIST BOX

Click in an open list box, then type the first letter of the item you want to select. WordPerfect will scroll through the list box and automatically select the first item beginning with that letter. The technique works with all Windows applications.

Step 2: Supply the template information

- Press the **Personal Info command button** to view the information that is currently stored with the ExpressDoc templates. If necessary, change the existing data so that it reflects your personal information. Click **OK** to return to the dialog box in Figure 4.10b.
- Enter the semester and year as shown in Figure 4.10b, then click **OK** or press the **enter key.**
- You will again see a message indicating that the Autofill macro is executing, after which you will see the table for your class schedule.
- Save the document as **MYSCHED.WPD.**

Step 3: Disable the cell locks

- Click anywhere within the table.
- Press the **Tab, Shift+Tab, up,** and **down arrow keys** to move from one cell to the next. Do not be concerned if you cannot access the top row in the table.
- Pull down the **Table menu.** Click **Format.**
- Click the **Table option button** to produce the dialog box in Figure 4.10c. Check the box to **Disable Cell Locks** at the bottom center of the dialog box. Click **OK.**
- Use the arrow keys to move from cell to cell within the table. This time you should be able to access every cell.

Step 4: Add a row

- Click in cell A4 (the first empty cell in the leftmost column).
- Pull down the **Table menu.** Click **Insert** to produce the dialog box in Figure 4.10d.
- Click the option buttons to insert a row after the current row. Click **OK.**
- Pull down the **Table menu** a second time. Click **Insert.** Click the option button to insert a column after the current column. Click **OK.**
- Type **Instructor** as the heading in the new column.
- Save the document.

DELETING ROWS AND COLUMNS

The Del key does *not* delete the selected cell, row, or column in a table, but rather the contents of the selected cells. You must use the Delete command in the Table menu to delete rows or columns from a table.

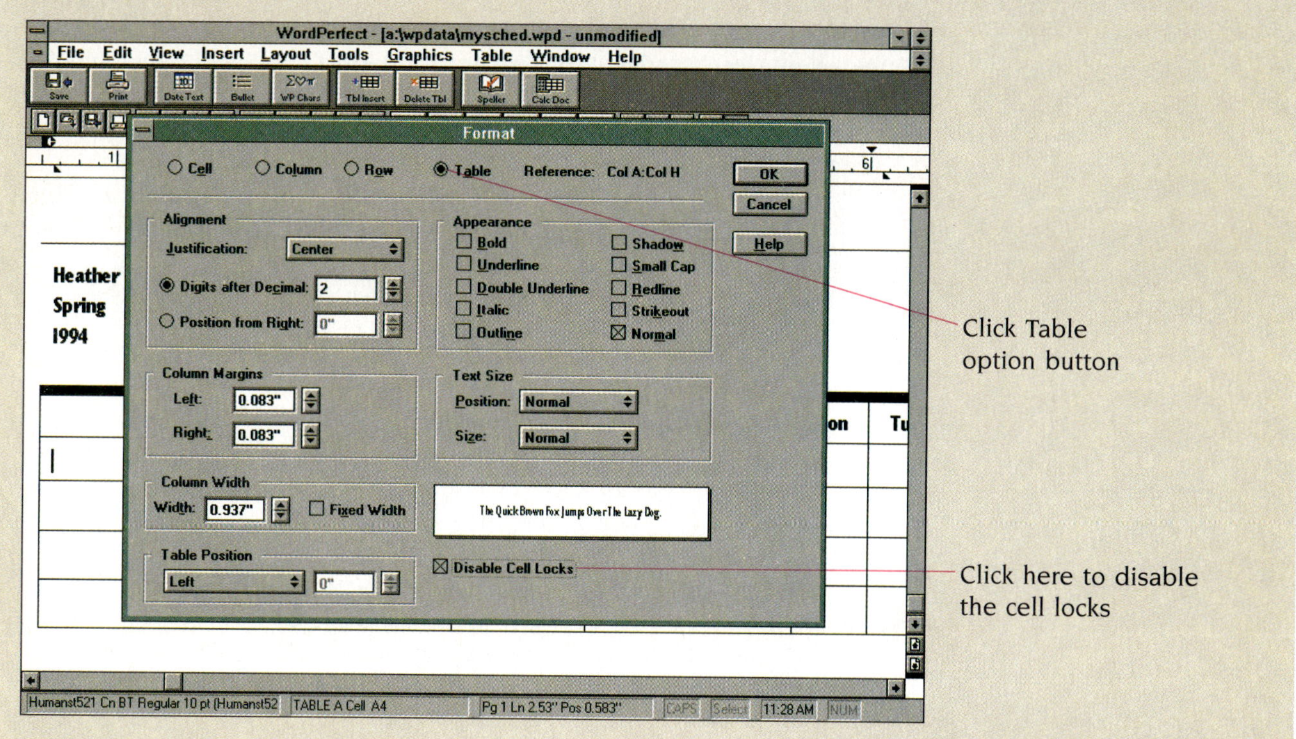

(c) Disable Cell Locks (step 3)

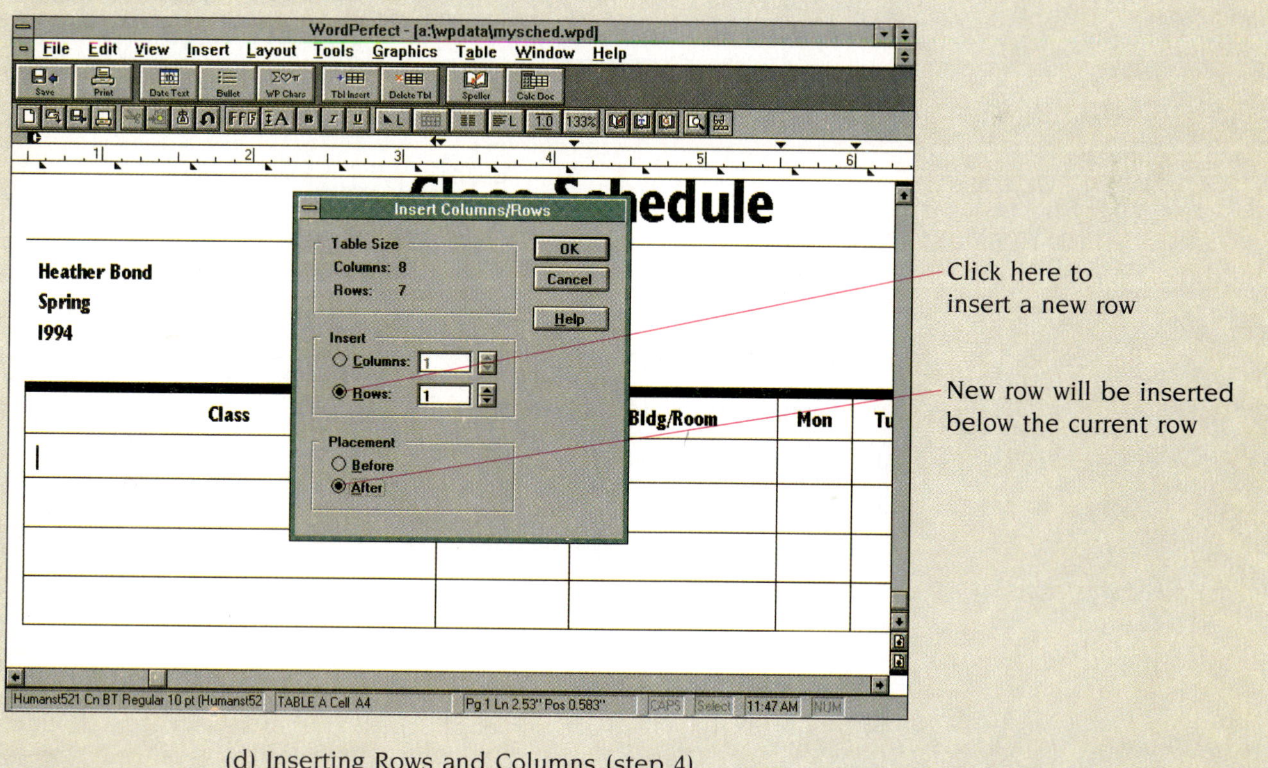

(d) Inserting Rows and Columns (step 4)

FIGURE 4.10 Hands-on Exercise 3 (continued)

Step 5: Complete the table

- Enter your class schedule as shown in Figure 4.10e. Change the font and justification as follows:
  - — Select the five rows containing the course information. Pull down the **Layout menu.** Click **Font.** Click **Arial.** Click **10** points. Click **OK.**
  - — Drag the mouse over the first two columns as shown in Figure 4.10e. Use the Justification icon on the Power Bar to center the text in the selected cells.
- Click outside the selected cells to see the effect of the formatting change.
- Save the schedule a final time. Print your schedule.

Step 6: The Daily Planner

- Pull down the **File menu.** Click **Template.**
- Scroll through the open list box until you can select the **PLANDAY** template.
- You will see a message indicating that the Autofill macro is executing, after which you will see the table in Figure 4.10f.
- Move through the table and enter your activities for the day.
- Save the document as **MYDAY.WPD.** Print the table.

Step 7: The Calendar

- Pull down the **File menu.** Click **Template.**
- Scroll through the open list box until you can select the **CAL_SIDE** template.
- Enter the month and year as shown in Figure 4.10g. Click **OK.**

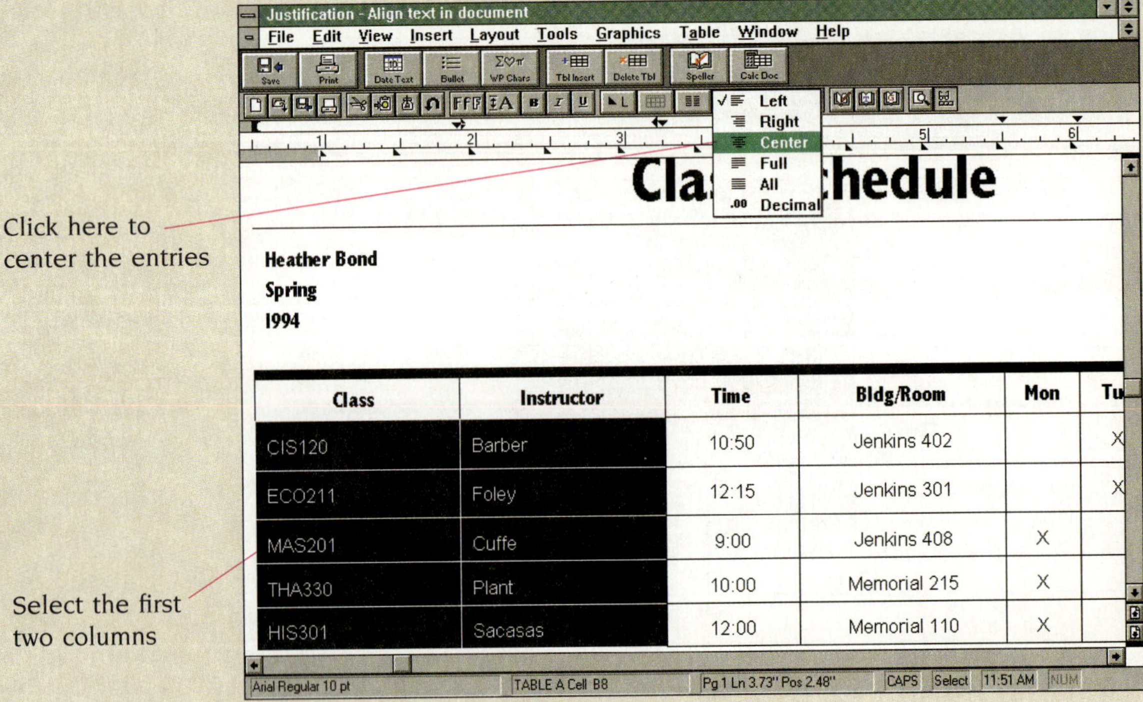

(e) The Completed Schedule (step 5)

FIGURE 4.10 Hands-on Exercise 3 (continued)

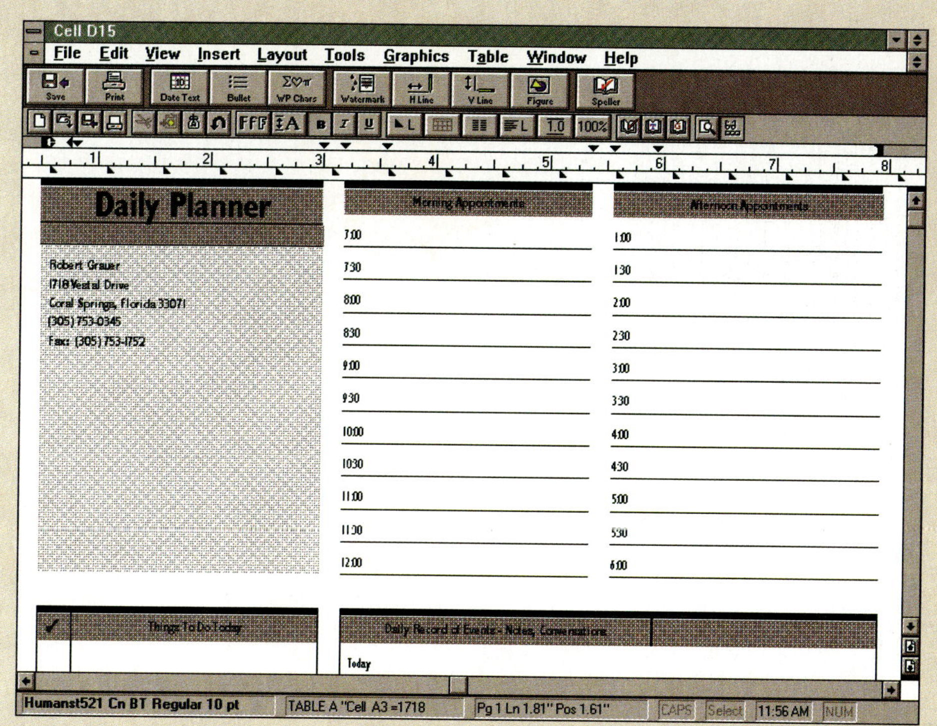

(f) The Daily Planner (step 6)

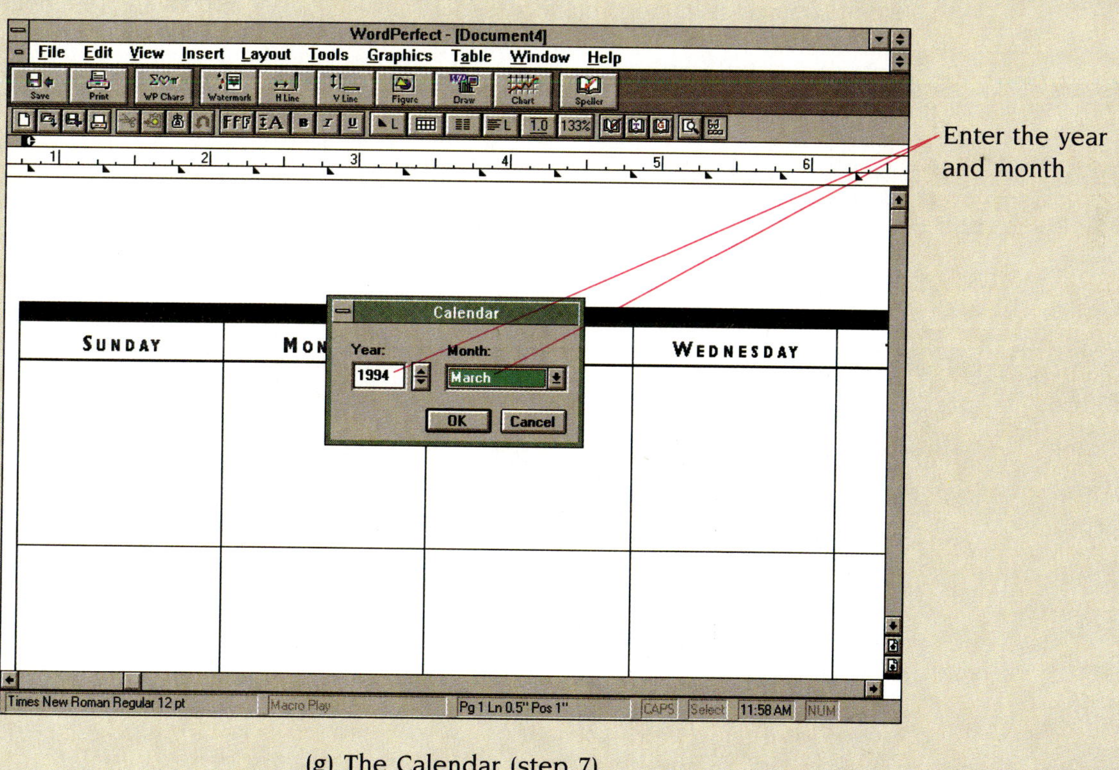

(g) The Calendar (step 7)

FIGURE 4.10 Hands-on Exercise 3 (continued)

- Be patient while WordPerfect creates the calendar. You will see a continual message at the bottom left of your screen as the different days are inserted into the calendar.
- Click the cell for any specific date and enter an appropriate note. Change the font and justification as appropriate.
- Save and print the calendar.
- Exit WordPerfect.

SUMMARY

A header consists of one or more lines that are printed at the top of every (designated) page. A footer is text that is printed at the bottom of every (designated) page. Page numbers may be added to either a header or footer. The Go To command is useful in long documents as it moves directly to a specific page or other designated position.

The Bullets & Numbers command creates a bulleted or numbered list. The bullet symbol and/or the numbering scheme can be changed by selecting the desired option within the associated dialog box.

A style is a set of formatting instructions that are saved under a distinct name. Styles automate the formatting process and provide a consistent appearance to similar elements within a document. Change the style, and you automatically change the appearance of all elements defined by that style. Styles are defined on the character, paragraph or document level.

The Create command in the Table menu is the first step in defining a table. Other commands in the Table menu insert or delete rows or columns, join or separate cells, or apply borders and shading. Many of the 45 ExpressDoc templates included with WordPerfect are tables that can be used as the basis for your own documents.

Key Words and Concepts

Autofill macro
Bookmark
Bulleted list
Bullets & Numbers command
Cell
Character style
Create Table command
Delete Column command
Delete Row command
Disable cell locks
Document style
ExpressDoc template
Footer
Go To command
Header
Insert Column command
Insert Row command
Layout Header/Footer command
Layout Style command
Numbered list
Page Numbering command
Paragraph style
QuickCreate
Style
Table Format command
Tables feature

Multiple Choice

1. What is the easiest way to move quickly to any of three major topics in a 20-page term paper that is undergoing continual revision?
   (a) Determine the starting page number for each topic, then use the Go To command to move to the appropriate page

(b) Define a bookmark at the beginning of each topic, then use the Go To command to move to the appropriate bookmark
(c) Drag the scroll box on the scroll bar to the approximate position in the document of the appropriate topic
(d) All of the above are equally acceptable

2. Which of the following can be stored within a paragraph style?
(a) Typeface, size, and attributes
(b) Margins and justification
(c) Both (a) and (b)
(d) Neither (a) nor (b)

3. What is the easiest way to change the justification of five paragraphs scattered throughout a document, each of which has been formatted according to the same style?
(a) Select the paragraphs individually, then click the icons on the tool bar to change the formatting
(b) Select the paragraphs at the same time, then click the icons on the toolbar to change the formatting
(c) Change the format of the existing style, which changes the paragraphs
(d) Retype the paragraphs according to the new specifications

4. In which view do you see page numbers?
(a) Page
(b) Draft
(c) Both (a) and (b)
(d) Neither (a) nor (b)

5. Which of the following numbering schemes can be used with page numbers?
(a) Roman numerals (I, II, III . . . or i, ii, iii . . .)
(b) Regular numbers (1, 2, 3 . . .)
(c) Letters (A, B, C . . . or a, b, c . . .)
(d) All of the above

6. Which of the following is true regarding headers and footers within a document?
(a) Every document must have at least one header
(b) Every document must have at least one footer
(c) Both (a) and (b)
(d) Neither (a) nor (b)

7. Which of the following is true regarding headers and footers within a document?
(a) A different header can be established for odd and even pages
(b) A different footer can be established for odd and even pages
(c) Both (a) and (b)
(d) Neither (a) nor (b)

8. Page numbers can be specified in:
(a) A header but not a footer
(b) A footer but not a header
(c) Either a header or a footer
(d) Neither a header nor a footer

9. Which of the following is true regarding the styles within a document?
   (a) One style can be applied to many paragraphs
   (b) One paragraph can have many styles
   (c) Both (a) and (b)
   (d) Neither (a) nor (b)

10. Which of the following modifications can be implemented on an ExpressDoc template?
    (a) A new row may be added or an existing row deleted
    (b) A new column may be added or an existing column deleted
    (c) Both (a) and (b)
    (d) Neither (a) nor (b)

11. What happens when you press the Tab key from within a table?
    (a) A Tab character is inserted just as it would be for ordinary text
    (b) The insertion point changes to the next column in the same row or the first column in the next row if you are at the end of the row
    (c) Both (a) and (b)
    (d) Neither (a) nor (b)

12. Which of the following is true about a WordPerfect table?
    (a) Every row must be the same height as every other row
    (b) Every row must contain the same number of columns as every other row
    (c) Both (a) and (b)
    (d) Neither (a) nor (b)

13. The Edit Go To command enables you to move the insertion point to:
    (a) A specific page
    (b) A specific cell within a table
    (c) A bookmark
    (d) All of the above

14. Which of the following is true about the ExpressDoc templates?
    (a) Every ExpressDoc template must be based on a table
    (b) Every ExpressDoc template must contain one or more fields
    (c) Both (a) and (b)
    (d) Neither (a) nor (b)

15. Which of the following is a *false* statement regarding lists?
    (a) A bulleted list can be changed to a numbered list and vice versa
    (b) The symbol for the bulleted list can be changed to a different character
    (c) The numbers in a numbered list can be changed to roman numerals
    (d) The bullets or numbers cannot be removed

ANSWERS

1. b	**6.** d	**11.** b
2. c	**7.** c	**12.** d
3. c	**8.** c	**13.** d
4. a	**9.** a	**14.** d
5. d	**10.** c	**15.** d

EXPLORING WORDPERFECT

1. Use Figure 4.11 to match each action with its result; a given action may be used more than once.

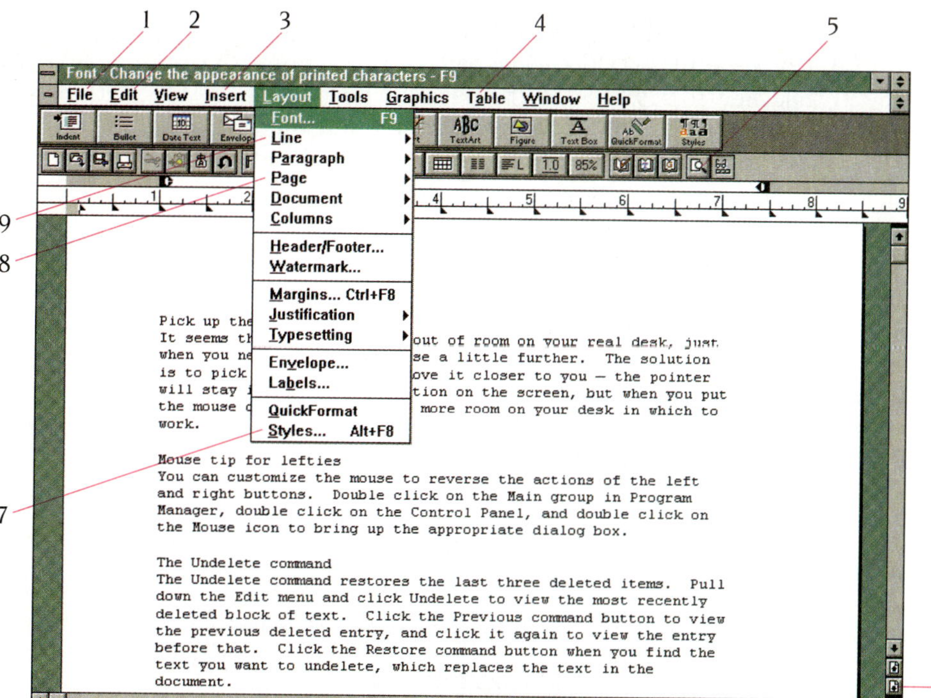

FIGURE 4.11 Screen for Problem 1

Action		Result
a. Click at 1	___	Insert page numbers in a document
b. Click at 2	___	Create a numbered list
c. Click at 3	___	Edit an existing style
d. Click at 4	___	Prevent widows and orphans in the document
e. Click at 5	___	Scroll down one page in the document
f. Click at 6	___	Zoom to full page view
g. Click at 7	___	Create a 4 × 12 table
h. Click at 8	___	Go to a specific page number
i. Click at 9	___	Create a bulleted list
	___	Open an ExpressDoc template

2. Styles, headers, and footers: Open the document WINDTIPS.WPD on the data disk and use it for the remainder of the exercise.

   a. What is the name of the style in effect for the text of the individual tips? What are the specifications for this style? Change the specifications to include a different typeface and/or a different type size.

   b. What is the name of the style in effect for the tip headings? What are the current specifications for this style? Change the specifications for the style to include a different typeface, boldface or italics as appropriate, and/or a different type size.

c. Create different headers for the even and odd pages; the title of the document, *48 Windows Tips,* is left justified on the even header, whereas the odd header should right justify the authors' names, *Grauer and Barber.* Both headers are to be set in 8 point capital letters. Change the top margin to .75 inch to accommodate the header.

d. Create a title page: 48 Windows Tips by Grauer and Barber. Add a second line somewhere on the page indicating that the tips were prepared for you (and include your name) so that the instructor will know the assignment came from you. Do not print a header on the title page.

e. Include page numbers at the beginning (end) of the header similar to the way the page numbers appear in a book. The page number is to appear before the text of the header on an even page and after it on an odd page.

3. Sports fans: The tables feature is perfect to display the standings in any league, be it amateur or professional. Figure 4.12, for example, shows hypothetical standings of the NFL and was a breeze. Pick any sport or league that you like and create a table with the standings as of today.

AMERICAN CONFERENCE *Standings as of October 25, 1993*				
EAST	Wins	Losses	Ties	Percent
Miami	5	1	0	.833
Buffalo	5	1	0	.833
New York Jets	2	4	0	.333
Indianapolis	2	4	0	.333
New England	1	6	0	.149
Central	Wins	Losses	Ties	Percent
Cleveland	5	2	0	.774
Pittsburgh	4	3	0	.571
Houston	3	4	0	.429
Cincinnati	0	7	0	.000
West	Wins	Losses	Ties	Percent
Kansas City	5	1	0	.833
L.A. Raiders	4	2	0	.667
Seattle	4	3	0	.571
Denver	3	3	0	.500
San Diego	2	4	0	.333

FIGURE 4.12 Table for Problem 3

4. The table in Figure 4.13 exists on the data disk but without formatting and with missing data. Retrieve the document PROB0404.WPD from the data disk, then implement the necessary commands so that your document matches ours. Better yet, change the formatting and improve on our design. Be sure you add a row to the bottom of the table with prices for a Pentium configuration. (Add $400 to each of the prices in the previous row.)

A sleek, fast machine is within your grasp!

CHEETAH COMPUTERS

Our tremendous sales volume enables us to offer the fastest, most powerful series of 486 computers at prices almost too good to be true. Each microprocessor is offered in a variety of configurations so that you can get exatly what you need. All configurations include a local bus video, a 15 inch monitor, a mouse, Windows 3.1, and DOS 6.0

	Configuration 1 *4Mb RAM* *130Mb Hard Drive*	Configuration 2 *8Mb RAM* *245Mb Hard Drive*	Configuration 3 *16Mb RAM* *540Mb Hard Drive*
486SX-25Mz	$1695	$1995	$2295
486DX-33Mz	$1895	$2195	$2495
486DX2-50Mz	$2095	$2395	$2695
486DX2-66Mz	$2295	$2595	$2895

FIGURE 4.13 Table for Problem 4

5. ExpressDocs and Time Management: WordPerfect supplies ExpressDoc templates for a daily, weekly, and monthly calendar.

   a. Use the PLANDAY template to create a detailed schedule for your busiest day next week.
   b. Use the PLANWEEK template to show your activities for next week.
   c. Use either the CAL_SIDE (landscape) or CAL_UP (portrait) template to create a monthly calendar.
   d. Which of the templates do you think is most useful? Remember, time management is one of the keys to success in school and in the workplace.

6. Exploring Coach: Answer the following with respect to Figure 4.14.
   a. What command(s) produced the dialog box in Figure 4.14?
   b. What is the difference between the Coach and the WordPerfect tutorial?
   c. Use Coach to guide you through a procedure you know—for example, headers and footers. Do you find it helpful?
   d. Use Coach to guide you through a procedure you don't know—for example, footnotes. Do you find it helpful?
   e. What is the difference between a footer and a footnote?

FIGURE 4.14 Dialog Box for Problem 6

Celebrity Golf Tournament		
Foursome	Tee Time	
Date	Fee	

FIGURE 4.15 Table for Problem 7

7. Graphics: A table may contain a graphic image in addition to text as shown by the document in Figure 4.15. (The golfer in the figure is included in the clip art supplied with WordPerfect.) Graphics are discussed in the next chapter, but we think you are ready now. It's not complicated; in fact, it's really very easy; just follow the steps below:

   a. Create the 3 × 3 table.
   b. Join the cells in columns one and two of row one and type the heading. Enter the text in the remaining cells as shown in the figure. Press the enter key three or four times to extend the cells in rows two and three.
   c. Join the cells in column three to create a single cell to hold the golfer.
   d. Pull down the Graphics menu. Click Figure. Double click the WPWIN60\GRAPHICS directory on drive C if it is not already open.
   e. Scroll through the list box containing the file names of the clip art images; click INKGOLF.WPG, then click OK to insert the golfer into the table.
   f. Add the finishing touches by changing fonts and/or using the Line/Fill command to add shading or borders to selected cells.

   Of course, it isn't quite that simple, but we think you get the idea. Good luck and feel free to improve on our design.

8. Graphics: The table in Figure 4.16 uses two different graphic images to describe the honeymoon packages. Reproduce the table in the figure or create a different design. By now you've mastered tables so you are on your own. Go to it!

FIGURE 4.16 Table for Problem 8

Milestones in Communications

We take for granted immediate news of everything that is going on in the world, but it was not always that way. Did you know, for example, that it took five months for Queen Isabella to hear of Columbus' discovery, or that it took two weeks for Europe to learn of Lincoln's assassination? We've done some research on milestones in communications and left the file for you (COMMUN.WPD). It runs for two, three, or four pages, depending on the formatting, which we leave to you. We would like you to include a header, and we think you should box the quotations that appear at the end of the document (it's your call as to whether to separate the quotations or group them together). Please be sure to number the completed document and don't forget a title page.

The Term Paper

Go to your most demanding professor and obtain the formatting requirements for the submission of a term paper. Be as precise as possible; for example, ask about margins, type size, and so on. What are the requirements for a title page? Is there a table of contents? Are there footnotes or end notes, headers or footers? What is the format for the bibliography? Summarize the requirements, then indicate the precise means of implementation within WordPerfect for Windows.

Forms, Forms, and More Forms

Every business uses a multitude of forms. Job applicants submit an employment application, sales personnel process order forms, and customers receive invoices. Even telephone messages have a form of their own. The office manager needs forms for everything, and she has come to you for help. You remember reading something about a tables feature and suggest that as a starting point. She needs more guidance so you sit down with her and quickly design two forms that meet with her approval. Bring the two forms to class and compare your work with that of your classmates.

The Shareholders' Meeting

Your job as CEO also includes the requirement to address the stockholders at the annual meeting. You'll need some charts with the equivalent information as an annual report (use your imagination) but in bulleted form with a much more limited amount of text. The charts should have a consistent look, be done in a larger type size, and be printed with landscape orientation. Use WordPerfect for Windows to create a suitable presentation (six charts will do). ExpressDoc templates may help. You might also explore the availability of presentation graphic programs to achieve the same result.

5

Desktop Publishing: Creating a Newsletter

CHAPTER OBJECTIVES

After reading this chapter you will be able to:

1. Create a multicolumn document and vary the number of columns in a document.
2. Use the Border/Fill command to box and/or shade text.
3. Define an embedded object; distinguish between the server and client applications, and between the source and destination documents.
4. Insert a graphic into a document; move and size the graphic; use WP Draw to edit the graphic.
5. Use TextArt to create graphic effects with text.
6. Discuss the importance of a grid in the design of a document; describe the use of white space as a design element.

OVERVIEW

Desktop publishing evolved through a combination of technologies including faster computers, laser printers, and sophisticated page composition software to manipulate text and graphics. Today's generation of word processors has matured to such a degree that it is difficult to tell where word processing ends and desktop publishing begins. WordPerfect for Windows is, for all practical purposes, a desktop publishing program that can be used to produce all types of documents.

The essence of desktop publishing is the merging of text with graphics to produce a professional-looking document without reliance on external services. Desktop publishing will save you time and money because you are doing work that used to be done by others; in practice it is not so easy because you are doing work that was done by others who were skilled and experienced in their respective areas. Suffice it to say that in addition to learning the commands within WordPerfect to implement desktop publishing, you also need to be familiar with the basics of graphic design.

This chapter focuses on desktop publishing as it is implemented in WordPerfect; it also includes a brief introduction to graphic design. We show you how to create a multi-column document, how to import graphic images, and how to edit those images as embedded objects. We include an introduction to WP Draw and TextArt, two applications that are optionally installed with WordPerfect. We conclude with several guidelines to help you create a more polished document.

THE NEWSLETTER

The entire chapter is driven by the newsletter of Figure 5.1, which illustrates the most basic capabilities of desktop publishing. These include the ability to:

- Switch fonts within a document
- Use newspaper-style columns
- Include graphic elements
- Preview the document on the screen and manipulate its various elements

The hands-on exercises in this chapter help you create the newsletter(s) in the figure. We think you will be pleased at how easy the process is and hope that you go on to create more sophisticated designs.

Figure 5.1a shows the newsletter as it exists on the data disk. We supply the text, but the formatting is up to you. Figure 5.1b shows the newsletter at the end of the first hands-on exercise. It contains balanced newspaper columns, a masthead within thick parallel lines, and a shaded box to emphasize a specific paragraph.

THE SKIER'S HI

Contest Winner
Congratulations to Carol Vazquez Villar, who submitted the winning entry for our logo. Carol wins a pair of skis, boots, and poles, which she promises to show off at our next outing.

Warming Up
Ever pull a muscle skiing your first mogul? You should have stretched before you started — right? Not according to a panel of sports medicine experts put together by the National Strength and Conditioning Association.

Warming up, not stretching, is the most important thing you can do to prevent injuries. Muscles that are cold are not very pliable and thus are susceptible to injury. Even stretching should be put off until you warm up with a few minutes of light skiing (on the bunny hill, perhaps) to increase your metabolic rate and raise your body's core temperature. When should you stretch? After your exercise — when your muscles are warm.

Better Fit Than Fat
There is nothing like finishing a meal with a delicate French pastry or a luscious chocolate mousse, but how much will that indulgence cost in calories? And what will you look like on the beach if you keep treating yourself to such delights?

Exercise is important to weight control, giving you more caloric leeway in your diet and suppressing your appetite. The number of calories burned during physical exercise depends on many factors — how big you are (thinner, smaller people burn fewer calories at the same activity level as heavier, larger people), how hard or fast you work out (the harder the labor or faster the speed, the more calories you burn per minute), the air temperature (the colder the weather, the more calories you burn), the clothes you wear, the type of activity you choose, and the amount of time you spend doing it.

Some sports burn more fat than others. Start-Stop activities, such as tennis or sprinting, are primarily carbohydrate burning activities and use 60–70% carbohydrates and only 30–40% fat. Continuous sports on the other hand, such as walking, jogging, or skiing, consume 50–60% fat and 40–50% carbohydrates.

Any strenuous workout, be it jogging, energetic walking, biking, or swimming, is fine. The important thing is to make a commitment to exercise regularly, at least three to five times a week, every week. If you haven't exercised in a while, start off slowly and gradually build up to the level that you desire.

Exercise and Income
According to a recent Gallup poll, the higher a person's income, the more likely he or she is to exercise; for example, in households with an income over $30,000, 68% of the men and 60% of the women exercise regularly. In addition, people with college degrees are more likely to exercise than those with only high school diplomas.

The Sun and Your Skin
If you have blond or red hair and your eyes are blue, green, or gray, you are more prone to skin cancer. The harmful rays of the sun are the ultraviolet (UV) ones. Unlike the infrared rays that are screened by the clouds, the UV rays go right through. So even on overcast days you need to protect your skin with a sunscreen with a high SPF factor. The best sunscreens are those that contain PABA esters and benzophenones that protect against both UVA and UVB rays.

As a precaution against skin cancer, examine brown spots, birthmarks, moles, and sores that don't heal within two weeks. See your doctor immediately if you notice any change in shape or color.

Nastar Races
Ski our new slalom course on Saturday, March 15 at 5:00 PM, then meet friends and family at the lodge for dinner in front of the fireplace. Robert Plant, from the ski patrol not the concert circuit, will be our pacesetter. Can Robert beat 52 seconds setting the pace? Can you?

(a) Text for the Newsletter

THE SKIER'S HI

Contest Winner
Congratulations to Carol Vazquez Villar, who submitted the winning entry for our logo. Carol wins a pair of skis, boots, and poles, which she promises to show off at our next outing.

Warming Up
Ever pull a muscle skiing your first mogul? You should have stretched before you started — right? Not according to a panel of sports medicine experts put together by the National Strength and Conditioning Association.

Warming up, not stretching, is the most important thing you can do to prevent injuries. Muscles that are cold are not very pliable and thus are susceptible to injury. Even stretching should be put off until you warm up with a few minutes of light skiing (on the bunny hill, perhaps) to increase your metabolic rate and raise your body's core temperature. When should you stretch? After your exercise — when your muscles are warm.

Better Fit Than Fat
There is nothing like finishing a meal with a delicate French pastry or a luscious chocolate mousse, but how much will that indulgence cost in calories? And what will you look like on the beach if you keep treating yourself to such delights?

Exercise is important to weight control, giving you more caloric leeway in your diet and suppressing your appetite. The number of calories burned during physical exercise depends on many factors — how big you are (thinner, smaller people burn fewer calories at the same activity level as heavier, larger people), how hard or fast you work out (the harder the labor or faster the speed, the more calories you burn per minute), the air temperature (the colder the weather, the more calories you burn), the clothes you wear, the type of activity you choose, and the amount of time you spend doing it.

Some sports burn more fat than others. Start-Stop activities, such as tennis or sprinting, are primarily carbohydrate burning activities and use 60–70% carbohydrates and only 30–40% fat. Continuous sports on the other hand, such as walking, jogging, or skiing, consume 50–60% fat and 40–50% carbohydrates.

Any strenuous workout, be it jogging, energetic walking, biking, or swimming, is fine. The important thing is to make a commitment to exercise regularly, at least three to five times a week, every week. If you haven't exercised in a while, start off slowly and gradually build up to the level that you desire.

Exercise and Income
According to a recent Gallup poll, the higher a person's income, the more likely he or she is to exercise; for example, in households with an income over $30,000, 68% of the men and 60% of the women exercise regularly. In addition, people with college degrees are more likely to exercise than those with only high school diplomas.

The Sun and Your Skin
If you have blond or red hair and your eyes are blue, green, or gray, you are more prone to skin cancer. The harmful rays of the sun are the ultraviolet (UV) ones. Unlike the infrared rays that are screened by the clouds, the UV rays go right through. So even on overcast days you need to protect your skin with a sunscreen with a high SPF factor. The best sunscreens are those that contain PABA esters and benzophenones that protect against both UVA and UVB rays.

As a precaution against skin cancer, examine brown spots, birthmarks, moles, and sores that don't heal within two weeks. See your doctor immediately if you notice any change in shape or color.

Nastar Races
Ski our new slalom course on Saturday, March 15 at 5:00 PM, then meet friends and family at the lodge for dinner in front of the fireplace. Robert Plant, from the ski patrol not the concert circuit, will be our pacesetter. Can Robert beat 52 seconds setting the pace? Can you?

(b) At End of Exercise 1

FIGURE 5.1 The Newsletter

Figure 5.1c displays a more interesting design that contains a graphic, columns of different widths, and a vertical line to separate the columns. This version is developed in the second hands-on exercise. The final newsletter in Figure 5.1d uses a different graphic, which is superimposed on the entire document and is assigned to you as a problem at the end of the chapter.

Typography

Typography, the process of selecting typefaces, styles, and sizes, is a critical element in the design of any document. The basics were presented in Chapter 2 where we distinguished between a serif and a sans-serif typeface. Serif typefaces are preferable for large amounts of text. Sans-serif is preferable for headings and titles. Type size is measured in points. There are 72 points to the inch.

Typography influences the appearance of a document more than any other element. Good typography goes almost unnoticed, whereas poor typography calls attention to itself and distracts from the document. There are no hard and fast rules—only guidelines and common sense. What works in one instance may not work in another.

One generally accepted guideline is to limit the number of typefaces in a document to two, but to use multiple styles and sizes of those typefaces. Use boldface and/or italics for emphasis. Vary the type size to distinguish between headings, subheadings, and text.

You should also choose a type size that is consistent with the column width. The larger the type size, the longer the line. Conversely, the shorter the line, the

THE SKIER'S HI

Contest Winner
Congratulations to Carol Vazquez Villar, who submitted the winning entry for our logo. Carol wins a pair of skis, boots, and poles, which she promises to show off at our next outing.

Warming Up
Ever pull a muscle skiing your first mogul? You should have stretched before you started — right? Not according to a panel of sports medicine experts put together by the National Strength and Conditioning Association.

Warming up, not stretching, is the most important thing you can do to prevent injuries. Muscles that are cold are not very pliable and thus are susceptible to injury. Even stretching should be put off until you warm up with a few minutes of light skiing (on the bunny hill, perhaps) to increase your metabolic rate and raise your body's core temperature. When should you stretch? After your exercise — when your muscles are warm.

Better Fit Than Fat
There is nothing like finishing a meal with a delicate French pastry or a luscious chocolate mousse, but how much will that indulgence cost in calories? And what will you look like on the beach if you keep treating yourself to such delights?

Exercise is important to weight control, giving you more caloric leeway in your diet and suppressing your appetite. The number of calories burned during physical exercise depends on many factors — how big you are (thinner, smaller people burn fewer calories at the same activity level as heavier, larger people), how hard or fast you work out (the harder the labor or faster the speed, the more calories you burn per minute), the air temperature (the colder the weather, the more calories you burn), the clothes you wear, the type of activity you choose, and the amount of time you spend doing it.

Some sports burn more fat than others. Start-Stop activities, such as tennis or sprinting, are primarily carbohydrate burning activities and use 60–70% carbohydrates and only 30–40% fat. Continuous sports on the other hand, such as walking, jogging, or skiing, consume 50–60% fat and 40–50% carbohydrates.

Any strenuous workout, be it jogging, energetic walking, biking, or swimming, is fine. The important thing is to make a commitment to exercise regularly, at least three to five times a week, every week. If you haven't exercised in a while, start off slowly and gradually build up to the level that you desire.

Exercise and Income
According to a recent Gallup poll, the higher a person's income, the more likely he or she is to exercise; for example, in households with an income over $30,000, 68% of the men and 60% of the women exercise regularly. In addition, people with college degrees are more likely to exercise than those with only high school diplomas.

The Sun and Your Skin
If you have blond or red hair and your eyes are blue, green, or gray, you are more prone to skin cancer. The harmful rays of the sun are the ultraviolet (UV) ones. Unlike the infrared rays that are screened by the clouds, the UV rays go right through. So even on overcast days you need to protect your skin with a sunscreen with a high SPF factor. The best sunscreens are those that contain PABA esters and benzophenones that protect against both UVA and UVB rays.

As a precaution against skin cancer, examine brown spots, birthmarks, moles, and sores that don't heal within two weeks. See your doctor immediately if you notice any change in shape or color.

Nastar Races
Ski our new slalom course on Saturday, March 15 at 5:00 PM, then meet friends and family at the lodge for dinner in front of the fireplace. Robert Plant, from the ski patrol not the concert circuit, will be our pacesetter. Can Robert beat 52 seconds setting the pace? Can you?

(c) At End of Exercise 2

THE SKIER'S HI

Contest Winner
Congratulations to Carol Vazquez Villar, who submitted the winning entry for our logo. Carol wins a pair of skis, boots, and poles, which she promises to show off at our next outing.

Warming Up
Ever pull a muscle skiing your first mogul? You should have stretched before you started — right? Not according to a panel of sports medicine experts put together by the National Strength and Conditioning Association.

Warming up, not stretching, is the most important thing you can do to prevent injuries. Muscles that are cold are not very pliable and thus are susceptible to injury. Even stretching should be put off until you warm up with a few minutes of light skiing (on the bunny hill, perhaps) to increase your metabolic rate and raise your body's core temperature. When should you stretch? After your exercise — when your muscles are warm.

Better Fit Than Fat
There is nothing like finishing a meal with a delicate French pastry or a luscious chocolate mousse, but how much will that indulgence cost in calories? And what will you look like on the beach if you keep treating yourself to such delights?

Exercise is important to weight control, giving you more caloric leeway in your diet and suppressing your appetite. The number of calories burned during physical exercise depends on many factors — how big you are (thinner, smaller people burn fewer calories at the same activity level as heavier, larger people), how hard or fast you work out (the harder the labor or faster the speed, the more calories you burn per minute), the air temperature (the colder the weather, the more calories you burn), the clothes you wear, the type of activity you choose, and the amount of time you spend doing it.

Some sports burn more fat than others. Start-Stop activities, such as tennis or sprinting, are primarily carbohydrate burning activities and use 60–70% carbohydrates and only 30–40% fat. Continuous sports on the other hand, such as walking, jogging, or skiing, consume 50–60% fat and 40–50% carbohydrates.

Any strenuous workout, be it jogging, energetic walking, biking, or swimming, is fine. The important thing is to make a commitment to exercise regularly, at least three to five times a week, every week. If you haven't exercised in a while, start off slowly and gradually build up to the level that you desire.

Exercise and Income
According to a recent Gallup poll, the higher a person's income, the more likely he or she is to exercise; for example, in households with an income over $30,000, 68% of the men and 60% of the women exercise regularly. In addition, people with college degrees are more likely to exercise than those with only high school diplomas.

The Sun and Your Skin
If you have blond or red hair and your eyes are blue, green, or gray, you are more prone to skin cancer. The harmful rays of the sun are the ultraviolet (UV) ones. Unlike the infrared rays that are screened by the clouds, the UV rays go right through. So even on overcast days you need to protect your skin with a sunscreen with a high SPF factor. The best sunscreens are those that contain PABA esters and benzophenones that protect against both UVA and UVB rays.

As a precaution against skin cancer, examine brown spots, birthmarks, moles, and sores that don't heal within two weeks. See your doctor immediately if you notice any change in shape or color.

Nastar Races
Ski our new slalom course on Saturday, March 15 at 5:00 PM, then meet friends and family at the lodge for dinner in front of the fireplace. Robert Plant, from the ski patrol not the concert circuit, will be our pacesetter. Can Robert beat 52 seconds setting the pace? Can you?

(d) Student Assignment (problem 6)

FIGURE 5.1 The Newsletter (continued)

smaller the type size. Avoid very narrow columns because they are choppy and difficult to read. Overly wide columns can be just as bad because they seem to go on indefinitely.

Columns

The ***Columns command*** in the Layout menu lets you define newspaper-style columns in which text flows continuously from the bottom of one column to the top of the next. All you do is specify the number of columns and the space between columns. WordPerfect does the rest. It calculates the width of each column according to the left and right margins on the page and the space between columns.

The dialog box in Figure 5.2 defines three ***newspaper columns*** with .25 inch between each column. The columns will be different lengths because WordPerfect fills the first (leftmost) column from top to bottom, then fills the middle column, then moves to the column on the right. ***Balanced newspaper columns,*** on the other hand, contain the same amount of text and are of equal length. You can appreciate the difference by clicking the appropriate option button and viewing the schematic within the dialog box. (Parallel columns are not discussed.)

The two-inch width for each column is computed automatically based on left and right margins of one inch each and the one quarter inch spacing between columns. The margins and the space between the columns, a total of 2½ inches in this example, is subtracted from the page width of 8½ inches. The remaining 6 inches is divided by three, resulting in a column width of two inches.

Execution of the Columns command defines a column specification, which remains in effect until a new specification is defined. Execution of the Columns command also turns the column feature on, causing the text in the document to be displayed in columns from that point on, until the column feature is turned off. Columns can be toggled off and on by checking (not checking) the ***Column Off command.***

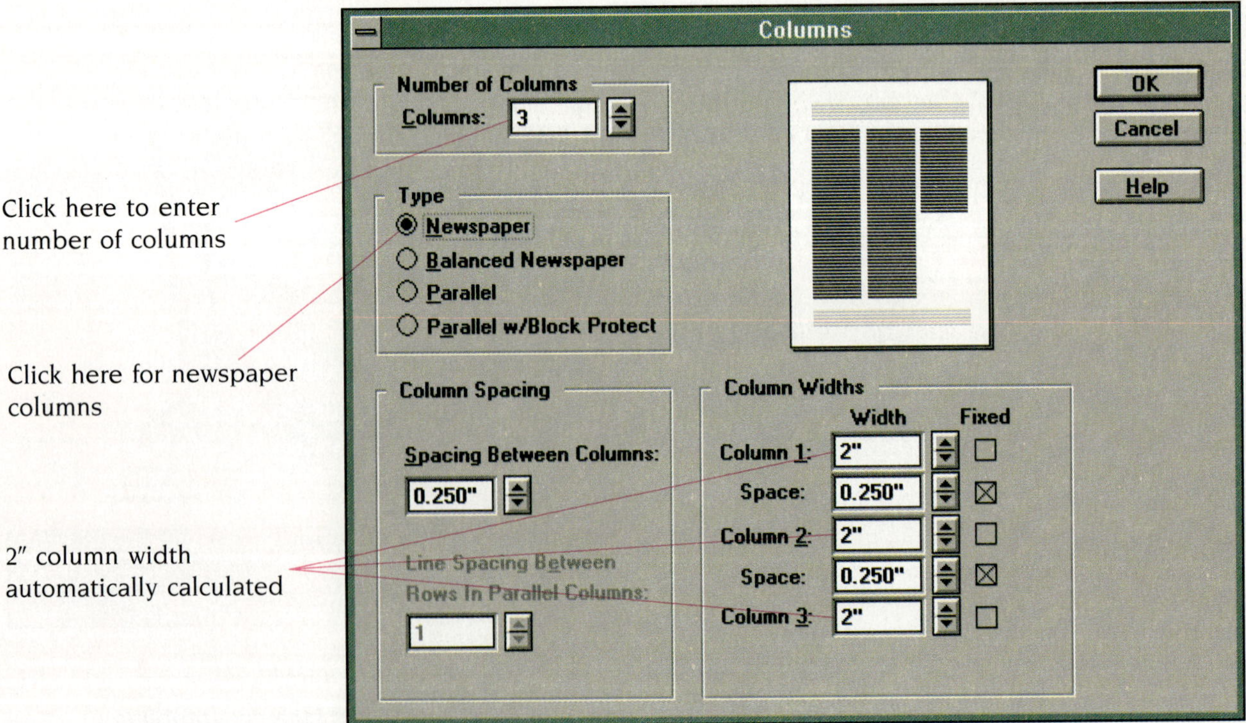

FIGURE 5.2 The Columns Command

COLUMN BREAK

Press Ctrl+Enter to force a column break and begin subsequent text in the next column. Do not force a column break with Balanced Newspaper Columns as the breaks are created automatically to balance the columns.

Border/Fill Command

The ***Border/Fill command*** places a full or partial border around the selected paragraph(s) and optionally shades the area within the border. The command is executed from the ***Layout menu*** and lets you create boxed and/or shaded text, as well as horizontal and/or vertical lines. The command was used in the newsletter to produce the bold horizontal lines above and below the masthead and the shaded box announcing the Jungle Jog.

IN THE ABSENCE OF CLIP ART

Boxes and/or shading add interest to a document when clip art is not available. Horizontal rules (lines) are also effective to separate one topic from another, emphasize a subhead, or call attention to a ***pull quote,*** a phrase or sentence taken from the article to emphasize a key point.

HANDS-ON EXERCISE 1:

Newspaper Columns

Objective To create a document with balanced newspaper columns; to box and shade text within selected paragraphs. Use Figure 5.3 as a guide for the exercise.

Step 1: Load the practice document

- Load WordPerfect.
- Pull down the **File menu.** Click **Open.** Select the **WPDATA** directory.
- Double click **NEWSTEXT.WPD** to retrieve the document containing the text of the newsletter, leaving you free to concentrate on its design.
- Pull down the **View menu.** Click **Draft.** Pull down the **View menu** a second time. Zoom to **Page Width** as shown in Figure 5.3a.
- Save the document as **MYNEWS.WPD** so that you can return to the original NEWSTEXT.WPD if necessary.

Step 2: Newspaper columns

- Click immediately in front of **Contest Winner,** the place where column formatting is to begin.
- Pull down the **Layout menu.** Click **Columns.** Click **Define** to produce the dialog box in Figure 5.3b.

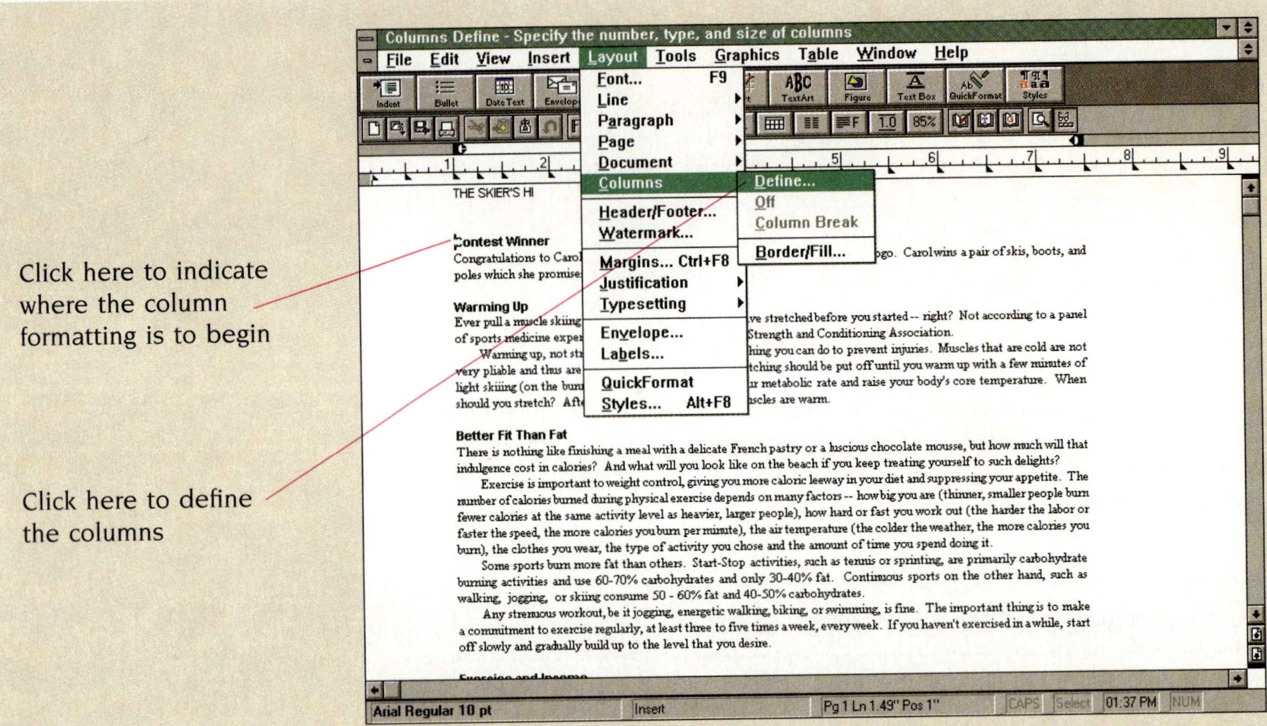

(a) The Practice Document (step 1)

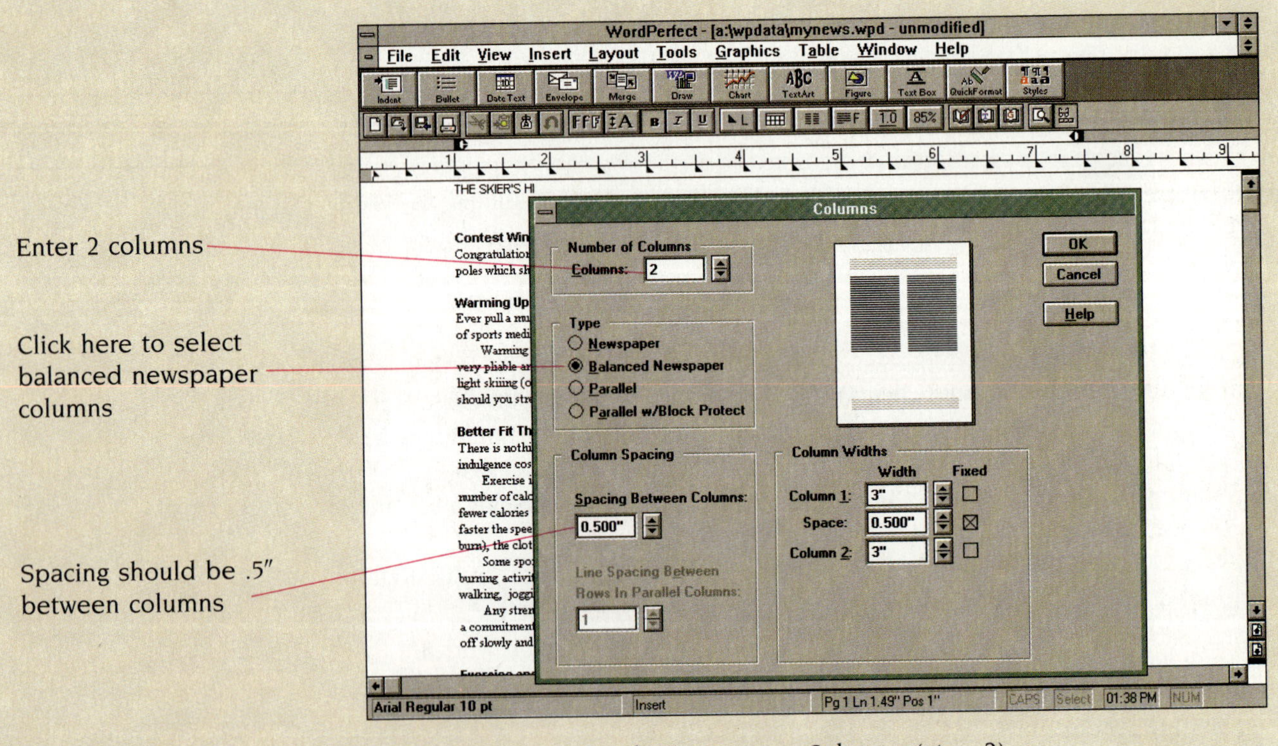

(b) Newspaper Columns (step 2)

FIGURE 5.3 Hands-on Exercise 1

- Check that the number of columns is set at **2** and that the spacing between columns is **.500** inch.
- Click the **Balanced Newspaper** button as shown in the figure.
- Click **OK** to exit the dialog box and return to the document.
- Save the document.

THE COLUMN ICON

Use the **Column icon** on the Power Bar to define columns in a document. Click the icon, then drag the mouse down the list to choose the number of columns; release the mouse to create the columns.

Step 3: Reveal Codes

- Pull down the **View menu.** Click **Page.** Click the **Zoom icon** on the Power Bar to view the **Full Page.** You should see two newspaper columns, and the columns should be of equal length.
- Press **Alt+F3** to open the Reveal Codes window as shown in Figure 5.3c. Click immediately before the Col Def code as shown in the figure to see the column definition.
- Press **Alt+F3** to close the Reveal Codes window.
- Click the **Zoom icon** a second time and return to **Page Width.** Pull down the **View menu** and return to Draft view.

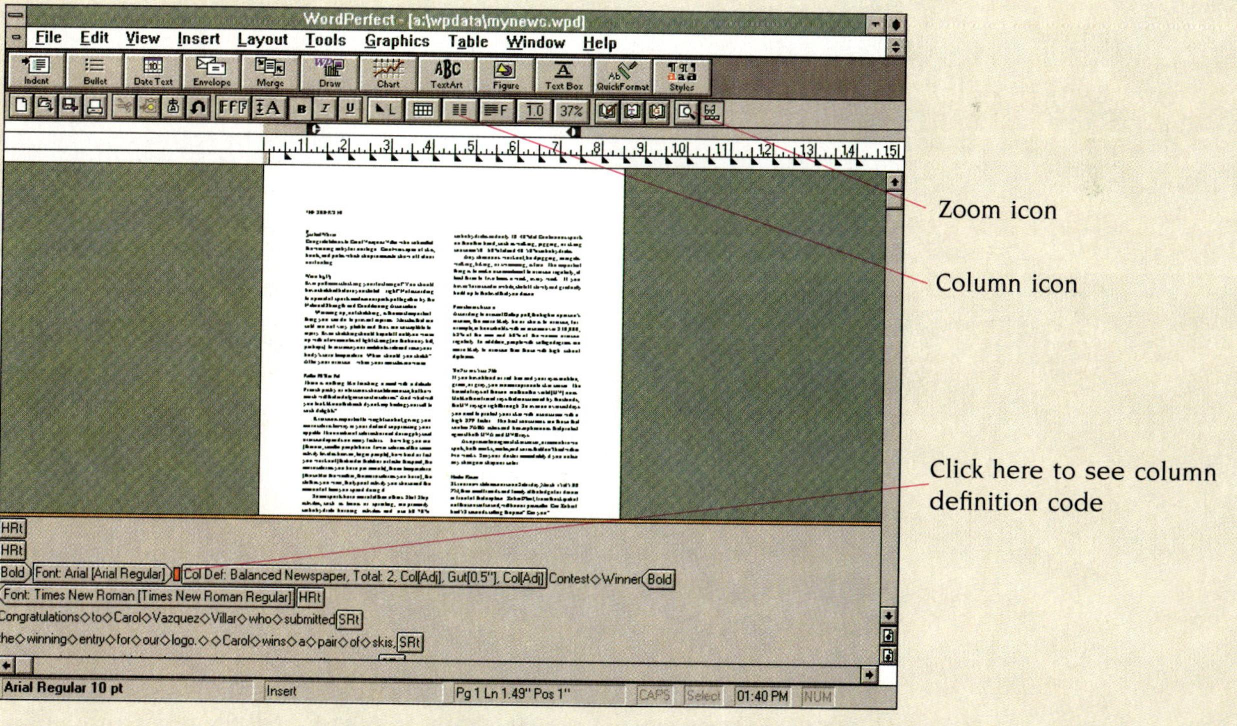

(c) Reveal Codes (step 3)

FIGURE 5.3 Hands-on Exercise 1 (continued)

TURNING COLUMNS ON AND OFF

The Column Off command toggles columns on and off once they have been defined. Just move the insertion point to where you want the columns to begin (or end), then set the columns on or off. To delete columns altogether, press Alt+F3 to open the Reveal Codes window, then move the insertion point just before the column definition code. Press the Del key to eliminate the code, and the columns will disappear.

Step 4: Create the masthead

- Press **Ctrl+Home** to move to the beginning of the document.
- Select the title of the newsletter as shown in Figure 5.3d.
- Double click the **Font icon** on the Power Bar to produce the dialog box in the figure.
- Change the font to **60 pt Arial Bold.** Click **OK.**
- Check that the title is still selected. Click the **Justification icon** on the Power Bar and center the title.
- Save the document.

Step 5: The Border Style command

- Check that the title is still selected.
- Pull down the **Layout menu.** Click **Paragraph.** Click **Border/Fill** to produce the dialog box in Figure 5.3e.
- Click in the **Border Style box.**
- Click the Border Style for thick top and bottom lines as shown in Figure 5.3e.
- Click **OK.** Click outside the title to deselect it in order to view the parallel lines.
- Save the document.

Step 6: The Border/Fill command

- Press **Ctrl+End** to scroll to the end of the document.
- Select the last paragraph and its heading as shown in Figure 5.3f.
- Pull down the **Layout menu.** Click **Paragraph.** Click **Border/Fill** to produce the dialog box in Figure 5.3f.
- Click the **Border Style box.** Click the Border Style for a single line around the selected text.
- Click the arrow for the **Fill Style drop-down list box,** then click 10% as shown in Figure 5.3f.
- Click **OK** to exit the dialog box and return to the document.
- Click outside the selected text to deselect it and view the shading.
- Save the document.

Step 7: The completed document

- Click the **Zoom icon** on the Power Bar to see the **Full Page** as shown in Figure 5.3g.

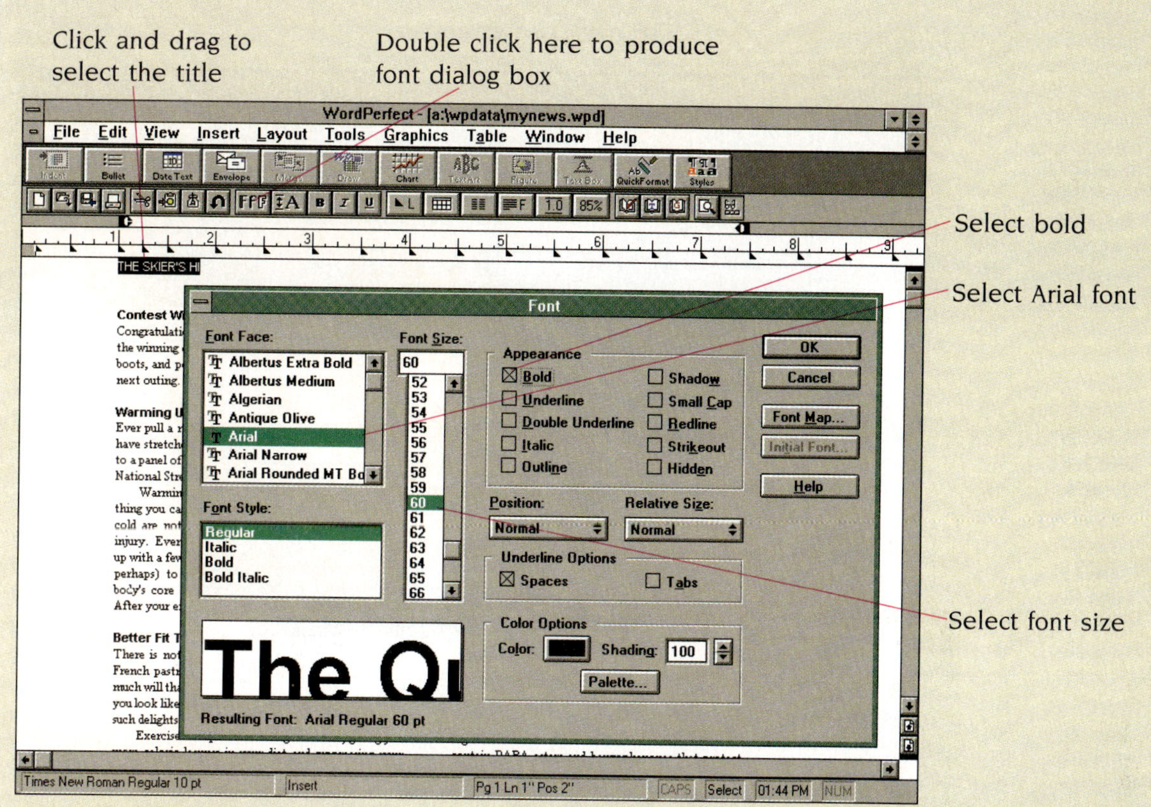

(d) Create the Masthead (step 4)

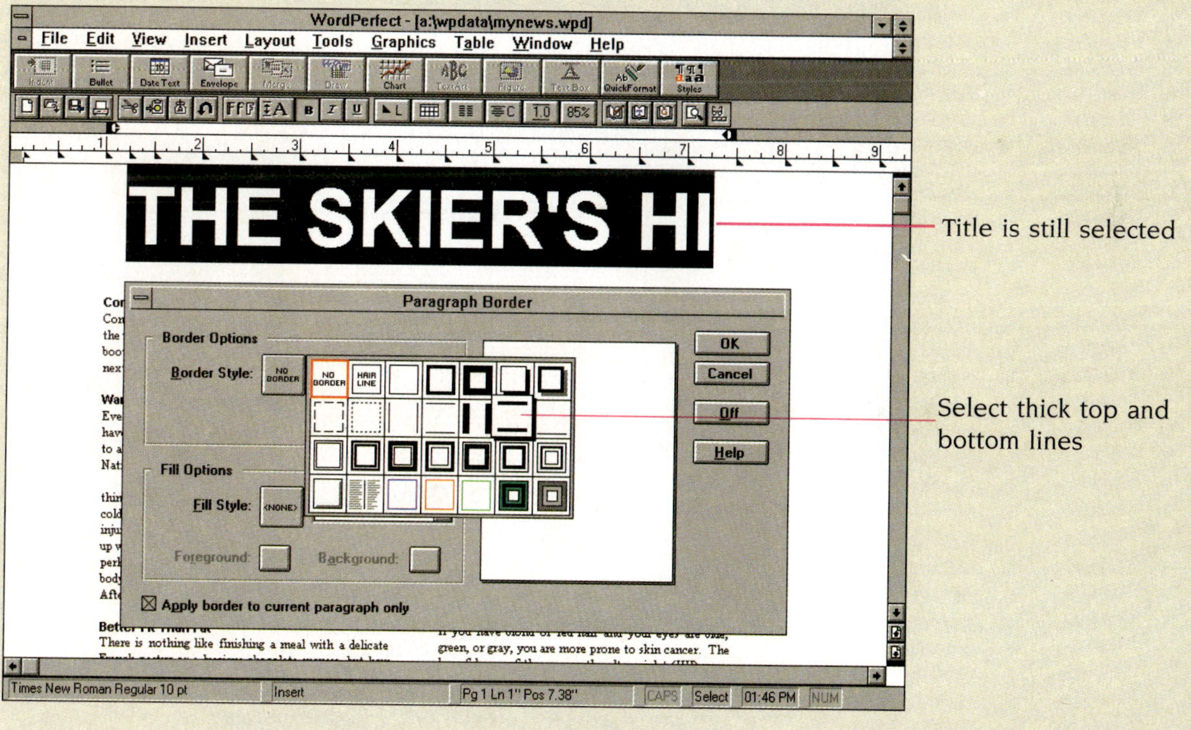

(e) The Border Style Command (step 5)

FIGURE 5.3 Hands-on Exercise 1 (continued)

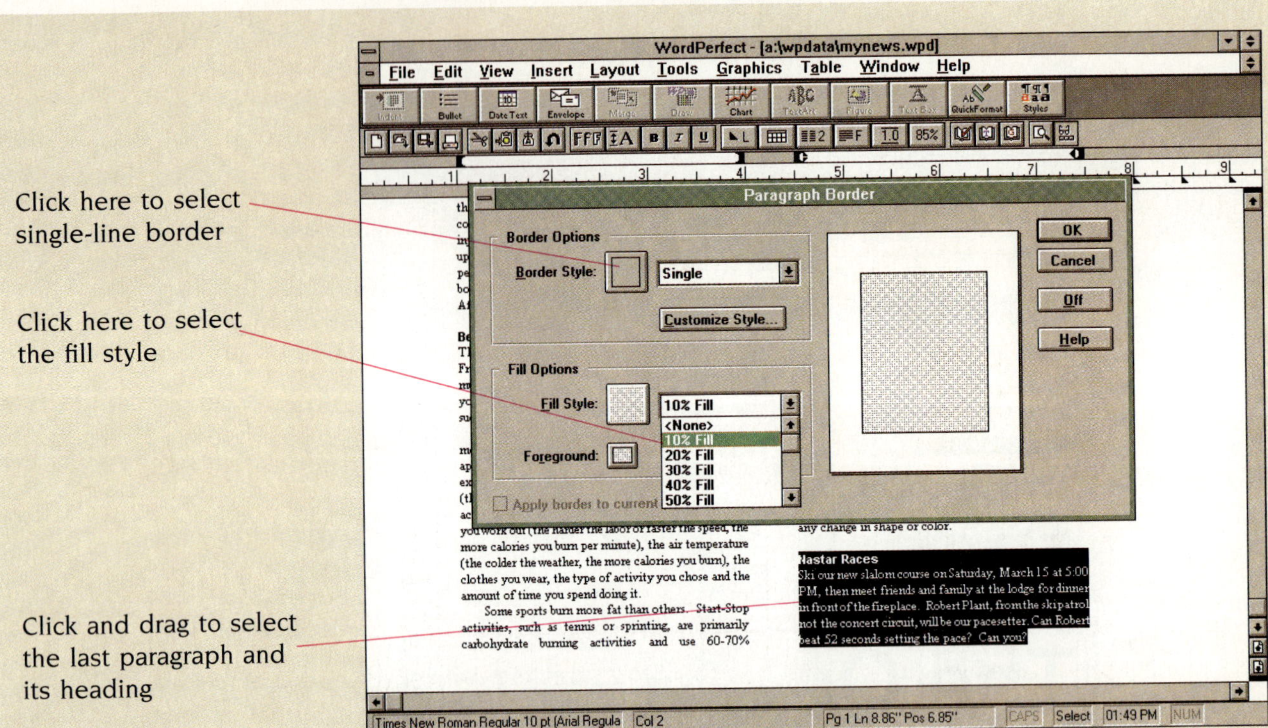

(f) The Border/Fill Command (step 6)

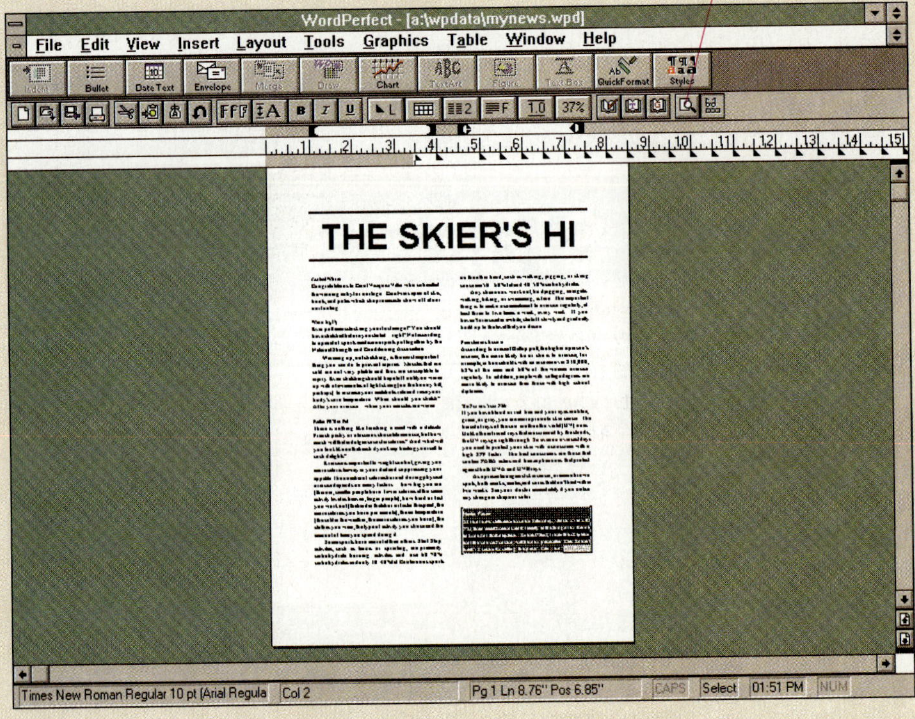

(g) The Partially Completed Newsletter (step 7)

FIGURE 5.3 Hands-on Exercise 1 (continued)

- The masthead is centered in large type within two parallel lines. The text of the document is in two balanced newspaper columns.
- Exit WordPerfect.

MOVING FROM COLUMN TO COLUMN

Click anywhere in a document to move from one column to the next. Press **Alt+Home** and **Alt+End** to move to the top and bottom of a column, respectively. Press **Alt+Left arrow** to move to the previous column and **Alt+Right arrow** to move to the next column.

GRAPHIC ELEMENTS

One of the primary advantages of Windows is the ability to create a ***compound document***—that is, a document containing data from multiple applications. The newsletter in this chapter is created in WordPerfect, but it contains an ***embedded object*** (the skiing graphic) that was created in ***WP Draw,*** an entirely different application. In this example WordPerfect is considered the ***client application*** and WP Draw is the ***server application.***

The concept of a client/server relationship can be applied to every Windows application. If, for example, you import a Lotus spreadsheet into a WordPerfect document, WordPerfect will be the client application and Lotus will be considered the server application. In similar fashion you can use WP Draw to create an image that will be imported into a Lotus spreadsheet, in which case Lotus would be the client application and WP Draw the server.

Clip Art

WordPerfect supplies a limited amount of ***clip art*** (graphics) that can be inserted into a document. The graphics are found in a separate ***GRAPHICS subdirectory*** that is created automatically when WordPerfect is installed.

The ***Figure command*** in the ***Graphics menu*** is the easiest way to insert an image into a document. The command produces the dialog box of Figure 5.4a, which lets you select and preview a picture, then insert it into a document. The list of available graphics is displayed in the filename list box. Select (click) a graphic, such as SLALOM.WPG (WordPerfect graphics files have the extension WPG), then preview the graphic in a separate window as shown in Figure 5.4b. Click the OK command button to insert the graphic into the document. Note, too, the selection of the \WPWIN60\GRAPHICS subdirectory in the directory list box, which specifies the directory containing the graphic images.

Once a graphic has been inserted into a document (e.g., the newsletter), you can change its size and/or position within the document. Clicking the object selects it and enables you to move or size the object within the document. You can also double click the object to load the server application (WP Draw in this example) and modify the graphic.

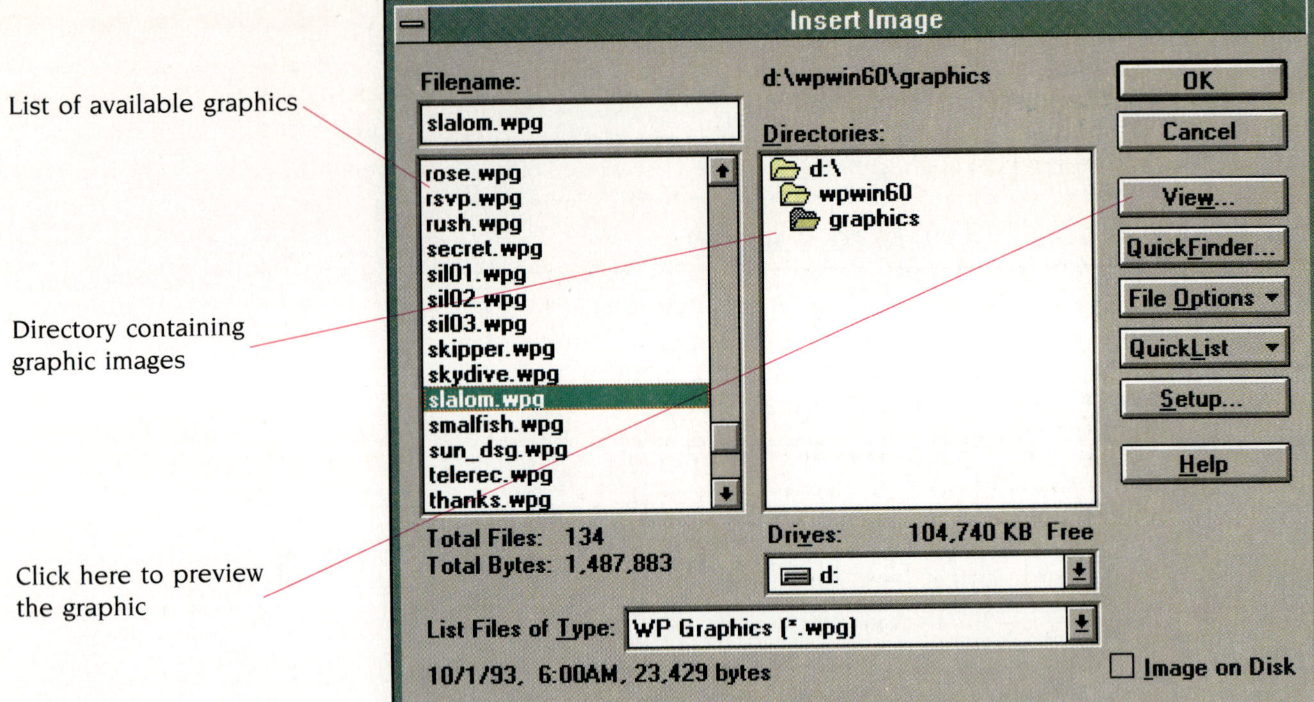

(a) Insert Image Command

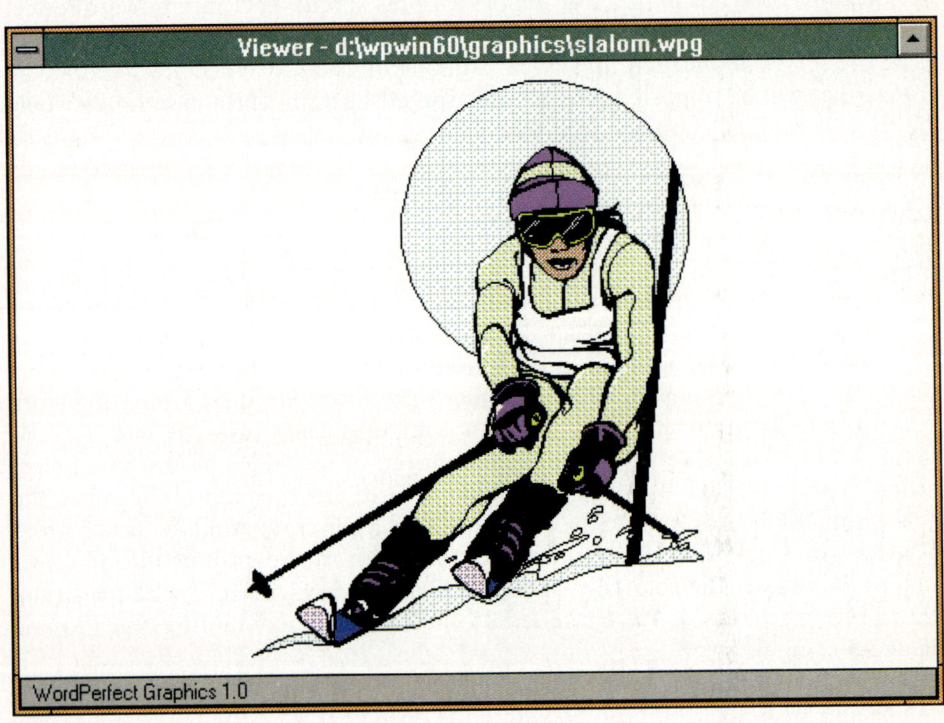

(b) View Command

FIGURE 5.4 Clip Art

CREATE A MIRROR IMAGE

A mirror image is one of several effects you can achieve by using the ***Image Tools*** provided in WordPerfect. Point to the graphic, then click the right mouse button to produce the Graphics ***QuickMenu.*** Click Image Tools, then click the (horizontal or vertical) mirror image icon, a pair of facing (horizontal or vertical) arrows, to flip the image.

TextArt

The right clip art image adds immeasurably to a document, but what if you cannot find an appropriate graphic? WordPerfect anticipates this situation and includes a second application, ***TextArt,*** that enables you to create special effects with text. It lets you rotate and/or flip text, display it vertically on the page, shade it, slant it, arch it, or even print it upside down. You can use any TrueType font installed on your system. You can even use different colors provided you have a color printer.

The ***Insert Object command*** is used to access TextArt from within a WordPerfect document. TextArt is considered the server application and WordPerfect the client. Create a document in the usual fashion, then pull down the ***Insert menu,*** click ***object,*** and select TextArt from the Object Type list in Figure 5.5a. Do not be concerned if you do not see all of the object types displayed in the figure, because you may not have the server applications associated with those objects. You should, however, see WP Graphic and TextArt because these applications are included with WordPerfect.

Figure 5.5b displays the TextArt window in which we create a logo for the Miami Ski Club. Just type the text in the appropriate text box, click the sketch containing the desired effect, and enter the dimensions for the height and width. Pull down the File menu to insert the TextArt object into the WordPerfect document, exit TextArt, and return to WordPerfect.

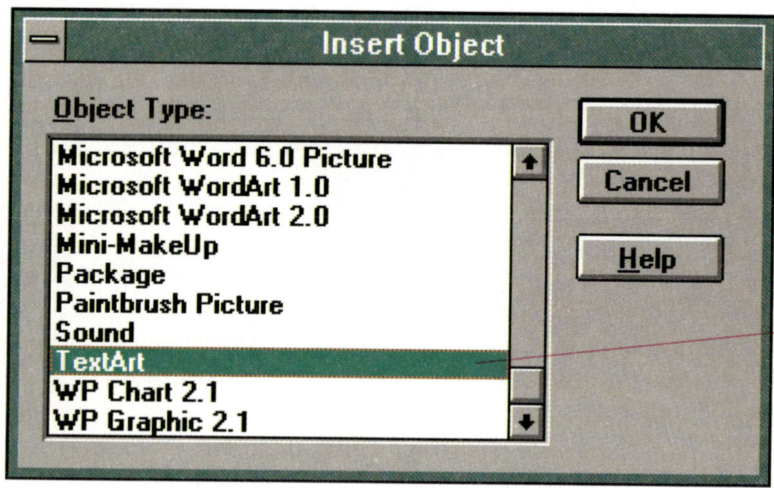

(a) Insert Object Command

FIGURE 5.5 TextArt

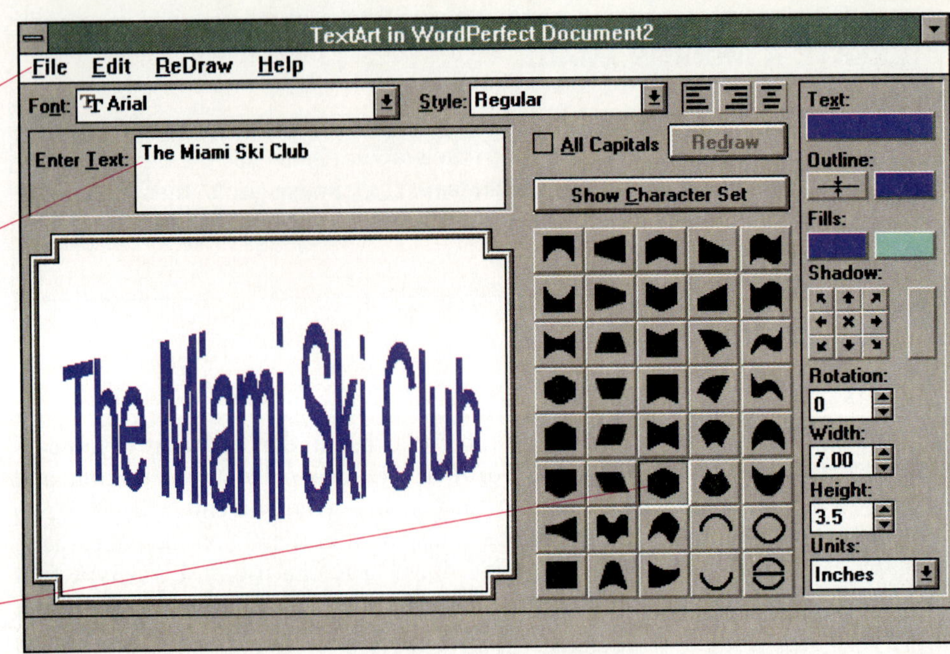

(b) TextArt Window

FIGURE 5.5 TextArt (continued)

> **THE COMMON USER INTERFACE**
>
> The common user interface is one of the major advantages of Windows and means that you are already familiar with a new application even before you begin to use it. In addition, **on-line help** is available for WP Draw and TextArt as it is for every Windows application. So too is the **Undo command,** which is found in the Edit menu.

A Compound Document

Figure 5.6 combines text, the clip art image of the slalom skier, and the text art logo to create a compound document. WordPerfect is the client application. WP Draw and TextArt are each considered a server application.

Look carefully at the figure and you will see the sizing handles that indicate the skiing graphic is selected. The graphic is contained in a graphics box that can be modified by command buttons on the ***Graphics Feature Bar.*** (The Feature Bar is displayed automatically whenever a graphic is selected.) The command buttons are used in the next hands-on exercise and are described briefly below:

Caption	Adds or edits a figure caption.
Content	Changes the content of a graphics box; for example, substitutes one figure for another.
Position	Changes the position of the graphics box on the page.
Size	Changes the width and/or height of the graphics box.

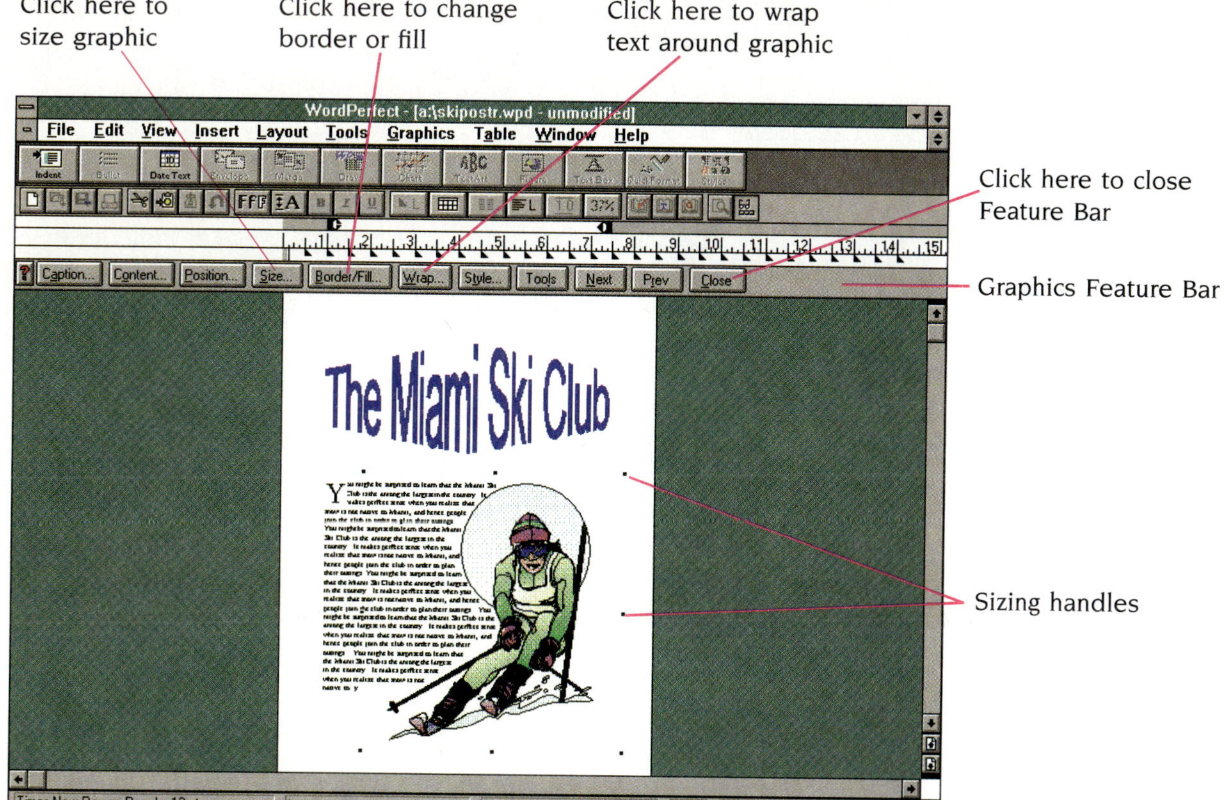

FIGURE 5.6 A Compound Document

Border/Fill	Changes the border and/or shading associated with the graphics box.
Wrap	Determines how text flows around a graphics box.
Style	Changes the style of the box.
Tools	Displays a palette to change the image; for example, flips the image vertically or horizontally.
Next	Selects the next graphics box in the document.
Prev	Selects the previous graphics box in the document.
Close	Exits the graphics box and cancels the display of the Feature Bar.

DROPCAPS

D***ropcaps*** add interest to a document and are created through the Dropcap macro. Move the insertion point to the beginning of a paragraph; that is, the position in the document where the dropcap is to appear. Pull down the ***Tools menu,*** click Macro, and click Play. Click the File selection icon, click Dropcap as the name of the macro, then click the Play command button. Type the letter in the Dropcap Character dialog box. Click OK.

Hands-On Exercise 2:

Graphics

Objective Insert a graphic into a document, move and/or size the graphic within the document; and use WP Draw to edit the graphic. The end result of this exercise is the newsletter of Figure 5.1. Use Figure 5.7 as a guide in the exercise.

Step 1: Load the newsletter

- Pull down the **File menu.** Click **Open.** Double click **MYNEWS.WPD** to retrieve the newsletter from the first exercise.
- Save the file as **MYNEWS2.WPD** so that you can always return to the newsletter as it existed at the end of the first exercise.
- Pull down the **View menu.** Click **Draft.** Pull down the **View menu** a second time. Zoom to **Page Width** as shown in Figure 5.7a.

> **THE COACH**
>
> The ***Coach*** is a series of interactive lessons within the Help facility that provides step-by-step instructions for various features in WordPerfect. Pull down the Help menu, click Coach, click Graphics, then click OK to let Coach guide you through the process of inserting and modifying a graphic.

Click here to insert a graphic figure

Place insertion point here

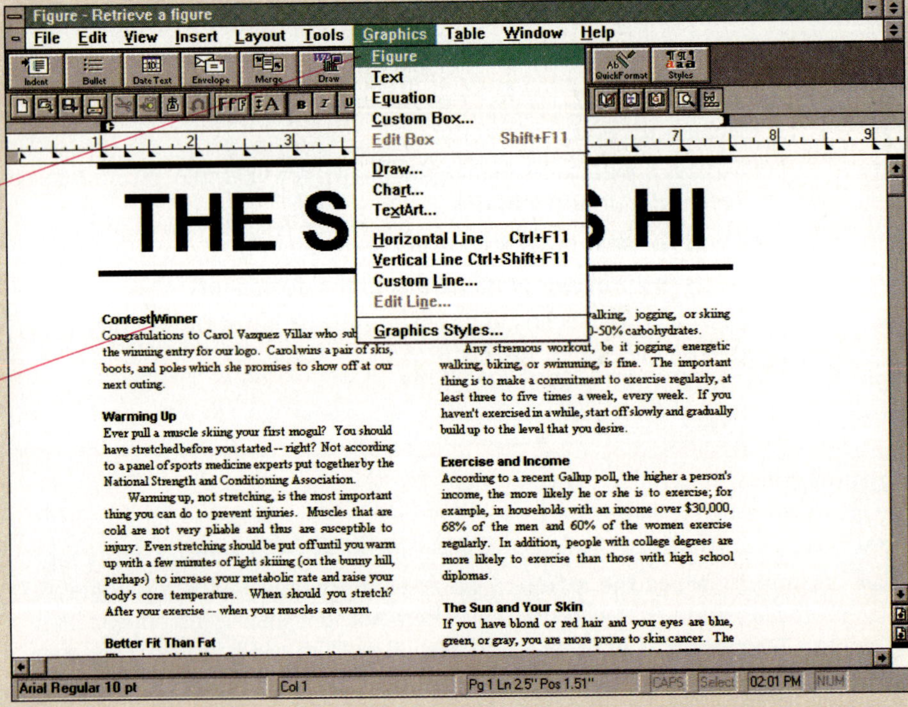

(a) The Newsletter and the Graphics Menu (step 1)

FIGURE 5.7 Hands-on Exercise 2

Step 2: Add the graphic

- Click within the phrase **Contest Winner.**
- Pull down the **Graphics menu.** Click **Figure** to produce the dialog box of Figure 5.7b.
- The GRAPHICS subdirectory should already be open, but if not, you must indicate to WordPerfect where the clip art can be found.
  - — Click the arrow in the Drives list box, then click drive C. Scroll in the Directories list box until you come to the root directory C (C:\).
  - — Double click **C:\.**
  - — Scroll through the list box until you come to the **WPWIN60** directory.
  - — Double click **WPWIN60.**
  - — Double click the **GRAPHICS** subdirectory.
- The list of available figures is contained in the Filename list box. Each figure is stored in a separate file.
- Scroll through the list box of filenames until you find **INKSKIER.WPG.** Click that filename.
- Click the **View command button** to view the graphic before bringing it into the document. Double click the control-menu box in the Viewer window to close it.
- Click **OK** to insert the figure into the document. Do *not* be concerned if the placement, size, or other attributes of your figure are different from the original newsletter.
- Click outside the graphic to deselect it.
- Save the newsletter.

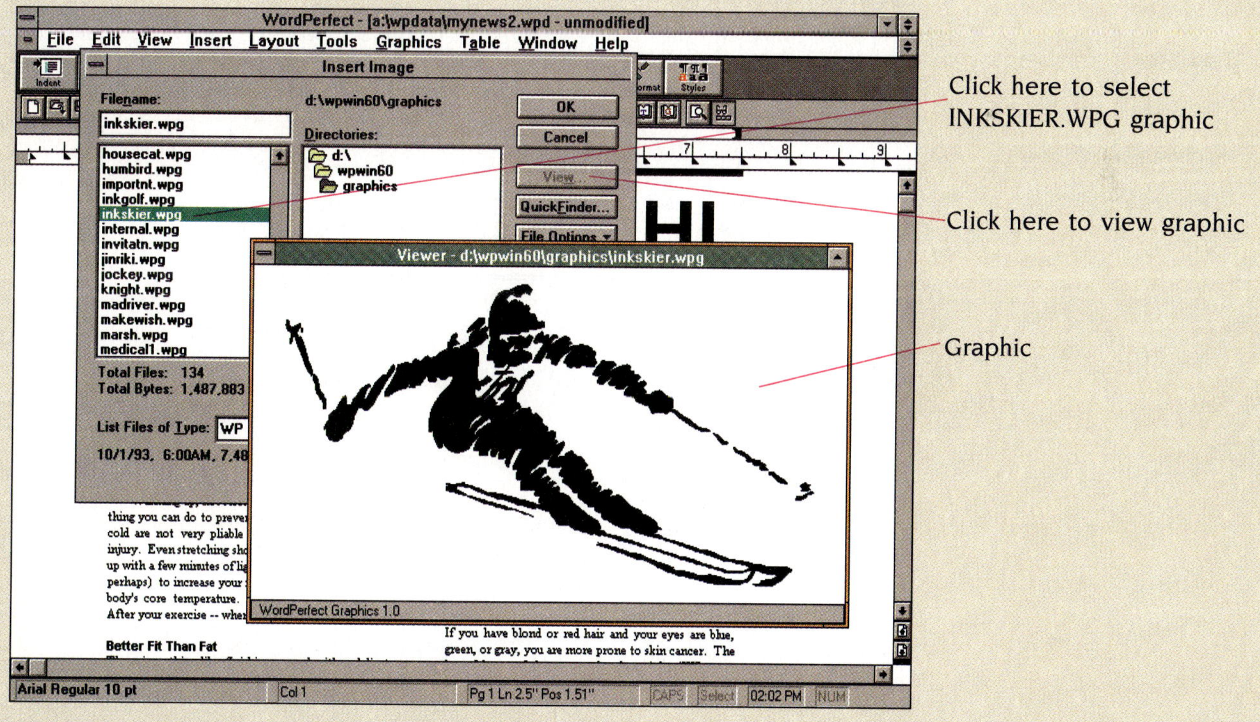

(b) Inserting a Figure (step 2)

FIGURE 5.7 Hands-on Exercise 2 (continued)

TROUBLESHOOTING

The GRAPHICS subdirectory referenced in this step, as well as the WP Draw application used later in the exercise, are optional components of the installation process and may not be available on your system. If you are unable to complete any portion of the exercise because these elements are not present, ask your instructor about reinstalling WordPerfect to include the missing components.

Step 3: Move and size the graphic

➤ The procedure to move and size the graphic is identical to the procedure in any other Windows application:

— To select the graphic, click anywhere in the graphic; that produces the eight sizing handles as shown in Figure 5.7c. (When you are finished working with the figure, click outside the skier to deselect the object.)

— To move the graphic, select it, then press and hold the left mouse button (the mouse pointer changes to a four-sided arrow) as you drag the graphic to a new location in the document.

— To size the graphic, point to any of the eight sizing handles (the mouse pointer changes to a double arrow), then press and hold the left mouse button as you drag the handle outward (inward) to increase (decrease) the size of the graphic.

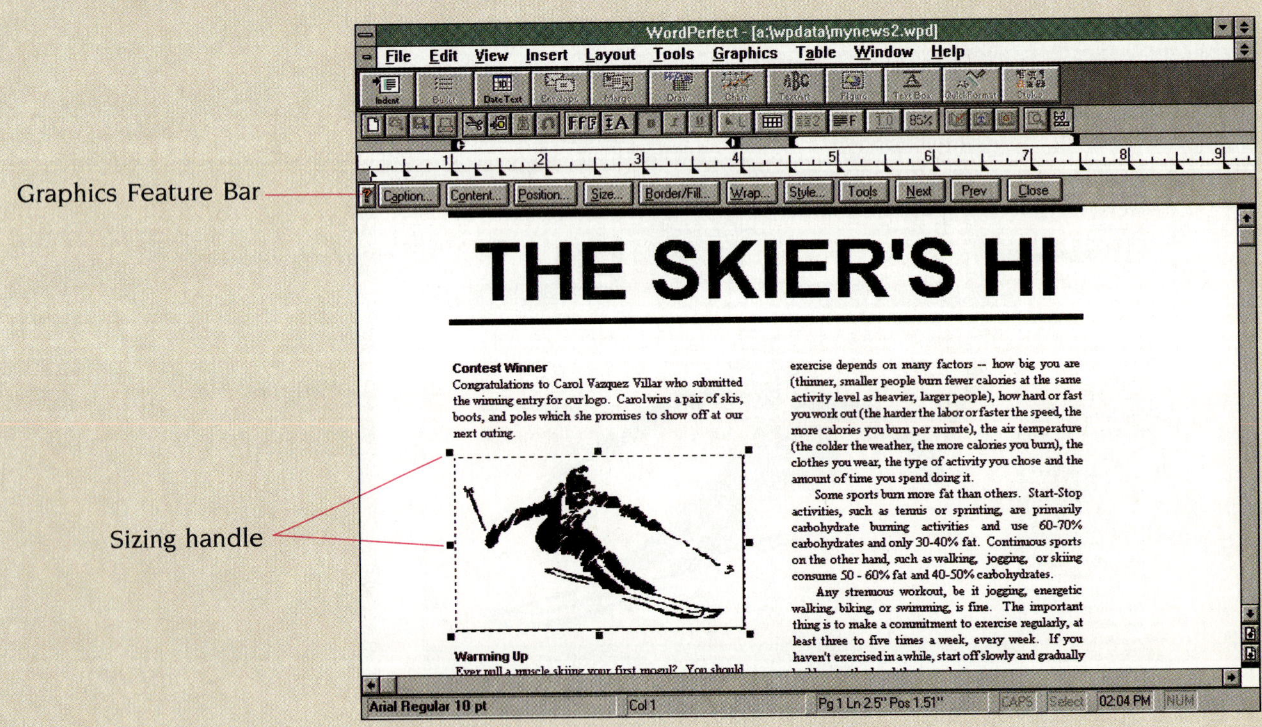

(c) Moving a Graphic (step 3)

FIGURE 5.7 Hands-on Exercise 2 (continued)

— To undo a moving or sizing operation, click outside the graphic to deselect it, then click the **Undo icon** on the Power Bar.

➤ Save the newsletter.

MOVING AN OBJECT

Use the Graphics Feature Bar if you are having difficulty moving an object with the mouse. Select the object, click the Position command button, choose Put Box on Current Page as the placement option, then manually enter the horizontal and vertical coordinates. Click OK to return to the document. It may be necessary to repeat this procedure once or twice, but you will achieve the precise position you want.

Step 4: The Graphics Feature Bar

➤ The skier in our newsletter appears without a border and without text on either side. The Graphics Feature Bar lets you change these and other options by clicking the appropriate command button.

➤ Select the graphic if it is not already selected.

— To change the way the text wraps around the graphic, click the **Wrap command button** on the Graphics Feature Bar to display the dialog box in Figure 5.7d. Choose the option you want, then click **OK.** (You may need

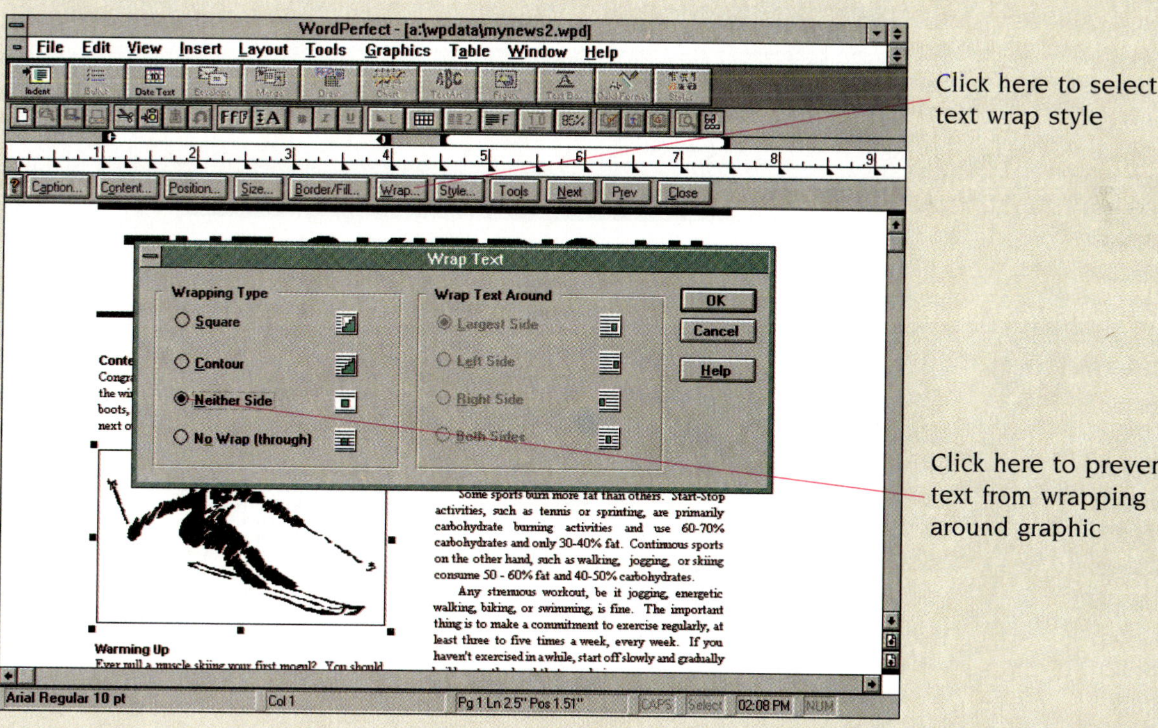

(d) The Graphics Feature Bar (step 4)

FIGURE 5.7 Hands-on Exercise 2 (continued)

to move and/or size the graphic to see the effects of changing the Wrap option.)

— To change the border around the graph, click the **Border/Fill command button** on the Graphics Feature Bar, choose the Border Style you want, then click **OK.**

— To undo either operation, click outside the graphic to deselect it, then click the **Undo icon** on the Power Bar.

➤ Save the newsletter.

> **DISPLAY THE FEATURE BAR**
>
> If you select a graphic and the Feature Bar does not appear, click the right mouse button to access the QuickMenu. Click Feature Bar and the Feature Bar will appear on the screen immediately below the Ruler Bar.

Step 5: Image Tools

➤ Point to the graphic, then click the **right mouse button** to produce the Graphic QuickMenu.

➤ Click Image Tools to display the tool box in Figure 5.7e.

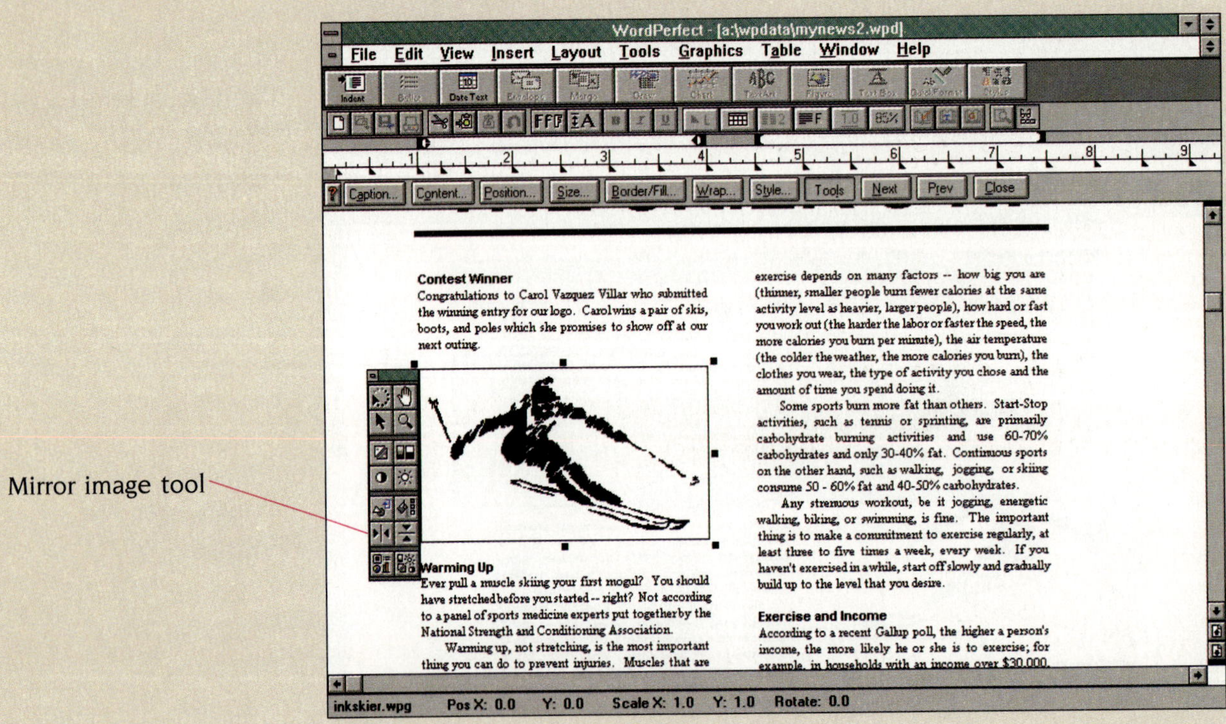

(e) Image Tools (step 5)

FIGURE 5.7 Hands-on Exercise 2 (continued)

- Click the icon to create a mirror image along the vertical axis, causing the skier to face left rather than right.
- Click the adjacent icon to create a mirror image along the horizontal axis, turning the skier upside down.
- Choose the image you like best for your newsletter. (You can click each icon a second time to return the skier to its original position.)
- Save the newsletter.

Step 6: Add your name to the graphic (WP Draw)

- Move the mouse pointer anywhere over the graphic. **Double click** the left mouse button to load WP Draw (the application that created the graphic), producing the screen in Figure 5.7f.
- Pull down the **Text menu.** Choose an appropriate font and type size in bold italics.
- Click the **Text tool** (the capital A in the tool box).
- Click and drag anywhere in the drawing area to create a text box to hold your name.
- Release the mouse. Type your name. Click outside the text box to deselect it.
- Double click the **control menu box** for WP Draw to exit the drawing program and return to your document. Click **Yes** to save the changes in MYNEWS2.WPD.

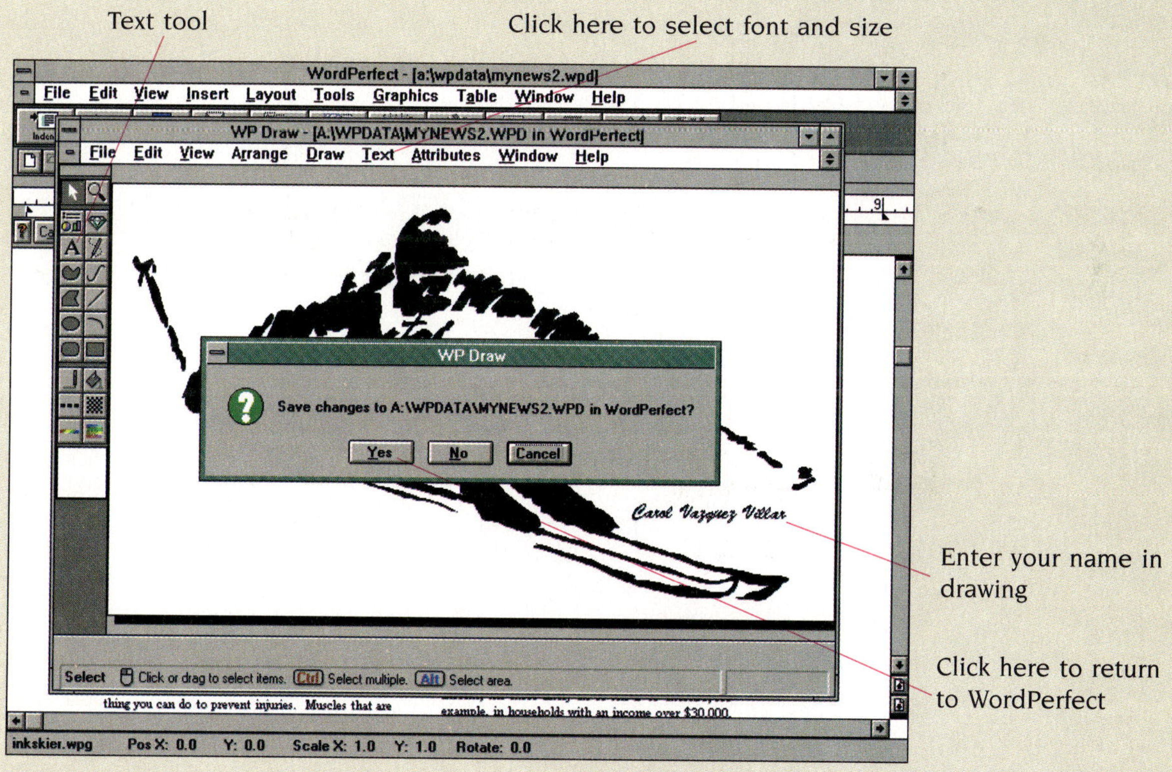

Text tool

Click here to select font and size

Enter your name in drawing

Click here to return to WordPerfect

(f) WP Draw (step 6)

FIGURE 5.7 Hands-on Exercise 2 (continued)

TO CLICK OR DOUBLE CLICK

Clicking an object selects the object (e.g., the skiing graphic) and produces the sizing handles. Double clicking an object loads the application that created it. All of the clip art supplied with WordPerfect is associated with WP Draw, and thus double clicking the art automatically loads WP Draw and opens the graphic for editing. You are then able to edit the graphic using the commands in the drawing program.

Step 7: The finishing touches

- Click anywhere outside the figure to deselect the graphic.
- Change the justification.
  - Click immediately in front of Contest Winner, then drag the mouse to the end of the document to select the text of the entire newsletter. Pull down the **Justification icon** on the Power Bar and change to left justification.
- Change the column definition.
  - Click anywhere in the text of the newsletter.
  - Pull down the **Layout menu.** Click **Columns.** Click **Define.**
  - Change the width of the first column to two inches and click **OK;** the width of the second column will change automatically.
- Change the border around the masthead.
  - Click anywhere in the masthead.
  - Pull down the **Layout menu.** Click **Paragraph.** Click **Border/Fill.** Click the Border Style box and choose a different border. Click **OK.**
- Add a line between the columns.
  - Click in the text of the newsletter.
  - Pull down the **Layout menu.** Click **Columns.** Click **Border/Fill** to produce the dialog box in Figure 5.7g.
  - Click the Border Style that produces a line between the newspaper columns. Click **OK.**
- Save the newsletter.

USE THE RULER BAR

The width of a column can be changed by dragging the appropriate column width marker on the Ruler Bar. You must explicitly change the width of every column; that is, changing the width of one column does not change the width of the neighboring column but increases or decreases the space between columns.

Step 8: The completed newsletter

- Pull down the **View menu.** Click **Page.**
- Click the **Zoom icon** on the Power Bar to zoom to **Full Page** to display the completed newsletter as shown in Figure 5.7h.
- Save the document a final time, print the newsletter, then exit WordPerfect.

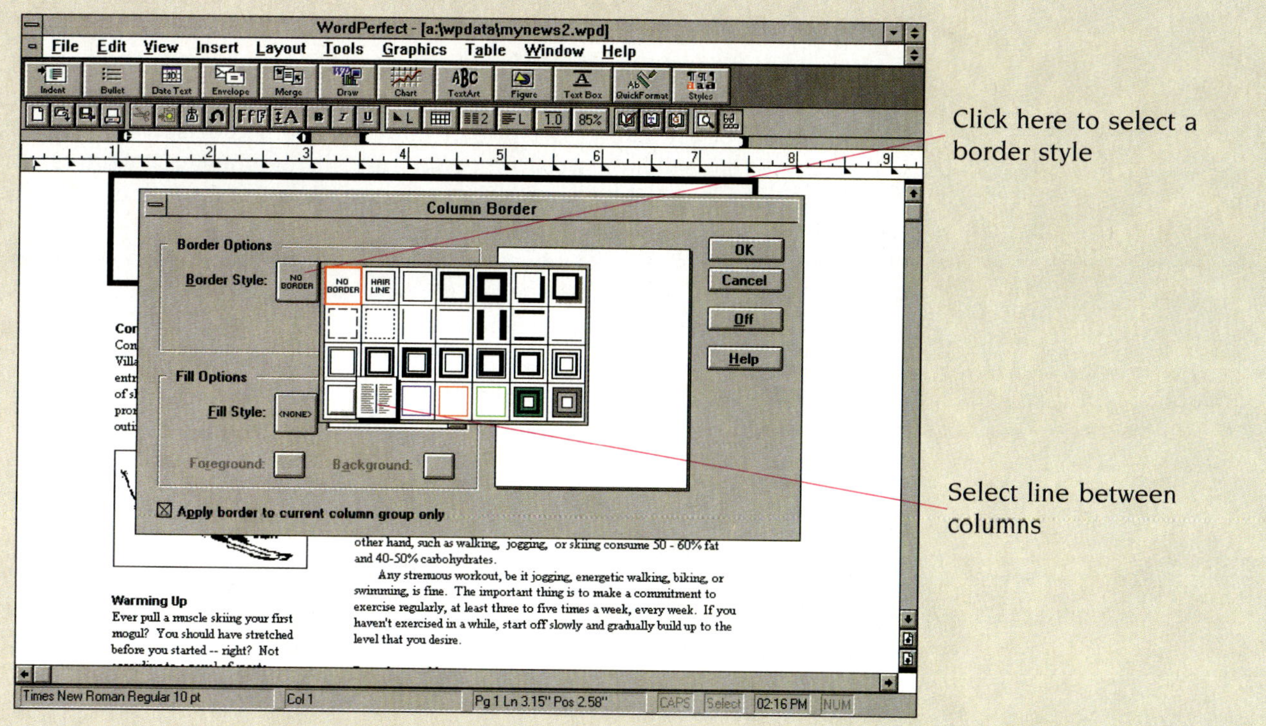

(g) The Column Border Command (step 7)

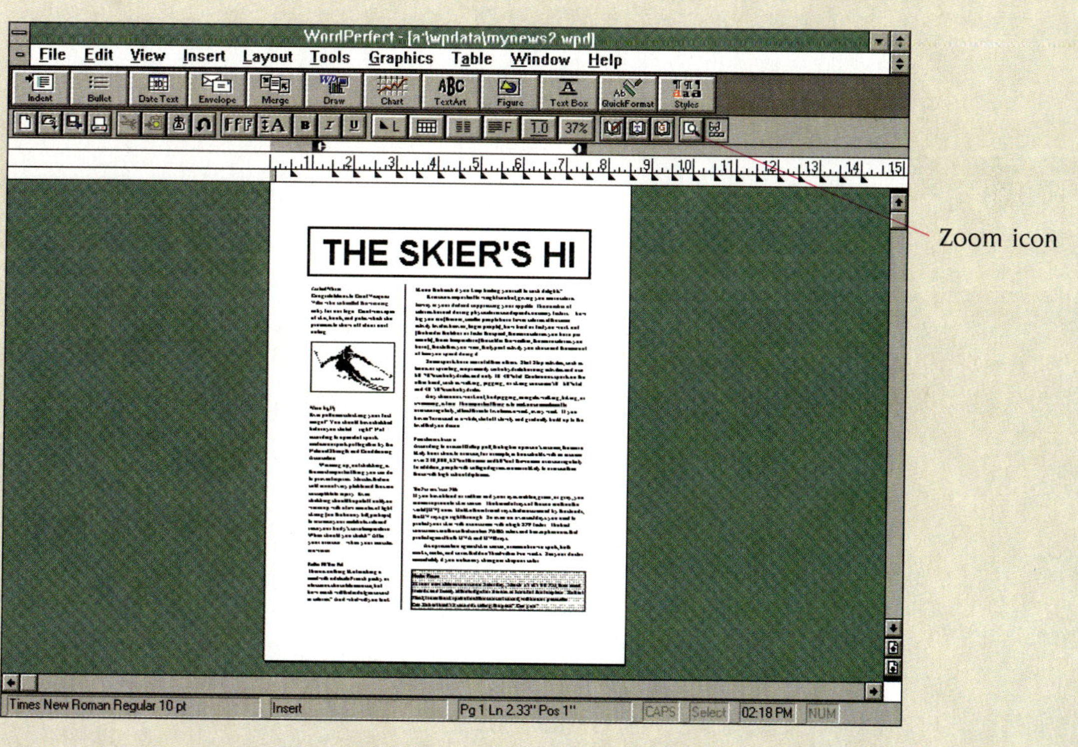

(h) The Completed Newsletter (step 8)

FIGURE 5.7 Hands-on Exercise 2 (continued)

ELEMENTS OF GRAPHIC DESIGN

We trust you have completed the hands-on exercises without difficulty and that you were able to reproduce the newsletter. Realize, however, that the mere availability of WordPerfect and a laser printer does not guarantee success in desktop publishing, any more than a word processor turns its author into a Shakespeare or a Hemingway. Other skills are necessary and so we conclude with an introduction to basic principles of graphic design.

Much of what we say is subjective, and what works in one situation will not necessarily work in another. Your eye is the best judge of all and you should stick to your own instincts. Experiment freely and realize that successful design is the result of trial and error. Seek inspiration from others by maintaining a file of publications, with examples of both good and bad design, and use the file as the basis for your own publications.

The Grid

The design of a document should be developed on a ***grid,*** an underlying, but *invisible,* set of horizontal and vertical lines that determine the placement of the major elements. A grid establishes the overall structure of a document by indicating the number of columns, the space between columns, the size of the margins, the placement of headlines, art, and so on. The grid does *not* appear in the printed document nor on the screen.

A grid may be simple or complex, but is always distinguished by the number of columns it contains. The three-column grid of Figures 5.8a and 5.8b is one

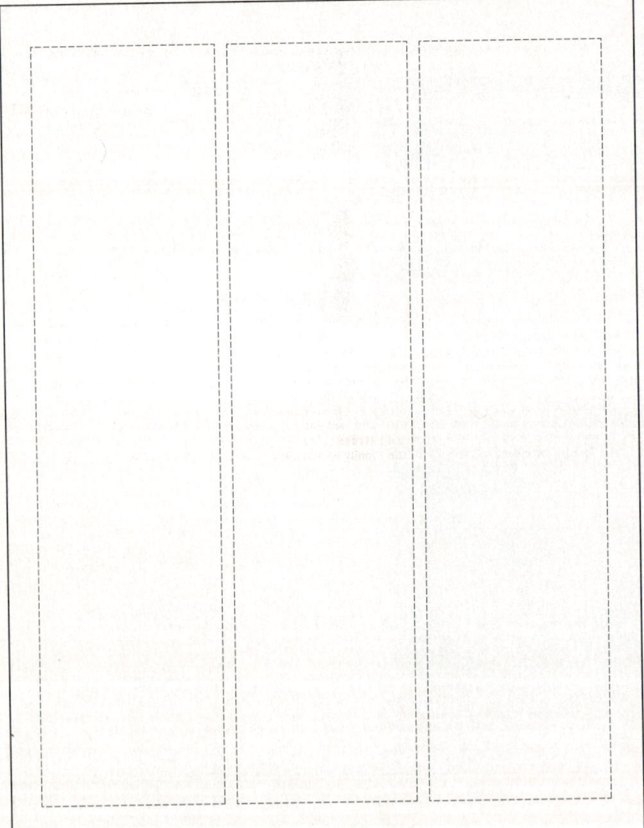

(a) Empty Three-column Grid

Nocando

He felt more and more pressure to play the game of not playing. Maybe that's why he stepped in front of that truck.

People wonder why people do things like this, but all you have to do is look around and see all the stress and insanity each person in responsibility is required to put up with. There is no help or end in sight. It seems that managers are managing less and shoveling the workloads on to their underlings. This seems to be the overall response to the absence of raises or benefit packages they feel are their entitlement. Something must be done now!

People wonder why people do things like this, but all you have to do is look around and see all the stress and insanity each person in responsibility is required to put up with. There is no help or end in sight. It seems that managers are managing less and shoveling the workloads on to their underlings. This seems to be the overall response to the absence of raises or benefit packages they feel are their entitlement. Something must be done now!

People wonder why people do things like this, but all you have to do is look around and see all the stress and insanity each person in responsibility is required to put up with. There is no help or end in sight. It seems that managers are managing less and shoveling the workloads on to their underlings. This seems to be the overall response to the absence of raises or benefit packages they feel are their entitlement.

People wonder why people do things like this, but all you have to do is look around and see all the stress and insanity each person in responsibility is required to put up with. There is no help or end in sight. It seems that managers are managing less and shoveling the workloads on to their underlings. This seems to be the overall response to the absence of raises or benefit packages they feel are their entitlement. Something must be done now!

People wonder why people do things like this, but all you have to do is look around and see all the stress and insanity each person in responsibility is required to put up with. There is no help or end in sight. It seems that managers are managing less. Something must be done now! ▼

(b) Three-column Grid

FIGURE 5.8 The Grid System of Design

of the most common and utilitarian designs. Figure 5.8c shows a four-column design for the same document, with unequal column widths to provide interest. Figure 5.8d illustrates a five-column grid that is often used with large amounts of text. Many other designs are possible as well. A one-column grid is used for term papers and letters. A two-column, wide and narrow format is appropriate for textbooks and manuals. Two- and three-column formats are used for newsletters and magazines.

The simple concept of a grid should make the underlying design of any document obvious, which in turn gives you an immediate understanding of page composition. Moreover, the conscious use of a grid will help you organize your material and result in a more polished and professional-looking publication. It will also help you to achieve consistency from page to page within a document (or from issue to issue of a newsletter). Indeed, much of what goes wrong in desktop publishing stems from failing to follow or use the underlying grid.

UNEQUAL COLUMNS

Add interest to a document by creating columns of different widths. Pull down the Layout menu, click Columns, and click Define. Enter the number of columns and the spacing between columns. Click the check box to fix the width and/or spacing of individual columns, then click the up (down) arrow to increase (decrease) the width of individual columns. WordPerfect will automatically change the other columns to match your specifications.

(c) Four-column Grid

(d) Five-column Grid

FIGURE 5.8 The Grid System of Design (continued)

White Space

White space, or space that is free of text and art, is underutilized by most newcomers to graphic design. White space is essential, however, to provide contrast, and to give the eye a place to rest; conversely, the lack of white space makes a document crowded and difficult to read as seen in Figure 5.9a.

White space is introduced into a document in several ways, but not every document will use every technique. White space will appear:

- Around a headline; surrounding a headline with white space gives it additional emphasis.
- In the page margins (left, right, top, and bottom); a minimum of one inch all around is a generally accepted guideline.
- Between columns in a multicolumn layout; the wider the columns, the more space is required between the columns.
- Between lines of text.
- In paragraph indents and/or the ragged line endings of left-aligned type.
- Around a figure to emphasize the art.
- Between paragraphs through use of a paragraph spacing command. This subtlety increases the space after a hard carriage return and gives a more professional appearance than double spacing between paragraphs, which adds too much space.

White space can be used as a design element by leaving a column empty (or almost empty) as was done in Figures 5.9b and 5.9c. The use of vertical white

An Uninviting Morass of Text

I came to his garden alone, while the dew was still on the roses. Sweet fragrances and the song of birds filled the air. His voice I heard, soft and clear, saying that this is an organic garden. All the flowers, shrubs and trees were so beautiful not because of chemicals, but because of supplying the correct natural nutrients needed by each of them. There were no harmful insects because these plantings were strong and full of vitality. The birds, which also doubled as bug snatchers, were attracted by the various flowers and berries. Indeed Mrs. Crabtree was a lucky woman to have such a delightful garden and such an inspired man as Adam to tend it.

I came to his garden alone, while the dew was still on the roses. Sweet fragrances and the song of birds filled the air. His voice I heard, soft and clear, saying that this is an organic garden. All the flowers, shrubs and trees were so beautiful not because of chemicals, but because of supplying the correct natural nutrients needed by each of them. There were no harmful insects because these plantings were strong and full of vitality. The birds, which also doubled as bug snatchers, were attracted by the various flowers and berries. Indeed Mrs. Crabtree was a lucky woman to have such a delightful garden and such an inspired man as Adam to tend it.

I came to his garden alone, while the dew was still on the roses. Sweet fragrances and the song of birds filled the air. His voice I heard, soft and clear, saying that this is an organic garden. All the flowers, shrubs and trees were so beautiful not because of chemicals, but because of supplying the correct natural nutrients needed by each of them. There were no harmful insects because these plantings were strong and full of vitality. The birds, which also doubled as bug snatchers, were attracted by the various flowers and berries. Indeed Mrs. Crabtree was a lucky woman to have such a delightful garden and such an inspired man as Adam to tend it.

I came to his garden alone, while the dew was still on the roses. Sweet fragrances and the song of birds filled the air. His voice I heard, soft and clear, saying that this is an organic garden. All the flowers, shrubs and trees were so beautiful not because of chemicals, but because of supplying the correct natural nutrients needed by each of them. There were no harmful insects because these plantings were strong and full of vitality. The birds, which also doubled as bug snatchers, were attracted by the various flowers and berries. Indeed Mrs. Crabtree was a lucky woman to have such a delightful garden and such an inspired man as Adam to tend it.

I came to his garden alone, while the dew was still on the roses. Sweet fragrances and the song of birds filled the air. His voice I heard, soft and clear, saying that this is an organic garden. All the flowers, shrubs and trees were so beautiful not because of chemicals, but because of supplying the correct natural nutrients needed by each of them. There were no harmful insects because these plantings were strong and full of vitality. The birds, which also doubled as bug snatchers, were attracted by the various flowers and berries. Indeed Mrs. Crabtree was a lucky woman to have such a delightful garden and such an inspired man as Adam to tend it.

I came to his garden alone, while the dew was still on the roses. Sweet fragrances and the song of birds filled the air. His voice I heard, soft and clear, saying that this is an organic garden. All the flowers, shrubs and trees were so beautiful not because of chemicals, but because of supplying the correct natural nutrients needed by each of them. There were no harmful insects because these plantings were strong and full of vitality. The birds, which also doubled as bug snatchers, were attracted by the various flowers and berries. Indeed Mrs. Crabtree was a lucky woman to have such a delightful garden and such an inspired man as Adam to tend it.

I came to his garden alone, while the dew was still on the roses. Sweet fragrances and the song of birds filled the air. His voice I heard, soft and clear, saying that this is an organic garden. All the flowers, shrubs and trees were so beautiful not because of chemicals, but because of supplying the correct natural nutrients.There were no harmful insects because these plantings were full of vitality. The birds, which also doubled as bug snatchers, were attracted by the various flowers. ▼

(a) Crowded Page

A Page Should Leave a Place for the Bird to Fly

I came to his garden alone, while the dew was still on the roses. Sweet fragrances and the song of birds filled the air. His voice I heard, soft and clear, saying that this is an organic garden. All the flowers, shrubs and trees were so beautiful not because of chemicals, but because of supplying the correct natural nutrients needed by each of them. There were no harmful insects because these plantings were strong and full of vitality. The birds, which also doubled as bug snatchers, were attracted by the various flowers and berries. Indeed Mrs. Crabtree was a lucky woman and to have such a delightful garden and such an inspired man as Adam to tend it.

I came to his garden alone, while the dew was still on the roses. Sweet fragrances and the song of birds filled the air. His voice I heard, soft and clear, saying that this is an organic garden. All the flowers, shrubs and trees were so beautiful not because of chemicals, but because of supplying the correct natural nutrients needed by each of them. There were no harmful insects because these plantings were strong and full of vitality. The birds, which also doubled as bug snatchers, were attracted by the various flowers and berries. Indeed Mrs. Crabtree was a lucky woman and to have such a delightful garden and such an inspired man as Adam to tend it.

I came to his garden alone, while the dew was still on the roses. Sweet fragrances and the song of birds filled the air. His voice I heard, soft and clear, saying that this is an organic garden. All the flowers, shrubs and trees were so beautiful not because of chemicals, but because of supplying the correct natural nutrients needed by each of them. There were no harmful insects because these plantings were strong and full of vitality. The birds, which also doubled as bug snatchers, were attracted by the various flowers and berries. Indeed Mrs. Crabtree was a lucky woman and to have such a delightful garden and such an inspired man as Adam to tend it.

I came to his garden alone, while the dew was still on the roses. Sweet fragrances and the song of birds filled the air. His voice I heard, soft and clear, saying that this is an organic garden. Indeed Mrs. Crabtree was a lucky woman to have such a delightful garden and such an inspired man as Adam to tend it. ▼

(b) White Space

FIGURE 5.9 White Spaces as a Design Element

space in this fashion is a very effective tool. White space is *not* attractive, however, when it is trapped in the middle of a page as in Figure 5.9d.

Emphasis

Good design makes it easy for the reader to determine what is important. ***Emphasis*** is achieved in several ways, the easiest being variations in type size and/or type style. Headings should be set in type sizes larger than the subheadings, which in turn should be larger than body copy. The use of **boldface** is effective, as are *italics,* but both should be done in moderation. Shading, reverses (white letters on a black background), or simple boxes are also effective.

DO NOT, HOWEVER, EMPHASIZE LARGE AMOUNTS OF TEXT WITH ALL UPPERCASE LETTERS BECAUSE THE READER GETS LOST TOO EASILY. Nor is underlining effective, because the underline can interfere with the descenders on lower-case letters—such as g, j, p, and y—that extend below the base line.

Facing Pages

A multipage document such as a manual, newsletter, or brochure is typically viewed two pages at a time by the reader. If this is true for your publication, it makes sense to develop facing pages as a unit, as opposed to creating the pages individually. This is illustrated by Figure 5.10a, which shows individually balanced pages that do not look very well together. Figure 5.10b rearranges the same

(c) Emphasis

(d) Trapped White Space

FIGURE 5.9 White Spaces as a Design Element (continued)

Tall Ships and Iron Horses: The Golden Age of Transportation?

It is interesting that during the same period of time two vitally needed forms of transportation were developed. One, on the sea, working with nature's best principles to create a totally eco-friendly means of transportation, and the other, on land, working against established social systems, the ecology of land and air using combustion, land acquisitions, and the power of the bullet to subdue nature and the native societies. It takes time to learn from our mistakes, and even more time to repair the damage done to man and nature.

It is interesting that during the same period of time two vitally needed forms of transportation were developed. One, on the sea, working with nature's best principles to create a totally eco-friendly means of transportation, and the other, on land, working against established social systems, the ecology of land and air using combustion, land acquisitions, and the power of the bullet to subdue nature and the native societies. It takes time to learn from our mistakes, and even more time to repair the damage done to man and nature.

It is interesting that during the same period of time two vitally needed forms of transportation were developed. One, on the sea, working with nature's best principles to create a totally eco-friendly means of transportation, and the other, on land, working against established social systems, the ecology of land and air using combustion, land acquisitions, and the power of the bullet to subdue nature and the native societies. It takes time to learn from our mistakes, and even more time to repair the damage done to man and nature.

It is interesting that during the same period of time two vitally needed forms of transportation were developed. One, on the sea, working with nature's best principles to create a totally eco-friendly means of transportation, and the other, on land, working against established social systems, the ecology of land and air using combustion, land acquisitions, and the power of the bullet to subdue nature and the native societies. It takes time to learn from our mistakes, and even more time to repair the damage done to man and nature.

It is interesting that during the same period of time two vitally needed forms of transportation were developed. It takes time to learn from our mistakes, and even more time to repair the damage done to man and nature. ▼

In the days when travel was a real adventure, the journey was as important as the determination.

It is interesting that during the same period of time two vitally needed forms of transportation were developed. One, on the sea, working with nature's best principles to create a totally eco-friendly means of transportation, and the other, on land, working against established social systems, the ecology of land and air using combustion, land acquisitions, and the power of the bullet to subdue nature and the native societies. It takes time to learn from our mistakes, and even more time to repair the damage done to man and nature.

It is interesting that during the same period of time two vitally needed forms of transportation were developed. One, on the sea, working with nature's best principles to create a totally eco-friendly means of transportation, and the other, on land, working against established social systems, the ecology of land and air using combustion, land acquisitions, and the power of the bullet to subdue nature and the native societies. It takes time to learn from our mistakes, and even more time to repair the damage done to man and nature.

It is interesting that during the same period of time two vitally needed forms of transportation were developed. One, on the sea, working with nature's best principles to create a totally eco-friendly means of transportation, and the other, on land, working against established social systems, the ecology of land and air using combustion, land acquisitions, and the power of the bullet to subdue nature and the native societies. It takes time to learn from our mistakes, and even more time to repair the damage done to man and nature.

It is interesting that during the same period of time two vitally needed forms of transportation were developed. One, on the sea, working with nature's best principles to create a totally eco-friendly means of transportation, and the other, on land, working against established social systems, the ecology of land and air using combustion, land acquisitions, and the power of the bullet to subdue nature and the native societies. It takes time to learn from our mistakes, and even more time to repair the damage done to man and nature.

It is interesting that during the same period of time two vitally needed forms of transportation were developed. It takes time to learn from our mistakes, and even more time to repair the damage done to man and nature.

It is interesting that during the same period of time two vitally needed forms of transportation were developed. One, on the sea, working with nature's best principles to create a totally eco-friendly means of transportation, and the other, on land, working against established social systems, the ecology of land and air using combustion, land acquisitions, and the power of the bullet to subdue nature and the native societies. It takes time to learn from our mistakes, and even more time to repair the damage done to man and nature. ▼

(a) Pages Balanced Individually

FIGURE 5.10 Balance Facing Pages

material in a more appealing fashion. Use the Two Page view in WordPerfect to work on your document.

SUMMARY

The essence of desktop publishing is the merging of text with graphics to produce a professional-looking document without reliance on external services. Proficiency in desktop publishing requires not only knowledge of WordPerfect, but familiarity with the basics of graphic design.

A document can be divided into any number of newspaper-style columns in which text flows from the bottom of one column to the top of the next. Columns are implemented by clicking the Column icon on the Power Bar or by selecting the Columns command from the Layout menu. Columns may be toggled on or off throughout a document. Different column formats can be in effect at different places in the document.

The Border/Fill command in the Layout menu creates boxed and/or shaded text. It is also used to place horizontal and/or vertical lines around a paragraph and to place a line between columns. The View Page command at Full Page magnification (Zoom) is used to preview (and make final changes to) a document prior to printing.

The newsletter created in this chapter is an example of a compound document; that is, a document containing objects from multiple applications. The Insert Object command embeds the object from the server application—for example,

Tall Ships and Iron Horses: The Golden Age of Transportation?

In the days when travel was a real adventure, the journey was as important as the determination.

It is interesting that during the same period of time two vitally needed forms of transportation were developed. One, on the sea, working with nature's best principles to create a totally eco-friendly means of transportation, and the other, on land, working against established social systems, the ecology of land and air using combustion, land acquisitions, and the power of the bullet to subdue nature and the native societies. It takes time to learn from our mistakes, and even more time to repair the damage done to man and nature.

It is interesting that during the same period of time two vitally needed forms of transportation were developed. One, on the sea, working with nature's best principles to create a totally eco-friendly means of transportation, and the other, on land, working against established social systems, the ecology of land and air using combustion, land acquisitions, and the power of the bullet to subdue nature and the native societies. It takes time to learn from our mistakes, and even more time to repair the damage done to man and nature. It takes time to learn from our mistakes, and even more time to repair the damage done to man and nature. It takes time to learn from our mistakes.

It is interesting that during the same period of time two vitally needed forms of transportation were developed. One, on the sea, working with nature's best principles to create a totally eco-friendly means of transportation, and the other, on land, working against established social systems, the ecology of land and air using combustion, land acquisitions, and the power of the bullet to subdue nature and the native societies. One, on the sea, working with nature's best principles to create a totally eco-friendly means of transportation, and the other, on land, working against established social systems, the ecology of land and air using combustion, land acquisitions, and the power of the bullet to subdue nature and the native societies. It takes time to learn from our mistakes, and even more time to repair the damage done to man and nature.

It is interesting that during the same period of time two vitally needed forms of transportation were developed. It takes time to learn from our mistakes, and even more time to repair the dam-age done to man and nature. It takes time to learn from our mistakes.

It is interesting that during the same period of time two vitally needed forms of transportation were developed. One, on the sea, working with nature's best principles to create a totally eco-friendly means of transportation, and the other, on land, working against established social systems, the ecology of land and air using combustion, land acquisitions, and the power of the bullet to subdue nature and the native societies. It takes time to learn from our mistakes, and even more time to repair the damage done to man and nature. ▼

(b) Pages Balanced as a Unit

FIGURE 5.10 Balance Facing Pages (continued)

WP Draw—into the document created by the client application—for example, WordPerfect.

The successful use of desktop publishing requires knowledge of graphic design in addition to proficiency in WordPerfect. The use of a grid, white space, and appropriate emphasis are basic design techniques.

Key Words and Concepts

Balanced newspaper columns
Border/Fill command
Client application
Clip art
Coach
Column Off command
Columns command
Compound document
Desktop publishing
Dropcap
Embedded object
Emphasis
Figure command
Graphics Feature Bar
Graphics menu
GRAPHICS subdirectory
Grid
Image Tools
Insert menu
Insert Object command
Layout menu
Newspaper columns
Object
Pull quote
QuickMenu
Server application
TextArt
Tools menu
Typography
White space
WP Draw

Multiple Choice

1. Which of the following *must* be specified by the user in the Columns command?
   (a) The number of columns
   (b) The width of each column
   (c) The space between columns
   (d) All of the above

2. Which of the following is true about the grid system of design?
   (a) It is not appropriate for multicolumn documents
   (b) It can be used to position text but not graphics
   (c) Both (a) and (b)
   (d) Neither (a) nor (b)

3. Which of the following describes balanced newspaper columns as they are implemented by the Columns command in WordPerfect?
   (a) The columns are equal in length
   (b) The columns are the same width
   (c) The columns are separated by a vertical line
   (d) All of the above

4. Where (in which subdirectory) can you find the clip art supplied with WordPerfect?
   (a) In the same subdirectory as the document you are editing
   (b) In the WPWIN60 subdirectory
   (c) In the GRAPHICS subdirectory under the WPWIN60 subdirectory
   (d) In the WINDOWS subdirectory

5. What is the difference between clicking and double clicking an object such as the skiing graphic in the newsletter?
   (a) Clicking selects the object; double clicking loads the application that created the object
   (b) Double clicking selects the object; clicking loads the application that created the object
   (c) Clicking changes to Page Width; double clicking changes to Full Page
   (d) Double clicking changes to Page Width; clicking changes to Full Page

6. Which of the following is an embedded object in the newsletter?
   (a) The boxed masthead created by the Border/Fill command
   (b) The skiing graphic created by WP Draw
   (c) Both (a) and (b)
   (d) Neither (a) nor (b)

7. Which of the following is considered a *server application* with respect to the newsletter developed in the chapter?
   (a) WordPerfect
   (b) WP Draw
   (c) Both (a) and (b)
   (d) Neither (a) nor (b)

8. Which of the following is considered a *client application* with respect to the newsletter developed in the chapter?
   (a) WordPerfect
   (b) WP Draw
   (c) Both (a) and (b)
   (d) Neither (a) nor (b)

9. Which menu contains the Border/Fill command?
   (a) Edit
   (b) Layout
   (c) Tools
   (d) Graphics

10. Which type size is the most reasonable for columns of text, such as those appearing in the newsletter created in the chapter?
   (a) 6 point
   (b) 10 point
   (c) 14 point
   (d) 18 point

11. A grid is applicable to the design of
   (a) Documents with one, two, or three columns and moderate clip art
   (b) Documents with four or more columns and no clip art
   (c) Both (a) and (b)
   (d) Neither (a) nor (b)

12. Which of the following is *not* an appropriate place to introduce white space in a document?
   (a) Between columns of a multicolumn document
   (b) In the middle of a page
   (c) Vertically, by leaving the left column empty, or almost empty
   (d) Between paragraphs

13. Which of the following can be used to add emphasis to a document in the absence of clip art?
   (a) Pull quotes
   (b) Boxes and shading
   (c) Both (a) and (b)
   (d) Neither (a) nor (b)

14. Which of the following is a recommended guideline in the design of a document?
   (a) Use underlining and/or all upper-case letters to achieve emphasis
   (b) Use at least three different typefaces in a document to maintain interest
   (c) Use wider columns for larger type sizes
   (d) Use the same type size for the heading and text of an article

15. Assume that you create a memo using the Windows Write accessory, and that the memo contains a drawing created by Paintbrush.
   (a) Paintbrush is the client application
   (b) Write is the server application
   (c) Both (a) and (b)
   (d) Neither (a) nor (b)

ANSWERS

1. a	**6.** b	**11.** c
2. d	**7.** b	**12.** b
3. a	**8.** a	**13.** c
4. c	**9.** b	**14.** c
5. a	**10.** b	**15.** d

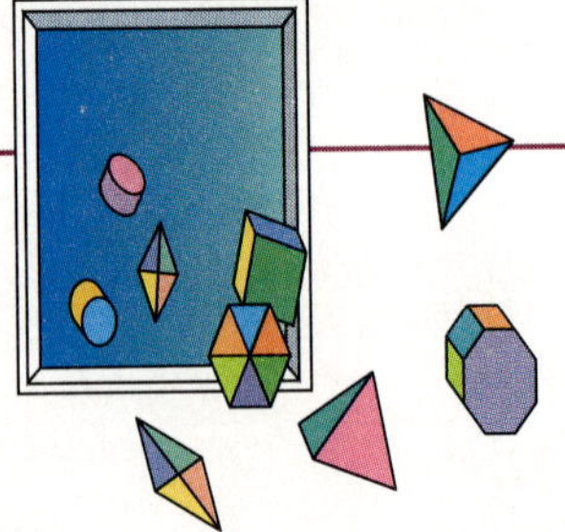

EXPLORING WORDPERFECT

1. Use Figure 5.11 to match each action with its result; a given action may be used more than once.

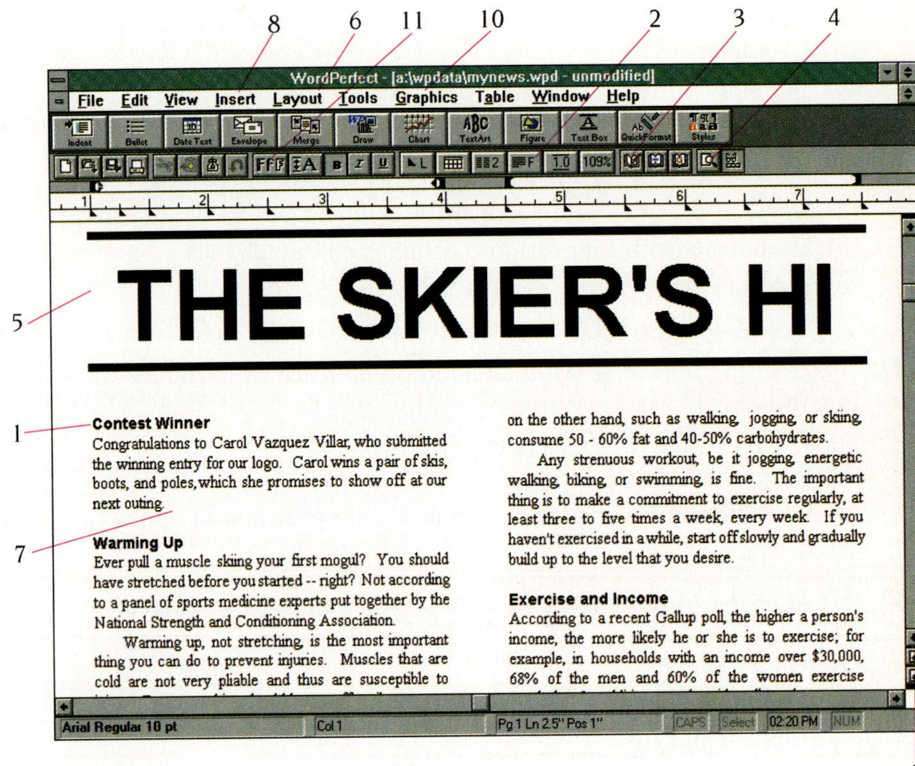

FIGURE 5.11 Screen for Problem 1

Action		**Result**
a. Click at 1, drag to the end of document, click at 2	___	Change to page view with zoom at full page
b. Click at 3	___	Change border around the masthead
c. Click at 4	___	Open the Reveal Codes window
d. Click at 5, click at 6	___	Shade the heading and article about the contest winner
e. Click at 7, click at 6	___	Change the masthead font
f. Click at 8	___	Change the justification for the newsletter text
g. Click and drag at 9		

h. Click at 10 ___ Add a piece of clip art

i. Click at 5, click at 11 ___ Spell check the newsletter

j. Click at 1, drag to 7, click at 6 ___ Change the column definition to a three-column layout

___ Add a text art object to the newsletter

2. Design your own letterhead containing your name, address, telephone number, hypothetical fax number and E-mail address, and any other text you want to include (e.g, Attorney at Law). Use horizontal (vertical) lines to offset the letterhead and/or a graphical logo.

3. Each part of Figure 5.12 contains two versions of the same page, one of which violates basic rules of design (on the left), and one that follows them. List several problems in the poorly designed page, then indicate how they were corrected in the revised version.

   As indicated in the chapter, the design of a document is a subjective process. Your taste is different from everyone else's, and thus there is no single correct answer to the problem. Nevertheless, we think that in every example the page on the right looks better than the page on the left. Tell us why.

A Special Report: Living Latin

Latin was one of the subjects which I really enjoyed in high school. Many people laugh at it because they say it is a useless, dead language. Churches do not even use it any more in their services, pity. Something like eighty five percent of the English language is derived from a mere ninety latin root words. I cannot express how useful it was to have an understanding of latin when it came to memorizing the order, phylum and classification of organisms in zoology class, later on in college. My creative writing classes also got a shot in the arm because of it. It was also interesting to find out the toll that the dark ages took on the European civilization which the Romans had established for centuries. Latin is indeed living. But it is living quietly in the essence of western civilization.

Latin was one of the subjects which I really enjoyed in high school. Many people laugh at it because they say it is a useless, dead language. Churches do not even use it any more in their services, pity. Something like eighty-five percent of the English language is derived from a mere ninety latin root words. I cannot express how useful it was to have an understanding of latin when it came to memorizing the order, phylum and classification of organisms in zoology class, later on in college. My creative writing classes also got a shot in the arm because of it. It was also interesting to find out the toll that the dark ages took on the European civilization which the Romans had established for centuries.

Latin is indeed living. But it is living quietly in the essence of western civilization.

Latin was one of the subjects which I really enjoyed in high school. Many people laugh at it because they say it is a useless, dead language. Churches do not even use it any more in their services, pity. Something like eighty-five percent of the English language is derived from a mere ninety latin root words. I cannot express how useful it was to have an understanding of latin when it came to memorizing the order, phylum and classification of organisms in zoology class, later on in college. My creative writing classes also got a shot in the arm because of it. It was also interesting to find out the toll that the dark ages took on the European civilization which the Romans had established for centuries. Latin is indeed living. But it is living quietly in the essence of western civilization.

Latin was one of the subjects which I really enjoyed in high school. Many people laugh at it because they say it is a useless, dead language. Churches do not even use it any more in their services, pity. Something like eighty-five percent of the English language is derived from a mere ninety latin root words.

I cannot express how useful it was to have an understanding of latin when it came to memorizing the order, phylum and classification of organisms in zoology class, later on in college. My creative writing classes also got a shot in the arm because of it. It was also interesting to find out the toll that the dark ages took on the European civilization which the Romans had established for centuries. Latin is indeed living. But it is living quietly in the essence of western civilization.

Latin was one of the subjects which I really enjoyed in high school. Many people laugh at it because they say it is a useless, dead language. Churches do not even use it any more in their services, pity. Something like eighty-five percent of the English language is derived from a mere ninety latin root words. I cannot express how useful it was to have an understanding of latin when it came to memorizing the order, phylum and classification of organisms in zoology class, later on in college. My creative writing classes also got a shot in the arm because of it. It was also interesting to find out the toll that the dark ages took on the European civilization which the Romans had established for centuries. Latin is indeed living. But it is living quietly in the essence of western civilization. It was also interesting to find out the toll that the dark ages took on the European civilization which the Romans had established for centuries.

Latin is indeed living. But it is living quietly in the essence of western civilization. It was also interesting to find out the toll that the dark ages took on the European civilization which the Romans had established for centuries. It was also interesting to find out the toll that the dark ages took on the European civilization. ▼

A Special Report: Living Latin

Latin was one of the subjects which I really enjoyed in high school. Many people laugh at it because they say it is a useless, dead language. Churches do not even use it any more in their services, pity. Something like eighty-five percent of the English language is derived from a mere ninety latin root words.

I cannot express how useful it was to have an understanding of latin when it came to memorizing the order, phylum and classification of organisms in zoology class, later on in college. My creative writing classes also got a shot in the arm because of it. It was also interesting to find out the toll that the dark ages took on the European civilization which the Romans had established for centuries. Latin is indeed living. But it is living quietly in the essence of western civilization.

Latin was one of the subjects which I really enjoyed in high school. Many people laugh at it because they say it is a useless, dead language. Churches do not even use it any more in their services, pity. Something like eighty-five percent of the English language is derived from a mere ninety latin root words. I cannot express how useful it was to have an understanding of latin when it came to memorizing the order, phylum and classification of organisms in zoology class, later on in college. My creative writing classes also got a shot in the arm because of it.

It was also interesting to find out the toll that the dark ages took on the European civilization which the Romans had established for centuries. Latin is indeed living. But it is living quietly in the essence of western civilization. It was also interesting to find out the toll that the dark ages took on the European civilization which the Romans had established for centuries.

I cannot express how useful it was to have an understanding of latin when it came to memorizing the order, phylum and classification of organisms in zoology class, later on in college. My creative writing classes also got a shot in the arm because of it. It was also interesting to find out the toll that the dark ages took on the European civilization which the Romans had established for centuries. Latin is indeed living. But it is living quietly in the essence of western civilization.

Latin was one of the subjects which I really enjoyed in high school. Many people laugh at it because they say it is a useless, dead language. Churches do not even use it any more in their services, pity. Something like eighty-five percent of the English language is derived from a mere ninety latin root words. ▼

(a)

FIGURE 5.12 Pages for Problem 3

A Special Report: Living Latin

Something like eighty-five percent of the English language is derived from a mere ninety latin root words.

Latin was one of the subjects which I really enjoyed in high school. Many people laugh at it because they say it is a useless, dead language. Churches do not even use it any more in their services, pity. Something like eighty-five percent of the English language is derived from a mere ninety latin root words. I cannot express how useful it was to have an understanding of latin when it came to memorizing the order, phylum and classification of organisms in zoology class, later on in college. My creative writing classes also got a shot in the arm because of it. It was also interesting to find out the toll that the dark ages took on the European civilization which the Romans had established for centuries. Latin is indeed living. But it is living quietly in the essence of western civilization.

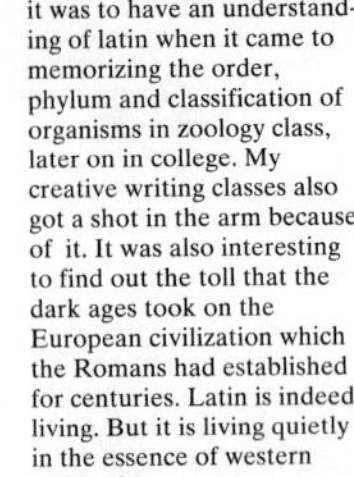

Many people laugh at it because they say it is a useless, dead language. Churches do not even use it any more in their services, pity. Something like eighty-five percent of the English language is derived from a mere ninety latin root words.

I cannot express how useful it was to have an understanding of latin when it came to memorizing the order, phylum and classification of organisms in zoology class, later on in college. My creative writing classes also got a shot in the arm because of it. It was also interesting to find out the toll that the dark ages took on the European civilization which the Romans had established for centuries. Latin is indeed living. But it is living quietly in the essence of western civilization.

Latin was one of the subjects which I really enjoyed in high school. Many people laugh at it because they say it is a useless, dead language. Churches do not even use it any more in their services, pity. Something like eighty-five percent of the English language is derived from a mere ninety latin root words. I cannot express how useful it was to have an understanding of latin when it came to memorizing the order, phylum and classification of organisms in zoology class, later on in college. My creative writing classes also got a shot in the arm because of it.

It was also interesting to find out the toll that the dark ages took on the European civilization which the Romans had established for centuries. Latin is indeed living. But it is living quietly in the essence of western civilization. I cannot express how useful it was to have an understanding of latin when it came to memorizing the order, phylum and classification of organisms in zoology class, later on in college. My creative writing classes also got a shot in the arm because of it. Latin is indeed living. But it is living quietly in western civilization. ▼

Latin is indeed living. But it is living quietly in the essence of western civilization.

A Special Report: Living Latin

Latin was one of the subjects which I really enjoyed in high school. Many people laugh at it because they say it is a useless, dead language. Churches do not even use it any more in their services, pity. Something like eighty-five percent of the English language is derived from a mere ninety latin root words. I cannot express how useful it was to have an understanding of latin when it came to memorizing the order, phylum and classification of organisms in zoology class, later on in college. My creative writing classes also got a shot in the arm because of it. It was also interesting to find out the toll that the dark ages took on the European civilization which the Romans had established for centuries. Latin is indeed living. But it is living quietly in the essence of western civilization.

Many people laugh at it because they say it is a useless, dead language. Churches do not even use it any more in their services, pity. Something like eighty-five percent of the English language is derived from a mere ninety latin root words.

I cannot express how useful it was to have an understanding of latin when it came to memorizing the order, phylum and classification of organisms in zoology class, later on in college. My creative writing classes also got a shot in the arm because of it. It was also interesting to find out the toll that the dark ages took on the European civilization which the Romans had established for centuries. Latin is indeed living. But it is living quietly in the essence of western civilization.

Latin was one of the subjects which I really enjoyed in high school. Many people laugh at it because they say it is a useless, dead language. Churches do not even use it any more in their services, pity. Something like eighty-five percent of the English language is derived from a mere ninety latin root words. I cannot express how useful it was to have an understanding of latin when it came to memorizing the order, phylum and classification of organisms in zoology class, later on in college. My creative writing classes also got a shot in the arm because of it.

It was also interesting to find out the toll that the dark ages took on the European civilization which the Romans had established for centuries. I cannot express how useful it was to have understanding of latin when it came to memorizing the order, phylum and classification of organisms in zoology class, later on in college. My creative writing classes also got a shot in the arm because of it. Latin was one of the subjects which I really enjoyed in high school. ▼

Latin is indeed living. But it is living quietly in the essence of western civilization.

(b)

Living Latin Bulletin

Published by The Romulus and Remus Society of Southern California — Januarious MXMXCIV

Managers Required to Study Roman Classics

Latin was one of the subjects which I really enjoyed in high school. Many people laugh at it because they say it is a useless, dead language. Churches do not even use it any more in their services, pity. Something like eighty-five percent of the English language is derived from a mere ninety latin root words. I cannot express how useful it was to have an understanding of latin when it came to memorizing the order, phylum and classification of organisms in zoology class, later on in college. My creative writing classes also got a shot in the arm because of it. It was also interesting to find out the toll that the dark ages took on the European civilization which the Romans had established for centuries. Latin is indeed living. But it is living quietly in the essence of western civilization. ▼

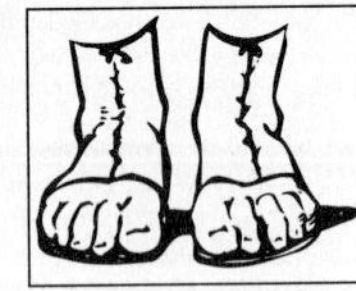

These Boots Were Made for Walkin'

Latin was one of the subjects which I really enjoyed in high school. Many people laugh at it because they say it is a useless, dead language. Churches do not even use it any more in their services, pity. Something like eighty-five percent of the English language is derived from a mere ninety latin root words. I cannot express how useful it was to have an understanding of latin when it came to memorizing the order, phylum and classification of organisms in zoology class, later on in college. My creative writing classes also got a shot in the arm because of it. It was also interesting to find out the toll. ▼

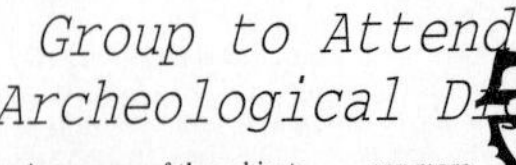

Group to Attend Archeological D

Latin was one of the subjects which I really enjoyed in high school. Many people laugh at it because they say it is a useless, dead language. Churches do not even use it any more in their services, pity. Something like eighty-five percent of the English language is derived from a mere ninety latin root words. I cannot express how useful it was to have an understanding of latin when it came to memorizing the order, phylum and classification of organisms in zoology class, later on in college. My creative writing classes also got a shot in the arm because of it. ▼

Living Latin Bulletin

Published by The Romulus and Remus Society of Southern California — Januarious MXMXCIV

Managers Required to Study Roman Classics

Latin was one of the subjects which I really enjoyed in high school. Many people laugh at it because they say it is a useless, dead language. Churches do not even use it any more in their services, pity. Something like eighty-five percent of the English language is derived from a mere ninety latin root words. I cannot express how useful it was to have an understanding of latin when it came to mem-orizing the order, phylum and classification of organisms in zoology class, later on in college. My cre-ative writing classes also got a shot in the arm because of it. It was also interesting to find out the toll that the dark ages took on the European civilization which the Romans had established for centuries. Latin is indeed living. But it is living quietly in the essence of western civilization.

Latin was one of the subjects which I really enjoyed in high school. Many people laugh at it because they say it is a useless, dead language. Churches do not even use it any more in their services, pity. Something like eighty-five percent of the English language is derived from a mere ninety latin root words. I cannot express how useful it was to have an understanding of latin when it came to memorizing the order, phylum and classification of organisms in zoology class, later on in college. My creative writing classes also got a shot in the arm because of it. It was also interesting to find out the toll that the dark ages took on the European civilization which the Romans had established for centuries. Latin is indeed living. But it is living quietly in the essence of western civilization. ▼

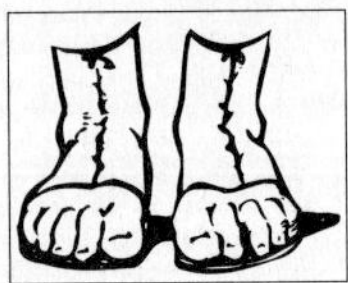

These Boots Were Made for Walkin'

Latin was one of the subjects which I really enjoyed in high school. Many people laugh at it because they say it is a useless, dead language. Churches do not even use it any more in their services, pity. Something like eighty-five percent of the English language is derived from a mere ninety latin root words. I cannot express how useful it was to have an understanding of latin when it came to memorizing the order, phylum and classification of organisms in zoology class, later on in college. My creative writing classes also got a shot in the arm because of it. It was also interesting to find out the toll that the dark ages took on the European civilization which the Romans had established for centuries. Latin is indeed living. But it is living quietly in the essence of western civilization. Latin is indeed living. It is living quietly in the essence of western civilization. ▼

(c)

FIGURE 5.12 Pages for Problem 3 (continued)

4. The flyers in Figure 5.13 were created from a graphic in the GRAPHICS directory that was imported into a document and sized (and moved) appropriately. Reproduce either or both of our flyers, or better yet, create your own.

Join the "IN" Crowd

What: **Graduate Business Association**

Where: **The Chart House**

When: **Monday, 7PM for cocktails and dinner**

(a) Join the "IN" Crowd

EXAMS DRIVING YOU CRAZY?

Join the CIS 120 Study Session!!

For those who don't know a bit from a byte
Come to Mahoney Hall this Tuesday night
We'll study the concepts that are not always clear
And memorize terms that hackers hold dear.

We'll hit the books from 7 til 10
And then on Thursday we'll do it again.
It can't hurt you to try us - so come on by
And give the CIS tutors that old college try!

(b) CIS 120 Study Sessions

FIGURE 5.13 Flyers for Problem 4

5. Typography: The best way to practice design and type selection is to create a simple document, then set that document in a variety of typefaces, type sizes, styles, and column arrangements. Accordingly, create a one-paragraph document containing the text below, then copy the paragraph several times until it takes at least a page.

There is a definite relationship between type size and column width. The smaller the type, the shorter the line; or conversely, the larger the type, the longer the line. In other words, the line length of a document set in 8 point type should be shorter than one set in 10 point type, which in turn should be shorter than one set in 12 point type.

Experiment with some (or all) of the following designs.

a. A two-column grid in various type sizes—for example, in 8, 10, and 12 point type. Use a serif typeface such as Times New Roman. Choose the type size you think most appropriate, then experiment with different alignments (left and full justification) and the use (omission) of a vertical line between columns. Vary the space between columns and/or the left and right margins until you arrive at a satisfactory design.

b. Use a three- (rather than two-) column grid and vary all of the design parameters from part (a)—that is, justification, type size, and the use (omission) of a vertical line between columns.

c. Add a sans-serif heading to randomly selected paragraphs from part (a) or part (b). Use a larger type size and/or boldface for the heading(s).

d. Create a masthead *without* the benefit of WP Draw; use the Format Border command to add horizontal line(s) as appropriate.

e. Add your name to the document and submit it to your instructor.

6. The Skier's Hi: Modify the newsletter at the end of the second hands-on exercise so that it matches the design in Figure 5.1d at the beginning of the chapter.

a. Change the view. Pull down the View menu. Click Page. Zoom to Full Page.

b. Change the masthead. Select the title of the newsletter, then choose a font other than Arial.

c. Select the graphic. Click anywhere on the skier to select the graphic and display the sizing handles.

d. Trouble shooting. If you are unable to select the graphic, pull down the Graphics menu and click the Edit Box. If the Feature Bar does not appear after selecting the graphic, click the right mouse button to access the QuickMenu, then click the Feature Bar; the Feature Bar will appear on the screen immediately below the Ruler Bar.

e. Change the graphic. Click the Content command button on the Feature Bar. Click the file icon in the Filename box. Scroll in the box to find and click SLALOM.WPG. Click OK. Click OK a second time, then click Yes to delete the current box contents.

f. Superimpose the graphic on the newsletter. Click the Wrap command button. Click No Wrap. Click OK.

g. Change the position. Click the Position command button. Click Put Box on Current Page as the placement option. Click OK.

h. Move and size the graphic. Drag the sizing handles to change the size of the graphic. Click and drag the graphic to move it within the document.

i. Remove the border. Click the Border/Fill command button. Click the Border Style box and select No border. Click OK.

j. Trouble shooting. It may be difficult to achieve the precise size and/or position using the mouse. Click the Size or Position buttons on the Feature Bar and enter the values manually in the dialog box.

7. Before and after: Answer the following with respect to Figure 5.14.

a. What is the name of the WPG graphic? In which directory is it found?

b. Which command is used to bring the graphic into a document?

c. What was done to produce the mirror image?

d. How was the image converted from color to black and white?

e. How would you add your name to either graphic?

8. An original newsletter: Design your own newsletter with at least one graphic from the clip art subdirectory. The intent of this problem is simply to provide practice in graphic design; that is, there is no requirement to write meaningful text, but the headings in the newsletter should follow the theme of the graphic.

a. Select a graphic from the clip art directory, then write one or two sentences in support of that graphic. If, for example, you choose MARSH.WPG, you could write a sentence describing how the wetlands are threatened and how important it is to protect the environment.

b. As indicated, there is no requirement to write meaningful text for the newsletter. Copy the sentences from part (a) once or twice to create a paragraph, then copy the paragraph several times to create the newsletter. Break up the text in the newsletter by creating *different (meaningful) headings* throughout the document.

c. Develop an overall design away from the computer—that is, with pencil

(a) Before

(b) After

FIGURE 5.14 Before and After Images (problem 7)

and paper. Use a grid to indicate the placement of the articles (headings), clip art, masthead, and other elements (e.g., a shaded box or sidebar). You may be surprised to find that it is easier to master commands in WordPerfect than it is to design the newsletter. Do not underestimate the importance of graphic design in the ultimate success of your document.

d. More is not better; that is, do not use too many fonts, styles, sizes, and clip art just because they are there. Don't crowd the page; and remember, white space is a very effective design element. There are no substitutes for simplicity and good taste.

9. A guide to smart shopping: Design a one- (or two-) page document with helpful tips to the novice on buying a computer. We have, however, written the copy for you and put the file on the data disk.

a. Open the file BUYING.WPD and print the document, which takes approximately a page and a half as presently formatted. Read our text and determine the tips you want to retain and those you want to delete. Add other tips as you see fit.

b. Consult a current computer magazine (or another source) to determine actual prices for one or more configurations, then include this information prominently in your document.

c. Create the masthead for the document using TextArt, then develop with pencil and paper a rough sketch of the completed document showing the masthead, the placement of the text, and special of the month (the configuration in part b).

d. Return to the computer and implement the design of part (c). Try to create a balanced publication that completely fills the space allotted; that is, your document should take exactly one or two pages (rather than the page and a half in the original BUYING.WPD on the data disk).

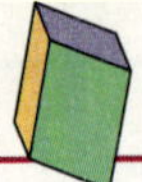

Case Studies

Before and After

The best way to learn about the do's and don'ts of desktop publishing is to study the work of others. Choose a particular type of document—for example, a newsletter, résumé, or advertising flyer—then collect samples of that document. Choose one sample that is particularly bad and redesign the document. You need not enter the actual text, but you should keep all of the major headings so that the document retains its identity. Add or delete clip art as appropriate. Bring the before and after samples to class and hold a contest to determine the most radical improvement.

Clip Art

Clip art—you see it all the time, but where do you get it, and how much does it cost? Some images are supplied with a word processor, but you grow tired of these and yearn for more. Scan the computer magazines and find at least two sources for additional clip art. Return to class with specific information on price and the nature of the clip art. Be sure to determine in advance how much disk space the clip art will require; the answer may surprise you.

The Invitation

Choose an event and produce the perfect invitation. The possibilities are endless and limited only by your imagination. You can invite people to your wedding or to a fraternity party. Your laser printer and abundance of fancy fonts enable you to do anything a professional printer can do. Clip art and/or special paper will add the finishing touch. Go to it—this assignment is a lot of fun.

The Flyer

It's rush week and you're the publicity chairperson for your fraternity or sorority. Needless to say it's highly competitive and you need effective flyers to attract new members. This is an absolutely critical assignment and people are counting on you. Don't blow it!

Paper Makes a Difference

Most of us take paper for granted, but the right paper can make a significant difference in the effectiveness of the document. Reports and formal correspondence are usually printed on white paper, but you would be surprised how many different shades of white there are. Other types of documents lend themselves to colored paper for additional impact. In short, the paper you use is far from an automatic decision. Research the subject and tell us what you find.

Countries of the World

Presentation programs such as Freelance and PowerPoint supply clip art, which includes maps and flags of foreign countries. Design a one-page travel brochure for a country you would like to visit. Open the presentation program, copy the appropriate clip art image(s) to the Windows clipboard, then paste it into the word processing document.

Appendix A: The Power Bar and Button Bars

WORDPERFECT POWER BAR

The ***Power Bar*** provides a shortcut for common editing and formatting commands. It is displayed in a fixed position toward the top of the WordPerfect application window immediately below the Button Bar. The Power Bar is shown below (its icons were described on page 6). The icons are intended to be indicative of their function; for example, the printer (fourth from the left) executes the Print command. You can also point to an icon, and its description will be displayed at the top of the screen.

The Power Bar cannot be moved from its position on the screen, but it can be customized as follows:

- To customize the Power Bar, pull down the File Menu, click Preferences, then double click the Power Bar icon. You can also select Preferences from the Power Bar QuickMenu, which can be accessed by clicking the right mouse button as you point to the Power Bar. Then:

  —To move a button, drag it to its new location on the Power Bar
  —To delete an icon, drag it off the Power Bar and release the mouse button or deselect the corresponding item in the Items list box
  —To add a button, select the corresponding item in the Items list box
  —To restore the default Power Bar, click the Default command button

- To hide (show) the Power Bar, pull down the View Menu and click the Power Bar command.

WORDPERFECT BUTTON BARS

In addition to the Power Bar, WordPerfect offers a series of ***Button Bars*** for more advanced but less frequently used commands. There are 12 different Button Bars in all, but only one Button Bar can be displayed at a time. (The Button Bar is displayed in addition to the Power Bar.) The Button Bars are shown below. As with the Power Bar, you can point to a button and its description will be displayed at the top of the screen.

Equation Editor

Font

Generate

Graphics

Layout

Macros

Outline

Page

Preferences

Tables

WordPerfect (Default)

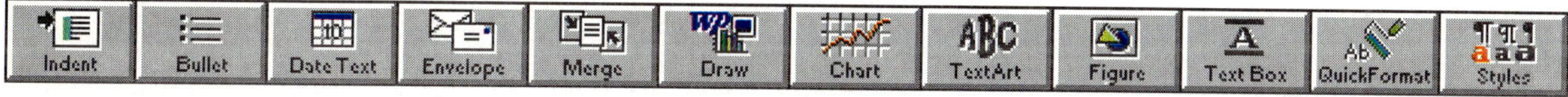

WordPerfect 5.2

The WordPerfect Button Bar is displayed by default and appears immediately below the Menu Bar. You may move this (or any other Button Bar) to a new location on the screen, customize its appearance, or suppress its display.

- To hide (show) a Button Bar, pull down the View Menu and click the Button Bar command. You may also toggle its display on and off by clicking the Button Bar icon on the Power Bar.
- To select a different Button Bar, pull down the File Menu, click Preferences, and double click the Button Bar icon. Select the desired Button Bar, click the Select command button, and then click Close to exit the Preferences dialog box. You may also click the right mouse button when pointing to the current But-

ton Bar and then select the desired Button Bar from the Button Bar QuickMenu. (Only one Button Bar may be selected at a time.)

- To move the Button Bar, pull down the File Menu, click Preferences, double click the Button Bar icon, and then select the Options command button. (You may alternatively select Preferences from the Button Bar QuickMenu). Select a new position for the Button Bar (Left, Top, Right, or Bottom) or let it float on the screen as a palette (window). Similarly, you can point to a blank area on the Button Bar (the mouse pointer will change to a hand) and drag the Button Bar to its new location at the edge of the screen, or to the middle of the document window if you want it to be displayed as a palette.
- To change the appearance of the buttons (to display them with text and picture, text only, or pictures only), pull down the File Menu, click Preferences, double click the Button Bar icon, and then select the Options command button. Select the desired appearance, which will also make a corresponding change to the size of the buttons on the bar. You may make the same change by selecting Preferences from the Button Bar QuickMenu.
- To customize the Button Bar, pull down the File Menu and click Preferences. Double click the Button Bar icon, select the desired Button Bar, and select the Edit command button. Alternatively, select Edit from the Button Bar QuickMenu. Then:

  —To move a button, drag it to its new location on the Button Bar

  —To delete an icon, drag it off the Button Bar and release the mouse button

  —To add a button, select the Activate a Feature option button in the dialog box, choose a category from the drop-down list (the categories correspond to the various menus on the Menu Bar), choose a Feature (command) from the open list box, and then click the Add Button command button.

  —Note that once the Button Bar has been customized it cannot be returned to its default appearance.

- To create your own Button Bar, pull down the File Menu, click Preferences, double click the Button Bar icon, and then select the Create command button. Assign a name to the Button Bar and then continue, following the same procedures as for customizing the Button Bar.

Index